CORPORATE CRIME: CONTEMPORARY DEBATES

D1564584

Corporate crime inflicts massive harm on employees, consumers, workplaces, economies, and the environment, but there are inadequate controls and few deterrent mechanisms, and sanctions are mild relative to the harm done. There is little agreement on remedies and praxis, reflecting an underlying diversity of opinion on the causes of corporate criminality.

Corporate Crime is a collection of original papers by many of the world's leading experts on corporate crime, and covers its causes, extent, and control. It presents discussions of all the major areas of corporate criminal conduct and looks at the relationship between corporate structure and corporate crime. It opens up debate on appropriate control strategies to deter perpetrators and minimize harm. The discussions focus on strategies to control the social, economic, and political costs of various kinds of corporate crime – within the corporate organization and the fields of finance, occupational health and safety, and environmental degradation.

FRANK PEARCE is a professor in the Department of Sociology at Queen's University. His publications include *Crimes of the Powerful*; *The Radical Durkheim*; and *Global Crime Connections: Dynamics and Control*, a collection he edited with Michael Woodiwiss.

LAUREEN SNIDER is a professor in the Department of Sociology at Queen's University. Her publications include *Bad Business: Corporate Crime in Canada*.

EDITED BY
FRANK PEARCE AND
LAUREEN SNIDER

Corporate Crime:
Contemporary Debates

UNIVERSITY OF TORONTO PRESS
Toronto Buffalo London

© University of Toronto Press Incorporated 1995
Toronto Buffalo London
Printed in Canada

ISBN 0-8020-0667-1 (cloth)
ISBN 0-8020-7621-1 (paper)

Printed on acid-free paper

Canadian Cataloguing in Publication Data

Main entry under title:

Corporate crime : contemporary debates

Based on the conference, Corporate crime: ethics,
law and the state, held Nov. 12–14, 1992.
Includes index.
ISBN 0-8020-0667-1 (bound) ISBN 0-8020-7621-1 (pbk.)

1. Commercial crimes – Congresses.   2. Corporations
– Corrupt practices – Congresses.   I. Pearce, Frank.
II. Snider, Laureen, 1944–   .

HV6768.C67 1995   364.1'68   C95-930820-2

University of Toronto Press acknowledges the
financial assistance to its publishing program of the
Canada Council and the Ontario Arts Council.

For Patricia Reddy, John Connelly, and Cecelia Pearce
and in memory of George Pearce

Contents

viii Contents

Part V
Crimes against the Environment

Contributors

HAROLD C. BARNETT is a professor of economics at Rhode Island University. Publications include *Toxic Debts: The Superfund Dilemma* (forthcoming).

JOHN BRAITHWAITE is a professorial fellow in the Law Program at the Australian National University, Canberra. Publications include *Not Just Deserts: A Republican Theory of Criminal Justice* (1990).

KITTY CALAVITA is an associate professor of sociology at the University of California at Irvine. Publications include *Inside the State: The Bracero Program, Immigration and the INS* (1992).

JOSEPH DIMENTO is a professor of law and society in the School of Social Ecology at the University of California at Irvine.

GILBERT GEIS is emeritus professor of sociology at the University of California at Irvine. Publications include *White Collar Criminal* (1968).

HARRY GLASBEEK is a professor at Osgoode Hall Law School, Toronto. Publications include *The Changing Workplace* (1992).

COLIN GOFF is a professor in the Department of Sociology at the University of Winnipeg. Publications include *Corporate Crime in Canada* (1978).

TED HAINES is an occupational health physician and clinical researcher at McMaster University, Hamilton, and LAMP Occupational Health Centre. His areas of interest are work-related upper-extremity disorders and the effectiveness of occupational health interventions.

CARL KEANE is an assistant professor of sociology at Queen's University, Kingston.

MICHAEL LEVI is a professor of criminology at the University of Wales College of Cardiff. Publications include *Regulating Fraud: White Collar Crime and the Criminal Process* (1987).

WAYNE LEWCHUK is a professor in the Labour Studies Programme at McMaster University, Hamilton. His current research projects include a SSHRCC-funded study on the regulation of occupational health hazards in industrialized market economies and a labour-based study of working conditions.

LEA ANNE MORAN is a research coordinator in the Department of Surgery at McMaster University, Hamilton. As an epidemiologist with anthropological training, she has a particular interest in study design regarding quality of life.

CHARLES NOBLE is a professor of politics at California State University at Long Beach. Publications include *Liberalism at Work: The Rise and Fall of OSHA* (1986).

ROBERT PAEHLKE is a professor of politics at Trent University, Peterborough. Publications include *Environmentalism and the Future of Progressive Politics* (1989).

FRANK PEARCE is a professor of sociology at Queen's University, Kingston. Publications include *Crime's Global Connections* (1993).

PATRICIA PEPPIN is an assistant professor of law at Queen's University, Kingston. Publications include articles in the *Canadian Bar Review*.

HENRY N. PONTELL is a professor of sociology at the University of California at Irvine. Publications include *A Capacity to Punish: The Ecology of Crime and Punishment* (1984).

R. JACK RICHARDSON is an associate professor of sociology at McMaster University, Hamilton. Recent publications include 'Directorship Interlocks and Corporate Profitability' in *Administrative Science Quarterly* and articles on the trust industry and free trade in the *Canadian Review of Sociology*.

LAUREEN SNIDER is a professor of sociology at Queen's University, Kingston. Publications include *Bad Business* (1992).

W. T. STANBURY is UPS Foundation Professor of Regulation and Competition Policy at the University of British Columbia, Vancouver. Publications include *Canadian Competition Law and Policy at the Centenary* (1991).

STEVE TOMBS is a reader in organizational sociology at John Moore's University, Liverpool. Publications include articles in the *British Journal of Criminology*, the *Journal of Human Justice*, and the *Sociological Review*.

ERIC TUCKER is an associate professor of law at Osgoode Hall Law School, Toronto. Publications include *Administering Danger in the Workplace* (1990).

DAVE VERMA is a professor at McMaster University, Hamilton, and director of the Occupational Health Laboratory. He worked previously as an occupational hygienist in several provinces and in the United Kingdom and India.

VIVIENNE WALTERS is an associate professor of sociology at McMaster University, Hamilton. Publications include *Health and Safety Approaches in the Workplace* (1992).

KERNAGHAN WEBB is an adjunct professor of law at Carleton University, Ottawa, and senior policy analyst with the federal Office of Consumer Affairs. Publications include *Pollution Control in Canada: The Regulatory Approach in the 1980s* (1988).

PETER CLEARY YEAGER is an associate professor of sociology at Boston University. Publications include *The Limits of Law: The Public Regulation of Private Pollution* (1991).

Acknowledgments

The editors would like to thank the sponsors and all the participants in the conference 'Corporate Crime: Ethics, Law, and the State,' out of which this book grew. The conference, held 12–14 November 1992, was made possible by contributions from the Social Science and Humanities Council of Canada and from Queen's University – specifically, the Faculty of Arts and Science, the School of Graduate Studies and Research, the Faculty of Law, and the Departments of Philosophy, Political Studies, Psychology, and Sociology. We would also like to thank all those who participated in the conference as chairpersons, discussants, and presenters. We would like to thank in particular our research assistants, Ross Macmillan, Martha Roberts, Jackie Chelsky, James Williams, and Chris Anderson, for their pivotal contributions and their logistical and organizational support.

The book would not have come to fruition without the help of June Pilfold, of the Department of Sociology, and Natalie Forknall and Cheryl Corcoran, of the Faculty of Arts and Science. We also acknowledge with gratitude the help of Virgil Duff, of the University of Toronto Press, and of three anonymous reviewers, who made constructive suggestions. Anthony Woodiwiss, Steve Gill, and Steve Tombs provided us with significant theoretical input. Our families – Bill McLatchie; Cameron and Carolina McDonald; and Elaine Stavro-Pearce and Rory and Blake Stavro-Pearce – provided invaluable moral and intellectual support.

CORPORATE CRIME: CONTEMPORARY DEBATES

1

Introduction

FRANK PEARCE AND LAUREEN SNIDER

This book examines various kinds of corporate crime, focusing on its causes, extent, and control. It brings together scholars interested in corporate crime from a number of the Anglo-American democracies and from many disciplines. These people work in Canada, the United Kingdom, the United States, and Australia, and their disciplinary backgrounds range from law and business to economics, political science, and sociology. In their papers, written specially for this volume, we find complex examinations of a number of common themes.[1]

There is widespread agreement on the seriousness of corporate crime and the massive amount of harm it causes to economies, employees, consumers (particularly the poorest and least powerful), workplaces, and to the air we breathe, the water we drink, and the natural resources on which life on earth depends. There is agreement, too, on the inadequacy of controls, the paucity of deterrent mechanisms, and the mildness of sanctions imposed relative to harm done, although the efficacy of control varies broadly both over the different types of corporate crimes and from locality to locality, as well as from country to country.

But there is much less agreement on remedies and praxis, reflecting an underlying diversity of opinion on the causes of corporate criminality. Causes, and therefore solutions, can be found at the micro, or social-psychological levels, at the level of organizational structure, and at macro, or super-structural levels. The utility and potential of criminalization as a remedy for corporate crime, the appropriateness of corporate as opposed to individual criminal liability, the role and potential of government and specifically of regulatory agencies, and the utility of formal remedies versus informal remedies – those outside the law – are all hotly debated. Both the controversies and the consensus are reflected in this book.

The articles in part I look at the context within which corporate crime is committed, analysed, and controlled. Chapter 2, by the editors, Pearce and Snider, examines the controversy over the decline of the nation-state in an era characterized by global trading blocks, trans-national corporations, and the internationalization of capital. Neo-conservative economics, combined with yet another crisis of capitalism, this one fuelled by the panic of the right at the declining rate of surplus extraction in the period since the Second World War, unleashed a frenzy of deregulatory activity that has attacked both the philosophy and the resources of regulatory regimes. The apparently increasing weakness of the nation-state, combined with the attack on regulatory agencies and regimes, has left many observers wondering whether the battle against corporate crime has been irrevocably lost. Pearce and Snider argue, first, that the nation-state retains more power than the rhetoric of capital admits; second, that the new post-Fordist capitalist regimes are less successful than their supporters claim; and, third, that independent national and international regulatory schemes must be developed and advanced and can prove effective.

In a related vein, John Braithwaite, in chapter 3, shows the potential of policies based in the nation-state – in this case, Australia – to challenge and control corporate crime. Braithwaite argues that a 'new republicanism' is emerging in Australia, and perhaps in New Zealand and Canada as well, which reflects a resurgence of civility, notions of fairness, and a linking of power and privilege to accompanying obligations. He distinguishes this from liberal legal individualism, which privileges rights and individuals above duties and communities. The argument is rich in paradox: Braithwaite sees no problem in advocating the symbolic use of criminal law while abandoning it, except as a final alternative, in practice. Against corporate crime, the most useful strategy, he argues, escalates from initial persuasion to deterrence to incapacitation (defined as loss of licence to operate rather than incarceration). The compliance technique employed throughout is one of dialogue with offenders and their victims, bringing offenders face to face with the consequences of their deeds, rather than stressing threats, confrontion, and resulting loss of face.

Braithwaite presents three case studies illustrating the potential and the achievements of this model. Reforms to federal regulatory law governing quality of care in nursing homes in Australia culminated in the drawing up of thirty-one consensually derived standards that inspectors are now required to enforce. Residents and nursing-home operators meet with the inspectors, who report on their findings back to residents and operators in onsite meetings. The resulting combination of 'dialogue, empowerment of victims and responsible pyramidical enforcement has effected real improvement in a troubled industry' (Braithwaite 1993, 15). Two cases in the area of trade practice – one on false advertising in the carpet industry, the other a massive fraud involving misrepresentation to aboriginal people in the insurance industry – illustrate the potential of republican philosophies for securing redress and facilitating cooperation from offending corporations. The third study describes an experiment by Australia's Trade Practices Commission in allowing the pharmaceutical industry to police itself through self-regulation for a three-year trial period. Again, successful results are reported.

Braithwaite does not, however, mention the ideological climate and structural conditions that underlie these apparent successes. It is not clear, then, how much of this model is transferable to areas where the relations of capital, state, and citizens are different and where definitions of the responsibilities of capital and the requirements of 'good corporate citizenship' dramatically differ. Conditions as they are in Australia are probably more the exception than the rule. All the same, the model provides much for both activists and scholars to incorporate and to use.

In chapter 4, Gilbert Geis and Joseph DiMento offer a critique of the principle of corporate criminal liability. It is almost unknown in civil law countries and, they argue, serves no demonstrable purpose that could not be fulfilled equally well by more creative use of individual criminal liability. They set out to demolish the five key rationales for corporate criminal liability – the metaphysical argument and the arguments of expediency, efficiency, deterrence, and ease of redress. They conclude that the alleged benefits are at best not proven, and at worst, fallacious, mischievous, and socially harmful.

Chapter 5, by Patricia Peppin, describes the precedents and decisions that constitute present-day law on pharmaceutical products and analyses law from the perspective of key feminist goals. Peppin demonstrates that women in Western societies have a very different relationship with modern medicine and the drugs that doctors dispense than do men. Women are the primary consumers of medical care and of prescription and non-prescription drugs. The reasons are complex – biological (women live longer), economic (women are more likely to be poor), and structural and sociological (some women and many doctors accede to stereotypes of women as dependent and acquiescent to authority, particularly of the male variety). Moreover, research and treatment of women's diseases are notably underfunded. When key feminist goals of gender equality, affirmation of difference, control over one's body, and avoidance of harm are applied to pharmaceutical law, the sexism inherent in the legal status quo is revealed in striking detail. Ageism (prejudice against the old) and class prejudice are also apparent but not fully developed or theorized here.

The four chapters of part II examine corporate form and organization. In chapter 6, Harry Glasbeek looks at the futility of corporate criminal liability. He argues that the conceptualization of the corporation must be recognized as an ideological construction rather than an 'objective' attempt by university-based scholars to understand the nature of the modern corporation. He sees the work of lawyers and economists, especially those in the Law and Economics movement, as inherently political. The enthusiasm with which economic theories that legitimate the unfettered operation of free-market forces are embraced by mass media and the state is similarly ideological. The belief that corporate law scholarship is 'political machination' allows Glasbeek to agree with Geis and DiMento that abandoning corporate criminal liability would make no substantive difference – a somewhat surprising conclusion given that the principle has actually been used, especially in the United States, by judges seeking a legal mechanism to hold corporations responsible for harm inflicted.

Glasbeek starts from the premiss that lawyers and neo-conservative economists seek models of corporate governance that 'facilitate and justify the accumulation of wealth in private hands.' To do this, they must rescue capitalism from its inherent contradictions – those arising from the corporate directive to maximize profit versus 'the public interest' and, on an organizational scale, those generated by the separation of ownership (through shareholders and boards of directors) and management. The chapter sets out and analyses three theories on the nature of the corporation that have dominated the academy, law, and the state since the rise of incorporation as the key vehicle of capital accumulation – the corporation as a fiction created by the state; the corporation as a natural person with all the rights and responsibilities of such a being; and the contractarian approaches, which view the corporation as 'rational economic man.' The chapter focuses on the last-named because this model has gained immense intellectual and political respectability in recent decades. Contractarians argue that corporations must be free to pursue the goal of profit maximization; hence, regulatory bodies, directors representing labour or other broader interests, restrictions on take-overs, and all other 'fetters' simply impede the efficient operation of market forces and thus add costs and slow the generation of wealth. A variant of this theme is added by institutionalists, who tackle the theoretical implications of the separation of ownership and control by envisaging investors as freely choosing corporations as devices to reduce their costs of investing.

After exploring various attempts to unseat this form of reasoning, Glasbeek argues that the model is intellectually and internally consistent. It therefore represents a major challenge to those who seek to restrain capitalism. However, it is convincing only if one accepts the model's central and guiding assumption – that rational economic man relentlessly pursuing the goal of profit maximization in market relationships represents the only, and the most desirable, form of economic 'development.' The quest of humans to provide for their material needs is basic to our continued survival on this planet; is it true that, out of the many and varied models people have tried throughout history, only one, the pure capitalist model, is viable? And, furthermore, are we convinced that this model is the least destructive of all other human needs and values?

Steve Tombs is interested in the intersection of corporate form with occupational health-and-safety law. Accordingly, in chapter 7, he describes the various and much-heralded 'postmodern' organizations, characterized by fragmentation, or 'decentralization' (if in large firms), or small size (if independent); increased autonomy and responsibility and decreased surveillance over these units; corporate cultures emphasizing involvement, interaction, participation, and risk-taking; increased emphasis on market conditions, consumer demand, and new technologies; and 'down-sizing' through contracting out of as many functions as possible. Tombs recognizes the contradictions, inconsistencies, and sheer wishful thinking that characterize much of the literature on this subject, particularly as it describes the corporate sector in most developed countries. Nevertheless, his question is useful, if necessarily somewhat speculative. To the degree that postmodern organizations may represent the reality of the future, and the values that inspire them reflect wish fulfilment among today's business and academic elites, what are the implications for the occurrence, detection, and control of safety crimes?

Tomb's answer is sobering. When a decentralizing approach was applied to the chemical industry in the United Kingdom in the late 1980s, one result of the creation of more centres of power within corporations was the removal of any central unit with responsibility for monitoring safety. Many decentralized units did not even bother collecting data on compliance, a virtually certain signal of low priority. Moreover, safety was 'commodified' internally; it became a product merchandised by an internal unit, subject to the same requirements of cost-efficiency as others. Decentralization also led to reduced numbers of employees responsible for safety, to more work being contracted out (and thus performed by poorly trained and poorly paid workers), and weaker unions. Tombs sees several potential rays of light, however. New corporate forms are still in their infancy, and it is hard to predict which versions will become dominant. Moreover, they contain numerous contradictions, and employees might be able to wrest decision-making power and increased democracy of form and substance from the interstices.

In chapter 8, Peter Yeager contributes a richly textured analysis of managers' perceptions of morality in their day-to-day responsibilities as corporate actors, and the implications of those perceptions for societal control over unethical and/ or illegal behaviour. His work reinforces and substantiates, on a micro-level, the macro level contradictions of capitalism that are discussed by Tombs (chapter 7) and Keane (chapter 9), and that are implicit in Peppin's work (chapter 5). Yeager shows how these contradictions translate into personal conflicts experienced by managers between, for example, the corporate goal of maximizing profit, as transmitted by management in policy directives, and the directives of common morality – to be honest and straightforward with customers and fellow employees and respect their best interests. However, because personal ethical issues are publicly and privately inadmissible in corporate culture, these conflicts are translated into tensions between professional ethics and values and organizational requirements.

Yeager bases his study on interviews with managers at all levels, from CEOs to first-line managers, in all key units, with two companies, one in banking (46 interviews) and one in high technology (25 interviews). The research team found strong evidence of a moral division of labour, with conflicts between different levels in the organization. The aforementioned denial of ethical issues, not surprisingly, reinforces utilitarianism or pragmatism in decision-making. Yeager reinforces the observations of Tombs and Keane that decentralized management exacerbates this tendency by placing even more responsibility on low-level managers.

The implications for social change give cause for hope, if not for optimism. Yeager's study highlights the importance of professional value systems and ethics as culturally acceptable points of resistance to instrumental or dishonest corporate goals. Managers feel comfortable using them to argue against strategies that they see as unethical; there is potential, then, to strengthen and reinforce the salience of professional systems of ethics, since professional identifications constitute part of the background of a high percentage of corporate executives and managers. Yeager also points out that externally imposed regulations such as law will work to strengthen managers' ethical positions only when they are perceived as moral in themselves. Too often, the passage of new regulatory laws can be interpreted as political – a way for politicians who do not understand business to curry favour with constituents, provide a competitive advantage to large firms, or enrich the companies in the constituency of the politician sponsoring the legislation. The first way to ensure that this is not the perception is to ensure that it is not the reality – a point that takes us back to Braithwaite's observations about the importance of dialogue and consensus in generating compliance.

Carl Keane (chapter 9) analyses new corporate forms that involve decentralization, which he calls 'loosely coupled systems.' The high levels of uncertainty generated by the complex and contradictory demands of capitalism have long been recognized as potentially criminogenic. But when a corporation attempts to cope with an uncertain environment by decoupling, the resulting form may be more rather than less criminogenic. Keane first describes the traditional large-scale corporate pyramid, using General Electric as an example, and then lists the benefits and the dangers of loose coupling. While conferring greater flexibility, cost-effectiveness, responsiveness to markets, and more knowledge of local environments and conditions, loose coupling can also increase the motivation for and decrease the mechanisms of control over illegal behaviour. Keane provides numerous examples of the potentially disastrous effects of both organizational and individual decoupling on the environment, worker safety, and the like.

The articles in part III look at financial crimes, beginning with Michael Levi's subtle analysis in chapter 10 of serious fraud cases in the United Kingdom. Levi puts empirical clothing on several crucial issues in the regulation and control of such offences. In no developed Western country is business crime treated in the same manner as 'conventional' crime, although the monetary damage caused by the latter is minuscule. Levi illustrates some of the reasons for this state of affairs. First, the globalization of financial services means nation-states now compete for investment, and 'too much' (as well as 'too little') regulation puts a country at a competitive disadvantage. Second, there are special difficulties in reconstructing complex corporate dealings for any kind of tribunal – criminal, civil, or administrative. This is particularly true with respect to criminal courts, where cases must be reconstructed years after the offences occurred, before judges (and juries) who lack expertise in the areas concerned, and with substantiation provided by witnesses who have professional reputations to maintain and who are therefore motivated to reconstruct cases in ways that do least damage to themselves. Third, there is the fact of moral ambiguity – whatever one's normative judgment, influential segments of the public do view financial crimes committed by distinguished senior executives differently from those committed by unemployed youth or by rogue 'cowboy' capitalists. A consequence of this attitude is that less pressure is exerted on state bodies to act, or to act punitively.

Levi takes all these complexities, and more, and shows how they complicate notorious fraud cases such as *Guinness* and *Blue Arrow.* He also gives an overview of the regulatory agencies involved and their very different budgets, powers, rationales, and modes of operation. It is clear that criminal prosecution is not successful with many massive frauds, and not cost-effective even if convictions are obtained. However, Levi is keenly aware of the symbolic value of criminalization and concludes with the apt observation that 'the mode in which we deal with crime is legitimately a site for struggle.' In other words, the applications of social control will differ across nation-states in line with the particular historical, ideological, social, and economic factors shaping each struggle.

For the United States, Kitty Calavita and Henry N. Pontell (chapter 11) explicate the massive savings-and-loan debacle which broke in the United States in 1988 but whose repercussions are ongoing. They describe the causes and ramifications of the many and varied illegalities involved in this series of crimes and seek to explain the relatively aggressive and punitive response (compared with the response to other corporate crimes) of the federal government and the systemic inadequacies that ultimately stymied its efforts. Government interest in prosecution is explained by differentiating kinds of corporate crimes – an elementary 'sorting' that too many theorists neglect. Financial crimes of this sort threaten not only the organization and its consumers/investors but also undermine the financial viability of capitalist markets, thereby threatening the crucial ability of capital to raise, trade, and manipulate shares. While this situation does not automatically wipe out national differences in responding to fraud, it does, as Levi's chapter illustrates, provide a stimulus to action.

However, Calavita and Pontell show that even the massive resources of federal agencies in one of the world's richest, and most prosecutorially inclined, countries were woefully insufficient to handle the investigation and prosecution necessary for frauds of this magnitude. Even investigating and prosecuting only the most serious cases proved impossible. 'Damage control' therefore became the chosen option. This example illustrates the practical limitations of wholesale adoption of criminalization, whatever its benefits symbolically and from an egalitarian perspective, if anything close to full enforcement is envisaged.

Chapter 12 looks at competition law in Canada. W.T. Stanbury looks at the history of enforcement against individuals and companies involved in conspiracy, misleading advertising, price maintenance, and unfair competition, and argues that individuals (as well as corporations, where appropriate) should be held accountable for illegal anti-competitive acts. This has not been the practice under Canada's Competition Act or its predecessor (from 1889 to 1986), the Combines Investigation Act. Stanbury's arguments for holding the individual accountable relate to the literature of social psychology and deterrence as well as organizational theory. The empirical part of the chapter sets out the history of the prosecution of individuals, showing that although sanctions have been small in relation to harm done, they have been on the rise in recent decades. Stanbury concludes with a discussion of the politics of business law, from its instigation to its enforcement – an analysis that clearly shows the success of business interests in shaping law, regulatory agencies and the judiciary to their own advantage.

Part IV addresses dilemmas of safety and health in the workplace. Despite the ideology of street crime, people are statistically much more likely to die on the job than down a dark alley in a major city. All three chapters in this part combine theory and data to reach their conclusions, but Tucker (chapter 13) and Noble (14) are perhaps more concerned with conceptual issues, pointing out the theoretical weaknesses in regulatory processes pertaining to occupational health and safety; Walters and her colleagues (chapter 15) illustrate these problems.

In chapter 13, Eric Tucker posits three distinct periods: 1830–80, the era of market regulation, when workers were required to sue their employers to prove negligence; 1880–1970, the era of command and control, characterized by statutes enforced by inspectors backed up by courts; and 1970 to the present, the so-called third wave of regulation, wherein workers have the right to be informed of workplace dangers, to refuse unsafe work, and to monitor workplace conditions. Like every author who has studied the field, Tucker concludes that the results have been disappointing overall, despite some 'improvement in material and ideological conditions that situate future struggles.' As Tucker points out, the definition of 'reasonable risk' is constantly being renegotiated and reconstructed, with its limits usually being defined by the possibilities of profitable production in the particular industry and the particular nation-state. Thus, improvement is contingent on the relations of power among workers, capital, and the state, and the dominant ideologies arising from these. With present conditions and trends apparently limiting rather than increasing the bargaining power of workers, he finds it difficult to be optimistic about the possibilities of the present stage of reform, even though the province of Ontario, the site of his analyses, has strengthened rather than weakened the legal rights of workers, on paper, during the last decade.

Charles Noble comes to similar conclusions in chapter 14 by looking at the rather different situation that characterizes federal occupational health- and-safety law in the United States. He recognizes that, historically, workers have made 'substantial gains' and discusses five basic regulatory strategies he sees as dominating the American scene. The success of any and all of them, however, depends ultimately on political will and on the power of workers, employers, and the state. His analysis focuses on the history and record of the Occupational Health and Safety Act (OSHA), presenting useful data that update his 1986 book. The data certainly provide ample documentation of his conclusion that labour is too weak in the United States to allow legislation to work to its advantage.

Vivienne Walkers and her co-authors report in chapter 15 on face-to-face interviews conducted with managers and workers' representatives in seven unionized workplaces in Ontario. Their fascinating results show how third-wave reform works in practice – or, rather, why it does not work as originally envisaged. Both workers and managers tend to emphasize workers' culpability and individual responsibility while putting little emphasis on risks generated by the nature of work or the social relations of production. Workers have a less significant role in redefining hazards than expected, in part because they allow management to define reasonable and unreasonable risks – and this despite the fact that only unionized workplaces were sampled. The situation would in all likelihood be more extreme in non-unionized firms. The recession has also weakened workers' clout, as they fear for their jobs, while managers have gained power. The result is less overt conflict between management and labour, but one cannot conclude that the workplace has been made safer.

None of the authors in part IV mentions the potential of outside monitoring groups to make a difference in occupational health and safety. Indeed the role of such bodies in this area of corporate crime has been minimal, reflecting dominant cultural beliefs (and practices) that define conditions on the job as, in some senses, private matters to be resolved by those directly affected – employers and employees. State intervention is now seen as legitimate in extreme situations, but, overall, how bosses treat employees is ideologically privatized. Contrast the minimal role of outside pressure groups here with the very different situation in environmental regulation. There citizens' pressure groups operate in conjunction with capital, labour and the state to create a very complex set of options and statagems.

Robert Paehlke's analysis of environmental law and policy (chapter 16) opens part V. Paehlke, though unwilling to condemn criminal law outright, argues that it has many practical disadvantages, not the least of which is its politically unfashionable status at the present time. His article is an exercise in model-building and prediction, with an emphasis on policy alternatives. Paehlke starts with an overview of a number of issues surrounding definition and regulation of environmental offences. He looks at the harm represented by each and points out that most environmental offences are complex. It may take several generations and require intricate regression analyses to determine the part played by environmental carcinogens (such as toxic waste) in causing disease. This makes it extremely difficult to attribute blame, a necessary precondition for prosecution. And because blame is problematic and everyone is responsible for problems such as human overpopulation and the destruction of rain forests, no one is (legally) to blame. An allied complexity is the difficulty in attaching self-interest to environmental concerns. Self-interest has been a major factor in actions forcing governments to enact and enforce legislation, and its relative (though not absolute) absence in environmental offences constitutes a major political problem. So does the fact that environmental protection does not fit easily into right/left categories. In theory, this should make it easier to build national coalitions, but, in practice, with forces on the right and the left both promoting economic growth, albeit for different reasons, it makes policy formulation more difficult. Finally, Paehlke points out that the trans-national, global nature of environmental offences conflicts with the local or national emphasis and power base of most activists.

Looking at policy options in the future, Paehlke foresees major problems. Governments will be forced to accede to demands of growth coalitions, coming from both the right and the left, if recession and unemployment continue unabated. He excoriates environmentalists for paying too little attention to the human pain some environmental struggles have caused. However, if environmentalist pressure groups were to address issues such as the political implications of jobless growth and explore policy alternatives compatible with environmental protection, this outcome would be avoided. Paehlke suggests numerous possibilities that combine environmental protection with protection of people – for example, job-sharing, substance bans, and revenue options that remove subsidies from environmentally harmful industries and encourage job creation in environmentally friendly activities.

In the end, Paehlke takes a pragmatic approach to environmental protection. He is willing to explore and endorse all options, from the creation of new criminal offences such as environmental manslaughter and greater regulatory sanctions (beloved of the command-and-control schools) to the economic, market-based incentives favoured by new right deregulationists, to cooperative strategies. The approach is somewhat postmodern, recalling Tombs' discussion, in that it emphasizes flexibility and specificity and calls for the use of whatever tools are most applicable to the situation in question.

Chapter 17 is a case study by Harold Barnett of attempts by U.S. federal agencies in United States to force industrial corporations to clean up their environmental messes. Barnett begins with a history of attempts by the Environmental Protection Agency and the Congress to clean up hazardous waste sites by setting aside vast sums of money to create what is called a Superfund. The purpose of Superfund was to clean up hazardous waste sites, force polluters to pay their share, and get the public to contribute the remainder. Over 60 per cent of the total cleanup bill, estimated to be between $100 billion and $300 billion, was thought to be recoverable from the offending corporations. However, aggressive enforcement, stressing punitive sanctions and litigation, has achieved little, except to increase the personal fortunes of an endless variety of lawyers and professional lobbyists. After more than a decade of wasted effort, a compromise solution has been suggested, and this is what Barnett seeks to analyse. The compromise minimizes confrontation in favour of policies that involve all parties (reminiscent of Braithwaite's prescriptions) and seeks to use flexibility and negotiation instead of the blame and rigidity that have characterized the approach taken to date.

Barnett employs a structuralist analysis to describe the failures of the original strategy, pointing out the effects of tensions between policies dictated by the state's contrasting needs for accumulation and legitimacy. Applying the same framework to the compromise now being employed, he comes up with a choice of two conclusions – one pessimistic and one optimistic. Each is consistent with structuralist analyses, but the optimistic allows more room for agency and struggle and relies more heavily on concepts of enlightened self-interest.

Kernaghan Webb, in chapter 18, offers an overview of regulatory offences in Canada (with particular emphasis on environmental law) and a strong defence of the superiority of regulatory over criminal law. Webb argues that the practical problems of criminal law, particularly the necessity of proving 'mens rea,' make it inefficient in comparison with the relative flexibility provided for regulatory offences. In the latter, the onus is on defendants to prove that they have exercised 'due diligence' or that a 'reasonable' mistake of fact occurred. The standard of reasonableness is objective, not subjective, so the corporation cannot escape responsibility by claiming that its officers believed the incorrect fact that caused the offence if a reasonable layperson would not have made that mistake. Webb also argues that regulatory offenders are held by the standards of strict liability to a higher standard of conduct than they would be under criminal law, because of the aforementioned standards of proof. The onus in regulatory law is less on the state to prove culpability and more on the defendant to prove that he or she took reasonable care. This is entirely appropriate, given the privileged positions that those in regulated sectors enjoy, but it does – or should – make it harder for offenders to escape responsibility.

Webb also argues that new criminal laws are not necessary to cover environmental damage because relevant offences in Canada's Criminal Code can be applied where intentional harm or negligence is suspected. And regulatory offences already make use of fines and penal sanctions to punish offenders, who are thus not getting off more easily than they would under criminal law. Moreover, Webb thinks that Canadian governments, notoriously lax in the past, are becoming increasingly interested in enforcement, pushed by tort actions and due diligence defences that make governments complicit in the offence if their actions are deemed insufficient. He cites the establishment of separate enforcement units for environmental offences in Ontario, Quebec, and British Columbia. And he sees evidence that the federal Supreme Court, spurred by Charter of Rights cases, is finally developing a distinctive approach that legitimates the imposition of penal liability, including imprisonment, for regulatory offenders.

It could be argued, conversely, that Webb's well-developed and carefully reasoned chapter overlooks the ideological advantages of criminalization – its ability to attract media attention and to symbolize evil. The ideological significance of criminalization means that a criminal prosecution that ends in acquittals may be more successful, in terms of pressing politicians and corporations into socially responsible behaviour, than ten convictions under regulatory law. Webb's approach also assumes that active countervailing groups will be present, pressing governments and courts to carry out their duties. This is not the case for the vast majority of complex, boring regulatory offences, overseen only by the understaffed and weak regulatory agency and a usually inert Parliamentary opposition.

Colin Goff (chapter 19) focuses on attempt by fifteen citizens in Nova Scotia to challenge two major multinational corporations – an American pesticide manufacturer, Dow Chemical, and a Swedish company operating pulp-and-paper mills. Residents in affected areas have struggled since 1976 to prevent air and ground spraying of dangerous chemicals, allegedly necessary to kill the spruce budworm destroying the forests and thereby indirectly threatening the main source of jobs and prosperity in the area. In 1982–3, local residents obtained a temporary injunction against the spraying but then had to prove in court that the substances being sprayed were indeed harmful to people. Not surprisingly, they lost.

Goff discusses the trial in detail, pointing out that the ideology of scientism reinforced the perception that witnesses called by the multinationals were 'objective' and 'unbiased,' whereas those called by the plaintiffs were well-meaning victims of misguided 'zeal.' In fact, later documents revealed that the so-called objective evidence was not only reversed by later studies, but was based on fraudulent data. Goff also points out that, even though the plaintiffs lost the case, environmental causes were advanced by the judge's decision to accept the idea that citizens had a right to intervene in the process through a class-action suit and, hence, that they had a stake in the outcome, even though they were not 'directly' involved, according to traditional legal reasoning and precedent. Finally, Goff points out the importance that regional disparities of wealth and power within developed countries in the First World play in environmental politics, with the relatively small and capital-hungry province of Nova Scotia being a case in point.

NOTES

1 The book came out of a conference held at Queen's University in Kingston, Ontario, in

November 1992. The conference brought together scholars, activists, and practitioners
interested in corporate crime from many different disciplines and several nations.
Some of the papers presented at the conference were rewritten and edited, and these,
with the addition of the introduction and chapter 2, 'Regulating Capitalism,' comprise
the book.

PART I

Controlling Corporate Crime

2

Regulating Capitalism

FRANK PEARCE AND LAUREEN SNIDER

Any study dealing with corporate crime and regulation today must address questions about the continuing viability of the nation-state. Legislation originating in national (federal) or provincial (state) levels has been the main vehicle for controlling the offences of corporations in Western democracies. However partial and inadequate regulation has been, there is no comparable countervailing body with the motivation or ability to oversee the vast agglomerations of privilege and power known as corporations.

Recently, moreover, the nation-state has been undermined both externally and internally. Internally, ethnic tensions, the rise of interest-group politics, increasing unemployment, and lower standards of living have led to unprecedented levels of cynicism and discontent with politicians and politics. Externally, the power of trans-national corporate bodies has grown exponentially, fuelled by technological advances that have freed capital from national or temporal boundaries, the corporate takeover frenzy of the 1980s, and the proliferation of free-trade zones. These new mega-corporations are not responsible to any nation-state, as they do not need a geographic centre or headquarters in the traditional sense and operate around the world, moving capital and resources with lightning speed. The ability of the weakened nation-state to handle the reinforced power of private capital, and the viability of the nation-state in an era of free trade become crucial issues.

This chapter explores these issues, beginning with an examination of the economic philosophies that facilitate these structural and ideological transitions of the nation-state. Compared to most citizens in most other countries, the vast majority of those living in the twenty-four countries that are members of the Organization for Economic Cooperation and Development (OECD) have a dramatically better standard of living. On average, they work fewer hours, live longer, are healthier and better housed, have access to a greater volume and

range of goods and services, are more mobile, and, through their easy access to
a range of mass media, are exposed to more information. They have better education and better medical care and, through unemployment benefits, welfare,
workers' compensation, and pensions, are much more secure.

A historical perspective on the same OECD countries shows an equally dramatic improvement in life within them compared to a hundred years ago. These
particularly prosperous nations are also pivotal in international trade – in 1988,
over 80 per cent of such trade occurred between them. Further, they are the core
of the three emerging trade blocs – those based in Europe, the Americas, and the
Pacific Rim – which, in turn, incorporate virtually all the other dynamic
national economies – including southern Europe, Mexico and Chile, and the
four Asian 'tigers' (Hong Kong, Singapore, South Korea, and Taiwan).

In all these states, the dominant form of economic organization is capitalistic
– that is, these are market economies based on private property, with markets in
capital and in labour (in Canada, the United Kingdon, and the United States, for
example, over 80 per cent of individuals are employees). The limited-liability
corporation is the main legal mechanism through which capital is brought
together and interacts in the various marketplaces. The activities of the organizational entity supported by this legal form are, of course, the major subject of
this book. This type of enterprise makes possible dispersed individual
shareholding, which, along with significant institutional shareholding, is
believed to invalidate simple class polarizations. For example, in 1990, 24 per
cent of the adult population in Britain and 25 per cent in the United States
owned shares. In the former nation, these individuals owned 21.3 per cent of all
shares, unit trusts 5.9 per cent, insurance companies 18.4 per cent and pension
funds 30.4 per cent (Whitfield 1992, 314–15). It is estimated that, by the end of
this century, institutional investors will hold 85 per cent of outstanding equity in
Britain, 55–66 per cent in the United States, and 60–65 per cent in Canada
(Phillips 1992, 82).

Within most of these national economies, a limited number of corporations
own most of the economically productive assets and appropriate most of the
profits; they are the major employers and fund most commercially based
research as well. For example, in the 1980s, the top five hundred U.S. corporations were responsible for over 75 per cent of all sales, received as much as 85
per cent of profits, and owned nearly 90 per cent of all assets (Cherry et al.
1987, 311). The Canadian economy is, if anything, even more concentrated –
six conglomerates control 723 companies, and, according to the Canadian
Bankers' Association, 'nine families control 46 per cent of the value of the most
important companies on the Toronto Stock Exchange' (cited in Clement 1988,
7). The German economy is led by approximately thirteen interrelated groups,

which generally integrate financial and industrial concerns (J.F. Scott 1979, 91–2), and the Japanese economy is structured around a limited number of groups of corporations, or *keiretsu* (Clegg 1990; J.F. Scott 1979, 92–3). Indeed, of the one hundred largest economies in the world in 1989, forty-seven were corporations, not countries. In 1992, Exxon, General Motors, Itochu, and Sumitomo all had sales revenue in excess of $100 billion a year – more than the gross domestic product of Denmark, Finland, and Norway combined. Many Japanese, American, and French banks own assets worth as much, if not more (*Forbes* 19, July 1993, 142; Green and Sutcliffe 1987, 21).

Such large corporations produce the bulk of the internationally traded goods and services, and they often produce them globally. For example, in the 1980s, the computer company Motorola, while maintaining in the United States its corporate headquarters and facilities for all aspects of its production process, had overseas operations that included design centres in Hong Kong, Japan, and Switzerland; wafer-fabrication plants and testing centres in France, Scotland, and West Germany; and assembly plants in Malaysia, the Philippines, and South Korea (Henderson 1989, Figure 4.2, pp. 56–7). Not surprisingly, then, most OECD-based trade occurs between and within the large corporations themselves (U.N. Centre of Transnational Corporations 1984; Knox and Agnew 1989, 192).

The correspondence of affluence with trade within and between these countries and large corporations is seen by many as a vindication of the corporate-capitalist market system and a demonstration that there is a generalized benefit from trading between different economic units with varied forms of comparative advantages (Dunning 1979; World Bank 1989; but see N. Smith 1984).

What needs to be explored further, however, are the differences as well as the similarities between these nation-states. What, for example, is the nature of and relationship among their economies, states, and societies? We also need to know how, why, and with what consequences these have changed over time. Relatedly, we need to know about changes in their relationship to the international economic and political order and, indeed, about changes in that order itself. Neither the descriptions nor the explanations of these phenomena are theory-neutral. Although the theorists frequently fail to acknowledge this fact, their analyses depend on the paradigms within which the theorists themselves are operating.

A NEO-LIBERAL WORLD ORDER?

One way of understanding the nature and development of contemporary societies is expressed in modernization theory, encapsulated in Lipset's less- than-modest description of the United States as 'The First New Nation' (Lipset 1968), which he generously expanded to include a backward Canada in *Continental Divide* (Lipset 1990). In these two words, Lipset makes clear that we have seen the future and it is 'Amerika.' Using more complex arguments, Daniel Bell thinks the United States is leading the way by becoming a post-industrial society, characterized by the 'centrality of theoretical knowledge and the expansion of the service sector as against a manufacturing economy' (Bell 1976; xix).[1]

In this chapter, our focus is more on two other ways of describing contemporary societies, both of which have been significant – the one in structuring the policy of governments, the other in disarming the politics of resistance. The economic understanding developed by the Chicago school has influenced the entire developed world, and the American, British, and Chilean governments, to mention but three, have redesigned their states and economies to follow its dictates. The economic and political understanding generated by some uses of the concept of post-Fordism, in contrast, has helped undermine collective resistance to the global power of capital. Allegedly, the combination of consumer demand for more differentiated and high quality products and a new capacity to provide for such 'niche' markets – short production runs of new products that can be produced frequently, quickly, and cheaply, thanks to the development of flexible general-purpose machines and computer-integrated design and production – has made old-style economies of scale less important than economies of scope (R. Murray 1985, 44). For Leadbetter (1989), this means that old class based identities and strategies are no longer relevant; our goal, instead, should be 'power to the person.'

In the view of the Chicago school, everybody's lawful pursuit of self- interest in the free market produces an efficient allocation of resources, maximizes production, enhances individual self-satisfaction, and promotes liberty and freedom of choice. According to this view, then, the market is the most just and effective regulator of economic conduct (Stigler 1952). Indeed, using the 'economic model of man' (and it is men who are modelled) as a basis for understanding human conduct and organizing legal institutions can, it is believed, produce more rational policies in every area of the modern state, including crime control, welfare provision, and education (Becker 1963; Kelman 1987).

The Chicago school also recognizes that, although production can and does take place through ad hoc, temporary contractual relationships with independent agents, there are often fewer transaction costs – 'search and information costs, bargaining and decision costs, policing and enforcement costs' (Dahlman 1979) – for entrepreneurs if they develop permanent, centralized, authoritative organizations (firms). By so doing, they spare themselves the necessity of continuously renegotiating and monitoring contracts. Furthermore, it may be advantageous to them as well as socially efficient to develop very large organizations indeed. Thus, current trends to concentration in parts of U.S. industry indicate efficiencies resulting from engineering and production developments, new distribution techniques, or new control-and-management techniques (Bork 1978, 205–6; Williamson 1975, 101, 102, 104). Firms often grow through mergers which these enable firms to exploit economies of scale more quickly than they could by internal expansion and place assets in the hands of superior managers and punish or displace inefficient or corrupt managers (Posner 1976, 96). Furthermore, an authoritative order is a more efficient way to settle conflicts than is haggling or litigation, and conflicts between independent firms can be settled by fiat rarely, if at all. In North American, 'efficiency is the main and only systematic factor responsible for the organizational changes that have occurred' (Williamson 1983; see also Chandler 1969, 1977, 1990).

A perfectly contestable market characterized by optimal behaviour can exist within a full range of industry structures, including even oligopoly (Bork 1978, 221–2) and monopoly. In part because of the growth of international competition, potential entry into a market disciplines behaviour almost as effectively as would actual competition *within* the market even in highly concentrated industries (E. Bailey 1981; Baumol 1982; see Snider 1991 for an illustration of this belief in the revision of competition law in Canada). This analysis vastly extends the domain of the invisible hand. Firms, then, arise, survive, and grow when they are the most efficient way of organizing production. Equally, they may decline or be restructured under different circumstances. In other words, this theory also explains the kinds of changes in corporate form described by Elizabeth Moss Kanter (1989) and discussed below.

Chicago economists have been at the forefront of the movements to deregulate the British and American economies, and they have encouraged the development of such free trade zones as the maquilederos. They argue that any kind of state intervention in the economy poses tremendous dangers to the working of market rationality. For, although state activities are usually justified as being necessary to correct allocative problems caused by market failure, they in fact function primarily to redistribute resources in a socially inefficient way. The effect of the activities of regulatory agencies, for example, is that consumers end up paying higher prices than is necessary to the benefit of small groups of highly motivated and well-organized actors – established (and inefficient) firms, full-time regulators, and pork barrel politicians (cf Stigler 1971; Peltzman 1976). Regulation also benefits 'politically motivated' entrepreneurs such as environmentalists and compliant regulators and politicians (Weaver 1978; J. Wilson 1980). To avoid these consequences, regulation is best achieved by a combination of market forces and private litigation.

Occupational safety and health, for example, can be viewed as a good, bought and sold as part of the wage bargain. Some workers who 'do not value additional safety very highly relative to additional income – whether because they are poor, have high pain thresholds, or just do not care' (R. Smith 1982, 213) – knowingly select hazardous jobs because they receive substantially better compensation than they would in safer ones (Viscusi 1979, 1983).[2] In an equilibrium situation, the worker's total compensation (wages plus the marginal cost of safety per worker) will be equal to the value of the worker's marginal product. At that point, the supply of safety will reflect workers' demands for protection and the resource costs of reducing risk (Viscusi 1983, 136; see also Chelius 1977). These resource costs include those of workers' compensation and other insurance, of investing in safe technology and work practices, and of litigation (Oi 1977).[3]

Chicago economists have also been prominent as advisers in eastern Europe since the collapse of the 'communist' economies[4] and in the privatization movement that has swept the world in the last decade. They admit that under some conditions of market failure – a high initial fixed-cost capital investment, when economies of scale are realized only with high- volume production but where there is only a limited market – monopoly may be economically rational. Under these circumstances, in theory, a state enterprise would be 'unlikely to exploit customers by raising prices as much as would a profit-oriented firm' (Foreman-Peck 1989, 134). However, they argue that, in reality, the primary beneficiaries of such state monopolies have been their underworked, overpaid, inefficient managers and unionized employees, not consumers (Brittan 1988: 164). Moreover, conditions of natural monopoly, always rare, are becoming ever rarer with new technologies.

It is also argued, by these and other economists, that universal provision of welfare discourages participation in the labour market and artificially inflates wages for all areas of economic activity. Similarly, paying for utilities from taxation or by charging a standard flat fee is seen as less efficient than charging user fees. If income redistribution is to be a goal of government policy, it is better achieved by a program of targeted income support (Fine 1990, 111–37). Keynesian policies also cause problems, since credit expansion sustains unprofitable producers. Such state activities generate inflation, increase uncertainty and discourage productive investment. The state should aim instead to achieve stable prices, to restrict the money supply, and remove barriers to competition in labour, product, and financial markets, hence encouraging innovation (Clarke 1988, 60). Allegedly, the success of the four Asian 'tigers' results from their having embraced such free-market policies.

By 1991, more than eighty-eight countries had privatized public assets. In mixed economies, the privatization wave was initiated by Pinochet in Chile after the murder of Salvador Allende and was an integral element of the Chilean 'miracle.' Britain followed, with estimated sales of £87 billion between 1979 and 1992 (Whitfield 1992, 141), in its attempt to establish a dynamic 'people's capitalism.' Between 1984 and 1988, Canada sold off all or part of forty governmental organizations, for $4.6 billion (Mosco 1989, 208–9). This international trend has been caused by the coming to power of governments influenced by these economists (who argued that selling off assets allowed for the most efficient way of engaging in economic production and facilitated a necessary decrease in government debt)[5] and by pressure from the International Monetary Fund (IMF), particularly on countries caught in the 'debt trap' by the explosion of credit in the 1970s and the subsequent collapse of commodity prices.

This process of privatization in traditionally mixed economies has of course provided new market opportunities for many firms, particularly in the financial, manufacturing, and service sectors. Since, increasingly, the only way of producing and distributing goods and services is by capitalist enterprises in a global market economy, the world now looks like a more 'rational' place. There has been a concomitant attempt to reduce the role of the state to that of nightwatch, providing nothing except security from enemies without and within and a feeble safety net for the 'deserving poor.'

The agents of this new hegemonic strategy have been large multinational companies, right-wing governments and politicians, particularly from the United States and Britain, and right-wing academics. As Cox (1993b, 266) has pointed out, their ideas have developed within such unofficial bodies as

the Trilateral Commission, the Bilderburg conferences, the Club of Rome, the more esoteric Mont Pelerin Society among others – and then endorsed through official consensus making agencies like the OECD. A new doctrine defined the tasks of states in relaunching capitalist development out of the depression of the 1970s. There was, in the words of a blue-ribbon OECD committee, a 'narrow path of growth' bounded on one side by the need to encourage private investment by increasing profit margins, and bounded on the other by the need to avoid kindling inflation.

The government-business alliance formed to advance along this narrow path ruled out corporative-type solutions like negotiated wage and price policies and also the expansion of public investment. It placed primary emphasis on restoring the confidence of business in government and in practice acknowledged that welfare and employment commitments made in the framework of the post-war social contact would have to take second place.

These policies have been rigorously pursued under pressure from the IMF and the World Bank (Petras and Morley 1990, 5; Whitfield 1992, 283–5).

This reduction in the power and role of the state has several consequences. It makes democratic demands less articulable, less realizable, and hence, if they are designed to constrain capital, much less effective. Employers in both public and private sectors are convinced that it is too expensive to regulate or pay 'decent' wages or benefits and that the requirement of competing in a global marketplace demands a few roll-backs and benefit reductions. They are also convinced (despite the evidence below) that government regulatory structures are counterproductive and inefficient. Bargaining takes place in a world where reducing the deficit has become the number-one economic priority (even if the deficit is caused by borrowing for productive investment), an article of faith now with governments of every political stripe. These ideological changes mean that progressive forces have lost legitimacy and the indirect leverage it provides, as well as losing bargaining power because of structural changes in the nature of capital and allied reductions in the percentage of workforces in unions.

The reduced role of the state has other effects as well. In the different settings where capital and other groups – workers, consumers, communities, and nation-states – are players, capital has a tremendous relative (but not absolute) advantage. The reduction in the power of the state has immensely increased 'the structural power of capital' (Gill and Law 1993), particularly that of the massive, geographically mobile multinationals. If the state does not provide goods and services, governments have to persuade capital to provide them, and they do so in a world where capital increasingly holds the best cards.

We are all becoming aware of the negative consequences of unbridled and unregulated industrial growth. Global warming, depletion of the ozone layer, and poisoning of the atmosphere, sea, and land may now be on the political agenda, but, for the well-being of many of us, this may be too little and too late. Furthermore, the continuous occurrence of high-tech disasters and the more routine damage inflicted by industry on working people and communities in developed and underdeveloped, capitalist and Stalinist regimes warn us of the general dangers of industrialization when it is beyond democratic control (Perrow 1984; De Bardelon 1985; Cook 1989; Pearce and Tombs 1989, 1993; Medvedev and Sakharov 1991; M.R. Reich 1991).

A NEW HEGEMONY?

These ideas represent a particular way of conceptualizing economic activity, the global economy, and the role of the state. This conception, we argue below, conceals as much as it reveals. The move to privatization has been associated with a non-contingent increase in inequality – generally, the lower the wage and benefit level, the fewer the 'natural monopolies' (Fine 1990, 124–6). This, combined with deregulation and the move away from progressive taxation, has led to a tremendous shift in resources and power to capital (Edsall 1984; Field 1989; Hudson and Williams 1989; Phillips 1991; Bartlett and Steele 1992; Whitfield 1992; Wilson 1992). The welfare state has become at best a 'workfare state' (Fine 1990, 129; Jessop 1993).

Despite the theory's status as a dominant, hegemonic 'truth,' it is far from clear that private enterprise is unequivocally more efficient than public, or state, ownership.[6] Many public enterprises, such as SNCF and other nationalized European rail networks, have been economically efficient. Others, like the Norwegian North Sea natural gas company (Statoil Group) and the French Société nationale Elf Aquitaine Group, Thomson CSF (*Forbes* 19 July 1993, 134), and Renault (*Globe and Mail* 7 September 1993, B11), have also been profitable. Moreover, private enterprise has sometimes showed profits only because it was able to avoid the restrictions imposed on state enterprises. It has demanded, for example, the freedom to enter new markets or raise finance commercially (Whitfield 1983, 37). It has repudiated obligations to provide workers with a living wage or a reasonable pension and evaded obligations to implement employment equity.[7] It has sought to reject obligations to service all income levels, as opposed to providing for those with the ability to pay the price demanded. It would not be willing to subsidize other companies, whereas the nationalized British coal industry in the 1950s had to subsidize the private-enterprise steel industry (Jenkins 1959). Historically, more nationalizations have occurred because private enterprise failed to run key industries effectively and/or because of a need to resolve *for capital* a more general crisis of accumulation (Jessop 1990, 157) than because the state recognized the need for a natural monopoly (see, with regard to Britain, Chile, and Mexico, for example, Whitfield 1992, 281–2).[8]

Private companies have involved themselves inprovision of public services only when opportunities to make profits were relatively poor elsewhere, and, as argued above, they sought to serve only those with an ability to pay, leaving sizeable minorities without heat, electricity, or health care. Such practices reproduce pre-existing inequalities and limit the production of healthy, well-educated working people. They waste human lives and human resources. Perhaps, in assessing the impact of economic activities, it is important to go beyond the narrow confines of the rate of profit, partial productivity statistics, or even consumers' satisfactions. Economics, after all, 'is concerned with the efficient use of resources, and many economic activities which may be non-commercial (i.e., non-profitable for the enterprises concerned) may prove still to be *economic* – in the sense that for the economy as a whole the total gains exceed the total costs incurred' (Donaldson and Farquar 1988, 141).[9] Indeed,

Macro measures like the GNP and GDP can also be misleading because they treat the flow of goods and services (and the generation of incomes) as the sole basis of the GNP. Yet, these include defensive use of many resources with extremely high opportunity costs. For example, it is more rational to treat the use of resources required for environmental cleanups as a cost and to subtract this from the GNP and to treat as costs the waste of the potential use of resources generated by problems created by the private automobile, centralisation, urbanisation and contemporary. (Waring 1988, 292–3)

We would argue that meaningful criteria for judging efficiency should 'include an assessment of the ability to innovate in the widest sense,' since 'the dynamics of entrepreneurial performance must surely be a major factor in explaining differences in the growth of total factor productivity' (Fine 1990, 131–2). Further, it is important to explore which specific kinds of activities contribute to the growth of the economy as a whole and particularly how they link into other key manufacturing activities. In the United Kingdom, for example, 'the fate[s] of the coal, steel, and water industries are closely tied together' (Fine 1990, 133). Even in Britain, the indifference shown by Magaret Thatcher's governments to the kind of economic activity engaged in has been, at least gesturally, replaced recently by a concern with some kind of industrial policy. Moreover, state-owned utility companies, under no intrinsic pressure to increase or maintain revenues and hence profitability, are much more likely to develop ecologically sound, energy-saving policies than are capitalist enterprises.[10] And it is surely no accident that countries with the most 'pure,' market-driven versions of capitalism also suffer the highest rates of violent, anti-social behaviour, forcing them to spend billions of dollars, through the state and private sectors, on social control (Christie, 1993).

None of the above is to argue that socialist experiments are confined to a model of either the command economy or crown corporations. True, crown corporations may be useful for controlling signficant aspects of economic activity, for setting standards, and for providing accurate information on the actual workings of specific markets (Pearce 1987), but other institutional forms are as important. Mondragon-style co-ops, consumer co-ops, co-ops of the unemployed who can earn a living wage by providing subsidized services for community- and ecologically oriented projects, and provision of social property via institutional funds are just a few examples of alternative forms of ownership that can be put in place (R. Murray 1985; Doucaliagos 1990; Lipietz 1992; Phillips 1992). It is more crucial than ever that non-capitalist forms of production and control be developed and collective forms of financing be provided, if any independence from the 'agenda' of international corporate capital is to be secured.

Overall, the general impact of economic policies predicated on the dictates of the Chicago school has been, at best, equivocal. There remains the possibility that the experiment with monetarism will prove disastrous in the long term, having destroyed the trust and suspension of disbelief that are necessary to make any social order (particularly an inegalitarian capitalist one) endure. But restricting the analysis to economic effects also provides cause for doubt.

The Pinochet dictatorship's IMF-monetarist–free market experiment of the late 1970s and early 1980s in Chile, for example, produced first a boom and then a devastating recession, as 'industrial production plummeted, thousands of small enterprises went bankrupt, the trade deficit worsened, and the living standard of the mass of the population deteriorated as wages declined and unemployment rose' (Petras and Morley 1990, 15–16).[11] The economy recovered from 1984 to 1989, but the benefits were restricted to a narrow (and often expatriate) elite. During a period in which profits of the country's top two hundred companies quintupled, 'the socioeconomic status of the Chilean masses worsened immeasurably: real wages declined by 15 per cent and minimum wage earners made 40 per cent less in 1987 than they did in the 1978–81 period' (Petras and Morley 1990, 15–16). Indeed, with the exception of the four Asian 'tigers' (Hong Kong, Singapore, South Korea, and Taiwan), the restructuring of the world's economy has increased rather than reduced disparities in wealth between developed and Third World countries. The role of less-well-developed countries in international trade has declined, and their debt burden and balance-of-payments deficit increased (Magdoff 1992, 63–70).[12]

Further, the globalization of economies and the increasing mobility of capital have heightened regional and global insecurity. The commodification of most productive activity and an increasingly pronounced emphasis on producing for international markets have made all countries, but particularly those of the Third World, dangerously vulnerable to global economic fluctuations (Waring 1988). If the older, so-called socialist models of development have failed in the Third World, there are clear signs that monetarist-inspired capitalist models have been at least equally unsuccessful.

AN ALTERNATIVE INTERPRETATION OF THE GLOBAL ECONOMY

The arguments and aims of the neo-monetarists, then, should be seen as identifying a trend, a set of emerging institutional arrangements, more a hegemonic project than a hegemonic reality. As Hirst and Thompson (1992) have recently argued, we should not become too carried away with the concept of a global economy, since activities by nation-states, regional organizations such as the European Union, and international bodies (not to mention military alliances) all play key and often opposed roles in the organization of economic activity. By 1984, the world had 365 intergovernmental organizations and 4,615 International non-governmental organizations (Held 1989, 196), many of which affect internal national policies. For example, British attempts to attenuate or abolish occupational and- health-safety environmental regulation have been thwarted in part by directives from the then European Community occasioned by some of the political fallout from the events in Seveso and in Bhopal, India.

Globalization depends, in part, on universalizing certain legal categories – the corporate form, or patent and intellectual copyright laws, for example. These social relations are not merely regulated by legal systems, they are partially constituted by them. National or trans-national institutions are therefore intrinsic to the operation of the global economy. Indeed, as Giddens points out, the relationship between states has a logic irreducible to that of the economic.[13] Globalization is usefully described as a set of contexts where a series of relatively autonomous logics obtain. After all, there is good reason to explain U.S. foreign policy in terms of an overall goal of benefiting large American corporations, while recognizing that strategically it has always needed to take account of the international political and military order. For example, the tactics dictated by the domino theory involved the support/domination of countries which, in themselves, were neither economically nor politically of great significance.[14]

Both international credibility and national strategies remain important in the struggle to achieve meaningful control of capital. For example, while in the 1980s financial markets in London and New York were significantly internationalized and deregulated, scandals such as Britain's Polly Peck crisis and the U.S. savings-and-loans crisis (Levi in this volume, chapter 10; Calavita and Pontell, chapter 11) have prompted development of new national modes of regulation. Moreover, moves to deregulate were and remain significantly more muted in Japan (*New York Times*, 16 May 1993). The changing fortunes of environmental regulation and deregulation (Yeager 1991) and the U.S. cleanup of toxic waste provide examples of situations too complex to sum up in a simplistic anti- or pro-regulatory formula (Barnett, in chapter 17 of this volume).

Nevertheless, effective global economic institutions to supplement if not replace the nation-state remain underdeveloped, and diffuse markets in currency, capital, commodities, and services remain unintegrated but interdependent. At the global level, there are no mechanisms to determine the relationship between what is produced for the different markets (and by whom) and the scale and nature of these markets. If too much money goes into investment compared to wages, then there will either be a crisis of overcapacity or an unrealistic inflation in the value of stocks and shares and property. In other words, as Black Monday (October 1987) suggested, global stock-market crashes remain a possibility. If unbridled capitalism in the nineteenth century was made viable only by the development of national forms of regulation, usually initiated, if not finally controlled, by oppositional social movements, then the same is probably true of any emerging new global economy (Cox 1993a). However, since, as Paehlke (chapter 16 in this volume) points out, emergent modes of control, both supranational and infranational, are only too often not subject to democratic control, democratization must be a major political goal.

NATIONAL AND INTERNATIONAL CAPITALISM

Capitalism as an economic system is fundamentally characterized by relations of antagonism – between capital and labour and between enterprise and enterprise. These antagonisms are sources of dynamism as well as instability. An enterprise cannot rest on its laurels; it must always seek, through all available means, to protect or increase its market share. This is true of a single enterprise, of a cartel or group of national enterprises, or, indeed, of a national capitalist economy.[15]

How has capitalism, a system riven with and rendered unstable by antagonism among classes, enterprises, and nation-states, reached its present preeminence? The Chicago school of economics, as we saw above, does not address this issue. It assumes, rather, that market systems are the only 'rational' way to organize production and that rationality must eventually win out. The question has been considered, however, by scholars of the 'regulation school.' Like structural Marxists, they focus on the reproduction, development, and transformation of complex social entities. However, they try to go beyond the somewhat abstract and schematic general concepts of modes of production and social formations, and the somewhat functionalist concept of the state and reproduction that structuralists were prone to adopt. Their preference is to specify more closely the different forms that capitalist modes of production can and have taken. Given that endemic antagonisms, contradictions, and crises have made continuing accumulation improbable and regularly generated major ruptures and structural shifts, what mechanisms account for the continued survival and development of the capitalist mode of production?

The explanatory model developed by the regulation school is based on the related concepts of regime of accumulation, mode of growth, mode of regulation, and model of development:

An accumulation regime comprises a particular pattern of production and consumption considered in abstraction from the existence of national economies which can be reproduced over time despite its conflictual tendencies. A national model of growth comprises the pattern of production and consumption of a national economy considered in terms of its role in the international division of labour. Relatively stable accumulation regimes and national modes of growth involve a contingent, historically constituted, and societally reproduced correspondence between patterns of consumption and production. A mode of regulation refers to an institutional ensemble and complex of norms which can secure capitalist reproduction *pro tempore* despite the conflictual and antagonistic character of capitalist relations. And, finally, a model of development ... refers to a pattern of development based on a) a dominant paradigm of industrialization, b) an accumulation regime, and c) a mode of regulation. (Jessop 1990, 174)

This approach moves examination of regulation beyond enumeration and analysis of specific national regulatory bodies to broader, more systemic questions, which include analyses of institutional ensembles, class relations, and the relative strength of different class forces. It allows one, for example, to assess strategically the significance of particular tactics undertaken by regulatory agencies. Extensive consultation and the sparing use of prosecution for health-and-safety offences may be found in situations when capital has been forced to be compliant and is therefore generally following strict rules demanded by organized labour, or when capital has been able to deregulate health and safety (Snider 1991; Pearce and Tombs 1992). For scholars attempting empirical analyses and politicians evaluating regulation, lax, ineffective regulatory regimes will look very similar to effective, efficient institutions when 'success' is measured in terms of the number of complaints investigated and sanctions employed.

The evidence from the United States, one of the most successful capitalist economies throughout the twentieth century, suggests that the regulationist model, while useful, needs further refinement. Aglietta (1979), for example, argued that there had been two major regimes of accumulation and modes of regulation in the United States – extensive and intensive. The first was based on competitive regulation, and the barrier to sustained accumulation was primarily the limitations on the ability of the mass of the population to consume very much.[16] This situation created a 'realization problem' and a related speculative pressure, which inflated the value of stocks and shares. These class-related factors, and the decline in world trade, precipitated the Great Crash of 1929.

The second was based on the Fordist regime. The term *Fordism* to describes that stage of capitalism characterized by manufacture of goods through the use of large production runs over 24-hour cycles (yielding maximum economies of scale), maximum use of machinery, and correspondingly minute divisions of labour. Abundant consumer goods were thereby produced, and workers receiving high wages in the monopolistic industries that dominated key manufacturing sectors could afford to buy them. Wage increases were tied to increasing productivity and hence to the intensity of labour. Neo-Keynesian policies were instituted to create a social wage, administered by a bureaucratic welfare state. This approach created a (national) virtuous circle of rising living standards and rising productivity, rising wages and rising profits, economic stability and social harmony. It also produced inflation and workers dissatisfaction, as we shall see below.

Under Fordism, a continuous revolutionizing of the means of production occurred, which resulted in the overaccumulation of capital in the manufacturing sectors producing goods. However, the high degree of monopolization in this sector made it possible, at least for a time, for corporate executives to anticipate the ensuing devaluation of capital and destruction of productive capacity by launching an inflationary increase of prices and expansion in credit. Although the rising productivity of labour and the erosion of real wages by rising prices acted as countertendencies, they were insufficient to combat the tendency of the rate of profit to fall. Inflation and an increase in class conflict were the result. Class conflict over wages was exacerbated by dissatisfaction with working conditions associated with the autocratic Fordist production process. Machine-paced and repetitive, based on piece-work, and undertaken in shifts by unskilled workers, this mode of production is associated with high accident rates and occupational ill-health – gastrointestinal disturbances, sleeping problems, anxiety, depression, irritation, loss of appetite, accelerated heart rate, indeed, general morbidity (Navarro 1983, 550).

Aglietta's attempt to track the development of the American economy is partially successful, but it does not provide an accurate or complete analysis (Clarke 1988, 1990). The arguments need to be reformulated and supplemented. The vaunted success of American capitalism required two world wars to decimate the infrastructure and economic base of its major competitors. Indeed, the Second World War provided the definitive stimulus to the American recovery from the overwhelmingly destructive Depression of the 1930s (Dowd 1977, 105). And by the 1960s, it was clear that even the mighty United States could not sustain the heavy military spending required by the Vietnam War as well as the social expenditures necessitated by Lyndon Johnson's vision of a Great Society. It is unlikely that there has ever been a self-sustaining Fordist regime. Indeed, application of the generic term *Fordism* to describe a whole economic system and its subsequent use as a model to which specific systems are compared involve processes akin to abstract empiricism, with all the attendant consequences and intellectual baggage.[17] A more useful analysis would aim for greater specificity and explore the presence or absence of Fordist elements in different economic systems and then examine how these relate to other elements.

Japan is a case in point. Although elements of Fordist production techniques are apparent in productive processes there, they have been modified in significant ways. Moreover, the relationships among enterprises and between enterprises and the state are quite different than was the case in the United States. There are two groups of *keiretsu* – those firms interconnected, in a *zaibatsu* manner, by central banks or by trading companies, but in unrelated businesses; and the *kaisha*, large manufacturing companies that relate to smaller enterprises (and customers) in a sustained but more hierarchical manner. The latter produce particular kinds of commodities and hence develop very detailed and cumulative knowledge in specific areas. These 'enterprise groups' are a crucial (and dedicated) source of long-term finance for industrial investment. Other sources are the publicly regulated banking system and, more recently, internally generated profits. All three provide relatively cheap capital.

Coordination and long-term planning are encouraged externally by the Ministry of International Trade and Industry (MITI), which also actively promotes a modernizing small-business sector (Clegg 1990). Further, relatively low dividends on invested capital facilitate long term planning (K. Williams and Haslam 1990; T. Williams 1990); Thurow (1984), however, found that the average time horizon of firms in a thirty-firm U.S. conglomerate that he investigated was only 2.8 years, clearly inadequate for planning investments in processes with lifespans covering several product-generations. Furthermore national accounting practices and continuous stock-market evaluations in the United States (and in Britain and Australia) make it 'rational' for managers – assessed on performance at their 'profit centre' – to delay 'replacement of old or worn out equipment, replacing equipment eventually with technologically dated or inferior substitutes, and skimping on maintenance, research and personnel development' (Clegg 1990, 197). This situation may have disastrous consequences (Pearce and Tombs 1989, 1992; Pearce 1993).

In Japan, long-term planning, together with national investment strategies, lower executive salaries, intensive working styles and relatively low dividends on invested capital (K. Williams and Haslam 1990; T. Williams 1990) have given Japanese companies a clear advantage over their American rivals. In the case of automobiles and in many areas of electronics, Japanese firms have clearly outperformed those commonly recognized as American in origin. 'Between 1962 and 1982 the number [of 483 of the world's largest industrial enterprises] of U.S. origin dwindled from 292 to 213; while that of Japanese companies rose from 29 to 79; and that of developing countries from 2 to 23' (Dunning 1988: 82). The organizations in which Japan has the advantage all produce particular kinds of commodities, where the development of very detailed and cumulative knowledge in specific areas is a distinct advantage.

In large firms, relatively small salary differentials and status divisions are the norm, as are job rotation at all levels, legally enforced employment security, and seniority systems for core workers. During the post-1973 recession, the large Japanese companies laid off fewer employees than was true of U.S. firms, and they accepted a concomitant lower rate of return on total assets than did U.S. concerns (Clegg 1990). Workers are organized in self-managing small groups, with each individual continuously updating his or her skills and those of the group overall. This arrangement tends to involve workers actively in 'quality circle' and 'zero defect' movements (Itoh 1992, 201). Workers are flexible about the tasks they undertake and the hours they work. Further, companies make a relatively high capital investment per worker – roughly twice that of U.S. firms. Japanese capitalism also provides security of employment, the result not so much of the remnants of feudalism (Abegglen 1975) as of interwar and post–Second World War class conflict (Clegg 1990, 140), which led to attempts to legitimate these relations by offering job security to gain the loyalty of skilled workers in tight labour markets (Taira 1970; Woodiwiss 1992). Nevertheless, these conditions provide a rational basis for a much greater degree of loyalty than exists in U.S. companies.

Yet these conditions hold true only for people working directly for major Japanese corporations – almost exclusively male, white-collar workers, who constitute less than 30 per cent of the waged labourforce (Clegg 1990; 186). And these employees put in at least 13 per cent more hours than do similar Americans and 31 per cent more than do West Germans; in an average year, they have 23 per cent less free time than do Americans and 45 per cent less than do West Germans (Itoh 1992, 204). Moreover, within the actual enterprise, workers have few rights. Their unions are basically company unions, their union representatives are often also their supervisors (Beynon 1985), and managerial authority is absolute (Woodiwiss 1992, 141). Innovation, quality, 'just-in-time' production, low cost, and flexibility are in part attributable to complex subcontracting systems in which subcontractors employ less secure, poorer-paid workers. And may of these latter enterprises are partly owned but effectively controlled (relatively cheaply through a 20 per cent or so share) by the major automobile manufacturers themselves (Stinchcombe 1990).[18] This strategy made it possible to achieve productivity increases (between 1975 and 1985) at a rate twice as fast as the rise in real wages (Itoh 1992, 203) and to expand nominal production by auto firms (between 1965 and 1980) by 600 per cent while raising per-capita fixed investment by only about a third as much (Cusamo 1989, 215).

All this suggests that 'the Japanese miracle,' with long-term collaboration between large firms and their primary subcontractors producing high-quality products at low cost, was achieved only by heavy dependence on specifically

Japanese social relations and by 'outsourcing to low wage areas' (Powell 1990, 321).[19]

None of Asia's four tigers' fits classic free-market models terribly well either. In all cases, the state has self-consciously specified and developed particular industries. Strategies have included development of state-owned industries, which are joint ventures between the state and private capital; control of investment by nationalizing the banks and/or by providing cheap credit or subsidies to selected industries; and provision of protection from international competition. In Hong Kong, a low-wage economy has been made significantly less harsh by the state's provision of education and medical care and low-cost public housing for about 85 per cent of the working class and by cheap food supplied by the Republic of China at below market prices. The state's ownership of all land has enabled it to combine these measures with low individual and corporate taxes, since it generates revenue by leasing land to businesses. Singapore also has a highly developed welfare state. And Taiwan, according to Gini analysis, has one of the most egalitarian income distributions in the world.[20] The similarities with the Japanese model are obvious and include active measures to marginalize trade unions (Clegg 1990; Henderson 1993). Finally, the IMF has recently acknowledged that China itself, with its own version of a mixed economy, is now the fourth-largest economy in the world, and one of the fastest growing (*Globe and Mail* 25 May 1993, B1). It is these (national) structural factors, rather than some cultural phenomenon such as 'Asian capitalism,' that explain the success of these economies (Woodiwiss 1993a).

There was, in fact, a third major model of successful growth, also incorporating Fordist elements, that emerged by the late 1950s – the Swedish model. As in other nation-states, large corporations in Sweden were crucial to economic development, but their relationships to each other, to smaller companies, to employees, to trade unions, and to the state were all quite distinctive. In Sweden, the private manufacturing sector has long been dominated by a small number of family owned large firms – 'fifteen families and two corporations have majority ownership in 200 large industrial companies employing almost half of those employed in private industry' (J.F. Scott 1979, 71). These firms developed a close working relationship with both the state and the trade unions, themselves intimately tied to the electorally dominant Social Democratic party, in what has been an extremely creative form of corporatism.

Swedish Social Democrats believed that (speculative) capitalism was inherently irrational and that a countervailing power made up of the state and institutionalized unions was needed to make it operate efficiently and humanely. Their aim – in which they were largely successful – was to raise the material level of working-class people as a whole, to create a situation where there was 'equal pay for equal work and reasonable and fair pay differentials,' with 'work for everyone,' including part-time work at a living wage (Backstrom 1988, 2468). Through their 'active market policy,' involving job retraining, generous unemployment benefits and moving costs, information on employment possibilities, and public works jobs, they helped structure the labour market and determine the composition of jobs and skill levels (Navarro 1983, 528). Implementation of these policies and many others was decided in a tripartite manner with participation from labour, capital, and government.

This regime produced a high-wage, relatively skilled, highly productive economy with low unemployment and few low-wage jobs (Clegg 1990, 225–30). Further, whereas management's right to manage was left relatively intact until the 1970s – indeed, until that time there was a somewhat consumerist, welfare-state orientation – in a challenge to Fordism there developed a general concern with the quality of life, particularly at work. New kinds of team work, including a single team building a whole car – the Volvo solution – produced a kind of de-differentiation (Clegg 1990) that helped deal with some of the work-induced anomie (Durkheim 1984) associated with Fordist productive techniques. Moreover, having observed the rapid internationalization of Swedish capital, the state pushed to limit the extent to which profits could be invested outside the country, via the Meidner plan, to socialize ownership of the enterprises themselves (Meidner 1978; Abrahamson and Brostom 1980) and to develop workers' control of the organization of production.

In the 1980s, the average Swedish worker was among the highest-paid in the world. If one figures in the social wage (free health care, social welfare payments, unemployment payments, child care provision, maternity and paternity leave, and so on), their good working conditions, their short working week, and their long, generous holidays, they were the best paid. Furthermore, unions had won the right to representation on the boards of most companies and the right to bargain over the organization of many aspects of the work situation. Shop stewards and safety representatives garnered increasingly greater powers and greater protection. Under the Work Environment Act of 1977, safety representatives and safety committees could help plan new premises, work processes, and working methods, and, famously, the former had the right unilaterally to stop any dangerous process until an inspector arrived.[21]

Capital retained a significant degree of power despite the advances of social democracy. Although firms could avoid taxation of profits by allowing for state and union control over investment decisions, they still retained the right to invest them overseas or to pay them out in dividends. Nor did capital surrender any significant control over production. In part because of the threat (and the subsequent reality) of the internationalization of competition, the internationalization of its own production, and a significant decline in the global economy, the truce between capital and labour broke down in the 1980s, and capital gained greater independence. The SAF (the employers' federation) became increasingly vocal, and successful, in national politics, resulting in cutbacks in the welfare state and total repudiation of the Meidner plan (Pontussen 1987, 24–31). Perhaps Swedish social democracy, by not attacking capital's fundamental power – its ownership of the means of production – left itself open to counterattack. We have here a different form of economic organization, which, for a time at least, proved highly effective for employers and the state, and which offered superior employment and living conditions for working people.

Some regulation theorists (Lipietz 1988; Jessop 1993) believe that new forms of viable national and international organization and regulation may now be emerging. Some of these forms are viewed positively, some negatively – Jessop, for example, sees the 'Schumpeterian workfare state' as providing no more than 'the best possible political shell for post-Fordism' (1993, 7). Others are more hopeful. Charles Leadbetter, of *Marxism Today* and the *Financial Times*, argues that, in Fordist regimes, there was an assumption that the social democratic state would look after collective social interests and that economic decisions should and would take this fact into account. However, the welfare state did not work; it was overly bureaucratic, paternalistic, and inefficient, and it could produce only mass-quality products for mass populations (Leadbetter 1989, 139).

When's the world economy became bedevilled by stagflation and mass markets were allegedly saturated, demands by consumers for more differentiated and better products were initially frustrated.[22] Now, however, these demands are seen as providing a way out of the crisis. Not only do smaller production units make old-style corporate bureaucracies unnecessary, but the need to recruit individuated, skilled, flexible, and autonomous workers has led to decentralized bargaining and rendered traditional unions unnecessary. These new employees define themselves in a postmodern way; their identities are fluid, their lifestyles idiosyncratic and transient. This shift further reinforces product differentiation. Old, class-based identities and oppositions, and affiliated demands for universal state services or nationalized industries, become obsolete.

Although Leadbetter and allied theorists acknowledge that the new societies will be capitalist and 'riven with – inequalities in income, wealth and power' (Jacques and Hall 1989, 23), they play down this fact and discount the social forces that could challenge it.[23] Thus, Leadbetter has advocated an incomes policy 'formed around a publicly declared minimum standard of living,' and a policy that eschews state or trade-union ownership of the means of production in favour of workers' ownership through share purchase (1989, 147). The state would exist only to provide public space, not necessarily public services, on the model of the public park where a range of private activities, from boating to selling ice-cream to sunbathing, are possible. 'The state is vital to ensuring a space continues to exist and is developed; but beyond that its direct role depends on whether it is the most efficient provider of services' (1989: 148–9).

This analysis ignores the fact that those running the ice-cream vans would probably be employed by a multinational using part-time workers on subsistence wages with no benefits. The company would soon demand the concession to run the boats on the lake and eventually push for privatization of the park so that it could charge sunbathers user fees. It might well sell sunblock to provide protection from the depleted ozone layer caused by another component of its activities, and then sell medical services to those who contracted skin cancer!

More sophisticated approaches to the emergence of new economic forms are found in the work of 'network analysts' (Powell 1990), particularly as this relates to flexible specialization and industrial districts (Hirst and Zeitlin 1991). These theorists have challenged the assumptions of conventional economists, including the Chicago school. They refuse to reduce viable forms of economic organization to *either* the hierarchical and authoritarian firm *or* the free market. Markets may be elements of complex social organizations, but they depend on other social forms for their very existence.[24] Many successful, 'networking,' flexible, and innovation-generating ways of organizing production have never been explored. Examples include creation and reproduction of economic districts, the facilitation of cooperative relations between groups of enterprises, promotion of viable small enterprises, and the development of independent, skilled workforces that would move from firm to firm, with a significant amount of infrastructural and coordinating activity undertaken by the local state.

These kinds of networks are not a hybrid form of organization, but an analytically distinct way of organizing collective behaviour, particularly of the economic sort. They make possible unified collective action, which is denied to those involved in bureaucratic firms and markets, both of which assume and generate people who act as egoistic, rational calculators. The networks generate, instead, a more sustained, cooperative, trusting, and less calculative attitude. Information about new processes, products, changes in tastes and modifications in reputations would tend to be disseminated spontaneously. It becomes relatively easy to translate new ideas quickly into new products. For example, in the textile industry, thanks to computer-aided design (CAD), a new design that formerly took over three weeks to put together now takes six hours (Mytelka 1991, 122). Relations of production are transformed while efficient production is facilitated.

These approaches have been very successful, particularly where there is a high rate of innovation and a demand for quality and low-batch, customized production for targeted customers. Such networks can already be found, to varying degrees, in Silicon Valley, California, in Massachusetts; in the Alsace region of France; in the English Midlands; in Baden-Württemberg, Germany; and in Emilia Romagna, Italy (Sabel et al. 1989).

Although development of these industrial districts certainly challenges the notion that large, hierarchical, impersonal, bureaucratic corporations are the only efficient form of organization, they too have problems that their advocates have thus far failed to confront. First, their success depends not just on local factors but on fiscal policies generated by the national state, for it must maintain conditions of sustained demand for their products (Thompson 1989). Second, large-scale capital itself has learned from the profitability of such experiments and has appropriated elements of this model to its own ends. R.M. Kanter (1989), for example, has argued that the number of people employed by corporations has decreased, internal markets and decentralized profit centres have developed, and an openness to extra-organizational inputs and partnerships has produced organizations that are more viable, creative, and flexible. Changes in market focu and *modus operandi* have already taken place at Exxon, IBM, Xerox, and Kodak (in 1992, the first-, third-, fourteenth-, and sixteenth-largest U.S. corporations, respectively – *Forbes* 19 July 1993, 182–3). Thus such models may be co-opted, with their cooperative tendencies removed or reconfigured to serve the interest of immediately increased profits. Fiscal control remains centralized, and the accompanying decentralization of production may have deleterious as well as beneficial effects (Pearce 1993; in this volume, Tombs, chapter 7, and Keane chapter 9).

We have already seen that Japan has constructed itself on a national level as an industrial district. Increasingly, international joint ventures between firms in very different markets are being forged – automobile, steel and telecommunications firms provide recent examples (Dunning 1988; Adams and Brock 1991: 57–8). Trans-national corporations can combine these new forms with their other economic advantages – including those derived from economies of scale and those derived from monopoly power – to reassert their dominant positions. Economies of scale remain important: the last twenty years have seen a diminution in the number of car producers, a growth in their size, and the maintenance if not enhancement of large production runs (Callinicos 1989). As well, there is no evidence that demand for mass-consumption goods has decreased, and the differences between these and so-called niche products are often minuscule. More flexible technologies may in fact have the potential to increase the rates of change of design, to improve quality, and sometimes to reduce the size at which production runs become viable. We question, however, the technological determinism inherent in many of these analyses.[25] These changes, combined with the globalization of production, mean that trans-national corporations are, in some ways, creating global industrial districts. Thus, both of the schools discussed tend to underestimate the power and resourcefulness of corporate capitalism and its ability to appropriate potentially liberating technologies and subordinate their use to its own goals (Mosco 1989).

Moreover, both nationally and internationally, a minority monopolizes ownership and control of productive assets. So, for example, in the United States in 1983, the richest 1 per cent of families owned 'a fifth of all real estate (and over twice that much of the commercial real estate), three fifths of the corporate stock, and over four-fifths of all the trust assets owned by all of us' (Zeitlin 1989, 145). Most of these stock holdings, like those of a minority of commercial banks, are in the largest corporations, which also receive investment funds from the same minority of banks and insurance companies, and from other major institutional investors, which are effectively controlled by a minority of wealthy shareholders, large corporations, and other institutional investors (Zeitlin 1989, 30–6, 66). Such relationships always seem to enrich and empower the same groups – those who have majority or minority but controlling interests in companies and other institutions 'control not only the capital represented by the small shareholder and the institutional investor, but also that represented by debt obligations (bonds, mortgages, short term loans) and internally generated funds (undistributed profits and depreciation and depletion allowances). Together these have accounted for approximately 90 per cent or more of all sources of corporate financing in North America and Britain since the 1960s' (Phillips 1992, 73).

This is an appropriate point to return to Jessop and the prognoses of regulation theorists. He argues that recent years have seen 'a "tendential shift" from the Keynesian welfare state, and a "hollowing out" of national states in advanced capitalist countries' (Jessop 1993, 7–8). Thus states have lost power to international bodies or, conversely, to 'emerging horizontal networks of power – which bypass central states and link regions or localities' at regional or local levels (Jessop 1993, 7–8). Internationalization of financial and product flows limits the autonomy of states while forcing them to adopt policies geared to attracting new investment, particularly in knowledge-intensive industries and technologies. He is not arguing that these changes will automatically produce a viable regime of accumulation, nor that they are an inevitable outcome of current technological and economic changes. However, the power of capital has vastly increased, with the result that people and their communities have less ability to influence or block hurtful changes, and that changes will take place on levels other than that of the nation-state.

We would argue that it would be wrong to conclude from the foregoing that such transformations leave nation-states helpless. Specific political decisions and programs make nation-states weaker or stronger than they might otherwise be. For example, Article 2010 of the Canada–United States Free Trade Agreement (FTA), called 'Monopolies,' states that

if national or provincial programs are introduced in Canada, for example, an auto insurance scheme such as is found in British Columbia and Saskatchewan, the government would be required to give advance notice to the United States to 'engage in consultations' if Washington asked for them, and be prepared to modify the program in order to eliminate any adverse effect or loss of business – real or potential – to American companies. This last requirement includes being prepared to compensate American corporations affected by the program's implementation. A graphic example of this reality was seen in 1991, when the Ontario government backed down on its 1990 election promise and scrapped a long-standing NDP commitment to introduce a provincial auto-insurance plan after learning that State Farm, the largest U.S. auto insurance company, claimed that under the FTA $1.3 billion would be owed by Ontario as compensation to U.S. auto-insurance companies. (Orchard 1993, 169)

Although the above provides an example of a nation restricting its scope through trade agreements, this outcome is not inevitable. Given sufficient pressure, agreements can be reopened, renegotiated. There is already some evidence that there is a 'post-globalization' movement against the liberalisation of international financial activity (Cox 1993). Reasons include a general fear of major international financial crises; the uncertain future of such interstate bargains, including some among the countries of the European Union; and the declining benefits of liberalization for its major early proponents, the United States and the United Kingdom (Hellenier 1994). Similarly, renegotiation, even of GATT,[26] could also be used to widen protection for relatively powerless groups, the environment, and similar causes. Further, Gordon (1988, 58–9) has offered evidence that the most important factors determining foreign direct investment in different countries are the size of the home market, the degree of political stability, and price/exchange-rate stability. Other factors include the condition of the infrastructure, the skill levels of the workforce, and, to a lesser extent, wage levels. Most of these criteria are compatible with a range of different state structures and economic policies, even in the absence of successful struggles to modify these criteria or remove low-wage options. Lipietz (1992) has argued that the post-Fordist world order does not necessarily have to be neo-liberal. Instead, within countries, increased worker involvement in production decisions, an increase in leisure time and employment could be brought about by reducing the standard working week. Unemployed people or local municipalities could provide subsidized services for community groups and ecologically oriented projects, thereby allowing workers to earn a living wage.[27]

In conclusion, it appears to be feasible to conceptualize strategies that include state planning, state ownership of enterprises, particularly 'natural' monopolies, a welfare state based on universalistic principles (Holland 1975; Wainwright 1992); and similar advanced policies where historically and culturally appropriate. It is both possible and desirable to develop state-funded research and testing laboratories to allow independent assessment of corporate products and similar institutions to check corporate power and minimize corporate abuse. Indeed, it is absolutely essential for progressive scholars as well as activists in oppositional social movements to provide countervailing initiatives, now that traditional progressive forces in the welfare state (unions, for example) have been so seriously wounded on both structural and ideological levels.

NOTES

1 For critical comments on Lipset, see D. Smith (1970); on pluralism, see Pearce (1976); on Bell, see Mosco (1989); and on American modernism, see Woodiwiss (1993a).
2 Viscusi was an adviser to OSHA during the 1980s.
3 See the discussion of these issues by Noble (1986, and chapter 14 in this volume); Tucker in (chapter 13 this volume).
4 These are better described as command economies controlled by 'Hobbesian' states. For sophisticated critical assessments of the relationship between eastern European 'socialist' social formations and socialism, see van der Pijl (1993) and Cox (1993a).
5 In Britain privatization sales were used to lower the Public Spending Borrowing Requirement – Whitfield (1992, 141–51). However, by 1993 this amount had soared again and will reach £50 billion in 1993–4. It is suggested that the privatization of roads could bring in £75 billion (*Observer*, 30 May 1993 27). A similar argument – the need to slash the national debt – is being used to justify sale of twenty-one state-owned companies in France, including Banque Nationale de Paris, the insurance firm Assurances Générales de France, the drugs group Rhone-Poulenc, and the Elf-Aquitaine oil group (*Globe and Mail*, 27 May 1993, B4). In fact, pre-privatization France was in better shape than privatizing Britain in terms of its government debt (in 1991) and current-account deficit (1992), though worse off in terms of interest payments as a percentage of revenue (*Globe and Mail* 24 April 1992, B4).
6 The conclusions that can be drawn from current studies on the relative efficiency of state and private enterprises are at best ambiguous – cf. the evidence (as opposed to the authors' conclusions) in Parris, Pestieau, and Satnor (1988) and in Foreman-Peck

(1989). Nevertheless, neither private nor state-run enterprises are immune from organizational inefficiencies, poor judgment, deficient information, or unanticipated changes in circumstances. For example, both private and state-owned banks suffered the negative consequences of the Third World debt crisis and of the recent global collapse of the urban property market (George 1992).

7 Documentation of the decline in the conditions of work – people work harder, for longer hours, and with less security, fewer rights, and a lower rate of remuneration – is provided in Whitfield (1983, 56–7; 1992, 272–3). In Britain between 1981 and 1993, 'an estimated 250,000 public service employees have been made redundant or transferred to private companies on lower wages under the government's compulsory competitive-tendering and market-testing policies ... A survey by the Low Pay Unit found that enrolled nurses who had their jobs contracted out in private nursing homes received between only £1.70 and £2.40 an hour, while their counterparts in the NHS were getting £4.50 an hour.' (Dean Nelson 'Tories Multi-million Pound Blunder: Pay Cuts after Tendering broke ec law'; *Observer*, 9 May 1993, 3).

8 Nationalization has been part less of a socialist than of a nationalist-capitalist strategy – relatively successfully implemented in France, never adequately so in Britain. In the latter country, when it has occurred, it has often involved compensation to previous owners, providing an unreasonable burden of reparation payments on public industries (Jenkins 1959). With wonderful symmetry, the sale of nationalized industries and other state-owned assets has only too often been at fire-sale prices (Whitfield 1992, 281–2).

9 By these criteria, in Britain, Thatcherite policies that speeded deindustrialization, decline in housing quality and in the rate of building new houses, and overbuilding of offices (*vide* Canary Wharf and the concomitant increase in homelessness) must be seen as extremely economically inefficient.

10 One example is French energy policy after 1973 (Parris, Pestieau, and Satnor 1988, 124–5).

11 In Chile, 'the income share for top and bottom fifths of the population went from 44.5 per cent and 7.6 per cent, respectively, in 1969, to 654.6 per cent and 4.4 per cent in 1989' (Letter from Catherine Ornenstein in the *New York Times*, 16 May 1993, 38F).

12 Recent moves to represent national income through accounting procedures associated with the measure of GDP (as opposed to GNP cf. U.S. Department of Commerce 1991, 8) have concealed some of the severity of these problems. Income earned from assets physically located within a country, but owned overseas, is counted as part of the GDP, even when it is repatriated by the foreign owners (Waring 1988).

13 Although he reifies it as a distinctive level or plane of reality by describing it as a dimension (Giddens 1990, 70).

14 For a complex exploration of the way in which U.S. domestic and foreign policy has

been driven by the goals and contradictions confronting large-scale U.S. capital, see Kolko (1976).

15 Weber saw a clear connection among a 'capitalist state,' a consolidated 'national' capitalism, and the necessity of imperialist ventures (Weber 1980) – it was necessary to devise mechanisms to ensure the effective leadership of, and reproduction of, both the national economy and the nation-state. Since 'big business' often pursued ways of making profits and supported political programs that undermined the national interest (Borkin 1978, 24–5; Weber 1978, 140, 994, 1,430) Germany needed a political system that would force big business to define its own interests in a broad and long-term manner by recognizing its mutual interdependence with the other social groups necessary for economic reproduction, even including the 'responsible' working class (Weber 1978, 1,428; 1980, 445–7). Parliamentary democracy was a useful means of achieving this end. 'True' politicians, partisan and dedicated, with a 'will to power and responsibility' (Weber 1946, 115), preferably men of independent means (rentiers) (Weber 1978, 1,427), were needed to win the struggle to gain the confidence of both their party and the masses (Weber 1978, 1,459). This leadership would be authoritarian, for not only did Weber believe that 'once chosen, the leader then says shut up and do what I say' (Weber, cited in Giddens 1972, 19), but he also made it quite clear that 'the vital interests of the nation stand, of course, above democracy and parliamentarianism' (Weber 1978, 1,383).

16 Application of Taylorist techniques (Aglietta 1979, 114) and Fordist redesign of work around the possibilities of machinery (Hounshell 1984, 251–3) dramatically increased productivity and the percentage of unskilled labour (Levine 1988, 27–33). However, expensive fixed capital costs made assembly-line production dependent on economies of scale and hence required a large, standardized market. This demand was concentrated in the producer-goods sectors. Incomes from profit, interest, and rent rose dramatically, while wages remained stagnant (Aglietta 1979, 94), and the number of unemployed – fuelled by the influx of rural labour – high (I. Bernstein 1966, 41–82).

17 See Althusser and Balibar (1970), Willer and Willer (1973); Hindess and Hirst (1975). For a defence of regulation theory against such charges, and a construction of it in a mode akin to a realist epistemology, see Jessop (1990). For additional critiques of the version of Fordism/post-Fordism, in *New Times* (Hall and Jacques 1989), see Hirst (1989); Rustin (1989); and Hirst and Zeitlin (1991).

18 In 1983, while Nissan directly employed only approximately 30 per cent of production workers, the Nissan group controlled about 78 per cernt of firms involved in the production process, and the Toyota group, approximately 73 per cent; in the United States, GM controlled about 43 per cent, Ford about 36 per cent, and Chrysler 28 per cent (Cusamo 1989, 190). Toyota has as many as 30,000 tertiary, 5,000 secondary, and 220 primary subcontractors. Of the last named, 80 per cent had plants in the pro-

duction complex surrounding Toyota in Toyota City. As one moves from primary to
tertiary subcontractors, in part because of an ability created by the micro-electronics
revolution to spread factory and office automation, an increasing proportion of the
workforce is made up of non-unionized, poorly paid housewives.

19 Although the health of core workers is better looked after in large Japanese companies than in comparable U.S. ones (Wokutch 1992), the majority of these workers are
in white-collar posts. Moreover, given that a great deal of money is invested in their
training and that they have contracts until the age of fifty-five, it makes sense for
companies to take care of their health. No such rationale exists for workers employed
by subcontractors. There is a practice of subcontracting more hazardous jobs to
smaller companies, which generally provide much poorer working conditions and
less continuity of employment. Not surprisingly, then injury rates for workers in
enterprises with fewer than thirty workers are nearly twenty times those for workers
in enterprises that employ more than 1,000 workers (Reich and Frumkin 1988: 809).
Most part-time, temporary, and seasonal workers are women, underemployed rural
labourers, *Burakumin* (untouchables), or of Korean descent. State regulation tends to
follow a compliance model (Hawkins 1984), of the type that prevails where capital is
dominant and no real countervailing power exists (Pearce and Tombs 1990, 1991;
Snider, 1991). Although, formally, occupational health and safety are organized
according to a corporatist, tripartite model, and there is some evidence of managerial
and worker involvement within the plant and a reasonably professionalized inspectorate (Wokutch 1992), in practice they are dominated by the large corporations and
their narrow, partisan view of the appropriate balance between costs and benefits.

20 The Gini coefficient is a measure of the degree of inequality, based on the degree of
divergence between actual distribution of a country's income between the ten deciles
of a population and what the distribution would be if every decile received the same
income (Green and Sutcliffe 1987, 150–3).

21 Occupational health services improved dramatically and were under the control of
safety committees. The evidence on accident rates is less clear – they seem to have
neither worsened nor improved dramatically in the last decade. Reforms do not seem
to have been translated into new workplace practices. Capital and the labour inspectorate have focused on designing safety into new processes but have not sought significant input from workers and unions. Safety committees have been more involved
with immediate workshop issues than in planning of production, and even there they
have lacked effective power – only a minority of their complaints and recommendations are acted on (Tucker 1992, 110–11).

22 Since the 1920s, even in the case of motorcars, there has always been product differentiation – a range of models has been offered, and, thanks to the 'genius' of General
Motors, there have been yearly model changes (Hounshell 1984. 13). 'Fordist' production equipment always had some flexibility and was never totally dedicated.

23 For a superb critique of the role of 'postmodern' scepticism in the equivocal tone of recent writings of Stuart Hall, see Norris (1993).

24 See Polanyi (1957), White (1981), Clegg (1990), and Perrow (1991).

25 Moreover, there is a general tendency to play down the consequences of monopoly and oligopoly. In monopolistic situations, firms will increase prices as much as they can to maximize revenue, but, in oligopolistic situations also, they have little incentive to decrease prices and few problems in increasing them. They also have a mutual interest in restricting the range of products and in limiting innovation. Oligopoly combined with horizontal integration makes 'predation' easy (Adams and Brock 1991, 32–5) and, combined with vertical integration, allows large firms to dominate suppliers, competitors, and customers (Adams and Brock 1991, 72–8). Firms can also dictate the conditions under which they will invest, or continue to invest, in particular communities, states, or countries. Deunionization, environmental deregulation, and financial incentives are all demanded by them, and offered to them (Kazis and Grossman 1982).

The day before the *Financial Times of Canada* ran a feature indicating which U.S. states provided good incentives for Canadian companies investing in that country – tax concessions, subsidies, low wages, anti-union laws – the *New York Times* published the results of the EPA's survey of the more polluted states, and there was considerable overlap. The former paper's list comprised Ohio, Tennessee, Illinois, Georgia, Florida, Michigan, and North Carolina. In the *New York Times* (13 October 1991, 10F), it transpired that Ohio and Tennessee were among the most polluted states for both air and water; Illinois, among the most polluted for air and measurably worse than average for water; Georgia and Florida were measurably worse than average for both air and water; and Michigan and North Carolina were measurably worse than average for water; see also Natural Resources Defense Council (1991).

26 There was some progress in arguing for workers' rights in the 1994 GATT negotiations. For an example of a developed argument, see Kimon Valaskakis 'Wanted: A GATT Agreeemnt That Covers Workers' (*Globe and Mail*, 22 April 1994, A21).

27 Lipietz also explores how, on a global level, trade, deficits, debts, and development could be ordered more constructively, to avoid maintenance of consumerism in the First World and displacement of life-endangering and ecologically destructive economic activities to the Third World. In fact, a per-capita energy tax on all countries could provide an interesting, effective, and ecologically sound way of transferring wealth – 1 North American uses as much commercial energy as 2 Germans, 3 Japanese, 16 Chinese, or 1,072 Nepalese (Gordon and Suzuki 1990, 211).

3

Corporate Crime and Republican Criminological Praxis

JOHN BRAITHWAITE

In this chapter, I seek to describe the essence of the theoretical, empirical, and applied projects in the area of corporate regulation in which I have been engaged over the past decade and to explain its relationship to my general theoretical and empirical work. That essence, I argue, is republican – a label that would not necessarily be accepted by many of my co-authors and colleagues in the political endeavours that I describe.

Republicans are in a paradoxical position – they believe in undertaking collective intellectual enterprises with non-republicans, and they believe that dialogue with people who reject republican theory can produce practical agreement on political action. None of the republican ideas discussed here are my own; all have been generated out of dialogue with colleagues, particularly after joint fieldwork in companies from whose executives (and regulators) we stole and developed ideas. Very few of these people would identify themselves as republicans. My thirty-one co-authors bear the responsibility for my republican concepts, even as they reject the theory or hesitate to embrace it. Even more colleagues have been involved in the political struggles that I describe as republican praxis (from my perspective).[1] My own contribution in practical action has been smaller, much smaller, than in my writing.

The purpose of this chapter is to demonstrate that republicanism need not be a romantic longing for a lost Greek polis. I want to show how it is a practical philosophy for political winners, not just for political dreamers. My conviction about my own country is that it is very slowly transforming itself from liberal to republican democracy.[2] I hope that Australia will rewrite its constitution for the centenary of federation in 2001 to declare itself a republic. If it does not do it then, eventually it will. Even without the constitutional icing, the cake is changing below the surface. This chapter provides some minor examples of this happening. But more fundamental changes in the way law has been written and read by the High Court during the past decade has seen progressive divergence from the liberal individualism of English law. My colleague Paul Finn (1989) has shown how notions such as duty to neighbours, linking of power with obligation, regard for others, basic fairness, reasonable expectations, unconscionable conduct, unfair detriment, and unjust enrichment are Australianizing law and unmooring it from English-style legal individualism. Finn discerns similar trends in New Zealand and Canada.

The changes in Australia have motivated the linking of my work in criminal justice and business regulation to a wider project entitled 'Reshaping Australian Institutions: Towards and beyond 2001.' This endeavour will rethink most of Australia's key institutions, engaging over one hundred scholars; it has already produced fifty books. Most of these folks are not republicans; some are fervent anti-republicans. Republicans should be practical dreamers, who take seriously intellectual life and the central place of the university, who believe that good things can come of big collective endeavours that involve dialogue with people with whom one does not agree. Thomas Jefferson is a republican role model because his practical accomplishments were linked to his capacity to work with liberals.

It is only this year that I started writing papers like this that bring together the most important things going on in two sides of my life – the ideas most important to me as a scholar and the struggles most important for the activist in me. I hope that readers will forgive a style that is unusually personal for a collection such as this. The paper looks only at what I consider to be good ideas and successful struggles. There have been countless bad ideas and failed struggles along the way. Dishonesty, I hope, is not the main reason for suppressing them. Rather, there are some important ways in which we learn more from successful models than from failures. I am a 'model-monger' because I believe that this is how the weak (such as environmentalists) can achieve great victories against the strong (such as business). Model-mongers float a large number of reform models until they find one that strikes such a resonant appeal that it catches powerful adversaries off balance (Braithwaite 1994). An effective model-monger will always have more defeats than victories.

Yet model-mongers should be triumphal, since triumphs are what others model and triumphalism is important in motivating the powerless, sustaining their self-efficacy to struggle against the odds. This is why it is also important to have a political vision, to engage in theoretically driven model-mongering. The academy of researchers into corporate crime has not been very helpful to those engaged with practical struggles against corporate crime because of a disabling structural determinism that has tended to see the power of business as unassailable (contrast Snider 1990; 1991). A sociology of modelling empowers by showing that the shape of the world is not fully determined by the push of a mute past; the pull of humanly articulated futures also plays a role (Braithwaite 1994). Models have power independent of the resources of those who peddle them, because they enable the weak to set the terms of reform debates when their models strike a responsive chord. Models deliver a structural advantage to the weak over the strong. Model-mongering is not for the strong, because it dangerously destabilizes extant orderings of power.

This chapter first outlines four perspectives towards business regulation that I see as implied by republicanism: taking crime seriously; nurturing dialogue as an alternative to the criminal process; pursuing 'empowerment'; and seeing multiple motivations and contradictory regulatory effects. Next, I give three examples of republican praxis in Australia: the new nursing-home regulations; the new trade practices enforcement; and communitarian control of corporate crime in the pharmaceutical industry. I conclude by explaining the significance of such reforms of criminal justice and business regulation for wider and deeper societal changes.

WHAT REPUBLICANISM REQUIRES

Philip Pettit and I think that maximization of republican liberty should be the objective of criminal justice policy. We have outlined what such an objective means elsewhere (Braithwaite and Pettit 1990; Pettit with Braithwaite 1993; Braithwaite, in press). The basic idea is that criminal justice systems ought to be designed to maximize republican liberty or dominion. Dominion is a social conception of liberty that depends on structural and subjective assurance that the liberty is resilient. Egalitarianism is also built into the definition; one cannot enjoy dominion without equality of liberty prospects. Pursuit of republican liberty therefore entails very different policies from pursuit of the individualistic freedom in liberalism. With only the loosest of justification in terms of the objective of maximizing dominion, I posit the four concerns that are followed through below into instances of republican praxis.

Taking Crime Seriously

What do republicans say to deconstructionists who insist that what is a crime is an arbitrary and historically contingent matter, reflecting perhaps the momentary perspective of those in power? Republicans should not be dismissive of the deconstructionists' observation. We think, however, that the world would be a worse place (in terms of dominion) if we abandoned the concept of crime. Good consequences are achieved by describing spousal assault or breaches of occupational health and safety as crimes. My experience of negotiating some of the agreements discussed below is that it is an empowering moment when one is dealing with resistant or chain-dragging executives to say: 'Gentlemen [they always are men], what we are talking about here is criminal conduct by your company.' The concept of crime has deep traditional meanings in all Western societies which the consequentialist should want to put to good use. This, of course, is as true of consequentialists who want to destroy freedom (by calling flag-burning a crime) as it is of republicans who wish to defend it. But it seems to me that criminalization has increased liberty with respect to most of the types of conduct that are criminalized in the West.

Liberty is poorly served, however, by the way Western societies enforce the law against the conduct that it criminalizes. A great deal of 'crime' would be responded to better in the ways advocated by abolitionists – as troubles, problems of living, conflicts, and the like. So we do not have to choose between feminists who want to criminalize rape on the one side and deconstructionists or abolitionists on the other. We can, and should, have our cake and eat it on this issue. That is, we can define conduct of a certain type as crime, while not labelling or punishing it as crime in most cases. There need be no tension between struggling to clarify criminal law while problematizing particular instances of conduct that might fit the definition. In the first enterprise, the deconstructionist will be foe; in the second, friend.

Like left realists, therefore, Pettit and I think that republicans should take crime seriously as a politically progressive concept. There is a progressive effect in writing a book called *Corporate Crime in the Pharmaceutical Industry* that upsets people in the industry because they do not think of the conduct described as criminal. At the same time, the republican must struggle against retributivists who want to treat crime as a master category: 'If the conduct fits the definition of crime, it must be treated as a crime.' As we have shown elsewhere, this essentialism must be resisted because it has bad consequences for dominion (Braithwaite and Pettit 1990).

Nurturing Dialogue

Republicans believe in dialogue, reasoning with wrongdoers, seeking to effect change by persuading criminals that the harm they are doing to others should stop and be compensated. This approach relates to the belief that voluntary change and internalization of moral commitment deliver superior protection to the community (when it can be obtained) than coerced change. But it relates as well to the value of dialogic, participatory social control itself within a meaningful community. This is where liberals think that republicans are utopian. Liberals think that communities do not exist in which dialogic social control is possible. In this view, the liberal is both myopic and politically mischievous – myopic because liberals do not look beyond geographical neighbourhoods in their search for community, and mischievous because liberal individualist ideology has been the major destroyer of community during the past two centuries. 'Can't' implies 'ought not' when it comes to liberals looking for community. Republicanism is constitutive of community; liberalism is deconstitutive of it.

A variety of critical epistemologies also give good grounds for dialogue. I am afraid that epistemology does not interest me very deeply. I suppose that I am a pragmatist in the sense defined by William James (1978, 32) of having 'the attitude of looking away from first things, principles, "categories," supposed necessities; and looking toward last things, fruits, consequences, facts.' It seems to me that there are a good number of critical epistemologies that, however different they are in other respects, converge on James's conclusion that political truth 'is made in the course of experience.' The contemporary subjectivist heirs to the Aristotelian themes of phronesis and praxis are a varied bunch – Arendt (1958), Gadamer (1975), Barber (1984), Habermas (1984), and MacIntyre (1984a). Yet as Bernstein (1983), Handler (1988), and Dryzek (1990) have pointed out, these writers agree that the way to tackle the dilemmas of truth and method is through dialogue. Hence, while Gadamer (1975) can cause us to wring our hands worrying that there is no objective knowledge that we can apply to resolve contradictions, he also tells us that through dialogue citizens can acquire hermeneutical understanding and that the greatest threat to such understanding is abdication to experts such as lawyers.

Bernard Barber (1984, 108) expresses well the conclusion that uncertainty in metaphysics need not paralyse practical regulatory action:

The strong democrat would argue that the proper response to uncertainty and metaphysical failure is not passivity or toleration of all private judgments but rather a quest for forms of political judgment that do not depend on metaphysics, epistemologies, or independent grounds. The antidote to the loss of metaphysical faith is, precisely, politics, the cultivation of community judgment, rather than scepticism, anarchism, or that acquiescence of the modest that is called tolerance.

Indeed, objectivist philosophies also converge on the virtue of dialogic institutions. If you believe that liberty is an objective good that is subjectively experienced by individuals in different ways (as do Pettit and I), then there is virtue in institutions that empower individuals to discover and reveal their subjective liberty with others who might act to endanger or promote it. If you are an objectivist Popperian fallibilist, you must value dialogue for its capacity to draw out the refutation of falsehoods.

In short, there seem to be many grounds for doubting that truth and right will out from an objectivist, infallibilist political or legal program that rejects the need for dialogue. Hence, to pursue non-dialogic programs of the good and the right with unswerving dedication seems to run the risk of many tyrannies and failures. Of course, the recent failures and tyrannies of Marxism remind us of this fact forcefully, as do those of Western criminal justice systems. Edmund Burke (1910, 277) had warned us of the multitude of misfortunes caused by 'considering general maxims without attending to circumstances, to time, to places, to conjectures and to actors,' since 'if we do not attend scrupulously to these, the medicine of today becomes the poison of tomorrow.'

My suspicion is that MacIntyre (1984b: 500–1) is right when he concludes that disagreement on basic ethical paradigms is frequently compatible with consensus on the moral status of specific practical questions. My enterprise here is a case in point: it is easier to get large numbers of people to agree that dialogue is a good thing than it is to get any substantial number of people to agree with a republican or hermeneutical or fallibilist theory of dialogue. We see this in the decisions of our highest courts, where the justices agree a lot of the time, but rarely for reasons that are based in identical values or common abstract philosophies. This is why deconstructionists can play such havoc with their work. But if we take MacIntyre (1988, 364–5) seriously, we see that nihilism is not justified in the face of such deconstruction. Dialogue between incompatible traditions can see one tradition generate solutions for the other in terms that are coherent within the other tradition. After all the wooing and wondering among the justices, a supreme court decision, woven together from slender and contrary opinion, can knit a fabric of communal conviction that inspires civic purpose and practical problem-solving. The outcome can generally be regarded as sensible, but for several, philosophically incompatible reasons. In contrast, solitary criminal court judges who sentence corporations without any communal wooing and wondering about their remedy are at maximum risk of dishing up tomorrow's poison as today's medicine.

Pursuing Empowerment

For Habermas (1984), dialogic processes can facilitate communicative rationality only to the extent that inter-subjective reflective understanding is unconstrained by deception and domination. For most of us, Habermas's aspiration for uncoerced and undistorted dialogue among competent individuals is utterly utopian. Of course, ideals can be useful for measuring progress, even if they are never fully realizable. However, domination is such a recurrently intractable fact of life, the destruction of power so impossible,[3] that republicans are advocates of the alternative strategy of checking power with countervailing power (Braithwaite and Pettit 1990, 87–8). Ayres and Braithwaite (1992b) have argued for tripartism – fully empowering public interest groups as third players in regulatory proceedings with the state and the firm – for checking power. It can permit evolution of cooperation within negotiated regulation while preventing capture and corruption. The same conditions that make for 'win-win' solutions through cooperation can also allow capture and corruption – a dilemma that tripartism can avoid.

Republicans believe in an enriched conception of citizenship. Freedom is constituted by an active citizenry. But because entrenched centres of power, particularly of the corporate type, often seek to crush active citizens' groups, republicans must lobby for a state that empowers and gives resources to such groups. Poor and powerless citizens cannot enjoy liberty in a world of great inequality of wealth and power. For this fundamental reason, citizen empowerment vis-à-vis corporate concentrations of power is a central republican goal.

Seeing Multiple Motivations

Republicans like to deal with problems through dialogue partly because they prefer dealing with actors as responsible citizens. This approach extends to corporate actors, whom the republican seeks to nurture as responsible citizens. We see shame and pride as having enormous regulatory power in this connection. Indeed, reintegrative shaming and praise of virtue can constitute responsible citizens (Braithwaite 1989).

Eighteenth-century republicans were seen by their Hobbesian critics as naive in this regard. For Thomas Hobbes (1949) and David Hume (1963), institutions could not be based on the hope that citizens would be responsible. Rather, they should be designed for knaves. Geoffrey Brennan and James Buchanan (1985, 59) argue for institutions that economize on virtue; they think it likely that the harm inflicted by those who behave worst will not be compensated for by the good of those who behave better than average. Against this position, Ayres and Braithwaite (1992a), like Goodin (1980), argue that the trouble with institutions that assume that people will not be virtuous is that they destroy virtue. My own observations of business regulatory inspectors, as with police on the streets, is that if they treat people as knaves, knavery is often returned in full measure. Toni Makkai and I (Makkai and Braithwaite 1994) fail to find a general deterrence effect for compliance of nursing homes with the law. In some cases, deterrent threats increase compliance, and in others they make things worse. Burke told us about this – the medicine for today's case is poison for tomorrow's.

Some of the most brutish and nasty business people will put their best self forward, their socially responsible self, if they are treated as responsible citizens. Street-level law enforcement, with either common or corporate crime, seems to me about getting people who have multiple selves to put their best self forward. But what about when they don't? Debate over punishment versus persuasion for dealing with corporate criminals has proceeded on both sides from a much too static analysis. The argument is put that punishment is better than persuasion, or vice versa. Alternatively, the hypothesis is that we can pick which are the right cases for medicine and which for poison. I reject all three types of position in favour of a dynamic strategy – first, persuasion (try to get the regulated actor to put his or her responsible self forward); second, when citizenship fails (as it often will), shift to a deterrent strategy; third, when deterrence fails (as it often will for reasons detailed elsewhere [Ayres and Braithwaite 1992a; Makkai and Braithwaite 1994]), shift to incapacitation (e.g., licence revocation). We would think it terribly crude if debates about the international regulation of states were transacted in the discourse of the optimal level of military threats. We expect, and get, from even our most simple-minded political leaders, more subtle dynamic strategizing.

In relations between states, as in those between business and government, the best possible world is one where actors see themselves as having profound responsibilities for peacefully solving problems. The republican must aspire to nurturing responsible citizenship in pursuit of such a better world. However, the obligation to be vigilant on behalf of the dominion of the powerless requires that clear signals be given to business of willingness to toughen enforcement should there be abuse of trust. Displaying (rather than threatening) the possibility of upward escalation motivates cooperative regulation (Ayres and Braithwaite 1992a: chap. 2).

REPUBLICAN PRAXIS

Now I describe recent implementation of these principles in three domains in Australia: quality-of-care regulation in nursing homes, trade practices enforcement, and misrepresentation with promotional claims in the pharmaceutical industry. I do not discuss below the first principle – taking crime seriously – concentrating instead on the innovative, dialogic side of what has happened. In none of these areas has the criminality of the worst conduct been taken seriously enough. With nursing home regulation, there are Australian criminal cases, in some years running into double figures (if one adds up state and federal cases).

These in the past have resulted in wrist-slapping fines. Consequently, it is the closing down of the nursing home (incapacitation) that is most feared. This eventuality occurs once or twice in most years. For the first time, we are seeing a major homicide investigation, concerning the deaths of twenty-one residents in one home.[4]

If one adds state and federal enforcement, there are over a hundred criminal cases a year concerning consumer protection. Again, these result in wrist-slapping fines. The Trade Practices Act in 1977 dropped imprisonment as a sanction. The anti-trust side of the act is not even criminal, although possible civil penalties are much higher ($10 million) than the fines in any Australian criminal statute.

Of the three areas, misrepresentation of drugs has seen the most profound neglect of law enforcement. There have been botched investigations, but never a successful criminal prosecution.

Nursing Homes

A radical transformation of nursing-home regulation commenced in 1987. Together with Valerie Braithwaite, David Ermann, Diane Gibson, Anne Jenkins, and Toni Makkai, I have been studying these changes since before they started. We have been the primary consultants to the Australian government during this period, making many recommendations for changes, most of which have been adopted.

Our consultancy began just after the first feature of change was settled – complete rewriting of the law. Essentially, the old 'input' standards that required inspectors to measure the size of rooms, count toilets, and report cobwebs in the laundry were scrapped and replaced with thirty-one broad, outcome-oriented standards. These standards were developed by consensus. They were written by a working group in a process of intense dialogue with the industry, consumer groups, trade unions, and professional associations. The result has been extraordinarily high commitment by industry to the standards. Our survey of 410 nursing-home managers found that for none of the thirty-one standards did fewer than 95 per cent of managers view them as desirable; for most standards, more than 90 per cent found them practical as well as desirable (Braithwaite et al. 1992). Hence, dialogue secured industry's agreement and commitment, with a small number of (sometimes vocal) exceptions.

Support from the consumers' movement was not so strong. That group had been largely responsible for whipping up the atmosphere of scandal that led to two government reports and then the reform. Many in the movement (including me) suspected that the thirty-one standards were so broad and vague as to be unenforceable. Standards concerning 'freedom from pain,' 'privacy,' 'dignity,' and a 'homelike environment,' for example, seemed desirable but so inexplicit as to make enforcement impossible. In this, we have been proven wrong. Enforcement, while still inadequate, has increased considerably with the shift from input to outcome standards (Braithwaite et al 1992, chap. 11).

The critics have also been found to be wrong in asserting that a shift to thirty-one broad outcomes would make consistency of ratings (enforceability) impossible. The inter-rater reliability results are the most remarkable part of our findings. But first we can consider how radical the shift is by comparing it to the situation in the United States, where there are over five hundred federal quality-of-care standards for nursing homes. State-government inspectors enforce simultaneously both these and state standards, which in most jurisdictions exceed in number the federal standards. So their job is to check compliance with over one thousand standards, compared with thirty-one in Australia.

How did the United States come to have so many standards? The industry complained about inconsistency of ratings between one nursing home and another, and the consumers' movement complained about vagueness and unenforceability. Historically, legislators have dealt with such complaints by splitting one broad, vague standard into two or more standards with words that look more specific. The incremental pursuit of 'reliability,' however, cumulatively destroys reliability. Why? No inspection team can check compliance with a thousand standards. A compliance score depends on which subset of the standards the inspectors happen to check.

Agreement of one U.S. team with a citation issued independently by another team is the exception rather than the rule (Braithwaite et al 1991). In contrast, when our research team put its own trained inspector into fifty nursing homes to rate them independently at the same time as the government team was in the home, we found the thirty-one Australian outcome-oriented standards to be rated extraordinarily consistently. Inter-rater reliability on total compliance scores ranged from 0.93 to 0.96, depending on how and at what point the coefficient was calculated (Braithwaite et al 1991). Perhaps more remarkable, the average agreement of directors of nursing with the ratings given across the thirty-one standards was 92 per cent.

The key to the remarkable reliability of the Australian standards is dialogue with residents, with staff and management, and within the team itself. Dialogue with residents is, of course, about empowerment as well. As a result of the new regulatory process, the proportion of nursing homes with residents' committees increased from under 20 per cent in the mid-1980s to over 80 per cent by 1990. Most committees are still not actually empowering residents (Braithwaite et al 1992, chap. 8). However, in the most recent phase of reform, the government has committed substantial funds to supporting advocacy groups, which will assist residents' committees in making policy. We have also put recommendations before the minister to involve committees more directly in negotiation of plans to bring non-compliant homes back into compliance. To our research group, nursing-home regulation seemed a 'least-likely' case (Eckstein 1975) for empowerment of consumers. If there is success, then there is hope for the strategy on a wider front.

The new regulatory process is resident-centred. Australian inspectors spend a much larger proportion of their time than their U.S. or Canadian or British or Japanese counterparts[5] in sitting down with residents to get their definitions of problems, which ultimately decide the reliability of compliance ratings, even though observation and interviews with staff provide most of the facts that underlie the definitions.

Inspectors can become incredibly skilled at eliciting the perspectives of residents who are very sick, confused a lot of the time, even unable to speak. We have barely begun to write up the micro-transaction of this empowerment (Braithwaite et al. 1992). Here I want to deal only with how dialogue facilitates reliability in compliance ratings. Consider the standard most often attacked for 'subjectivity' – 'homelike environment.' Unreliability emerges here when inspectors follow 'objective' protocols, such as in some American states where the number of pictures on the walls is counted; staff plaster page after page of popular magazines around the walls of the institution! Subjectivity, not objectivity, is the path to reliability. A properly subjective approach on homelike environment involves talking to residents about whether they feel free to put up personal mementos in an area they define as their private space, whether there are spaces that they feel are inviting and homelike for chatting with friends, whether they feel there are inviting garden areas they can use. When the question arises, 'But is this complaint really an invasion of privacy?,' the answer is discovered through dialogue about the senses of privacy important to this resident. Disagreement is more likely when the question is resolved by pitting one inspector's conception of what privacy means against another's; consensus is more likely when both concentrate on the practical sense of privacy subjectively important to that resident. There will always be inconsistency in assessing whether privacy has been invaded. Resident-centred, contextual dialogue about privacy, in contrast, can often reach reliable conclusions.

Dialogue with staff and managers is responsible for the remarkable level of agreement of both directors of nursing and proprietors with compliance ratings. This dialogue occurs during the visit and, most critically, at a 'compliance discussion,' a group meeting within forty-eight hours of the initial visit. Between the two events, within-team dialogue takes place. At the compliance discussion, the team's preliminary findings are disclosed, standard by standard, to managers, sometimes representatives of staff and residents, and the proprietor or representatives from the church, if it is a church home. Disagreements are sometimes heated, even to the point of shouting and tears. Both inspectors and managers always get extremely nervous before them. In fact, I get nervous when I attend as an observer. There is a ceremonial quality to these occasions. Professional pride in on display; people are at risk of being shamed, before a group that matters to them, concerning fundamental issues of professional and business integrity. If it goes well for everyone, there is palpable elation afterwards. If serious allegations of fraud or neglect are put on the table, devastating cross-cutting emotions can be unleashed.

Often at the compliance discussion, debate will begin on the third stage of dialogue, over future action. The nursing home generally takes its problems of noncompliance back to a full staff meeting and often to a meeting of the residents' committee; the plan of action then comes as a proposal from the nursing home to the inspection team, which either approves it or initiates further dialogue.

Dialogue within the team is systematic and structured. After the initial inspection of the home, the team of two or three or occasionally more, infrequently with a member of the supervisory staff involved, works through each standard to record pluses and minuses. This, of course, is precisely what is impossible in the United States, with hundreds of standards. So the dialogue is disciplined by the standards and the need to write pluses and minuses for each of them and by the requirement to make judgments in terms of the outcomes that subjectively matter to residents. Some of the latter judgments are uncontroversial, of course. You don't need to ask residents if being burnt in a fire or given someone else's drugs matters to them. Debate on food, however, must be disciplined against discussion of what sort of food the inspectors like; the issue is what the residents in this facility like. These rules facilitate dialogue that generates rather robust agreement on standards.

If, after all this dialogue, the nursing home is led towards action that it does not think is justified, a new round of dialogue can be triggered with a standards review panel, consisting of representatives of the department, the industry, and consumer groups who were uninvolved in the first round. These are very rare, however.

When dialogue fails, the standard deterrent sanction is withholding of government benefits on new admissions to the nursing home for a period (usually until the problem is solved). If this fails, the nursing home can be closed. In some states, as an intermediate action, a receiver or administrator can be put in to run the facility.

The evidence seems quite strong (Braithwaite et al. 1992) that the new approach has improved the quality of care. This new approach is based on dialogue with all parties involved, empowerment of residents, and responsive enforcement – the three features, in addition to taking crime seriously, that, I argue above, republicans should pursue.

THE NEW TRADE PRACTICES ENFORCEMENT

After conducting a study of Australia's ninety-six most important business regulatory agencies during the mid-1980s, Peter Grabosky and I concluded that no agency 'has been able to impose as firm an enforcement orientation as the Trade Practices Commission [TPC]. If the commission is captured and weak, then we can only say that it follows from our study that *all* Australian regulatory agencies are so' (Grabosky and Braithwaite 1986, 91). At the time we did not know that I would become a part-time commissioner (1986–95). The TPC spends more on litigation than any federal agency apart from the Director of Public Prosecutions. It has been in court at some time with most of the nation's largest companies, and it wins much more often than it loses. While our regulatory agencies are pretty benign by U.S. standards, by Australian standards, the TPC displays an enforcement pyramid with tough options at the peak (such as divestitures) that it shows willingness to use. At the base of the pyramid, most complaints are dealt with by informal problem-solving – the company replaces a consumer's defective product, desists from a practice, recalls a product, or withdraws an advertisement. It is at the intermediate level that developments have been interesting from a republican point of view. I illustrate this point with two cases that are discussed (along with others of its type) in Fisse and Braithwaite (1993): Solomons Carpets and the insurance frauds on Aboriginal communities.

Solomons Carpets ran advertisements claiming a reduction of up to $40 per metre off the normal price. This representation was false; some of the carpets were no cheaper than the normal price. The matter came before the TPC in 1991. The commission had difficulty deciding what action to take. It was a less serious matter than others that were putting demands on its scarce litigation resources; it was also an area that the TPC did not regard as a top priority.

The commission decided to offer Solomons an administrative settlement that included voluntary compensation for consumers in excess of the criminal fine that was likely should it be convicted. The facts of the matter made court ordered compensation for consumers fairly unlikely, but a modest criminal fine probable. All the commissioners felt that Solomons would reject the administrative settlement because it would be cheaper for it to face the consequences of litigation. Even so, in the interests of consumers, they decided that the idea was worth a try. They turned out to be wrong, because of their erroneous assumption that companies make such decisions according to a deterrence cost-benefit calculus. Unknown to the TPC, there was also a 'soft' target within the firm, namely the chairman of the board, the retired patriarch of this family outfit. For him, as a responsible businessman, it made sense to accept the commission's proposal to use resources on correcting the problem for the benefit of consumers rather than on litigation and fines.

The chairman was dismayed at the prospect of allegations of criminality against his company and was concerned for its reputation and his family's. He was also angry with his chief executive officer (CEO) for allowing the situation to arise and for indulging in such a marketing practice. He sought the CEO's resignation and instructed his remaining senior managers to cooperate with an administrative settlement that included seven requirements:

1 compensation to consumers (legal advisers on both sides were of the opinion that the amount was considerably in excess of what was likely to be ordered by a court);
2 a voluntary investigative report to be prepared by a mutually agreed-on law firm to identify the persons and defective procedures responsible for the misleading advertising;
3 disciplining of those employees and remediation of those defective procedures;
4 a voluntary trade practices education and compliance program within the firm and among its franchisees directed at remedying problems identified and at improving trade practices compliance;
5 an industry-wide national trade practices education campaign funded by Solomons to get its competitors to increase their compliance with regard to advertising of carpets;
6 auditing and annual certification of completion of the agreed compliance programs by an agreed outside law firm at Solomons' expense; and
7 a press release from the TPC advising the community of all of the above and of the conduct by Solomons that initially triggered the investigation.

It should be noted that the press release attracted significant coverage in most major Australian newspapers. In addition, although it was not part of the deed of agreement, Solomons volunteered to conduct an evaluation study of the improvement (or absence thereof) in compliance with the act by its competitors as a result of the industry-wide campaign.

At low cost to taxpayers, the commission appears to have increased consumer protection. The company was required to undertake disciplinary action and to report the steps taken. It was also required to provide compensation that victims would not otherwise have received (without compromising their right to take further private action). The TPC was able to promote general deterrence by publicizing the nature and costs of the settlement.

The TPC has taken this strategy much further by using it successfully in the largest consumer protection cases in Australian history. A number of insurance companies engaged in widespread and systematic deceptive conduct, selling insurance policies to people living in remote Aboriginal communities. Insurance agents misrepresented the terms of the investment policies sold and used unconscionable selling tactics. The vulnerability of poorly educated, remote Aborigines to exploitation by authoritative men in white shirts from the city became clear during the TPC's investigation. Victims tended to assume that it must have been they who had done something wrong. On occasions when the commission's investigators knocked on the front door, the victims would flee out the back. Many shook continuously throughout their interviews, and some cried with fear.

The agents had cashed in on this vulnerability, a product of two centuries of white oppression and destruction of self-assurance. In one case, the customer was even told that he would go to jail unless he signed the policy. False representations were made to Aborigines that they would need to commit some of their existing unemployment benefits to a savings investment plan because when they turned sixty-five they would no longer be eligible for government welfare support. The saddest false representation was that the policy would pay generous funeral benefits. This is a matter of profound religious importance to Aborigines who live in communities away from their land. When they die, they must be taken back to be part of their country, their land, for ever. It can be prohibitively expensive to transport a body long distances along bush tracks.

There were many types of misrepresentation. One of the most common was that policy-holders could get their money back in two years. In fact, administration costs absorbed all the premiums paid during the first two years. Agents failed to inform holders that their policies would lapse unless the premiums were paid regularly. In most instances, the policies sold to the Aborigines lapsed because deductions from their wages could no longer be made when temporary employment ceased. In many cases, deductions continued, even after policies had lapsed.

In the first round of settlements negotiated by the TPC, the local Aboriginal community council participated actively in the negotiations and advanced a number of the key terms ultimately included in the settlement. Under the first deed, signed with Colonial Mutual Life (CML), refunds totalling $1.5 million have been paid to some two thousand policy-holders affected, even where claims were barred by the three-year limitation. Victims are getting 15 per cent compound interest on their investments, considerably higher than rates prevailing at the time of the deed. Some victims have received payouts well in excess of $10,000. CML also undertook to pay $715,000 into an Aboriginal Assistance Trust Fund for the benefit of Aboriginal people, including those in the communities affected by CML's unfair practices.

CML had as well to conduct an internal investigation in order to identify failings in compliance and the names of officers, employees, or agents who had engaged in or who had contributed to the unfair practices. It was then to undertake appropriate remedial and disciplinary action and to report the action taken to the commission. Specific action was to be taken in future to ensure that disadvantaged persons understood the nature and content of any insurance policy offered to them. CML was also required to put a senior manager in charge of compliance with the Trade Practices Act, to identify that person to the commission, and to have him or her report annually on progress.

The TPC and CML released a jointly prepared media statement summarizing the terms of the deed and called a press conference. The release spelt out CML's willingness to cooperate in resolving the matter. It also indicated the joint view of the signatories that the arrangement was in the best interests of the company, the commission, and the community. What happened within CML as a result? A cynic might be tempted to say that the agreement largely left CML free to return to unconscionable sales tactics. The outcome does not support this assessment. Members of the firm's board insisted on a purge. Over eighty employees or agents have been dismissed, including a national sales manager, state sales managers for Queensland and New South Wales, and Tri-Global, a major corporate agency that is contesting its termination in the courts.

One question mark surrounding the settlement is the confidential nature of the compliance and internal disciplinary report (see Fisse and Braithwaite 1993). Another concern is the limited criminal enforcement against individuals. One selling agent suffered a minor criminal conviction. However, there has been no initiation of criminal proceedings against senior managers.

The CML case and the related settlements in train represent a landmark in the

development of enforcement strategies geared to making corporations accountable for law-breaking. The commission built on the experience gained from the
Solomons Carpets affair and negotiated its way through a complex and large-
scale matter involving many major corporations, numerous corporate and individual agents of those corporations, and thousands of largely illiterate victims
located in some of the most inaccessible locations in a vast continent. There
were legion evidentiary and procedural problems, particularly time limits on
actions under the Trade Practices Act.

The TPC's approach in the CML operation involved an advance over the
Solomons strategy. Accountability was improved by having the agreed facts
formally endorsed by a court of law. Many more people were compensated, an
educational commitment was enshrined in the deed, the internal investigation
was rigorous, and a number of people lost their jobs as a result of the investigation. Most important, however, the case has triggered a wider, community campaign to reform insurance practices. Media coverage has been extensive. All
levels of the Australian polity have been touched by the shocking practices
revealed. Even the prime minister asked for a briefing on it. The minister for
justice has given a ministerial direction to the commission to conduct a wider
inquiry into the insurance industry and its sales practices. State consumer affairs
agencies are examining their neglect of consumer education for Aborginals.
Certain weaknesses revealed in the Insurance Contracts Act and the Trade Practices Act are likely to be remedied by parliament. Feverish deliberations are
under way within the industry itself about how to prevent such a damaging public-relations debacle from happening again. Thus the possibility of regulation
through a licensing regime for agents is back on the insurance industry's
agenda.

For some participants, the regulatory dialogue brought home their responsibility in a particularly compelling way. Top managers found themselves directly
confronted with the shame of the practices from which they and their companies
had benefited. The media and the courts were not the only forums in which
some people found themselves exposed. The top managers of Norwich, the second firm to sign a deed, was pressed into immediate contact with the victims as
part of the process leading up to settlement. This was an exacting and con-
science-searing experience. They had to take four-wheel–drive vehicles into
tropical northeastern Australia in order to participate in disputed negotiations,
during which the victims were given an active voice. Living for several days
under the same conditions as their victims, Norwich's top brass had to sleep on
mattresses on a concrete floor, eat tinned food, and survive without electricity
during the daytime.

Processes of dialogue with those who suffer from acts of irresponsibility are among the most effective ways of bringing home to us as human beings our obligation to take responsibility for our deeds. Traditional courts, where victims are treated as evidentiary cannon-fodder rather than given voice, have tended to be destructive of this human way of eliciting responsibility. These insurance cases illustrate how the 'accountability model' leaves space for encounters with victims which can both communicate the shame of the wrongdoing and heal it through acceptance of responsibility and putting right the wrong.

Another important feature of the negotiations was the part played by Aboriginal community councils. Councils also held out for stringent terms of settlement and made detailed suggestions as to the contents of the deeds. Their role was thus consistent with tripartite enforcement, in which consumer or other representative groups have a voice in the action taken. The tripartite model reduces the danger of enforcement agencies' entering into cosy deals. This is the principle of countervailing power that is so important from a republican perspective.

Both the insurance and the Solomons cases display resolute action in the middle of an enforcement pyramid. Both amount to 'net widening' of a productive sort. The negotiated settlement resulted in more of everything – deterrence, compensation, internal discipline, correction of standard operating procedures, compliance education, incapacitation, shame – than could ever have been achieved by a court case. Moreover, all of this was volunteered by the companies, though admittedly after some tough negotiating. But they offered so much more than they would have got away with in court fundamentally because top managers stood up and said that they wanted to be responsible corporate citizens. With the Aboriginal insurance cases, senior executives conducted negotiations out in remote communities where they met their victims and confronted the terrible circumstances that they had made worse. During the negotiations, all these companies said that they wanted to use the money that would be lost because of the debacle to put the problem right rather than spend it on lawyers to fight the commission. That was what they said, and that was what they did. The negotiating sessions were little shaming ceremonies, not completely unlike the nursing-home compliance discussions, that treated top managers as people whom the commission expected to act responsibly. When the TPC declined to treat them as knaves, knavery was not forthcoming; remorse and remediation beyond the requirements of the law were offered instead.

Again, we see here a strategy based on dialogic problem-solving, empowerment of victims, and responsive, pyramidal regulation. Rejecting this republican package in favour of standard liberal enforcement in the courts would have had less impact on reform of the industry and would have left Aboriginal victims worse off.

COMMUNITARIAN CONTROL OF CORPORATE CRIME IN THE PHARMACEUTICAL INDUSTRY

During the first half of the 1980s, I was involved in various attempts through submissions to government inquiries to strengthen regulatory enforcement, by the Department of Health and also by the TPC, concerning misleading claims in the promotion of pharmaceuticals. All these lobbying efforts failed. At the last failed attempt, a Public Service Board (1987) inquiry, the consumers' movement could see that the inquiry was heading in a worrying direction. It was going to find that given that there was no practical hope of the government providing the resources to regulate marketing claims effectively, the best approach was to give up the pretence of doing so and give self-regulation a try. So it switched tack. We reluctantly agreed to support a three-year trial of self-regulation, but only on condition that the industry commit itself to improving self-regulation in a variety of ways, that the TPC do an evaluation, and that if the TPC found self-regulation to have been a failure, the government should find the resources to regulate matters properly. The inquiry did indeed so recommend.

The TPC published the results of its fairly rigorous evaluation of self-regulations by the Australian Pharmaceutical Manufacturers' Association (APMA) (Trade Practices Commission 1992). The evaluation process was dialogic, culminating in a pre-decision conference attended by representatives of consumers, the medical profession, and the industry. The commission's conclusion, supported by all parties to the conference, was that the APMA's self-regulation had been more effective than government regulation had ever been. An independent chairman recommended by the TPC had run the scheme with greater toughness (even if still inadequate) in terms of sanctioning than the government had managed. The program had mobilized greater expertise of oversight than the government ever did or could, it put in place systematic pre-publication clearance of advertisements that Canberra could never have afforded, and it was kept on its toes by both the TPC's pending evaluation and repeated post-publication surveys of compliance with the APMA's Code conducted independently by the Australian Society of Clinical and Experimental Pharmacologists.[6] There is still a great deal to be done, as the commission found in its report. However, the view that self-regulation had performed better than had government regulation is not just my view and the TPC's. It is the view of every Australian consumer advocate I know who has been involved directly with pharmaceuticals regulation. In fact, Health Action International (one of the networks of the International Organization of Consumers' Unions) in 1992 surveyed implementation of the WHO's Ethical Criteria for Medicinal Drug Promotion in forty-two countries.[7] Australia obtained the highest score, with 26 out of a possible 37 points, followed by Sweden with 23; three countries scored zero!

It is not clear, however, that self-regulation is superior to government regulation. In principle, I still think that government is better placed to regulate pharmaceuticals promotion than an industry association. Such things should be decided not in principle, but out of a process of dialogue. If the other side promises something better than can be obtained under one's 'fine principles' and delivers it, pat it on the back, tell it that you were wrong (led astray by inappropriate application of the principle), and encourage it to keep up the good work, to improve further. Regulatory policy should not be framed out of an abstract, static analysis of what is the best strategy; it should be responsive to histories of success and failure to deliver the goods in a particular context. In the terms put forward in Ayres and Braithwaite (1992a, b), we should stand ready to adjust responsively up and down a pyramid of regulatory strategies.

During the same period, there sprung up in Australia the Medical Lobby for Appropriate Marketing (MaLAM), of which I am a member. The key players are doctors. MaLAM's strategy has been simple. Dr Peter Mansfield, the inspiration behind MaLAM, writes to a large number of doctors around the world who are members with information about a product that is being marketed inappropriately by a certain company in a particular country. These professionals then write to the company – generally at its First World headquarters, or in the nation where the offence occurred, or in their own country – demanding an explanation. A naïve strategy, hard-bitten advocates of state deterrence might say. Not really. It works enough of the time to make it an extremely cost-efficient method of social control for activists with scarce resources. Writing letters is cheap. Moreover, it is social control based on reasoned appeal to corporate and medical responsibility. Actually, it is not social control at all, but a method of dialogue. Sometimes MaLAM decides that it got things wrong and writes back to the company with an apology. Pharmaceutical executives, even some of the worst of them, do have a better side, a responsible side, to which appeals to professional and corporate responsibility can be made. When they don't put their responsible self forward, there are other strategies available – muckraking in the media and calls for state enforcement, for example, and, in extreme cases, threats of consumer or professional boycotts.

As well, pharmaceutical companies have self-interested reasons to listen and respond seriously to groundswells of professional concern. They survive in the marketplace by persuading physicians to prescribe their products. In other words, they depend for success on convincing health care professionals that they are trustworthy. Sometimes they decide that the best way to promote long-term success is to be trustworthy, to admit a mistake and put it right. Five of seventeen MaLAM letter-writing campaigns between January 1988 and June 1989 resulted in agreement by a company to alter claims or withdraw a product (Wade, Mansfield, and McDonald 1989). This rate increased to five out of nine for July 1989 to June 1990 (Mansfield 1991).

The strategy can be a strand in a web of controls over trans-national crimes that are beyond the reach of the state. I attempt elsewhere to show how MaLAM is interwoven with other threads in such a manner (Braithwaite 1993). Moreover, Fisse and Braithwaite (1993) explain, illustrating with cases such as that involving the Bank of Commerce and Credit International (BCCI) how state regulatory agencies and national courts might effect enforcement against transnational crime without depending on international laws or extraterritorial sweep of national laws; courts could mobilize republican institutions that use the concept of criminality, dialogue, empowerment, and enforcement pyramids.

CONCLUSION

Republican criminology can play a strategic part in a transition to twenty-first-century urban republics. It can show that republican ideas have potential for dealing even with our very worst problems and our most difficult people. With groups such as nursing-home residents, prisoners, and young Aboriginal offenders, coherent strategies of empowerment can succeed even with the most powerless. The solutions, of course, differ for each type of problem and each history of dialogue. Yet liberté, egalité, and fraternité are still the crucial republican aspirations.

Liberté

The police (private and public) are both one of the greatest threats to freedom and one of the institutions most crucial to assuring freedom. Large corporations that control private policing and the newest surveillance technology are such a deep threat to freedom that their worst excesses must be criminalized. A central republican task is to enshrine a bill of rights, which we in Australia still do not have. But we must avoid the mistake of the Canadian Charter of Rights and Freedoms, an eighteenth-century–style bill of rights that applies only to public abuse of power, that fails to come to grips with the greater concentrations of power in private hands today.

Egalité

Incarcerating a few corporate criminals strikes a rather trivial blow for equality.

Obversely, moving away from myopically punitive criminal justice can strike a major blow for the powerless. People often ask of my advocacy of family group conferences for dealing with youth crime: 'What will this do for the deeper structural problems of Aborigines?' My answer is, 'Quite a lot.' In this, I am not referring mainly to the fact that finding jobs and educational opportunities for young offenders is an important objective of these conferences. Rather, the criminal justice system is absolutely central to the oppression of Aboriginal people. In Australia, as in the United States, we have more young black males in prison than in higher education. That is our human-capital policy for black Australia. Family group conferences, as the pilot programs at Wagga Wagga show, and as the Maoris' experience in New Zealand reveals, are more promising alternatives (Braithwaite and Mugford 1992). Because they are dialogic, they empower and enrich all participants, including victims and the police. That is why the police have abandoned their traditional law-and-order posture to be leading supporters of the reform. Because Aborigines and the poor generally are overrepresented among both offenders and victims (including victims of corporate crime, as in cases such as CML), institutions that give voice to offenders and victims and their families profoundly redistribute power.

Giving poor offenders jobs instead of jail is obviously the way to go. But so is it a stupid human-capital policy to put our brightest and best corporate criminals in jail. Michael Milkin was one of the most talented people of this century; he transformed world capitalism in the 1980s with his idea of the junk bond. Alan Bond was one of the most talented, visionary people Australia has produced. What a waste to send him to jail instead of giving him a new public project rather more noble than winning the America's Cup, something that would benefit the poor in a major way – perhaps two decades of entrepreneurship on behalf of one of Australia's great charities, a major reintegrative feat of citizenship. Michael Milkin actually proposed a community service project – working with the banks to come up with some creative solutions to Third World debt. If anyone could have done that, Milkin – entrepreneurial citizen – could have. So I think that the United States may have made a serious mistake in not taking the offer seriously – in putting retribution ahead of egalitarian and republican values.

Fraternité

The trouble with the old socialists was structural determinism. They put people such as Lenin in power to erect structures that would create a new socialist man. The top-down vision failed to see that, in the absence of prior work in constituting responsible citizenship from below, it was carpenters such as Stalin who would be relied on to erect the structures. The efforts failed for reasons explained by the fallibilist critique of central control in Popper (1966), not to mention the subjectivist critique of objectivist tyranny (socialist man excluding women's truth). The structure-citizenship sequence in Marx must be replaced by citizenship-structure, or rather a developmentally recursive relationship between dialogue and structures. Republican citizenship still has profound appeal in the artistic traditions of Western peoples, whence the recent revival of *Les Miserables*. Caring citizenship and communitarian problem-solving can have their power most forcefully affirmed if we can deploy them where they seem least deserved and least plausible – with Milkin and Bond. Just as there was no way of socialism escaping the fact that its future depended on the citizenship values of Stalin, capitalism cannot escape the fact that its future rests with the citizenship of men such as Milkin. Marxism and libertarianism share the same structural blindness to this fact.

Most important, I hope the examples of communitarian problem-solving discussed above show that republican thinking can lead us to ways of grappling with the quality of nursing-home care, protecting powerless consumers, and the safe use of medicines that actually work. Problem-solving strategies that evince respect for enriched conceptions of liberty, equality, and community can actually increase the institutional competence of our efforts to tackle the troubles we sometimes call corporate crime.

NOTES

My thanks to Stanley Cohen, Philip Pettit, and participants at the Queen's University conference for critical comments on an earlier draft of this chapter.

1 There are so many that could be named that it is unfair to single some out. However, it behoves me to illustrate with people whose contribution in each area has been much greater than my own: with nursing-home reform, John Barber and Martin Derkley; with innovation in trade practices enforcement, Allan Asher and Bill Dee; and with reform of pharmaceuticals promotion, Peter Mansfield, Yong Sook Kwok, and Ken Harvey.

2 This doubtless seems a strange expectation about a country that is likely soon to see a decade of social-democratic national government terminated by a predominantly new-right, libertarian regime. But republicans need to be able to see plural sources of political change which, particularly in a federal system, frequently run deeper than the comings and goings of central governments.

3 Destroying domination is an especially dismal agenda with corporate crime, where large actors are by definition centres of power.

4 No one has ever gone to jail for a nursing-home quality-of-care offence, although people have been imprisoned for fraud in cases where 'ripping off' the government's benefits scheme was not unrelated to delivering care of shockingly poor quality.
5 We have done fieldwork with nursing-home inspectors in these countries as well.
6 R.F.W. Moulds and L.M.H. Wing, 'Drug Advertising,' *Medical Journal of Australia* 150 (1989): 410–11.
7 K. Harvey and D. Carandang, *The Impact of WHO Ethical Criteria for Medicinal Drug Promotion: A Study by Health Action International (HAI)* (The Hague: International Organization of Consumers' Unions 1992).

4

Should We Prosecute Corporations and/or Individuals?

GILBERT GEIS AND JOSEPH DIMENTO

Only dim echoes linger today in the jurisprudence of the United States, England, and Canada of the once-intense debate about whether it is proper – ethically, juridically, and in terms of effectiveness – to punish a corporation criminally rather than, or in addition to, punishing individuals within it. The position that corporations are fair game for criminal charges now has swept aside virtually all legal barriers that stood in its path (for a good review of this development, see Elkins 1976).[1] As one writer has noted: 'Early decisions in this area evidence a reluctance to convict a corporation of a crime requiring criminal intent, but now it is almost unquestioned that an agent's intent, knowledge, or willfulness may be imputed to the corporation' (B. Coleman 1975, 909).

We argue below that development of the idea of corporate criminal responsibility has been the result more of expediency than of either sound logic or empirical reasoning. This is to say not that the outcome is wrong, only that it has not been examined satisfactorily and that, if so examined, it *could* prove to be incorrect. Where it is available, empirical research is brought to bear on the issue; more often, we question claims about the advantages of corporate prosecution that fail to take adequate account of countervailing considerations or ignore alternative pathways that might equally well or more satisfactorily achieve the desired goals. The resolution of the issues addressed typically will be the equivocal Scots criminal-trial verdict: not proven.

The rationale that has led to far-ranging corporate criminal liability was set out by a Canadian court, which noted that corporations are 'more powerful and more materially endowed and equipped than are individuals and, if allowed to roam unchecked in the field of industry and commerce, they are potentially more dangerous and can inflict greater harm upon the public than can their weaker competitors' (*R. v. St. Lawrence Corp. Ltd.*, 1969; see also Caroline 1985). While these words accurately describe the corporate world, they hardly satisfactorily justify criminalizing corporate misconduct; there are, after all, much more powerful entities than corporations – such as political units and armies – that are not subject to criminal penalties, and control of corporate power does not necessarily demand use of criminal reins rather than other restraints.

Additional rationales behind the principle of corporate criminal responsibility were indicated in *United States v. Hilton Hotels Corp.* (1972). The facts are these: a purchasing agent of the hotel's branch in Portland, Oregon, had boycotted a merchant who refused to pay an assessment against the hotel's suppliers that allegedly was to be used to promote tourism to the city. For this act, the Hilton chain and the manager in Portland were charged with violations of the Sherman Antitrust Act, forbidding agreements that restrain trade.

The organizational defendant on appeal argued that both the chain's president and the manager had twice told the purchasing agent that he was not to participate in the boycott. The agent confirmed these warnings but said that his own anger at the recalcitrant supplier had overruled them. Granting these claims, the court none the less ruled that criminal liability could be imposed on a corporation 'without proof that the conduct was within the agent's actual authority, and even though it may have been contrary to actual instructions' (p. 1004). The judge insisted that it was 'reasonable to assume' that Congress had intended to 'impose liability upon business entities for the acts of those to whom they chose to delegate their affairs, thus stimulating a maximum effort by owners and managers to assure adherence by such agents to the requirements of the Act' (p. 1005). This congressional intent, if indeed the judge fathomed it accurately, represents the first in an array of assumptions about corporate criminal liability examined below. Is it not, for instance, as reasonable to assume that agents of corporations will be more willing to undertake illegal acts – and more susceptible to pressure to do so – because they appreciate that the corporate entity might well defend their crimes if it is jointly accountable for them?

On the question of corporate criminal liability, the judge in *United States v. Hilton Hotels Corp.* noted: 'Legal commentators have argued forcefully that it is inappropriate and ineffective to impose criminal liability upon a corporation, as distinguished from human agents who actually perform the illegal act' (p. 1006). One author the judge cited had suggested commonsensically: 'There has never been any doubt among lawyers that a crime committed on behalf of an association, corporate or incorporate, must in fact have been committed by individuals, and that therefore, guilt is always personal' (Canfield 1914, 472). The difficulty of enforcing personal responsibility for crime, this author maintained, is 'simply one of proof' (472). Another writer had insisted that if the criminal law 'takes care of individual responsibility the group will take care of itself' and that 'if we will pierce the corporate veil to strike down the guilty persons back of the corporate entity, when justice requires, we will also disregard this corporate veil and treat the persons back of it as human beings, instead of blindly striking ostensibly at the fiction and letting the blows take effect where they will' (Francis 1924, 319).

Unavailable to the judge at the time were Alschuler's (1991, 311) later, tart observation: 'One notable misuse of the criminal law occurred in 1909 [in the leading case of *New York Central*], when the Supreme Court upheld the imposition of criminal responsibility on a corporation ... The court uttered something vague about "public policy" and the power of the corporation in "modern times." It then upheld criminal punishment that could not truly be borne by a fictional entity but only by human beings whose guilt remained unproven.' For Alschuler (1991, 312), corporations are criminally scapegoated because people 'truly personify and hate the corporation.' They hate the mahogany panelling, the Lear jet, the smokestack, the glass tower, and all the people inside, Alschuler maintains. 'To superstitious people,' he writes, 'villains need not breathe; they may include Exxon and the phone company' (312).

Such reservations give way for the judge in the *Hilton Hotels* case to legislative judgment. That judgment is said to be reflected in the conclusion of the American Law Institute (ALI) (1956, 149): 'The great mass of legislation calling for corporate criminal liability suggests a widespread belief on the part of legislators that such liability is necessary to effectuate regulatory policy.' This statement, of course, avoids the real issue by use of the tautological sleight-of-hand deemed acceptable to defend judicial deference to legislative preference: if the elected law-makers think something necessary, and what they think is not unreasonable or unconstitutional, it then merits court approval. For us, though, there remain questions about the foundation and validity of the legislative wisdom. One question is whether corporate criminal liability really is necessary to carry out regulatory tasks, but more important, in terms of the present discussion: Does it accomplish this goal more satisfactorily than individual responsibility alone?

The *Hilton Hotels* decision offers one crucial piece of evidence: the Portland hotel manager had been acquitted of the Sherman Act charge while the corporation was found guilty, an outcome sustained by the appellate judge. Numerous intriguing questions suggest themselves. If the corporation could not have been charged criminally, would the manager, tried alone, have been convicted, possibly because the prosecutor would have made more strenuous efforts to determine his blameworthiness? Did the possibility of inculpating an impersonal corporate entity instead of another human being influence the jury and the judge? If the manager had been convicted, what would have been the consequences in terms of future illegal acts by the defendant, by managers in the chain, and by other vulnerable white-collar junior executives? Would Hilton Hotels have responded differently, locally and nationally, presuming that it responded at all to the verdict? Would the case have been prosecuted at all if the corporate entity could not have been held criminally liable?

Passing reference in the *Hilton Hotels* case is also made to Mueller's (1957) argument that it is a particularly regrettable violation of the crucial criminal law doctrine of *mens rea* to impose criminal liability on corporations if the acts committed by their agents are unauthorized. This reservation too is waved aside by the judge in terms of deference to legislative wisdom (p. 1006). Attention might have been paid, however, to Mueller's shrewd exegesis on the Model Penal Code commentary quoted in *Hilton Hotels* to justify laws imposing corporate criminal liability. He (Mueller 1957, 27) italicizes the ALI reporter's observation that it is '*pragmatic experience indicating their usefulness*' that undergirds these enactments (American Law Institute 1956, 147). Thereafter, Mueller quotes the phrase, cited in *Hilton Hotels*, about the 'widespread belief' among legislators in the value of corporate criminal liability for regulatory ends and then points out that the reporter, citing cases regarding corporate convictions and individual acquittals, laments that 'it is not clear what conclusions are to be drawn from the cited cases' and voices the hope 'that more could be pointed to in justification of placing the pecuniary burdens of criminal fines on the innocent [i.e. the corporation and its shareholders] than the difficulties of proving the guilt of the culpable individual' (Mueller 1957, 37; American Law Institute 1956, 150).

Mueller (1957, 27) scornfully summarizes the ALI's reasoning: 'This, I respectfully submit,' he writes, 'is not the ground upon which to perpetuate and enlarge corporate criminal liability!' For additional support, Mueller had drawn on Glanville Williams's reservations about the broad sweep of corporate criminal liability, shorthanded in Williams's observation that 'it seems to me that judges have not always looked where they are going' (G. Williams 1956, 137). Paraphrasing Williams, Mueller (1957, 28) writes: 'The law has developed the concept of corporate criminal liability without rhyme or reason, proceeding by a hit or miss method, unsupported by economic or sociological data. Moreover, instances are easily imaginable which completely disprove the popular belief in the efficacy of corporate criminal liability by suggesting its utter futility.'

Unattended to, since it was beyond the purview of the *Hilton Hotels* case, is Mueller's inventory of civil-law countries, which showed that in practically all of them such a doctrine does not exist, and only a natural person can incur criminal guilt.[2] During wartime, Mueller (1957 29) points out, a few civil-law countries had enacted economic legislation of limited applicability, some of it still in force, which held corporations criminally liable. But these laws permit exculpation of an organization that is able to demonstrate diligence in seeking to have the law obeyed. Otherwise, the ancient doctrine *societas delinquere non potest* – corporations do not commit crimes – prevails in jurisdictions in continental Europe. Mueller (1957, 35) concludes: 'A substantial portion of the world rejects corporate criminal liability after more thought and contemplation than has ever been given to the subject in this country.' Alschuler (1991, 311–12) insists, though offering no evidence, that the continental model results 'not only in greater fairness but also in more effective regulation.'

Mueller (1957, 35), following his review of continental codes, suggests that, without a comprehensive inquiry regarding the economic effects of the different approaches of civil-law countries and Anglo-American jurisdictions to corporate criminal liability, we ought 'at least ... to analyze the ... rationale of criminal liability of our law in the hope that it may shed some light on the utility or futility of subjecting corporations to criminal liability.'

RATIONALE

The most prominent arguments in support of the principle of corporate criminal liability are these:

1 A corporate body is distinctive from the sum of those persons who make up the organization; therefore, it is more reasonable to pursue the collectivity rather than the individuals who separately fall short of satisfactorily representing the culpable entity.
2 Punishing individuals rather than the corporate body is not an effective strategy, since for employees the risks associated with potential criminal liability will generally be less compelling than those related to failure to meet organizational demands.
3 The shame associated with criminal conviction will be a stronger deterrent on a corporation than on individual malefactors within it.
4 Corporations can be redesigned by court sanctions more readily than can individuals.
5 It is much easier for prosecutors to establish corporate criminal guilt than it is to discover and to prosecute guilty individuals.
6 Since the corporation almost invariably possesses much greater assets than the individuals who work for it, the opportunity for satisfactory redress of the

harm inflicted will be enhanced if the corporate resources can be attacked instead of those of its employees.

We analyze each of these items in turn with regard to its persuasiveness.

1 *Corporate Distinctiveness*

Abbott (1936) is one of many commentators who have expressed the idea that there is something significantly different between a corporate body and the aggregation of individuals employed by that organization: 'As has often been noted, it follows that a corporation has a personality of its own distinct from the personalities which compose it, a 'group personality' different from and greater than its constituent elements in the sense that the whole is greater than the sum of the parts' (p. 2; see also Boyden 1947, 352; Dicey 1905, 153; Fisse and Braithwaite 1988, 485).

There is no question that people in groups behave differently than people alone – each of us is the product of endless forces that consciously or, undoubtedly more often, unconsciously play into our behaviour. Our genetic structure, our childhood, the books we read, the motion pictures we saw, the conversations we overheard, the things we learned in school – all of these matters and endless others, like the corporate ethos, insinuate themselves into our personal behaviour. Obviously a decision rendered in the name of a corporate body, like that given in the name of a nation, may be an amalgam of innumerable contributions, but the law can separate out personal responsibility for particular segments and determine which persons ought to be held criminally responsible rather than abdicating that aim by resort to the fictive notion of a distinctive 'corporate personality.'

A further item in Abbott's catalogue of corporate traits – immortality – seems to us little more than a semantic sideshow. While the corporation assuredly can endure well beyond the lifespan of any or all of its members, criminal liability could be attached to the individuals within it who committed an illegal act at a particular moment. If the original culprits have moved on, they can be tracked down. If they have died by the time the crime is uncovered, this is no different from the consequences that fall out for the criminal justice system on the decease of a burglar or murderer before his or her law-breaking is unmasked.

In the end, the conclusion on corporate personality has to remain that enunciated so matter-of-factly and obviously by Mr Justice Brown in *Hale v. Henkle* (1906, 51): 'A corporation is, after all, only an association of individuals under an assumed name and with a distinct legal entity.' While this statement does not tell us whether that entity ought reasonably and practically to be held responsible for criminal behaviour, it does demystify the exotic and anthropomorphic idea that a corporate body comes to possess a beingness that can and should be differentiated from the persons who contribute to that result. J. Hall, in the same vein, points to the following observation in the *Harvard Law Review*: 'Just as an individual's moral blameworthiness depends on mental processes, corporate moral fault may be said to depend on internal processes' (Comment 1979, 1232). Hall's response is acerbic: 'Certainly anything can be *said*. But calling thinking and purposive action a "process" is questionable, and equating them to corporate processes is simply a play on words' (Hall 1982, 278).'

It does not appear rootless to prosecute human beings rather than inanimate corporate entities when no compelling reasons beyond the idea of a matter called a 'corporate personality' (Hallis 1930) exist. In social psychology, the concept of a 'group mind' (McDougall 1920), as one overview notes (Wegner, Giuliano, and Hertel 1985, 255; see also Knowles 1982), 'slipped ignominiously into the history of social psychology, and by its absence ordained the study of the individual as the prime focus of the field.' The same shift in perspective could be overdue in the jurisprudence of 'corporate crime.'

2 *Fear of Corporate Reprisal*

The fear of losing a job or failing to secure desired advancement obviously must be weighed in the balance by an employee who is directly ordered to, or who senses that a superior would be pleased if he or she were to, say, meet with competitors to fix prices in violation of anti-trust restrictions. In the infamous General Electric case, only one person so impelled refused on moral grounds to acquiesce to such pressure, indicating that he had signed an agreement not to do so and would not renege on his word. He was transferred to a position where such considerations were not relevant. Those who replaced this manager defined him as something of a pious old fuddy-duddy and saw no barriers to following instructions to meet with competitors to fix prices. But when apprehended, they uniformly denied, though we do not know whether truthfully or as a self-serving defence, that they had adequately appreciated that what they were doing was a criminal offence rather than merely a technical violation of a complex legal doctrine (Geis 1967). A General Electric executive who served a jail sentence for his role in the case said: 'They would never get me to do it again ... I would starve before I would do it again' (Geis 1972, 379). Apparently, had he known beforehand what he later came to know about his fate, at least this executive would have abstained from law-breaking, a result that might not have come about if he believed that he would be immune but that the corporation would be vulnerable to criminal prosecution. Both he and it, of course, were in fact prosecuted, and it has to remain uncertain whether that joint susceptibility is overkill, whether it dilutes individual responsibility, or whether it represents the most effective tactic for control of corporate crime.

As C.D. Stone (1975, xx) notes: 'We have arranged things so that people who call the shots do not have to bear the full risks.' Courts ought to be able to distinguish between an intolerable pressure to violate the law and a self-interested criminal act. Those who exert the pressure presumably should bear the criminal responsibility for its imposition. Just such a result ensued in an early reported case in which a foreman was found guilty for ordering the unlawful refilling of oil barrels, but the jury refused to convict the labourer who carried out the work, apparently on the ground that the subordinate employee had been coerced because of his fear of losing his job if he failed to do what he was told (*State v. Parsons*, 1982).

Baysinger (1991, 347–8) points out that individuals in organizations 'attempt to achieve their own personal objectives,' leading to problems of 'agent conflict, moral hazard or goal divergence,' so that it is not always true that the lawbreaker in the ranks is yielding to pressure – at least no more than the slum youngster who feels compelled by advertising or peer persuasion to steal a car. In addition, as Crane (1980, 45) has argued, 'making the manager criminally accountable gives him a weapon to resist pressures from his superiors.' In short, it seems at least arguable that criminal sanctions against a corporation (rather than or in addition to individuals) truly serve to reduce pressures on employees for acts that violate the law, especially if they come to appreciate that prosecutors often will be satisfied to charge the corporation rather than set out on what could be a wearisome attempt to place the blame on the responsible employee. Similarly, allowing individuals to plead in return for their testimony against the corporation, a common procedure, could undermine the prospect of their developing the integrity needed to resist the temptation of law-breaking. If a corporate employee comes to appreciate that he or she will bear a heavy punitive burden if detected, this knowledge may keep the person who realizes it honest, particularly since business people are presumed to be more rational in their behavioural calculations than street offenders (Braithwaite and Geis 1982).

3 Corporations Are More Deterrable

It is argued, among other things, that shame works wonders in leading a corporation to shape up after its wrongdoing has been exposed to public condemnation. Fisse and Braithwaite found from their interviews with corporate executives whose companies had been criminally sanctioned that they personally felt tainted, and they would recount stories of scorn and ostracism heaped on them and their families by their neighbours (Fisse and Braithwaite 1983). It seems likely that the derogation would be considerably greater were John Doe himself the object of prosecutorial action. In fact, one could argue that shame falling on employees totally innocent of wrongdoing is unreasonably unfair, a result to be avoided unless superordinate goals are being achieved.

Most economic theorists who study corporate crime maintain that when crimes are committed on behalf of an organization, it, rather than the individual culprits, should pay the price. They assume that the corporation has a superior ability to that of the government to locate and, if it believes it necessary, to punish individual malefactors (Posner 1980, 418). This line of reasoning resembles the ethically tainted idea of punishing a group because it will turn its anger on the wrongdoers in its midst. Other economists have insisted that the same efficient outcome will obtain whether liability is placed on the individual or on the firm (Kornhauser 1982, 1348–51).

The economists' views, however, are disputed by Coffee (1980, 422), who argues that 'more deterrence is generated by penalties focused on the individual than on the organization,' since personal gain and organizational loyalty appear to be the major ingredients in such offences (see also Coffee 1981, 409). The most reasonable guess appears to be that, in general, people will take greater pains to protect themselves from the law than to protect the entity that employs them. In addition, as Fisse (1980, 182) has noted, a possible 'worst danger' of focusing enforcement on the corporation is that 'if used without careful direction, it promotes a slide away from individual accountability or, in the vernacular, induces the *My Lai* syndrome.'

The power accorded the U.S. Securities and Exchange Commission in 1990 to go to court against individuals to bar them from any association with a public company, including service as an executive or director, possesses a particularly strong deterrent potential. If companies were not permitted to indemnify their officers either directly or through insurance programs for the expenses of defending legitimate causes against them, that would also undoubtedly aid the cause of deterrence (Bishop 1968).

4 *Corporations Can Be More Readily Refashioned*

Particularly pronounced in recent years has been the argument that the corporation represents a prime target for rehabilitation, since, after conviction, courts can sentence it to probation and, as part of that sentence, impose conditions that might render law-breaking less likely. Such conditions can include the appointment of an independent ombudsman, inauguration of better accounting procedures and quality-control standards, establishment of more open communication between executives and their underlings, and/or other remedies that seem likely to eliminate situations that appear to have been associated with the wrongdoing that got the corporation into trouble (Lofquist 1993).

The assumption here is that individual offenders are less amenable to rehabilitative efforts (Martinson 1974), and while they may be removed from the scene, the conditions that presumably gave rise to the wrongdoing will persist.

Such assumptions do not seem unreasonable. It is when analogies are drawn to street crime that weaknesses surface. After all, institutional conditions – poor schools, poverty, inadequate health-care facilities, unemployment – all form a significant part of the background for crimes such as car theft, muggings, and burglary. Why not, then, charge inadequate schools, hospitals, or welfare agencies with the crime, and as part of their punishment insist on remedial action.

It is self-evident that the analogous procedure for street offenders is not going to happen. Is that because we discriminate against street offenders and regard them as more responsible for what they have done? Or do we consider the surrounding atmosphere for them less compelling in regard to behaviour than the corporate ethos? Or is the matter nothing more than a pragmatic assessment of what is possible and what remains beyond the realm of public policy? May the policy be as wrong-minded (or right-minded) in regard to corporations as it would be for schools and welfare programs?

None of these questions addresses the empirical issue of whether altering corporate conditions is likely to prove more effective than punishing the individual. It may well be argued that civil liability or adverse publicity or simple decency will satisfactorily press the corporation to change its ways, while punishment directed at the individual will forewarn others in its employ regarding the jeopardy of illegal behaviour.

5 Corporations Are Easier Targets for Criminal Prosecution

A recurring argument for prosecuting corporations is that those within them who committed the offence often are not readily determinable and that the task of locating and charging individual officers or their subordinates is more 'arduous' (Carter 1980, 594) and 'burdensome' (Saltzburg 1991, 425; see also J. Hall 1979, 1249). Among other things, the paper trail often is more readily penetrated in regard to corporations, since they have no privilege against self-incrimination (Bellis v. United States 1974, 87–101). At the same time, though, officers of corporations often are more than willing to sacrifice the organization rather than their own hide, and they can obfuscate matters of responsibility to outside investigators. Braithwaite (1984, 324), who has interviewed many corporate officials, points out that 'the presumed diffusion of accountability in a complex organization sometimes can be a hoax that the corporation plays on the rest of the world, especially courts and sociologists!'

Coffee (1980, 462) notes that in terms of occupational health-and-safety laws that impose vicarious liability on corporate officers for negligent acts or omissions, the odds are high that any campaign to obtain tough penalties would be nullified when judges confronted 'flesh and blood' defendants with impeccable backgrounds, community ties, and tearful families. This conclusion, accurate enough, again raises the question of whether the opportunity to prosecute the corporation seriously undercuts efforts by law-enforcement personnel to locate an individual perpetrator and prosecute her or him more effectively.

There is an axiom that where penalties are high, individuals will fight while firms will settle (Coffee 1980, 463). Then there is the prosecutorial view that being able to threaten corporations with a criminal penalty will induce them to cooperate and, at times, to provide evidence against individual malefactors rather than to bear the burden of prosecution themselves (Coffee 1983, 143–254). These are the kinds of expedient considerations that have to be thrown into the evaluative cauldron.

It is frequently suggested that to prosecute the corporation rather than individuals almost invariably results in a financial loss for stockholders who themselves are innocent of any wrongdoing. For us, however, the dismissive resolution of this dilemma by Ralph Nader and his colleagues (Nader, Green, and Seligman 1976, 230) is persuasive: 'Part of the risk of an investment is that you may earn something you didn't expect ... or you may not earn something you do. The risk of loss comes with the territory.'

An analogy may help to pinpoint another ethical concern. Suppose the police come upon a car in a suburban garage in which a horde of money known to be stolen from a bank is found. The crime cannot be pinned on the mother, father, or either of the two sons whose garage it is. Would it be reasonable to prosecute the family unit criminally on the ground that its existence is by state licence and that each family member reasonably ought to suffer vicariously for the deed of any of them?[3]

6 *The Corporation's Greater Assets Make It a More Affluent Target*

The basic argument against punishing the corporation because it is wealthier than its employees is that the rich ought not to be prosecuted – at least not preferentially – merely because they have resources. The wealthy, however, can gain advantages from the criminal justice system merely because of their wealth. Few judges would insist on sending to a penal institution the burglar child of a rich family that said it would dispatch him or her to a military school known for its disciplinary regimen. The child of a poor family, committing the same offence, would be sent to prison. The seeming inequities of the administration of justice is not a sensible reason for adding to the roster. Perhaps one should focus on the losses suffered through the corporate act – or through the perpetrator's use of the corporate entity as a tool for crime (Lederman 1985, 325) – and prospects for reimbursement.

Resolution of issues of loss, however, historically has been the province of the civil law, and strong arguments would have to be mounted (and demonstrated) to support its movement to the criminal side. In practice, corporate criminal liability sometimes is employed as a threat in negotiating a civil settlement with a corporation (Crane 1980, 45; Fisse and Braithwaite 1988, 475).

CONCLUSION

The doctrine of corporate criminal liability is deeply embedded in American, Canadian, and English systems of criminal justice, and it is unlikely to be excised soon. Pursuing corporations rather than or in addition to individuals within them who violate the law is very advantageous. 'A criminology which remains fixed at the level of individualism is the criminology of a bygone era,' John Braithwaite (1989:148) has written, but he is describing what has happened, and not necessarily what might more reasonably have taken place or what exists in civil-law countries, which presumably are managing reasonably well with the approach that Braithwaite finds so archaic.

What are the dimensions of prosecution for corporate crime? A survey by the U.S. Sentencing Commission covering the period 1984–7 found that somewhat more than three hundred organizations were convicted each year of criminal offences. About 10 per cent of these bodies were large, publicly held firms or their subsidiaries with $1 million or more in sales and fifty or more employees, while fewer than 3 per cent traded stock (Cohen et al. 1988). A follow-up study for 1988–90 indicated a tendency over time to prosecute and convict larger companies (Cohen 1992). In 65 per cent of the cases involving organizations sentenced for non–anti-trust offences there also were individual codefendants who were convicted of the same underlying crime (Cohen 1992, 268).

We are not likely ever to know whether these figures accurately reflect the proportion of criminal wrongdoing by such groups. Nader and his colleagues (Nader, Green, and Seligman 1976) believe that the high representation of smaller companies can be traced to enforcers' desire 'to keep up a respectable numerical record,' which results in 'many small cases in, for example, the chrysanthemum or swimming suit industries' rather than big cases against companies in the automobile or steel industry.

Both the laws and the manner in which they are enforced raise intriguing questions about the ideological underpinnings of the strong move towards criminal punishment of corporations (see generally Pearce 1976). That the statutes exist at all probably signals a defeat for the powerful businesses, most likely because legislators, however much they cater to monied interests, will in the final analysis respond to their own interest in staying in office, which at times will depend on their support of legislation that business opposes. Business forces, however, reduced the penalties imposed on organizations under the U.S. Sentencing Commission's guidelines (Etzioni 1993), and they lobbied effectively to keep criminal sanctions out of the federal occupational health-and-safety laws except for offences that resulted in death. Besides, the larger businesses often have viewed criminal sanctions as useful: they have the resources to meet enforcement demands and the internal strength and legal expertise to protect themselves against the consequences of failure to do so, except in egregious instances such as the Exxon-Valdez oil-spill. Criminal sanctions then will most likely fall on their smaller competitors, placating the public and advancing the interests of the industrial giants (Shover 1980).

Punishing the corporation alone might well induce it to clean up its act, but such punishment, almost always a fine, could be regarded as not much more than an unfortunate consequence – some bad luck – and written off as another cost of doing business. Punishing perpetrator and corporation together appears to offer the best deterrence, although it remains to be demonstrated that such punishment produces the kinds of results claimed for it, which might more readily be achieved by concentrating all criminal resources on individual malefactors.

Ultimately, though, the issue of where deterrence is more readily accomplished remains unresolved, and it would require both cross-national study and exquisitely constructed experimental designs to begin to tease out a solid conclusion.

It also remains unclear whether allowing only civil penalties against corporations and focusing criminal penalties on individuals within them would represent a better policy than the one currently employed. Civil remedies are more flexible and potentially as severe, and they lessen the burden of proof considerably. Block, Nold, and Sidak (1981), in a study of price-fixing in the bread industry, concluded that civil suits, especially class-action suits, were more effective deterrents than criminal prosecutions. However, as Coffee (1981, 424–5) notes, 'the criminal process has a unique theatricality which can convey public censure far more effectively than the civil-law process.' Besides, criminal cases are finished in a shorter time and offer an opportunity to expedite restitution to victims (447).

The realm of discourse regarding corporate crime is suffused with rhetoric insisting that truth and wisdom have been located. Take, as but one example, Edelman's (1987) insistence that 'criminal sanctions can be an effective method of deterring illicit corporate behavior only when the corporation and its individual officers are prosecuted with equal fervor.' There is no proof for such an assertion – either as to its accuracy or to its fallacy – nor for the rousing observation that 'the social good now demands the use of all available means to control corporate power' (Elkins 1976, 129).

In essence, then, this chapter outlines some issues and makes a request (to which we hope to try to respond) for closer and, particularly, for empirical attention to the subject. Pending the outcome of such work, we would echo early sceptics, employing their words as a challenge for further inquiry. 'There is absolutely no evidence that corporate criminal liability is any more effective than personal criminal liability,' Mueller (1959, 94) wrote almost a quarter-century ago. L. Leigh (1969, 141), after a thorough study, concluded: 'Corporate criminal liability may well be an inefficient method. Its operation is indirect. It is essentially a blunt instrument, employed in circumstances where a scalpel might rather be required.' The issue remains fixed today at the position staked out by Francis (1924, 323): 'Until and unless it is demonstrated that the social good demands that corporations be held responsible for crimes, there is no sound reason for so holding them.' The neglect of efforts to demonstrate that claim of social benefit bedevils attempts to adjudicate corporate crime. In pressing for deeper attention to this matter, we repeat the admonition of the Seebohm Commission (Great Britain 1968, para. 455): 'It is both wasteful and irresponsible to set experiments in motion and omit to record and analyze what happens. It makes no sense in terms of administrative efficiency, and, however little intended, it indicates a careless attitude toward human welfare.'

NOTES

1 The vulnerability of corporations to criminal prosecution is most pronounced in the United States, from which much of the material in this chapter is taken. In England and Canada, criminal action against a corporation will be taken only if the illegal behaviour, in the words of Chief Justice Parker, was that of 'responsible officers forming the brain, or in the case of an individual, a person to whom delegation in the true sense of delegation has been passed' (*Magna Plant Ltd. v. Mitchell*, unreported, quoted in L. Leigh 1969, 37). The 'directing mind and will' theory is set out in *Tesco Supermarkets Ltd. v. Nattrass* (1972); but see Fisse (1971). For the Canadian version

of this doctrine, see *R.V. Canadian Dredge and Dock Co. Ltd.* (1985) and generally L. Leigh (1977).

2 Speculation by Bernard regarding the divergence on this matter resulted in three ideas: (1) there is no direct parallel in civil law to the nuisance offences that were the origin for corporate criminal liability in common-law countries; (2) prosecution of municipalities for failure to maintain roads and waterways was necessary to operate the highly decentralized governmental structure in England and the United States, but in France, the font of civil law, there was a large degree of centralization; and (3) there is a tradition of judicial interpretation in common-law countries that does not exist in civil-law jurisdictions (Bernard 1984, 13).

3 Carr (1907, 8), among others, has noted that 'it is possible to postulate a juristic person composed of husband and wife but separate and indistinguishable from them ... In England, we should probably call [such a juristic person] ... a corporation.'

5

Feminism, Law, and the Pharmaceutical Industry

PATRICIA PEPPIN

The feminist goals of equality, control over our own bodies, and avoidance of harm provide a framework for the analysis of laws on pharmaceutical products. Drugs and devices prescribed for treatment and contraception have particular effects on women. The regime of law compensating injury and regulating drug marketing is based on flawed assumptions, and these have a differential impact on women. Recommendations for change need to take account of differences among patients, broaden the concern for autonomy and bodily integrity, and incorporate equality as a goal.

FEMINIST GOALS

Feminist goals include equality, affirmation of difference, control over our own bodies, and avoidance of harm. The brief analysis that follows formulates these values, drawing on the work of a number of feminist theorists.

Gender equality is a central goal of the feminist movement. Achievement of equality for women as a group means moving beyond social structures based on the domination of women (MacKinnon 1987a, 32–45) through recognizing the historic condition of disadvantage and changing the social structures that replicate and produce it. Inequality in the distribution of power between the parties to a relationship raises the possibility of exploitation and vulnerability that should attract legal consequences. Feminist analyses attend to the power imbalances in relationships and to disadvantages based on stereotypes, historic conditions, and prejudice. Canadian constitutional jurisprudence uses this approach to interpret equality without discrimination under section 15 of the Canadian Charter of Rights and Freedoms (*Andrews v. Law Society of British Columbia*; *R. v. Turpin*; Women's Legal Education and Action Fund, Intervenor's Factum, in *Andrews v. Law Society of British Columbia*).

Affirming difference is an aspect of equality. It includes recognizing that achieving equality sometimes means treating people differently and rejecting social analyses that assume sameness of condition (Minow 1990). It also involves acknowledging differences among women, based on conditions such as disability, race, and age (Tait 1986; Spelman 1988; T. Williams 1990; P. Williams 1991), and trying to achieve a more subtle and complex understanding of social phenomena in themselves, as well as in relation to law (Smart 1989).

Control over our bodies is based on the idea of autonomy, but autonomy reconceptualized (Nedelsky 1989, see also O'Donovan 1985; Okin 1989) to include an understanding of political position and social condition (Sherwin 1989). It requires, in addition to avoidance of injury, freedom from external control, access to needed and beneficial procedures, and a sense of efficacy.

Freedom, as conceptualized by some feminist theorists, incorporates the rights to bodily integrity and dignity that are the foundation of tort law, as well as some ambivalent respect for that individual autonomy underlying liberal democratic theory (Bender 1988; 1990a; 1990b; Finley 1989). Feminist theorists have pointed to the unrecognized contingent nature of autonomy (Nedelsky 1989), to the unfounded assumption of equality that undergirds the goal of freedom, and to the acontextual and abstract notion of the individual inherent in conceptions of the autonomous actor (Gilligan 1982; Scales 1986; Lyons 1988). Alternative moral standpoints include an 'ethic of care' (Gilligan 1982; Bender 1988, 1990a, 1990b), with its focus on the relationship itself, and analyses of the contextual features of individuals' lives.

Harm avoidance includes freedom from intrusive, detrimental procedures and from those that commodify women's bodies. Harm must be assessed in terms of effects on women as a group. For instance, failure to disclose the risks of drugs used in in vitro fertilization may produce adverse effects for each individual and also breach her rights. As a process, it may produce desired benefits for infertile women but adverse effects for women as a group.

The next section explores women's health and drug treatment. The section following that sets out products-liability actions in general and the duty to warn in particular, focusing on the legal treatment of power and dependence inherent in the relationships among pharmaceutical company, doctor, and patient, exploring the assumptions on which actions are based. Finally, I use the feminist goals set out above to assess drug-liability actions.

WOMEN'S HEALTH AND DRUG TREATMENT

The regime of drug liability and regulation has particular implications for women. Women take more prescription and non-prescription drugs than men, and 'limited studies have suggested that adverse drug reactions are more common in women' (D'Arcy and Griffin 1986, 49). For instance, the Australian Adverse Drug Reactions Advisory Committee Report found that 1,375 of 2,503 suspected adverse drug reactions (ADRs) were reported by women, a ratio of 1.46:1 (D'Arcy and Griffin 1986). Moreover, it has been estimated that women with the same set of symptoms as men are more likely to be prescribed particular kinds of drugs, as the prescription rate for mood-altering drugs among older women indicates (Harding 1986, 66–7).

Elderly people, disproportionately women, take more prescription drugs. A survey of the retirement community of Dunedin, Florida, found that of 3,192 residents (2,009 women, 1,183 men), women were taking 3.5 medicines on average, while men were taking 2.8 (D'Arcy and Griffin 1986, 44). Over-drugging, sometimes for social control or through neglect, is a concern in all institutional settings. As well, elderly women have been reported to be particularly vulnerable to ADRs (Fincham 1991, 50). High-risk prescribing and questionable prescribing have been observed in a study of 63,268 elderly Quebec residents (Tamblyn et al. 1994). Defined as including prescribing for an excessive duration, drugs relatively contraindicated for elderly patients, and drugs with a risk of interaction, high-risk prescribing was more common among women, an observation attributed to the higher rate of prescription to women (Tamblyn et al. 1994, 1807). The general rate of prescribing was very high – only 166 (0.3 per cent) had not received a prescription in 1990, while the median number of prescriptions was higher for women (24) than for men (18) (p. 1804).

Women's health should be made the object of a concerted program of research and treatment. The mortality rate from breast cancer has remained virtually unchanged in the past twenty to twenty-five years, but the incidence went up at a rate of about 1 per cent per year between 1964 and the late 1980s (Canada, House of Commons, Standing-Committee, Sub-Committee on the Status of Women 1992, 3–4).

As Valerie Cotler put it, 'Research and design of contraceptives [are] stagnating ... "[I]n the United States today, the government spends less on contraceptive research in a single year than the Defense Department spends in 15 minutes"' (Cotler 1990, 130–1, quoting *Newsday*, 12 January 1989, 77).

Research samples and clinical trials have underrepresented and/or excluded women (Dresser 1992; Merton 1994). Although the evidence for gender inequality in participation and for any disadvantage to women may be considered equivocal and inadequate to determine the issue (Institute of Medicine 1994, 3, 47–9), it is most clearly the case with respect to clinical research on cardiovascular disease and AIDS (3, 49, 64–6). The issue has been addressed in the past few years through legislative, regulatory, and policy changes and proposals in the United States (132–42; Merton 1994, 390–400, 431–6) and has been receiving public attention. In its breast cancer report, the House of Commons sub-committee called for an audit of gender and race in research to be carried out by the federal government's cancer-research funding bodies and a comprehensive policy of inclusion in all health research (Canada, House of Commons, Standing Committee, Sub-Committee on the Status of Women, 1992, 31). The U.S. National Institutes of Health (NIH) has established the Women's Health Initiative, a $650-million, multidisciplinary, longitudinal study of the effects of certain factors on cancer, heart disease, and osteoporosis in women aged 50 to 79 (Friedland 1993, 1), to address this problem.

Because of underrepresentation and/or lack of sub-group analysis on the basis of gender by clinical researchers, the effects on women's bodies of particular diseases and drug therapies are, to too great an extent, untested. Extrapolation from male norms to female bodies has produced inadequate research (Ford 1986; Rosser 1989) and some harmful clinical results (Dresser 1992, 24, 26–7). Participation in clinical trials may provide access not only to new drugs but also to allied medical treatment and monitoring (Merton 1994, 378–9), an important benefit where universal health care is non-existent, as in the United States.

The most serious adverse reactions, involving harm on a mass basis, have occurred when women's health needs have been targeted by drug companies. Devastating harm has resulted from the following:

- inadequate warnings of the risk of stroke and death from contraceptives;
- poor labelling pertaining to the risk of toxic shock syndrome from tampons;
- the marketing of diethylstilbestrol (DES), a synthetic hormone, for preventing miscarriages. The drug proved no more effective than a sugar pill, but caused a rare form of vaginal cancer among DES daughters and has been linked to adenosis, cervical anatomical anomalies, and subfertility (Apfel and Fisher 1984, 43–58); genital-tract anomalies among DES sons; a greater risk of breast cancer among the women who took the drug DES (Dutton 1988, 87); and possibly conditions related to cancer and premature delivery among grandchildren of women who took DES (Marcotte 1990; Mascaro 1991; Overland 1991);
- A.H. Robins Co.'s ignoring of warnings about the wicking effect by which bacteria climbed the filamented string of the Dalkon Shield, which produced pelvic inflammatory disease, death, septic abortions, and infertility (Sobol 1991, 1–22; Regush 1993, 10–11);
- and, perhaps the best known example, the promotion in the early 1960s of thalidomide by Chemie-Gruenthal of West Germany as a completely safe

treatment for morning sickness. The drug caused serious physical disabilities among the children of the women who used it.

Worldwide, approximately 12,000 babies were born with thalidomide-induced disabilities (Silverstein 1993); in Canada, there were 125 such babies (War Amputations of Canada 1989, 1, 60–7). Since that disaster, 'there have been other – and, in a sense, greater – drug tragedies,' including DES (Dukes and Swartz 1988, 1). Moreover, 'several thousand asthmatic patients may have been killed by high dose isoprenaline aerosols because of a mistaken prescribing tradition. Benoxaprofen and Indosmos, though rapidly withdrawn, were each responsible for 70–100 deaths in Great Britain, arguably because they had not been adequately studied for their effects in old people or when used over long periods' (pp. 1–2, citations omitted).

Iatrogenic harm of this magnitude must be taken into account when assessing therapeutic benefits. Although accurate data on incidence are impossible to obtain because of inadequate surveillance after marketing commences, it has been estimated that over 100,000 Canadian women used the Dalkon Shield (Lord 1986, 27 n12) and that 150,000 have had breast implants (*Bendall v. McGhan Medical Corp.* 1993, 736). Physicians (Lucey 1992), drug regulators, and consumers (Slovic et al. 1991) all need information that will enable them to be vigilant when assessing the risks of particular innovations. The next section examines systems that monitor the behaviour of drug companies and the information available to health-care participants.

PRODUCTS LIABILITY AND THE DUTY TO WARN

Products liability has at its core concern for the adequacy of representations made by manufacturers for their products, protection of the bodily integrity of consumers, and promotion of autonomous decision-making. Products-liability actions aim at providing compensation for and deterring misrepresentations that would lead to reliance by consumers and harm from defective products.

Information is central to the increasing of consumers' autonomy. Unless consumers are warned of product risks, they are unable to assess the detriments and benefits and thereby make informed choices. The ability to protect one's bodily integrity is contingent on adequate information.

Products-liability law takes some account of the inherent advantage of a manufacturer over the consumer, arising from superior knowledge and control of manufacturing. In Canada, these obligations are imposed in negligence law in the common law provinces – that is, all but Quebec.

The principles derive from *Donoghue v. Stevenson*, the products-liability case over a snail in ginger beer that gave rise to the modern law of negligence in British common law jurisdictions. A breach of the standard of care in the manufacturing, bottling, assembling, distributing, or inspecting of products, which causes foreseeable harm to the ultimate consumer, where there has been no possibility of intermediate examination, will give rise to liability.

Manufacturers of products have a duty to warn of product risks of which they had actual, and presumably constructive, knowledge, as ruled in *Distillers Co. (Biochemicals) Ltd. v. Thompson*. For most products, this duty is discharged by direct warnings to consumers. For prescription drugs, however, it may be discharged indirectly. Under the 'learned intermediary rule,' the manufacturer may warn the consumer by transmitting warnings to the physician – the learned intermediary. The physician is under an independent duty, in the law of informed consent, to disclose the risks of proposed treatments.

The adequacy of the warning given by the manufacturer is measured in terms of the probability of the risk, the gravity of the harm, the burden of taking precautions, and, sometimes, the social utility. In the United States, more remote risks have been required to be disclosed by pharmaceutical manufacturers to doctors in duty-to-warn cases than by doctors to patients in informed-consent actions (Britain 1984, 386–9). Britain noted that 'drug manufacturers ... have been required to warn of dramatically less significant risks of adverse side effects than the one percent probability/high-magnitude guideline that emerges from most informed consent cases' (389). Too few prescription-drug cases exist in Canada to make the comparison, although a risk in the range of 1/5,000 to 1/7,500 was not too remote for rabies vaccine (*Davidson v. Connaught Laboratories*).

To succeed in an action for breach of the duty to disclose risks, the plaintiff must prove that the warning given by the drug company to the doctor failed to meet the standard of care, that the actual harm to the plaintiff was caused in fact and in law by the product, and that the causal link between the manufacturer and the consumer was not broken by an intervening cause.

Causation poses difficult questions for plaintiffs. For instance, was the drug the scientific cause of the injury in general and in particular (e.g., does pertussis vaccine cause brain damage in general, and did it cause the brain damage to this particular plaintiff, as in *Rothwell v. Raes*)? Did the defendant's product or some other manufacturer's product cause the injury (e.g., the indeterminate-defendant problem of which manufacturer produced the DES taken by the mother, causing the injury to her daughter, as in *Sindell v. Abbott Laboratories*)? Finally, would the plaintiff have declined the treatment if he or she had been adequately warned (e.g., would she have taken oral contraceptives if she had known the risk of stroke, as in *Buchan* v. *Ortho Pharmaceutical [Canada] Limited*)?

To establish a causal link between the company's failure to warn and the plaintiff's harm, the Court of Appeal in Ontario's leading pharmaceutical duty-to-warn case, *Buchan*, required the plaintiff to prove that she would not have accepted the treatment if adequate information had been disclosed to the doctor. This is a subjective test of legal causation, through which the value of autonomy is appropriately protected because of its emphasis on what the *patient* would have done.

In contrast, British Columbia's Court of Appeal has required the patient to prove that the reasonable patient in her shoes would have declined the breast implant if Dow Corning had made adequate disclosure to the physician, Dr Birch (*Hollis v. Birch*, decision reserved by the Supreme Court of Canada in *Hollis v. Dow Corning Corp.*, Feb. 1995). This test is objective with subjective elements, a standard usually more difficult for plaintiffs to meet. In the ten years since this standard was adopted in *Reibl v. Hughes* for actions pertaining to breach of the duty of disclosure between patients and doctors, plaintiffs have lost many informed-consent cases because of this factor (G. Robertson 1991).

When the pharmaceutical company has breached the duty to warn, it may still win the action if a court finds that the physician snapped the chain of causation between it and the patient. For instance, if the doctor has acquired information independently of the company but fails to disclose it, the manufacturer might be insulated from liability because the doctor might be an intervening cause. The court might consider the extent of reliance by doctors on the industry and the effects of promotional activities on disclosure, as the Ontario Court of Appeal did in *Buchan*. Most important, this court stated that a presumption arises that the physician, if adequately warned by the company, would warn the patient (*Buchan v. Ortho Pharmaceutical [Canada] Limited*, 682 [DLR]). This presumption was not applied by the British Columbia Court of Appeal in the breast implant case, *Hollis v. Birch*, in which two appellate judges found that Dr Birch knew of the risk and Madam Justice Prowse stated that he was warning 20–30 per cent of his patients (para. 105). Dow Corning was found liable, while the plaintiff obtained a new trial against Birch, after losing at trial. Dow Corning Corp. was granted leave to appeal by the Supreme Court of Canada, on a number of grounds: to argue that the two actions cannot proceed separately (one to decision and the other to a new trial), since the findings of fact and legal issues are common to both; to resolve the differences between subjective and contextualized objective cause in law standards in *Buchan* and *Hollis*; to determine whether the manufacturer's failure can be a proximate cause when the doctor knew but failed to warn of the risk; and to decide whether liability should be imposed when the

product failure could have been caused by a risk about which the manufacturer gave a warning.

Doctors have a duty to disclose certain information to patients. The Supreme
Court of Canada's decisions in *Hopp v. Lepp* and *Reibl v. Hughes* require them
to disclose to patients the nature and gravity of the proposed procedure, the
material risks, the alternatives, the answers to any questions, and any special or
unusual risks. Materiality includes what the doctor knows or should know the
patient would deem relevant to the decision. Significantly, risks with low probability but grave consequences such as stroke or death are material risks and
must be disclosed. Limited exceptions exist for common risks and waiver, while
therapeutic privilege is a disputed exception.

The Canadian disclosure standard includes the negligence standards of probability and gravity of harm but also the subjective, contextual components of
what patients deem relevant. Chief Justice Laskin emphasized that materiality
connotes objectivity according to what would reasonably be seen as influencing
the patient's decision to follow a recommended regimen of treatment and summarized the point by saying that scope and breach are both to be decided in light
of the patient's circumstances. The Supreme Court, then, clearly rejected the
professional standard of disclosure and went further than the reasonable patient
standard in emphasizing the subjective position of the patient (Picard 1984, 79–
80). Some later interpretations have focused on the reasonable patient for purposes of disclosure. In the Supreme Court's most recent decision, *Ciarlariello v.
Schacter*, Mr Justice Cory set out an objective, reasonable patient standard of
disclosure and then used the subjective and objective standards virtually inter-
changeably. Ontario legislation uses the reasonable patient standard.

Reasonableness plays an important role in the doctrine of informed consent in
many jurisdictions, either in setting the disclosure standard (what the reasonable
person would want to know) or in acting as part of causation (what the reasonable patient would have decided if properly informed). In either case, reasonableness is problematic from a feminist point of view (Bender 1988; Finley
1990; Chamallas 1992). When the 'reasonable man' was transmogrified into the
'reasonable person,' the values inherent in the concept remained static. Instead
of shifting from the male, white, middle-class, able-bodied norm to a more pluralist notion, what we see may be nothing more than 'false gender neutrality,'
which serves 'to disguise the real and continuing failure of theorists to confront
the fact that the human race consists of persons of two sexes,' with real physical
differences and very different assigned roles and access to power and opportunity (Okin 1989, 10). While the distinction between particularity and reasonableness may sometimes diminish in practice, the reasonableness standard may
make context irrelevant and mandate adherence to dominant standards.

ASSUMPTIONS OF THE DUTY TO WARN ACTION

The 'learned intermediary rule' and the principles around which the duty to warn is structured rest on four assumptions – that the 'single-source informational system' (McGarey 1984 131–7) will provide adequate warnings to consumers; that enough information is available in the system; that existing regulatory systems (the U.S. Food and Drug Administration [FDA] and Canada's Department of National Health and Welfare) can manage risk; and that compensation, a primary purpose of the action, is achieved. These assumptions are all flawed, in each case with particular implications for women.

Consumer Warnings

The manufacturer discharges the duty to warn by adequately warning the physician, who in turn is required to disclose information to the patient. The system assumes that physicians' warnings will be adequate and that physicians are willing and able to communicate with patients. A report by A. Paul Williams and Rhonda Cockerill for Ontario's Lowy Inquiry indicated that 'physicians with the largest volume practices ... are significantly less likely to engage their patients in reviews or discussions of drug use or to recommend reductions, suggesting that a significant proportion of the prescriptions written in the province are not accompanied by review or counselling' (Ontario, Pharmaceutical Inquiry, 1990, Appendix 7, viii). Unless doctors are willing to engage in a dialogue with their patients, patients will remain unaware of product risks.

The system assumes that the physician will mediate, filtering out some information as it is transmitted. Whether this leaves sufficient information will depend on the jurisdiction and the doctor's behaviour. In effect, though, the system increases patients' dependence on physicians and provides the potential, particularly in professional-disclosure jurisdictions in the United States, for paternalistic decision-making. If information is power, filtering of it decreases power and increases alienation. Non-disclosure of risk information also lulls the patient into a sense of security, reduces alertness to adverse effects, and depresses consumers' awareness of the inherent riskiness of drug-taking. For instance, one report indicated that 'overall the focus groups and survey found that Canadians have a high level of confidence in the safety of medical devices and faith in the system to ensure safety and effectiveness of medical devices ... based in part on an erroneous understanding of the testing systems ... Participants at one Montreal focus group were visibly startled and dismayed to learn that only 5% of medical devices are assessed by the federal government' (Canada, Medical Devices Review Committee, 1992, 2).

As Alan Styles has argued, the learned intermediary rule 'substantially over-states the ability and willingness of the medical community to act as a learned intermediary'; patients are not receiving adequate information and, as a result, do not use medications correctly, and the system 'ignores the benefits of having an informed patient' (Styles 1991, 123; see also Cook 1980, 260). Promotion of products to doctors is designed to affect prescribing practices, not only in the selection of product but in the assurances of efficacy and safety. One medical col-league found that the amount of junk mail she received one year equalled, and in the following year exceeded, her own weight (Duffin 1989, 112; 1990, 142).

In 1980, the FDA issued regulations requiring manufacturers to give product information directly to consumers, in the form of the so-called patient package inserts; the information was intended to supplement rather than supplant the doc-tors' warnings and the legal duty to inform (Styles 1991, 134–5). The FDA's stud-ies had shown that most patients were given inadequate information, conveyed in incomprehensible technical language that was soon forgotten (133–4). The American Medical Association and pharmaceutical associations fought the reg-ulations, which were withdrawn when Ronald Reagan took office (135–6). Direct warnings, imposed by the regulatory body, may be the only way to ensure that consumers have enough information to assess the effects of drug therapy.

In Canada, the Gagnon Report (Canada, Review of the Canadian Drug Approval System, 122) stated: 'The right of Canadian patients to be well informed must be met. Every prescription ... should be either prepackaged or the equivalent product information should be provided with the drug.' The report seemed to favour providing information in written form and recommended pub-lic access to the product monograph as well (119–20).

Inequality is inherent in the relationship between doctor and patient. The gen-ders of physician and patient may reinforce this disparity. Other conditions of disadvantage such as disability, race, age, or sexual preference may have an additional and complex impact. As a result, members of disadvantaged groups may be less able to elicit information about risks, and goals vis-à-vis products liability, and informed consent may be less likely to be met. When a lawsuit is brought, women will have more difficulty winning wherever a professional dis-closure or reasonableness standard is imposed. If women find it more difficult to win lawsuits, then they will be compensated less adequately for the same harm. The application of the law differs, producing different effects for the groups.

Adequacy of Information

There is good reason to believe that the information available about the adverse effects of drugs and devices is inadequate. Although the rate of ADRs is extremely difficult to ascertain, studies show that 'drug-related illness is the primary reason for 1% to 5% of medical visits, 3% to 23% of hospital admissions and 1 in 1,000 deaths' (Tamblyn et al 1994, 1,802, citations omitted). Commentators agree that underreporting of such effects is significant (Medawar 1992, 1–6).

There are many opportunities for drug risks to be missed:

- Patients may not identify the effect or may not report it to their physician.
- Physicians, most of whom are poorly educated in pharmacology, may not identify the effect or attribute it to the drug, or may not fill out the voluntary report effectively or at all.
- Hospitals may also miss the effect, fail to pick it up in the records, or fail to report it.
- Drug companies may discount information, be unable to evaluate poor information, or fail to transmit the information that they receive, although they are required to do so.
- The federal regulatory body may fail to collate or to respond to information received.

Systems for reporting ADRs in most countries are voluntary (Fletcher and Griffin 1991) and surveillance is not well developed (Consensus Workshop 1989; Canada, Review of the Canadian Drug Approval System, 1992, 113–16). Systems for spontaneous reporting vary considerably among countries and over time. 'The benefits of spontaneous reporting ... are offset by a number of serious deficiencies. The most troublesome deficiency is probably the high level of underreporting which is known to be universal in all spontaneous reporting systems' (Fletcher and Griffin 1991, 219). Their estimate of underreporting is in the 95-per-cent range (218–19). Dukes and Swartz (1988, 2–4) review studies estimating reporting of ADRs, rates of hospitalization caused by ADRs, claims paid by medical insurers, and incidence rates per capita of injury from drugs. They also find 'considerable under-reporting' (2) even in Britain, which has a stronger reporting system than the United States (Teff 1985, 599).

Fletcher and Griffin point to two other deficiencies in spontaneous reporting. First, there is 'a known tendency to bias' that originates in 'pressures from national regulatory authorities, the medical profession's perception of drug-related clinical events, reports in the scientific medical literature and ... coverage by the popular press and television.' As well, there are 'wide variations in reporting related to the therapeutic class of the drug, the organ system involved, the length of time the product has been on the market and the country responsible for the reports.' Second, it is very difficult to obtain reliable data on pre-scribing patterns to form the denominator in an analysis of the incidence of ADRs (Fletcher and Griffin 1991, 220).

The testing of new drugs prior to regulatory approval is carried out by the drug companies or by physicians participating in clinical trials set up by them. The regulatory agencies do not carry out pre-marketing trials of their own and do not, as a rule, use third-party laboratories to assess results of drug trials sub-mitted by the pharmaceutical companies.

The Canadian government contracts out the conducting of first-stage chemi-cal and, to a lesser extent, clinical reviews of new drug submissions to private consultants, instead of having them performed by officials in the Health Protec-tion Branch. The more intense, second-stage review is carried out internally. Designed to speed up drug approval, in response to heavy lobbying by the Pharmaceutical Manufacturers Association of Canada (PMAC), privatization of regulatory review may lead to less effective evaluation of drug companies' claims; private evaluators may depend on industry financing for their own research, and the level of expertise may not match that of the regulator (Fergu-son 1992). The Gagnon Report has recommended making contracting out an established feature; while acknowledging the potential for conflict of interest, the document simply proposed maintaining and reinforcing measures to prevent that (Canada, Review of the Canadian Drug Approval System, 1992, 66–8).

Knowledge of a drug is industry-constructed. As John Braithwaite has indi-cated, factors contributing to fraud in testing include not only the profit motive, which he cautioned should not be over-estimated, but also organizational stan-dard-setting, which controls the achievement of success and establishment of failure for individual researchers, work overload, misuse of honest researchers' work, and a system of scientific values that creates ownership of discovery and leads to unwillingness to find flaws in one's discovery (Braithwaite 1984, 92–5). Braithwaite said, 'There are many cases of drug companies concealing and misrepresenting dangerous effects of drugs noted by their own scientists' (55–6). A.H. Robins Co. knew of the fundamental defect in the Dalkon Shield – the wicking effect – because of a report from its own quality-control director and one of the device's coinventors, in the period during which it was launching the product (Sobol 1991, 6–7).

Testing prior to approval is limited in scope and concentrated first on healthy volunteers and then on persons with the disease. If a drug has a grave risk, but one with a very low probability, it may not show up in the clinical trial popula-tion. If the testing protocols do not draw on representative samples, knowable risks and benefits can be missed and may not show up until the post-marketing stages, when they are more likely to be overlooked. Because testing on women and members of non-white racial groups has been inadequate in the past, information on ADRs is less than complete. As Rebecca Dresser has said, 'As a result of the past over-representation of white men in research populations, physicians now frequently lack adequate evidence on whether women and people of colour will be helped, harmed, or not affected at all by numerous therapies now endorsed as promoting "human health"' (1992, 24).

Once the product is marketed, surveillance is not carried out in any systematic way. Adverse drug effects are left to be monitored by health professionals, hospitals, and drug companies; reporting to the manufacturer and regulator is carried out on an ad hoc basis (Sage 1988, 1021–2). In Canada, manufacturers must report ADRs, while in the United States they must report foreign as well as domestic ADRs. In both countries, health professionals report only on a voluntary basis (Canada, Gagnon Review, 1992, Table 4, 112).

Sophisticated post-marketing surveillance is essential to create an understanding of the effects of pharmaceutical products and to provide this information to doctors, the industry, government, and the patient. The Gagnon Report indicated that 'submissions to this review were almost unanimous in expressing that the current *ad hoc* procedures were inadequate, and underlined the importance and urgency of addressing this need' (Canada, Review of the Canadian Drug Approval System, 1992, 113) and recommended establishment of a pharmacovigilance program (111–18).

Regulatory System

The regulatory systems in Canada and the United States are, in worldwide terms, relatively strict and rigorous. Indications that they may have insufficient power to monitor devices effectively have surfaced concerning the silicon breast implant (Regush 1991, 1992, 1993; Kolata 1992). In general, requirements for approval of devices have not been stringent in either country, requiring considerably less than prescription-drug submissions and, in many cases, minimal documentation of safety or efficacy (Cotler 1990, 128). The thalidomide disaster and the Kefauver hearings in the United States led to tightening of drug regulation in the 1960s (Temin 1980, 120–40). Then 'the rapid diffusion of expensive medical devices, such as the computerized tomographic scanner, created a similar climate of concern for regulation' (King and Henderson 1991, 1,016), and the realization of the harm caused by the Dalkon Shield led to further reforms. In the United States, Congress passed the Medical Device Amendments of 1976, and in Canada six years later, pre-market review was extended to tampons, contact lenses. and implants. These measures obviously failed to prevent the problems now being revealed about breast implants. The U.S. Safe

Medical Devices Act of 1990 has strengthened regulation by requiring health care facilities to report problems, giving the FDA powers of emergency recall, creating a program to trace and contact users of particular devices, and requiring post-marketing surveillance by manufacturers. The changes 'make it more difficult for manufacturers to bypass the more rigorous premarket approval process' (Lynn 1991, 45).

Misrepresentation of data and non-disclosure of known risks are made possible because the regulatory systems rely on drug companies' honesty in disclosure. As John Braithwaite (1984, 51–100) has illustrated in his analysis of corporate crime, such honesty is not the invariable rule. Fraud and underreporting are difficult to detect, however, where the regulatory agencies are dependent on drug industry data, conduct few if any independent tests, and lack subpoena power. Joel Lexchin (1990, 1260) has called Canada's Health Protection and Promotion Branch's attitude to the drug industry a collegial relationship, amounting to clientele pluralism, in which the government relies on and cedes authority to the industry. The Sub-Committee on the Status of Women made similar points, describing the government's function as largely an auditing one, and questioned 'how adequately such policy serves the interests of Canadian women' (Canada, House of Commons, Standing Committee, Sub-Committee on the Status of Women, 1992, 49–50). It called for restructuring of the approval process for drugs and devices, recommending that the federal government explore the possibility of establishing an arm's-length agency to review and approve drugs and carefully consider mechanisms to support international harmonization in drug approval processes (35–6). The Gagnon Report made similar recommendations (Canada, Review of the Canadian Drug Approval System, 1992, 41–4, 31–6).

Joel Lexchin (1990) has noted gaps in the Canadian system that do not exist in the United States. When its regulatory systems were strengthened in 1963, the FDA set up panels to review pre-1963 drugs, banning 600 of approximately 4,000 products from the market. Such a review was not carried out in Canada (Lexchin 1984, 221). 'As late as 1982, Canadian authorities suspected that about 450 products were either completely worthless or lacked meaningful medical benefits' (Lexchin 1990, 1258).

Braithwaite has argued that, of the many lessons to be drawn from thalidomide, 'the most important of all concerns the need for international exchange of information on adverse reaction and the abolition of trade names for drugs. In the early 1960s when the adverse effects of thalidomide were being discussed, so inadequate was the international communication among drug regulatory agencies that companies could for some time isolate bad news about a drug to the country where the untoward research appeared' (Braithwaite 1984, 65–6).

Compulsory reporting by industry of adverse effects outside Canada, as recommended by the Gagnon Report (Canada, Review of the Drug Approval System, 1992, 80), is an essential step to remedying this problem. Canada relies on the manufacturers' reporting to the World Health Organization, which prepares a composite list of adverse effects.

In the United States, secrecy orders may 'seal potentially damning company documents that are produced in product liability suits' (Kolata 1992, 16), preventing participants from disclosing any of the evidence. Data about adverse effects from silicone breast implants not revealed to the FDA or Canadian officials had been made available eight years before in a products-liability action against Dow Corning but sealed as part of the court agreement (Kolata 1992, 1; Regush 1993, 102).

The tort system may secure compensation for some individuals, but at the cost of loss of deterrence and compensation for others. Litigation reveals to the public and government officials facts about the way the pharmaceutical industry operates. Gag orders prevent plaintiffs from building on previous litigation. Isolated plaintiffs may accept such conditions, for understandable reasons, but this allows the individualistic purpose of torts to work at cross-purposes to its latent role in public policy. As Stuart Schlesinger has pointed out with respect to silicone gel breast implants, it has been the plaintiffs' attorneys who have been raising questions about the implants: 'As was the case with the IUD device and DES, the federal and state agencies are 10 years behind private plaintiffs' attorneys who recognized the dangers of these products' (1992, 3).

Inadequate information in the system lulls consumers into a sense of security about products and induces undue reliance on manufacturers. Instead of acting efficaciously, consumers are reinforced in their trust – in products' safety and effectiveness and in the regulatory and tort processes to ensure safety and effectiveness. When trust is lost, and this is combined with feelings of low political efficacy, the result is alienation.

Access to drugs and devices that would permit greater control over our own bodies and a wider range of choice is also a feminist goal. One aspect is pressure to obtain access to experimental drugs prior to completion of clinical trials. For instance, demand for access to drugs seeming to indicate success in arresting AIDS, at a time when death was the only alternative, was wholly understandable. The ethical soundness of giving a placebo to an ill person is also a consideration.

Without double-blind studies, however, the benefits of the drug may be overestimated. Once the drug is released, the possibility of controlled experimentation disappears. For instance, the rationale for the FDA's withdrawal of breast implants from the market is the need for reliable data of the type obtainable from clinical trials. As FDA Commissioner David Kessler said, 'even after more than 30 years of use involving more than 1 million women, adequate data to demonstrate the safety and effectiveness of these devices does not exist' (Kessler 1992, 1713). George Annas (1989, 797) has stated that the argument made by advocates of early drug release, when individuals have no other treatment options, assumes that a drug is better than nothing; it is possible, however, that the treatment may hasten death, increase pain and suffering, and damage human dignity, as well as cost a great deal. The overall effect has been erosion of the distinction between therapy and experimentation and undermining of the regulatory process to serve the interests of industry, which threatens to change the FDA 'from a consumer protection agency into a medical technology promotion agency' (Annas 1989, 772).

As the anti-progestin drug RU 486, prescribed in combination with a prostoglandin to induce abortion, proceeds through the process of drug approval, women's safety must be kept at the forefront of attention (Raymond, Klein, and Dumble 1991). If the regulators are stringent in evaluating the RU/PG combination, including those risks and benefits observed to date (Charo 1992, 18), women may be able to secure safety, as well as access to a drug with significant benefits (Ricks 1989; Lees 1990; Rubin 1990; R.J. Cook 1991; Lader 1991; R. Cook and Grimes 1992). Like the new reproductive technologies, this combination of drugs may prove to raise more issues than merely choice, and the choice that is offered may prove to have deeper implications for the equality of women, in this and other societies.

Canada's Emergency Drug Release Program shares some of the same problems of 'cursory review' prior to release (Canadian Coordinating Office for Health Technology Assessment 1991, 4). Release is granted for a particular patient's needs, where the physician understands the risks and is willing to undertake them (Canadian Coordinating Office 1991, 17; Canada, Office of the Auditor General, 1987, para. 12.14). In reality, only the patient undertakes the physical risk. Although physicians are required to report any ADRs, fewer than half do so (Canadian Coordinating Office 1991, 4). Use of approved drugs for non-approved purposes poses similar problems.

The Gagnon Review's focus on delay in access to drugs is evident in its analysis of this release program. After acknowledging concerns about the safety of products released before review, its report stated: 'It is the responsibility of the physician to address safety concerns ... Drugs determined by attending physicians to be needed, even for non-emergency uses, should be accessible. That is the patient's right' (Canada, Review of the Canadian Drug Approval System, 1992, 124). The devolution of safety obligations to the doctor and away from the regulatory agency is highly questionable. It would also make decisions increasingly vulnerable to drug promotion. It is assumed that patients have a right to untested or unexamined products.

Compensation and Deterrence

Compensation, a primary purpose of tort actions, is based on principles of corrective, rather than distributive, justice. The remedy is individualized, with damages awarded for personal loss. As long as pay equity is not in place, women will recover less in damages than a man with the same job or one of equal value. Women who have chosen to stay at home or who have left the workplace will have their lost earnings undervalued, since unpaid labour is not compensable.

The substantive difficulties of proving negligence undoubtedly inhibit Canadian products-liability actions. Structural factors do as well. The cap on pain-and-suffering awards, more limited use of jury trials, the risk of paying the winner's costs as well as one's own under the cost-follows-the-event rule, representation of doctors by the Canadian Medical Protective Association, and the limits on class action suits, as well as on the benefits of the Canadian health care system and other forms of social programs for persons with disabilities (Danzon 1990; Coyte, Dewees, and Trebilcock 1991), all seem likely to reduce suits by injured consumers against manufacturers. The American experience of protracted, expensive, stressful litigation against pharmaceutical companies willing to litigate ferociously must also deter suits.

To date, no successful suit has been brought by a DES daughter or son against a manufacturer of DES sold in this country. No thalidomide suits were completed in any country, including this one (Braithwaite 1984, 73–4), although many were settled. Issues of jurisdiction (*Distillers Co. [Biochemicals] Ltd. v. Thompson*) and the *Sunday Times*'s right to publish information about company practices (Teff and Munro 1976, 1–26) were litigated. No Dalkon Shield litigation has been completed in this country; some Canadian women were made part of the U.S. action. Other actions by Canadians, against Pfizer Inc., manufacturer of the Bjork-Shiley heart valve, have been commenced in the United States. In spite of a rate of drug-related injury that appears substantial, few plaintiffs have alleged negligent manufacturing, design, or testing by a manufacturer of pharmaceutical products. In *Hollis v. Birch*, in the British Columbia Court of Appeal, the plaintiff lost her suit alleging negligent manufacturing by Dow Corning, won her duty to warn action against the corporate defendant, and won a retrial of the action against Dr Birch for breach of the duty of disclosure. The case against the manufacturer is under appeal to the Supreme Court of Canada; other suits against manufacturers of breast implants have started, and some Canadian women have joined the global settlement in the United States.

Canada has seen few tort actions against drug manufacturers. Only a handful of duty-to-warn actions against drug or vaccine manufacturers have been litigated, while several doctors have been sued for negligent prescription or breached duty to disclose. Governments have occasionally been made defendants in pharmaceutical products cases (*Lapierre v. Attorney General of Quebec*; *Rothwell v. Raes*). Undercompensation for drug-related injuries can be said to be the norm in Canada.

In contrast, the American products liability field involving manufacturers of prescription drugs and devices is extremely active. Even so, undercompensation exists in the United States as well (Dutton 1988, 257–8). Plaintiffs are reluctant to endure the trauma of litigation, particularly when the action may focus on the plaintiff's behaviour instead of the product. Not all the plaintiffs in DES actions were successful, particularly prior to the *Bichler* and *Sindell* cases. While some suits have produced ample awards, and sometimes substantial sums in the form of punitive damages, many awards have been small.

The drug MER/29, prescribed to reduce cholesterol levels, caused cataracts in hundreds of patients and involved 'not only deceptive advertising, but also, at best, gross negligence in research, and at worst, deliberate fraud' (Lexchin 1984, 74–5). Richardson-Merrell's sales, net worth, and net profits rose during and after the period of litigation and criminal convictions for violations pertaining to MER/29 (78–9). Under the corporate reorganization approved under U.S. bankruptcy law, A.H. Robins Co., responsible for death and the destruction of the reproductive lives of thousands of women by the Dalkon Shield, was able to limit its liability to the $2.3 billion paid to a trust to handle the claims. As a result, the company acquiring Robins – American Home Products Corp. – issued Robins shareholders stock 'worth four times the pre-bankruptcy price of their Robins stock. In fact, for the year 1987 while the company was in bankruptcy, Robins' stock had the highest rate of appreciation of any security on the New York Stock Exchange' (Sobol 1991, ix).

FEMINIST GOALS FOR PRESCRIPTION DRUGS AND DEVICES

Equality

Dependence and vulnerability are characteristic of the relationship between patient and doctor and of the attenuated relationship between patient and pharmaceutical company. In each instance, the patient is relatively powerless, dependent on the other for relief from suffering and reliant on the other's greater expertise. Patients' vulnerability arises out of their illness and their need. It is reinforced by their singularity – alone with disease or pain, and a recipient of treatment.

Disease is seen as a scientific entity, which can be controlled through drug therapy (Lexchin 1984, 209–11). Some diseases are constructed for which drug therapy is the solution – for instance, hormone replacement therapy for meno-pause. In either event, the political, social, and economic context of the patient's life is largely ignored as a possible source of disease or as a site for cures. The practice of medicine has been highly individualized and decontextualized.

This approach serves the interests of the drug industry, willing to sell means of quick intervention for difficult social problems. An environment of trust has been based on continuing public belief in the myth of continuous progress and ignorance of risks and nourished by exaggerated claims made to physicians, through sales agents of pharmaceutical companies and advertising. The undue reliance by doctors on drug companies and by patients on doctors needs to be tempered with enhanced capacity for efficacious and independent action by doctors and patients.

Creation of reliable data on ADRs is a vital component in making doctors more independent of the drug industry and in creating educated consumers. A requirement of direct warnings to consumers through patient package inserts and careful monitoring of the contents and presentation of labels would assist in breaking down the impediments preventing adequate information from reaching the patient. In addition, poor data-gathering and concealment of adverse data before marketing need to be stringently controlled. Ethical guidelines for research on human subjects need to be imposed for clinical trials in non-institu-tional settings and monitored in all settings.

In the legal relationship, the power imbalance needs to be made part of the analysis. First, reasonableness standards can be removed from the disclosure requirement and from causation analyses, to be replaced by subjective stan-dards. Second, analyses can be contextualized, taking into account the situation of the individual, including the network of connection, as well as the political context, based on any condition of disadvantage of the individual. The Supreme Court of Canada used such an analysis in *Norberg v. Wynrib*, a case of sexual abuse of patient by doctor, in which a prescription drug to which the patient was addicted was exchanged for sexual acts. All six judges decided in favour of Norberg's claim. In five of the judgments, equality analysis, in addition to ele-ments of the relationship, produced the legal framework.

Tort law takes power into account in other ways. The presumption that a doc-tor will disclose to a patient if adequately informed by the drug company par-tially remedies a difficult problem of proof for the patient. Another example is a reverse onus, sometimes imposed by courts when the defendant controls the means of proof or where fault has been proved but circumstances created by the defendant have made proof of causation impossible. Although courts have not applied these solutions to the problem of the indeterminate defendant in DES litigation, courts in California, New York, and other U.S. states have developed the market share liability analysis, which, while not an equality analysis per se, uses collective harm created by the defendants as the basis of its legitimacy.

Affirming Difference

Equality analysis in Canadian constitutional law rests on the premiss that difference may need to be recognized in order to achieve equality. The kind of decision-making that takes account of subjective factors and power relationships accommodates group and individual differences.

The stereotypical assumptions made about women's bodies in medical and pharmaceutical discourse are perpetuated through advertising and texts.

Research on women has been inadequate. Women have been underrepresented as research subjects, so that the effects of drugs on women's physiology have been inadequately understood. Female hormones and the cyclical nature of women's bodily lives need to be factored into the understanding of drug action. The underfunding of breast cancer research is one indicator of inattention to the nature of particular women's experiences.

In both Canada and the United States, female legislators called for increased research on women. Particular groups of women need to be assessed – younger and older women, heterosexual and lesbian women, women of different races.

Control of Bodies

The ability to control one's own body implies both freedom from external constraint and a sense of efficacy and personal power. While efficacy can coexist with trust – and the interplay of trust and efficacy may characterize the most confident of relationships – trust accompanied by low efficacy indicates dependence of the type apparent in doctor-patient and drug company–patient relations. When trust turns to mistrust, and is accompanied by low efficacy, the interaction is alienating.

Reducing dependence and increasing efficacy require profound attitudinal change, better communication of information by drug companies, creation of independent and adequate information for doctors and patients, and better drug and legal education for doctors.

Access to tested technologies necessary to women's health is an important aspect of control. Safety and efficacy remain important dimensions in the release of new drugs.

Avoidance of Harm

Both the regulatory system, designed to ensure that only safe and effective pharmaceutical products reach the market, and the tort system, with deterrence as one of its fundamental purposes, are intended to reduce harm. Because women take more drugs than men, the risk of harm for women as a group is greater. Similarly, because over-prescription is a problem among elderly people, and women seniors outnumber men, these groups are at greater risk.

A philosophy of cooperation with the industry and reliance on it can lead to an environment of receptivity to the industry's blandishments and the exercise of less control on behalf of consumers. The regulatory systems in both countries need strengthening in the areas of surveillance of adverse effects, maintenance of publicly accessible registers of adverse effects in the post-marketing period, third-party monitoring of clinical trials, and increased auditing of the industry's practices, including reporting of ADRs and promotional activities. In addition, staged release of drugs to the public, with enhanced post-marketing monitoring (Sage 1988, 1,021), could provide significant benefits.

In Canada, tort actions against drug manufacturers have been virtually non-existent. U.S. drug litigation has been considerably more extensive and, in some cases, has constituted 'mass tort' litigation. Even so, the American system undercompensates, as many injured consumers have chosen not to sue, have settled for inadequate amounts, or have lost their suits. Litigating against multinational corporations determined to deploy significant resources takes a particular kind of perseverance. Whether such litigation deters future harm is always a difficult and contentious question.

Even when a tort action is successful, against all odds – theoretical biases, practical impediments, and the inherent frailties of litigation – the calculation of damages itself is subject to bias.

CONCLUSION

Women are disadvantaged by the current liability scheme in the area of pharmaceutical products in North America. The learned intermediary rule is premised on a view of the physician as conduit and mediator of information between manufacturer and consumer. To the extent that the doctor-patient relationship and the manufacturer-consumer relationship are characterized by dependence, vulnerability, and inequality of power, patients' autonomy is subverted and made subject to an overriding concern for existing authority. Similarly, the products liability purpose of harm avoidance is undermined by the inadequacies of the current system of regulation and compensation. The feminist goals of equality, controlling our own bodies, and avoiding harm need to be achieved in the legal doctrine governing pharmaceutical products.

NOTE

I would like to thank Susan Fowler for her excellent research assistance; Yvonne Chisholm and Jo Ann Connolly for their effective assistance in finding research materials; Liz Fox, of the Queen's University Law Library, for making creative recommendations about sources; Alan Zuege for his careful checking of citations; and Sandy Tallen for producing the manuscript. I am grateful to the Law Foundation of Ontario and John D. Whyte, former dean, Faculty of Law, Queen's University, for providing funding for the research. I appreciate the comments made by participants in the conferences and workshops where this paper was presented: the Third International Conference on Health Law and Ethics, American Society of Law and Medicine, Toronto, July 1992; Feminism and Law Workshop Series, University of Toronto, Faculty of Law, January 1993; and the conference 'Corporate Crime: Ethics, Law, and the State.'

PART II

Corporate Form and Corporate Organization

6

Preliminary Observations on Strains of, and Strains in, Corporate Law Scholarship

HARRY GLASBEEK

This entire volume could be filled with the queer effects of the personification of industrial enterprises in mixing ceremony with the production and distribution of goods. Control of great organizations drifted out of the hands of those who knew the techniques of the business and into the hands of bankers. Stock manipulation became more important in control than efficiency of production. Organizations competed with each other in building magnificent structures for pure show and in order to gain dignity and prestige in the company of their peers. Great law offices grew up in New York to supply the infinitely complicated logic needed to keep the separate individuality of parent and subsidiary or affiliate corporations apart. Theological disputes produced a great literature as to what the 'real nature' of a corporation was which was assiduously studied in law schools. (Thurman W. Arnold 1937, 192)

Diverse and impressively sophisticated work is being done in the area of corporate crime. Without in any way seeking to be exhaustive, we mention that issues on the table include examinations of how best to apply criminal law to corporate deviance (e.g., Glasbeek 1984; Geis and Di Mento in this volume) how to theorize the corporation as a social being (e.g., Stone 1975; Ermann and Lundmann 1982; Sargent 1990; Wells 1993), whether or not to ascribe traits such as 'culture' to a corporation (e.g., Shover 1992), and even whether or not criminal law ought not to be retheorized (e.g., Sargent 1992). However, a totally different kind of scholarship is also going on, which does not focus on corporate crime but rather theorizes the corporation in order to legitimate it and, as a consequence, capitalism itself. This shapes and contours the corporate crime debate.

All the scholarship on corporate crime assumes that law has created the corporation and that criminal and other regulatory laws are political decisions that have been given a legal form. Necessarily, the metaphysical analysis of corporate-crime scholars and the prescriptions of others are contoured and shaped by the law. And the law has its own agenda.

Lawyers and economists, or, more specifically, lawyers imbued with the ideology and tenets of neo-conservative economics, see the corporation as a vehicle that has evolved and has been designed to serve the ultimate and unquestionably worthwhile aims of capitalism. In short, they see it as a means to promote private accumulation of wealth. Indeed, to them it is the most significant means by which to make capitalism work. These intellectual gatekeepers understand full well that the corporation is a peculiar tool, which constantly needs legitimating because it tends to undermine the core model that promotes and justifies private accumulation of wealth – namely, the de jure sovereign individual maximizing his or her opportunities to satisfy his or her own needs.

There always has been unease about the fact that doing business through the corporate form may betray the individualistic model and/or detract from the central proposition that owners of wealth should exercise dominion over their own property. Legal and economic scholars, therefore, seek models of governance of the corporation that facilitate and justify accumulation of wealth into private hands. They search for corporate theories that will yield the result they want: legitimation of maximization of private profits through the corporate form. To them, attribution of a theory is important *only* because it permits certain consequences and denies others. They will oppose theories that might lead to regulation that questions the legitimacy of the corporation as a single-purpose organization or that imposes unusual constraints on its ability to maximize profit.

This chapter sets out the way in which lawyers theorize about the corporation, concentrating on the most recent strains in such scholarship. Recent work facilitates and legitimates capitalist relations of production better than any other theory that had been used by lawyers and economists. Its 'drag-down' effect on adventurous and radical-thinking corporate-crime scholars is likely to be great. It is difficult for policy-makers to adopt views that run counter to the dominant and legitimated wisdom. Moreover, because many people who want to mediate the harsh effects of capitalism often feel the need to use the internal logic of the legal institution itself, progressive lawyers who, as a group, probably would support the overall aims of the corporate crime scholars frequently try to adapt the dominant legal theorizing to achieve their progressive aims. This tendency will make it even harder for scholars of corporate crime to achieve their goals.

We do not suggest abandoning the search for a corporate theory that recognizes the sociological reality of what is going on. We try merely to alert scholars with this aim that law and its functionaries tend to create, and continuously re-create, a hegemonic view of the corporation that blocks alternate regulation. It would be foolish to ignore this fact.

LEGAL CHARACTERIZATION AND FOCUS

Modern corporate legislation defines a corporation as a body corporate, incorporated under the relevant statute. It details the proper process of incorporation. The capacity of certified corporations is set out. Subject to anything to the contrary in the statutes, they are to have the rights, powers, and privileges of a natural person. The statutes provide rules that govern the extent to which the people who deal with such a body can rely on its capacity to do business. The remainder of the statutes' provisions are concerned with the duties and rights inter se of directors, managers, and shareholders.

The statutes do not say that the corporation is the same as a natural person and do not define its essence (if it has one). They merely give it attributes that will permit it to enter into legally binding transactions and to make some legal claims. The idea is to facilitate the capacity of this 'creature' to engage in business.

Lawyers, alongside philosophers and other theorists, have speculated on what the essence (if any) of the corporation is. It would be curious if they had not. After all, the modern corporate statutes do some astonishing things. The birth of a corporation is achieved without any period of gestation. Conception and birth are simultaneous. The creature is born fully mature and is potentially immortal. Further, it can spawn any number of new young, also born fully mature and with the parents' immortality. These almost magical properties beg theorization. And there has been no shortage of it. As long ago as 1938, Wolff noted that at least sixteen theories had been offered to conceptualize the corporation. For lawyers' purposes, the spectrum of explanation is constituted by three of these theories. Each has many nuanced variants, but that is not all that important to the legal scholars. As lawyers are interested in the consequences of attributing a character to a corporation, not the scientific purity of any particular theory, all three main theories have currency and sway with legal decision-makers at any one time. The law needs to be able to pick and choose.

The fiction theory argues that a corporation is an entity created by the state and, therefore, has the capacities and the powers that the state gives it. The state is seen as retaining a controlling role, which justifies its interventions if it chooses to make them. One of the difficulties of characterizing the corporation as an artificial device that is the creature of the state is that this is not the sort of person that needs the kinds of protections that individuals demand against state intervention. This is a problem because such protections are frequently sought and given. Another problem is that it is not easy to envisage that this state-created entity can act with malevolent or illegal intent because it is natural to assume that the state would not create an actor that could conduct itself illegally. Yet it is useful on occasion to treat the corporation as a responsible person. As time went on, this last difficulty made the natural entity or realist theory more appealing as a conceptual construct to progressive people.

The natural entity theory assumes that a corporation is an organization/entity with a life of its own; it is a real organism, not just an artifice. The government's role is that of an enabling agency, not of a controlling one. The state, therefore, ought to be as inhibited when interfering with the rights, powers, and privileges of the corporation as it is when it seeks to interfere with those of human beings. In addition, because the corporation is seen to exist not only as a separate legal entity to facilitate legal transactions but as a real being, it is easier to attribute a discrete will to it. This will is manifested in the conduct of certain central directors, officers, and employees, who, for some purposes only, are the corporation.

Contractarian visions of the corporation are most in vogue at the moment and have been particularly popular with U.S. theorists for the last twenty to twenty-five years. Most contemporary legal theorization in Canada also relies on this view.[1] Its understandings form the bulk of the discussion of the latter part of this chapter.

LEGAL CHARACTERIZATION MEETS THE REAL WORLD

What the corporation is supposed to facilitate is free market activities. But is the way in which the legal device can be, and is, manipulated antagonistic to the operation of an idealized market? This idealized view posits that private actors, rationally deploying their resources, assets, and capabilities, will meet demands formulated freely by other private actors. It is, therefore, crucial that the corporation be seen to behave as an individual, as a 'rational economic man.'

In England in the beginning, the corporation was created in such a way as to make this goal achievable. The grant of legal personality was seen as a privilege, restricted to those cases in which economic sense mandated its existence. Extension would undermine the notion of sovereignty by diminishing personal responsibility too much. Thus, for firms of less than twenty-five people, a partnership – in which each member of the firm was to be jointly and severally responsible for the liabilities of the business – continued to be considered the most appropriate business form. They could not incorporate. These joint ventures were to continue to be saddled with the same legal burdens as sole proprietors. But this balance between big and small enterprise was not maintained for long. The minimum number of enterprisers needed to get the privilege of incorporation as a matter of right was whittled down first to seven, then to one. At the same time, another major change occurred.

Initially, the privilege of legal personality for a many-member firm had not bestowed limited liability on the investors. This lack was soon remedied. Then, as the distinction between large and tiny firms was being rendered meaningless (legally speaking), a grant for limited liability to small firms was fought for and won. At this stage, the four elements had been put in place in England which, to this day, in Canada interrelate to undermine the claim of legitimacy made by free-market proponents that the corporate device does not distort the operation of their favoured economic model. These elements are separate legal personality, the limited liability of individual investors, and the possibilities of having one-person corporations and corporations with many investors.

Because the corporation is a legal person separate from its members, an investor, especially within non-traded, small corporations, can be any or all of the following: a major shareholder with limited financial responsibility for the debts and risk of corporate activities; an executive manager who can create risks that might hurt third parties and, perhaps, obligations in the corporation but that will yield benefits to the manager in his or her capacity as a shareholder; or a controlling shareholder and/or manager who can cause the corporation to enter into transactions with a business in which he or she has a direct interest as owner or shareholder. This ability to create benefits for an individual and to make the corporation responsible for the debts and obligations incurred is only mildly inhibited by rules regulating conflicts of interest and the like.

A problem of legitimacy therefore exists as a consequence of the legally created manipulative powers possessed by controlling investors in small corporations. Even some of the strongest proponents of the corporation as a device to facilitate market activities have been calling for the end of the privilege of limited liability in these kinds of situations. (Halpern, Trebilcock, and Turnbull 1988). While this kind of problem obviously is conceptually troubling for justifiers of corporate law, they have graver difficulties to resolve at the other end of the scale of enterprise.

While, in large, widely held, publicly traded corporations, most individual investors may not have sufficient manipulative power to benefit themselves at the expense of others, their ability to sell their shares, together with the benefits provided by limited liability, gives them a tremendous incentive to be passive – that is, not to be vigilant of their own interests, at least not as much as 'rational economic men' are supposed to be. From the economic model's point of view, this can be justified only on the basis that this passivity does not matter because the corporation, itself acting as a 'rational economic man,' is pursuing the shareholders' interests for them. And, not surprisingly, corporate law is designed to make this argument plausible.

As each individual investor contributes capital to the corporation, the corporation becomes the legal owner of all the bits of capital so invested. As a legal, property-owning person, it has the juristic standing to invest, sell, lease, buy, and so on. It is responsible for the debts of the enterprise and to make good the losses caused by it. It has the legal trappings of a sole proprietor.

A sole proprietor is expected to maximize profits, and, therefore, the managers of such a corporation should be pursuing goals that coincide with those of the investing shareholders. To ensure this end, the directors and managers are to be selected, elected, and appointed by the shareholders (though not always directly). They must then act in good faith (that is, not for themselves) and in the best interests of the corporation. The hope is that their view of its best interests is much the same as the shareholders' – whose capital the managers now control on behalf of the corporation – of what is in their best interest. This hope is sought to be realized by some concrete measures.

Although the corporation is the legal owner of the invested capital, the shareholders, who continue to think of themselves as proprietors, are treated as residual owners for some limited purposes by corporate law.[2] And, to assure shareholders that their interests as quasi-owners are pursued, they have been given a limited right to set into motion a derivative action when they can show that the corporation's best interests – which they feel coincide with theirs – are not being pursued by management. They also have a right to be bought out for a fair price when they dissent from directors' decisions, which, arguably, have been made in the corporation's best interests but may cause them a loss. Most important, they can claim redress when they can demonstrate that they have been unfairly prejudiced or discriminated against by directors or the corporation – the oppression remedy. But the problem of incoherence will not go away.

The directors have been granted wide, discretionary power to do things with, and to, the collectivized assets of individual investors. Such discretion 'to do' is potentially transmutable into 'power over.' The resulting problem of legitimacy can manifest itself if management asserts its power more obviously than usual. Then the legally created gap between the corporation and individual investors may become an unbridgeable political and economic gulf.

Berle and Means suggested that this gap had become very wide and deep in the United States of the 1920s. They found that, in large enterprises, professional managerial teams held de facto sway over the formal legal guardians – the board of directors – and therefore made the decisions.[3] For liberal, democratic capitalism the problem was acute: 'This fact destroys much of the economic justification of the institution of private property. The persons making the vital economic decisions are not those who suffer the consequences or reap the rewards of such decisions except by a very indirect and roundabout process. Likewise, to the extent that dividend payments are made to a group which does not actively participate in corporate affairs, the assumed equivalence between income and productive effort is broken.'[4] In the period after 1945, this issue was belaboured lovingly, particularly in the United States. During those optimistic times, the problem was seen as a challenge that could be confronted and tackled by liberal pluralist scholars.[5]

The very size of the corporations under managers', as opposed to owners', control and their centrality to the economy meant that managerial decisions had social, political, and economic effects on a scale normally attributed to governmental decisions. It was therefore appropriate, in the view of more progressive capitalism-favouring scholars, to make corporations responsible for the adverse effects of the conduct forced on them by unaccountable managers. The idea was to make the corporation a responsible citizen and to make its managers subject to checks and balances.[6]

Thus separation of ownership and control gave a push to the jurisprudential school, which treats the corporation as a natural entity able to form the same kind of intent as human beings are able to develop.[7] More directly, it was seen that, as managers were not committed to profit-maximization to the exclusion of all else, and because many groups were affected by their decisions, managers could be – and should be – asked to take into account interests other than those of the corporation (and/or those of the shareholders). To ensure this end, affected segments of the community should be protected by giving them rights of representation within the corporation, through, say, the appointment of specialist and/or independent directors who were to raise such concerns.

This debate led to many recommendations to restructure corporate governance, some of which are still being pushed and refined. Some proposals would have the corporation pursue profits in a manner more congruent with the way in which individual shareholders would seek to realize their goals as 'rational economic men.' Some, however, would treat the corporation as an entity with public responsibilities beyond economic efficiency and would put 'into play' the basic economic model and the kind of political economy that it justifies – namely, capitalist relations of production (Glasbeek 1988). Not surprisingly, there has been vehement reaction to this movement for change.

A REVISIONIST VIEW

To the proponents of classical economics, especially those in the United States, these developments were anathema. In his preface to M. Bruce Johnson's *The*

Attack on Corporate America (1978) – a title that said it all – one of the gurus of the contract-nexus school, Henry Manne, set out the need to develop an alternative vision. He argued that it was all too easy to pick on corporations, which, because of their size, their pervasiveness, and their apparent impersonality, were 'easily misunderstood.' He found 'near hysteria' in these malicious attacks: 'The past ten to fifteen years have witnessed an outpouring of corporate and business criticism as venomous as anything seen since Nazi "scholars" placed responsibility for the ills of an earlier epoch on the Jewish community.' This sad situation had arisen because there was not, as yet, 'a coherent and integrated economic theory of how large, publicly held corporations, and a corporate system, should operate in a free-market environment.'

In the 1970s, law-and-economics scholars (Alchian and Demsetz [1972], Jensen and Meckling [1976]), reached back for a long-neglected article by Ronald Coase – 'The Nature of the Firm.' Coase (1937) had argued that there was a lacuna in the work of economists. They accepted unquestioningly Adam Smith's postulates – namely, that, at a certain level of technology, the only constraints on consumers and individuals who wanted to pursue their own goals was a system of price-setting. The role that economists had given themselves was to discover how prices were determined, so that Smith's decentralized world could yield its beneficial results by removing anything that interfered with the operation of the 'invisible hand,' which should dictate prices so as to allocate resources in the most efficient way possible. Coase argued that concentration on the purchase of factors of production and the sale of the goods and services produced by them ignored internal relations within the organizations that purchased these factors and produced goods and services. He contended that certain kinds of business organizations were spawned because they offered an efficient way for rational economic men to participate in markets. This last premiss provides the launching pad for the most recent and influential theorization yet about the nature of the corporation.

One variant of this theory argues that isolated market transactions that create the need to get new information and to incur repeated transaction costs can make pooling of resources a more efficient way of doing business. Investors then will enter into a series of contracts with a group of other suppliers of resources and skills in a patterned way to enable them to produce much more than they could by engaging in discrete market transactions. This perspective sees firms as nothing but a bunch of contracts, by means of which participants seek to maximize opportunities. Participating individuals want their assets properly deployed and an appropriate share of the benefits produced.

In team production, coordinating activities must be given over to others, and, if there are many investors who have many business interests, it will be hard for them to monitor their managers. Further, because operations within a firm are coordinated, it is difficult to determine who contributes how much to any profits eventually produced. This situation creates incentives for 'shirking' – that is, incentives for some people to do less than they ought to do to deserve the share they appropriate. Classical economists, and many of their law-and-economics accolytes, argue that there will be no cluster-contracting by rational economic men – no business organization like a corporation – unless the contractors feel that they can overcome these kinds of problems.

As rational economic men, these scholars argue, contractors calculate the likely transaction costs when they enter into the clustered contractual arrangements that create the firm. If they believe that a combination of a discounted price for the share they pay and the existing and potential internal and external monitoring system will protect their investment well enough, they can participate with confidence. Contractarians view existing corporate structures as warranting that confidence.

They believe that agency costs arising from formation of a corporation are reduced by the normal governance structures of the corporation, the capacity and the natural inclination to add to the internal checks as need arises, and capital markets that structure the environment in which the corporation operates. Shareholders' rights to vote on decisions mean that, given sufficient information, they can protect their interests. Public trading of a corporation's shares means that, theoretically, their market value will reflect the extent to which managers are shirking – or are expected to do so. Managers, aware of such an accounting, understand that their prospects will be threatened if they are, or are thought to be, shirkers. They will seek to reassure investors by setting up monitoring mechanisms, such as independent directors and compensation committees. Additionally, genuine internal competition for managerial jobs will encourage incumbent managers not to shirk; reports on any way in which they favour their own interests at the expense of the corporation may cause them to be pushed aside. Capital markets also react unfavourably if managers render the corporation less competitive. Even more directly menacing to managers, if they fail to maximize profits, stock is likely to be undervalued in the capital markets, and alert investors may make a bid, believing that better managers would make a firm more profitable, even after a premium has been paid for shares.

In sum, forward-looking investors with good information can be confident that the calculable agency costs of entering into the cluster of contracts that make up a corporation can be kept reasonable. Accordingly, allowing others to administer their assets does not in any way transfer their control of these assets. To the contrary, investors remain true principals and the managers merely their agents.

This understanding thus rejects the managerialist argument of Berle and Means and of Cary altogether, by seeing the corporation as a bunch of contracts that are contiguous with market activities. There is no sharp boundary between the firm and the market.

There is another major variant of the theories based on Coase's work. Coase had argued that the firm was a vertically organized institution whose authoritarian, planned control was a substitute for the atomized, anarchic market, with its somewhat mysterious way of setting prices as a resource-allocating mechanism. Coase reasoned that whether a firm or organization would be used by investors would depend on how the transaction costs of establishing a hierarchically directed firm compared with those incurred by discrete, repetitive exchanges in the market. For Coase, this comparative work was to be the centre of economic studies of the firm. A group of scholars known as institutionalists, led by Owen Williamson (1975, 1984), has taken up this challenge by treating the firm as an alternative to the market – that is, as a separable institution. Institutionalists see the corporation as a vertically integrated organization in which people become involved to offset the disadvantages of individual participation in the market.

The argument is that, in the atomized market the nature of their resource, that is, their potential investment, may make some people too prone to exploitation by others, too prone to the effect of opportunism, particularly if, because of their position and the nature of what they can offer by way of investment, they cannot be sure that the terms of the exchange that they are willing to accept will not change. That is, they may feel that they have to agree to terms that are subject to unanticipated or unfavourable modifications by their contracting partners who enjoy more powerful economic positions. A vertically organized structure in which agency costs can be reduced and firm-specific investments might retain a value they would not have in a continuously changing and uncontrollable market may provide the safeguard that such vulnerable actors seek. Such would-be investors do not have to be presumed to be in a position to make completely informed decisions to favour such an arrangement, something which the more classical economic analysis with their almost devout belief in the rationality of economic man posit as a given for their contract-nexus arguments. That is, the institutional scholars' starting point is more realistic about human behaviour.[8] In the same way, the institutionalists acknowledge that the same institutional contractors might be a little shady, somewhat willing to be deviant, and that this tendency needs to be discouraged.[9] These theorists show themselves to be more sensitive than their classical economic colleagues.

The institutionalists argue that hierarchical corporate structures can eliminate many of the unacceptable side-effects of contractual relations between imperfect people with different kinds of investment resources. To them, the corporate firm is an island marked off from the market by a clearly delineated boundary, although, of course, the corporate institution interacts with the institution of the market. It is this that sets them apart from the contract-nexus people. But, like the latter they see the corporation as a transaction cost–reducing device for contracting parties. This means that they, too, see it as a *private* contract creation. Consequently, like their contract-nexus colleagues, the institutionalists believe that the corporation should be governed by rules and devices designed and accepted by the private contractors, as opposed to rules imposed by governments. The design of a corporation should reflect efficient cost-reduction, and there should be intervention with its governance only if it is crystal clear that, as a result of some failure in the contract markets, the contractors are unable to get the most efficient rules into place. Like the purer contract-nexus scholars, they justify existing corporate structures as efficient economic vehicles that reflect the values inherent in capitalist relations of production.

Enterprise conducted through the corporate structure is legitimated by both kinds of contractarian modelling. Because both kinds treat the corporation as a convenience that enhances coordinated contracting by private parties, they reduce the stature of the device itself. The corporation, once again, is a legal artifice, much as the fiction theory treats it. It is no longer seen as a real thing, a natural entity whose interests are human-like and, possibly, in conflict with that of the contractually related incorporators. Accordingly, it can claim the protection from state intervention guaranteed by documents such as Canada's Charter of Rights and Freedoms. After all, the 'real' claimants are the contracting parties, who, in essence, are merely using the corporate form as a convenient cloak. There is no need to make mystifying, and rather easily derided, claims that the corporation is a person, like you and I, entitled to protection of rights such as, say, privacy. Moreover, this kind of analysis is sufficiently distinct from the traditional fiction theory to stave off another difficulty.

If a corporation owes its separate existence to the state, as fiction theorists suggest, it is easier to win the argument in court that the state should be allowed to monitor its behaviour. Arguments against government intervention and surveillance lose resonance when they come from a creature created out of whole cloth by the government. Many of the early decisions by U.S. courts denied corporations, on this basis, the protection of the law against unreasonable searches and seizures and the privilege against self-incrimination (Tollefson 1992). By contrast, the contract-nexus and institutionalist approaches, while they continue to treat the corporation as a fiction, see it as privately created, with the government acting merely as an enabling agency during its creation. As a private 'fiction,' it has no obvious need for greater state surveillance than do human beings. The contract-nexus and institutional models provide corporations with legal and conceptual buffers against regulation.[10]

These models do away with the need to deal directly with the enigma created by the existence of two apparent property owners – the corporation and the investor – with all the ideological and legal baggage this brings along. By focusing on autonomous, free contracting, they explain why the investors, who have calculated that it is cost-efficient to delegate administrative tasks to others whom they can control, do not take a direct part in the deployment of their assets. They have not given up their sovereignty, nor are they acting as rentiers who have abandoned economic and moral responsibilities. On the contrary, they have measured the risks and taken steps to allocate their resources and responsibilities, just as sovereign rational economic men are supposed to do. Adam Smith's economic model is promoted, not brought into disrepute, by using the corporate structure. Those who saw apparently unchecked managerial control as an unacceptable, anti-capitalistic development misunderstood the constraints and limits on that control. The governance scheme of the corporation aims at ensuring that investors get the most 'bang for the buck,' and it will throw up new mechanisms for reducing agency costs as they are needed. Management will not get out of control as long as contracting parties can create appropriate incentives and disincentives.

These law-and-economics theories explain why people, acting as capitalists within capitalism, want to form, and be part of, corporations. The only serious counter-arguments that these theorists may have to confront is that capitalism is not working as it should and that, therefore, the corporation, as structured, may be something that can be questioned. If external markets are imperfect, the logic underpinning the corporation as an appropriate vehicle to deal with agency costs is undermined. And the undue influence the corporate sector exerts in social and economic affairs then becomes an ugly and potentially delegitimating phenomenon. There are clouds of this kind overhead, but the strong winds of contractarianism have the potential to clear the sky, sufficiently at least to persuade compliant governments to leave corporations alone. A few examples of how contractarianism works to defend the extant corporate structure follow.

Leading contract theorists, such as Jensen and Meckling, posited that stock prices will be discounted for ongoing and predicted shirking. This factor, they say, will cause management to set up monitoring devices to convince the markets that they are trustworthy. But, for this system to work, there needs to be a competitive, unbiased equity market of the kind that may exist in the United States. There, 63-plus per cent of all publicly traded corporations are widely held, not having any dominant, identifiable shareholders.[11] In Canada, 80-plus per cent of all publicly traded corporations are controlled by one or two major shareholders (Glasbeek 1984). On its face, there may be much less of a competitive equity market in Canada than there needs to be to have it work as a check on managerial shirking.

This kind of fact-based attack on contractarian theorizing does not destroy the contractarians' conceptualization. Rather, it leads to questions about whether Canada's equity markets are as imperfect as they seem to be or how much (or little) government intervention would be needed to bring the market closer to the ideal (Daniels and McIntosh 1991). The notion that the corporation, as a preferred and privately chosen form of business organization, should be left alone as much as possible is, therefore, not analytically undermined by revelations of 'momentarily' imperfect equity markets.

Similarly, contract-nexus theorists, such as Demsetz, argue that the equity markets are not the best monitoring device to control agency costs. They assume that unnecessary agency costs will be passed on to the consumers of goods and services produced by the corporation and that managerial incompetence and shirking will be punished as consumers stop purchasing the corporate outputs. It is this result, they contend, that will lead to the appropriate adjustments. In Canada, there may not be sufficient competition in many product and service markets to limit agency costs.

Here it is useful to digress slightly to underscore the internal flexibility of contract-nexus reasoning. If one possible source of agency cost–reduction is not available by means of forming a corporation, another may well do the trick. Bratton (1989) refers to this as the indeterminacy of contract-nexus theorization. But it makes the theory hard to disprove by reference to some specific market imperfections.

To return: if the argument is that competition in products and services is not intense enough to reduce corporate agency costs, two sets of responses are available to contract-nexus and institutionalist advocates. First, it is not true – there is more competition than there seems to be. The nay-sayers, it may be contended, are looking only at internal markets when they make their claims about lack of competition, not at regional or global trading and production. Second, if it is true that there are some competitive failures, what is needed is a different government-sponsored competition policy, not interference with corporate governance.

Obviously, this kind of debate can go on for ever without resolution and helps explain why so many Canadian scholars, working in a totally different environment to that in which their U.S. mentors are labouring, can accept their theorization without much question, indeed with acclaim.

The same kind of fact-crunching debate has taken place around the take-over and merger issue. The agency theorists argue that the threat of a take-over is an antidote to managerial opportunists. During the mad 1980s, however, the cry went up that this justified speculation (junk bonds) and deceit (insider trading and tipping). Worse, borrowing to launch take-over bids led to asset stripping and dismissal of workers to pay the bills so created. In short, it was argued that take-overs led not to increased efficiency, but rather to deviant behaviour and redistribution of wealth in favour of some shareholders at the expense of other shareholders and 'stakeholders,' such as creditors and workers in the firm. Proposals were pushed, therefore, to give corporate management the power to defend stakeholders when takeover bids were made. Defensive machinery, such as poison pills, white knights, the sale of the crown jewels, should all be made permissible to this end, provided that the managers did not use them as an excuse to protect their own interests in shirking. The old-line suggestion that independent, outside directors, some charged with looking after specific stakeholders' interests, should be given the role of overseen got a new lease on life. Contractarians' responses have been vigorous and plausible.

First, they point out that allowing corporate managers to make allocative decisions about other people's assets in order to protect some other groups' interests makes them, undemocratically appointed, taxation-like officers. This argument, of course, had been well worked out by Milton Friedman (1962). Relatedly, the argument of contractarians continues, because some directors and managers are required to represent certain special constituencies other than shareholders, they will be faced with serious, indeed insoluble political conflicts, as they will be forced to advocate certain interests at the expense of immediate and long-term profits. This difficulty will be compounded if they are directors with a general duty of care to the corporation. Given the internal logic of the corporate world, there is a lot of merit in the contractarians' responses (Glasbeek 1988a).

Second, the usual factual disputation is opened up by this kind of argumentation made in support of new kinds of corporate governance. Thus, contractarians contend that take-overs, in fact, are efficient. Using stock prices as an unbiased measure of efficiency, they have done empirical work to show that share prices of the taken-over corporations do not go down, as they would be expected to if, in fact, their values had been depressed as a result of the manoeuvring. Insofar as the allegations are that workers have paid an unfair price as a result of asset-stripping and/or 'downsizing' by the successful take-over bidder, empirical work is being done to show that few, if any, job losses have taken place that would (or should) not have occurred in any case (Daniels 1991; Howse and Trebilcock 1993).[12]

While all of this sounds incredible and is, therefore, contestable and contested (Hyde 1992; Stone 1992), these 'scientific' findings enable contractarians to argue that defensive mechanisms against take-overs, such as 'poison pills,' impose unnecessary fetters on the investors' ability to check agency costs caused by managerial shirking. Despite this argument, however, more than half of U.S. states have passed legislation allowing – but not forcing – managers to take stakeholders' (as well as shareholders') interests into account when considering take-over and merger bids. Contractarians see such laws as a perversion, a pandering to the lobbying undertaken to enable managers to exploit opportunities to shirk. Managers now can feather their own nest during a take-over bid while claiming to look after the corporation's best interest writ large; they can claim that they are protecting stakeholders when they reject premiums for existing shareholders.[13] This situation is regressive, say the contractarians; everything should be done to leave 'natural' market forces free to work, and, right now, they can work.

While Berle and Means's problematic was created by lack of incentive for shareholders to exercise their voices, economic circumstances have changed dramatically. Huge institutional investors want the corporation to maximize value and profits. They can – and should, say some contractarians – monitor management in ways that will ensure low agency costs. The model will work purely, just as it should. Certainly, it will guarantee far more efficiency than will attempts to protect all sorts of interests by creation of conflicting governance rules.

Of course, there is a debate among contractarians as to whether or not institutional investors, in fact, are interested in behaving as monitors, or even if they can (compare Coffee 1991, who says 'yes,' with Gartner 1992, who says 'doubtful'). But, if institutional investors may not be effective voices for shareholders, this is because of the restraints imposed by governmental regulations over institutions such as pension funds. Accordingly, to make sure that investors will want maximum profits, there should be deregulation of these investment houses. The irony is clear: to avoid regulation of the corporation, it may be necessary to deregulate other aspects of market activities. Perhaps this is as good an indication as any of the anti-regulatory thrust of contractarians, who claim to be merely efficiency-oriented and to have created value-free models to this end.

In sum, contractarian theorization is hard to fault empirically as long as the given – the virtue and superiority of rational economic men operating in an unfettered market – is not questioned. From within that framework, the contractarians have substantially relegitimated the corporation. This intellectual coup d'état has major ideological reach.[14]

PRELIMINARY CAUTIONS

For those who want to curb corporate power by using the internal logic of capitalism and the theories of legal essence of the corporation, the recent theories present a formidable barrier. Once one is inside the contractarian web of logic, it is virtually impossible to get out – progressives are like flies in a spider's web.

This is illustrated by recent searches for ways to protect workers from the ravages of capitalism's restructuring. The argument is made by people such as Stone, as well as by Howse and Trebilcock. The former is a progressive, social-ist lawyer; the latter are better described as liberal-conservative lawyers. These two wings of the legal-political spectrum use the same kind of argumentation to make their case.

They urge governors of corporations to take workers' concerns into account when making decisions; to this end, workers should be part of the governing structure. They use contractarian arguments to support this platform. They seek to exploit the self-advertised notion of contract theorists who claim that they are value-free and, therefore, indifferent as to who participates in the cluster-pattern contracts, and why. The salient point supposedly is that free, sovereign contract-ing is taking place to deal with agency costs. There should therefore be no a pri-ori reason why workers who contract to be employees cannot be treated as having, in essence, a contractual relationship with the corporation analogous to that between shareholders and the corporation.

These theorists argue that unionized workers have limited contracting power because of the restrictions imposed by collective-bargaining law and so cannot contract for adequate protections against dismissal. The corporation's decision-making rights in respect of their job security allow management to exploit the workers. In particular, when workers are hired and they need to be trained, they are likely to accept wage rates that reflect their inexperience. Once they are well-trained, their wages better reflect their actual productive value. As they get older, their wage rates are likely to outstrip their value to the corporation. In the absence of a contractual right against dismissal, management (usually different from the one that hired them) may seek to get rid of them. Workers who now have some skills, many of which are firm-specific, have no obvious way to recoup the earlier forgone wages. In this instance, the investment in the firm by the contractors (i.e., the workers) is so firm-specific that, given the constraining law of collective bargaining, the contracting workers should be given some cor-porate governance right to protect themselves against opportunism by the cor-poration's management.

The contractarians' response is the expected one. They say that unionized workers are not constrained by legal rules and, in as much as they are, have ways to protect themselves. Even though they cannot bargain, ex ante, in respect of a lifetime of work with any one corporation, a collective agreement is a not a once-and-for-all arrangement. Periodic and recurring collective bargaining enables workers to renegotiate terms of employment. Workers are therefore not caught in long-term, open contracts that can be changed by their employer at will (Williamson 1984).

Just as concerning disputes around the efficiency of equity and products markets and the effects of take-overs, an empirical morass is created. Policy-makers will hear a cacophony of contradictory, 'scientific' claims. At best, it will be hard for those who want workers to become part of governing structures to have those in power cause it to happen. They cannot make it obvious that their argument is more factually compelling than that made by the contractarians.

It is troublesome when a progressive such as Stone makes essentially the same arguments as Howse and Trebilcock, who are really nothing but hard-thinking, if well-intentioned, advocates of the status quo. Like them, she rests her case on a relatively minor factual difference between the employees and other contracts with the corporation. She points to the fact that workers are in a poorer bargaining position as a result of state-sponsored limitations on collective action. She does not dwell on what truly makes an employment contract distinct from other kinds of agreements.

Capital is a social relation, and the social relations of capitalism are reproduced through accumulation. Property owners engage in productive activities so that they can generate surplus value and convert it into constant and variable capital. That surplus value is to be extracted from workers who sell their only resource – their physical and intellectual abilities – like a commodity to employers who thereby gain the right to deploy this resource profitably. There are a few employers, while there are many workers who must sell their labour power in order to live. This difference makes the employment contract distinct from all other contracts; it is not a voluntary arrangement in any sense. Unlike the investment of a shareholder – the investment of surplus capital by a property owner who does not need this invested money to live on – a person who owns only her labour power is forced to enter into a contract for its sale. Further, because the worker sells her own labour power, she is to be the contracting party – a person who forms part of a cluster of contracts – at the same time as her labour power is the object of this cluster of contracts. The difference between the shareholder or lender who contracts with the corporation and the worker who does so is palpable.

To take but one example, occupational health-and-safety risks impose economic costs on the corporation, on shareholders, and on workers. If such a risk materializes, the effect on shareholders is not only diluted,[15] it is of a different kind. The losses they suffer are only economic. The worker may not only lose part of her income and her future earning potential, but also her enjoyment of life, her limbs, or her life itself. The investment of a person is simply not the same as the investment of spare capital.

This difference is also reflected in the way that different contractual relationships are interpreted by the law. Only an investment defined as a 'security' attracts protection by the security commissions that regulate capital markets on behalf of the corporate world. A 'security' is created, say the courts, when individuals have been enticed to invest money in a common enterprise with the expectation that they will earn a profit solely through the efforts of the promoter or of someone other than themselves; it is legally defined as the exact opposite of an employee's investment of her own labour power.[16] If the usually obfuscating law can recognize the real difference between a capitalist's and a worker's investment, serious analysts, especially progressive ones, should.

Yet it is easy to sympathize with those who seek to reform capitalism from within, even if this means abandoning class-based strategies. Parallel arguments were made by progressive lawyers, such as Harold Laski (1929), when, relying on the logic of their ideological opponents, they tried to use the emerging natural-entity conceptualization of the corporation to urge that it should be made tortiously and criminally responsible and also to lay the foundation for their argument that a similar-looking organization, the trade union, should also be recognized as a legitimate legal person. They hoped that this would help workers. This kind of abstract legal argumentation had, of course, minimal effect.

In a similar way, progressive labour activists, such as Stone, reach out for participation in corporate governance as a way to help workers. North American collective bargaining is failing workers during this latest capitalist restructuring, and boring from within is a more attractive alternative than it otherwise might be. Capitalism, however, is not going to be embarrassed by arguments, posited on contentious factual bases, into giving workers control over productive enterprises at a time when the employing classes have set out to roll back such gains as the working classes have made. More important, potentially, there is a negative aspect to this kind of legal politics.

The logic employed is that of contractarians who have a very limited view of contract, which reinforces the idea that rational economic men, relentlessly pursuing profit, will increase economic welfare, at the same time as political freedom will be enhanced because individuals decide for themselves what they will do with their resources and what they will demand by way of products and services. In short, the logic reflects the primacy of the promotion of welfare attained by giving private greed its head and the elevation of the politics of 'one dollar, one vote' over those of 'one person, one vote.' There are real risks in trying to help workers by reforming this schema from within. It may give it a legitimacy that it ought not to have.

To sum up, there have been, are, and always will be intellectual gatekeepers who will seek to legitimate extraction of surplus value, as the debates around the conceptualization of the corporation vividly show. Their most recent efforts will make it harder than ever for those who wish to develop the argument that a corporation, because it is larger than its component parts and has its own culture and essence, requires special forms of regulation. This means not that the progressives are wrong in their scientific quest for such a re-evaluation, just simply that the beauty of scientific argumentation has never been a match for political machination, which is what corporate-law scholarship is. It is this consideration that, to me, leaves the reasoning of those, such as Geis and DiMento, who would prefer to ignore the corporation when ascribing criminal responsibility – as most Europeans do – a more attractive strategy.

NOTES

1 The most vocal Canadian proponents are to be found at the University of Toronto Law School: e.g., M. Trebilcock, B. Chapman, R. Daniels, and J. MacIntosh. Law-and-economics jurisprudence is more fiercely pursued in this school than anywhere else in Canada.

2 For instance, upon dissolution, they are entitled to any capital that remains after all corporate obligations have been met; also certain decisions about the corporate constitution (e.g., amalgamation, sale, or lease of substantially all the assets other than in the ordinary course of business) require shareholders' consent. Shareholders also can maintain managerial power over a corporation by use of a mechanism known as a unanimous shareholder agreement. Typically they do so in family-type corporations.

3 Many recent empirical studies support these findings; see M. Mace, *Directors: Myth and Reality* (Boston: Division of Research, Graduate School of Business Administration, Harvard University, 1971); 'Directors: Myth and Reality – Ten Years Later,' *Rutgers Law Review* 32 (1979): 293; McDougall and Fogelberg, *Corporate Boards in Canada: How Sixty-four Boards Function* (London, Ont.: School of Business Administration, University of Western Ontario, 1968).

4 G.W. Wilson, untitled article, quoted in R.L. Campbell, ed, *Control of Corporate Management* (North York, Ont.: Captus Press 1992) 46, 47. Berle himself was later quoted as saying that, in the United States, one could find capitalism and capital, but no capitalists.

5 Separation of control and ownership had been detected, together with its attendant legitimacy problems, much earlier than 1932. In 1904, Thorstein Veblen had said that such separation had made managerial control the norm in large corporations. In the 1920s, John Maynard Keynes had made a similar point, as had William Z. Ripley. Capitalism's accumulation drive always threatens to destroy the theoretical model

used to justify it. The tendency to monopoly, with its incipient separation of owner-ship and control, is inherent. The fact that it was Berle and Means's study that was taken as the starting-point for debate was the result of the excellence and scope of their study and of the timing of its appearance. It arrived during the depression. Cap-italism and its devices were in crisis, and critical evaluation was sorely needed. The study justified capitalist relations of production because its findings showed that a central mechanism had strayed from the pristine capitalist model. If only this could be redressed ... !

6 One of the best-known pieces expressing an anti-managerialist bias was that of Cary, 'Federalism and Corporate Law: Reflections upon Delaware,' *Law Journal* 83 (1974): 663.

7 M. Horwitz, 'Santa Clara Revisited: The Development of Corporate Theory,' *West Virginia Law Review* 88 (1985): 173.

8 Although, like all the scholars of this genre, they seem to use strange terminology to state this very commonsensical position. They talk about the fact that economic actors have 'bounded rationality'; this means no more than that they cannot know or anticipate everything.

9 The slippery language to describe this characteristic moves from 'opportunism' to 'guile.'

10 This helps explain, to some extent at least, the great success of corporations under the Charter of Rights and Freedoms in Canada.

11 This, of course, is what led to Berle and Means's problematic raised by separation of ownership and control.

12 The argument is that good management would have led to job losses as a result of globalized production and pressures to replace expensive workers with less strongly organized ones and/or with machinery. Further, inasmuch as a take-over merchant engages in large-scale dismissals in order to meet the debt created by a successful take-over bid, it will be seriously constrained by the facts that, sooner or later, it will have to go to the labour market to get more workers and that the labour market, if it is func-tioning well, is likely to punish the corporation for engaging in crude opportunism.

13 An indication of how influential the contractarians are in Canada is that take-over defensive mechanisms have led to the same argumentation here as in the United States, even though it is clear that, because of Canada's densely integrated corporate structures, mergers are friendly and hostile take-overs rare. The Venture Economics database indicates that of nearly 1,200 mergers surveyed, only seven were hostile. But each hostile take-over and the few attempts to set up 'poison pills' attracts the kind of attention reserved for a major intellectual and social dilemma; see P. Dey and R. Yalden, 'Keeping the Playing Field Level: Poison Pills and Directors' Fiduciary Duties in Canadian Take-over Law,' *Canadian Business Law Journal* 17 (1990): 252; J. McIntosh, 'Poison Pills in Canada: A Reply to Dey and Yalden,' ibid., 323.

14 Have they found a riposte to Thorstein Veblen's acute observation that 'Bolshevism is a menace to absentee ownership. That is an unpardonable sin'?

15 Not only are the costs spread among many shareholders, but they affect them indirectly. Further, their personal obligations are limited. The corporation often can pass on the cost because of its oligopolistic position, and many of the costs are borne by other actors. Workers' compensation premiums are, in the end, paid for by workers' wages; taxpayer-supported medical and welfare schemes support much of the costs of the accidents; see Glasbeek (1988b).

16 *Pacific Coast Coin Exchange v. O.S.C.*, [1978] 2 SCR 112.

7

Corporate Crime and New Organizational Forms

STEVE TOMBS

This paper has emerged from two overlapping sets of interests.[1] One, and of much longer standing, is my concern with the regulation of occupational health and safety, specifically with the nature and prevention of safety crimes; the second involves arguments around the emergence of 'new' forms of organization.

The chapter considers, in schematic form, some of the relationships between these two areas of interest. It offers a selective outline of certain points of (actual and/or potential) contradiction and complementarity, and it raises many more questions than it answers. Yet I hope that it also suggests areas both for future academic inquiry and for political activity.

The first section emphasizes the legitimacy and significance of corporate crime as a focus of organizational research. The second presents an overview of the nature of a range of 'new' organizational forms. The third selectively considers aspects of the interrelationships between corporate crime and these new organizational forms, with particular reference to the organizational production of safety crimes. A brief conclusion indicates the potential fruitfulness of further pursuit of such lines of investigation.

CORPORATE CRIME AND ORGANIZATIONAL FORMS

Despite many attempts to define the term *corporate crime*, perhaps the most useful is that of Steven Box. Developing the work of Shrager and Short (1977) on organizational crime, Box (1983, 20–2) defines it as 'illegal acts of omission or commission of an individual or group of individuals in a legitimate formal organization, in accordance with the goals of that organization, which have a serious physical or economic impact on employees, consumers ... the general public and other organizations.'

Such a definition is particularly useful. First, in his reference to illegality,

Box concentrates on those acts of omission or commission currently proscribed by law. To focus thus on illegality avoids extending discussions to include acts or omissions that one finds morally blameworthy, socially harmful, and so on (see, for example, Kramer 1983, Simon and Eitzen 1990); such definitional extension weakens the critical force and analytical rigour of arguments about capitalist organizations and their operating contexts. Nevertheless, what Box's reference to illegality also allows is inclusion not simply of those acts or omissions proscribed by criminal law, but also those subject to other legal codes, namely administrative and civil law (Box 1983, Pearce 1992).

Second, the phrase 'omission or commission' clearly encompasses illegalities that occur through what is not done by organizations or their members and implies the need to transcend simplistic issues of intention, further calling into question individualizing understandings of crime. Thus corporate crimes are to be understood in the context of organizational structures, cultures, assumptions, modus operandi in various contexts, and so on, rather than by reference to the 'perverse personalities of their perpetrators' (Braithwaite 1984, 2).

For these reasons, Box's definition remains important. However, in its reference to the 'goals' of an organization, it becomes problematic. At the simplest level, organization theorists have long recognized difficulties in identifying the goals of any formal organization (Silverman 1970). To speak of organizational goals implies that organizations have a rational and consistent set of goals and that members are aware of these and can and do act on them.

However, the ascription of rationality to corporations, or even to groups within them, is a highly problematic and increasingly contentious exercise. Through empirical studies (Miller 1987; Jackall 1988; Brunsson 1989; Marchington and Parker 1990), as well as at the level of theoretical inquiry and development (Kreisberg 1976; Mintzberg 1983; Reed 1992), several things now seem clear. Corporations rarely act as unified, rational entities; major tensions and conflicts exist both within and between levels of management, partly as a consequence and partly as a cause of inconsistent organizational goals; and particular groups or levels of managers fail to act strategically even when they claim to recognize certain goals. It should be added, however, that while organizational or corporate rationality is problematic, many organizations present themselves as if they were rational actors (Keane 1992; Pearce and Tombs 1993). This general issue of rationality, then, is important, not least in the context of corporate crime and its regulation; some of the questions raised by these points are considered below.

Box's analysis of the nature of corporate crime is also highly sensitizing: he forces us to recognize the extent to which corporate attempts to minimize or control environmental uncertainties can produce contexts in which crime is either likely or inevitable. These uncertainties include internal 'sources of problems' (1983, 35–6), and the following discussion extends his intimations concerning such uncertainty within particular organizations.

More generally, Box's work emphasizes the (now-accepted) recognition that understanding the nature, structure, and functioning of organizational forms is crucial in understanding corporate crime. 'New' organizational forms are likely to affect the nature and incidence of corporate crime and require effective strategies for their regulation or prevention.

'NEW' ORGANIZATIONAL FORMS

We cannot here do justice to the range of existing and new or emerging organizational forms. Nevertheless, within the growing literature on organization, its theory, and the directions of its structures, a number of themes seem dominant, and here I outline some of the themes and characteristics commonly associated with new or emerging forms.

Given the variety of arguments around new organizational forms, and the eclectic selection of such arguments in what follows, it is worth beginning with the fundamental basis to such arguments – namely, that such forms can be understood partly in the context of a wider 'anti-modernism.' We can thus begin our discussion in terms of what these organizations are *not* (Keane 1992). They are distinct from that archetypal modernist organizational form, the bureaucracy. While the latter's nature and significance were first grasped by Max Weber (1964), its practical development was most famously pioneered by classical management theorists and advocates of 'scientific management.' As Morgan notes, it is based on the assumption that there is 'one best way to organize' (1986, 33). Moreover, the potency of this phrase, and of the prescriptions that follow from it, is such that when one thinks of 'organization,' and tries to evaluate its performance/practice, one often does so in terms of 'a structure of clearly defined activities linked by clear lines of command, communication, co-ordination and control' (33). In other words, we still tend to view organizations in a modernist sense.

More generally, such a view would include not simply 'organizations as machines' but all those conceptions couched in terms of some kind of systems metaphor. Thus, the theory that sees organizations as organisms, or as open systems adapting to their environments (Morgan 1986), remains one imbued with the totalizing ethic of modernism.

If it is inappropriate to view organizations as systems, as totalities, as (types of) unfolding entities of rationalization, how might we conceive of them? Several theorists have attempted to set out the key elements of new organizational forms.

Reed has characterized 'postmodern' forms of organization as predicated on a fragmenting and disorganizing dynamic and as entailing more decentralized, self-regulating, diffuse, and flexible arrangements (Reed 1992, 228). They are 'thought to generate a culture of expression and involvement within which autonomy, participation and disagreement are openly encouraged' (229). Intrinsic to these forms is 'perpetual problem-solving,' demanded by the requirement to 'stay ahead of the market' (232). Such forms 'facilitate the personal development of individuals within collectivities based on trust, and the relatively high level of risk-taking which that involves' (232). Thus the resulting culture 'celebrates, even luxuriates in, the dissolution and demise of the normative regimes and disciplinary practices associated with rational bureaucracy' (232).

Reed argues that this form of organizational specialization and coordination aims to be 'much more responsive to market change and technological advance' (231). Thus, citing Murray, he claims that these developments can best be summarized by the keyword 'flexibility – of plant and machinery as of products and of labour' (231).

Rosabeth Moss Kanter posits 'postbureaucratic' or 'post-entrepreneurial' organizational forms. The latter term conjures up 'the addition of entrepreneurial elements to established companies, moving them away from bureaucracy in order to play effectively the new business "game" ... In that kind of game, every element is in motion – technology, suppliers, customers, employees, corporate structure, government regulation – and none can be counted upon to remain stable for very long' (Kanter 1991, 65). Such forms are said to break fundamentally with bureaucracy (and its partner, hierarchy). They entail 'flatter, more focused organizations stressing synergies, entrepreneurial enclaves pushing newstream businesses for the future, and strategic alliances or stakeholder partnerships stretching capacity by combining the strengths of several organizations' (65–6).

In her discussion of 'synergies,' 'newstreams,' and 'alliances,' Kanter elaborates on these new forms of organization. Promotion of synergies is furthered by the designing of 'leaner, more co-operative, more integrated organizations with fewer layers of management and smaller corporate staffs' (66). In practice, promoting synergies means decentralizing and redeploying, that is, 'putting more responsibility in the hands of unit managers and reducing the need for approvals or checkpoints'; contracting out, that is, 'the divesting of all activities but the "central core,"' the ultimate extreme of which 'is represented by companies that are essentially marketing and financial shells working through vast networks of suppliers and dealers'; and turning services into business, whether by converting them into internal 'profit centres' or additionally requiring them to enter a wider market and sell these services 'on the outside' (66). New forms of organization that seek to promote synergies are networks or 'federations' of 'semi-autonomous divisions' (69–70), with increased emphasis on 'horizontal' rather than 'vertical' dimensions (70).

Strategic alliances and partnerships refer to 'developing close working relationships with other organizations' and allow companies to extend their reach without increasing their size (70). Such new relationships, or alliances, blur boundaries between organizations; they involve the creation of what might most simply be called networks, through which the 'extremes' of markets and hierarchies might be avoided.

Promotion of newstreams entails a 'flow of new business opportunities within the firm, creating small business start-ups within large corporations' (72). Newstreams facilitate diffusion of invention, innovation, risk-taking, and opportunity; they foster project rather than corporate identification and entail development of intra-organizational autonomy, which loosens 'traditional hierarchical authority' and 'respect for bureaucracy' (72–3).

According to Kanter, synergies, alliances, and newstreams differ radically from 'the old-style corporate bureaucracy.' They create organizational 'flexibility' (74).

Thus both Reed and Kanter set out a similar cluster of principles underlying new organizational forms and indicate the forms (structures) in which these principles become manifest. Heyderbrand places new organizational forms under a different generic term: 'postindustrial organizations or those emerging from the transition tend to have a postbureaucratic control structure even though prebureaucratic elements such as clanlike personalism, informalism, and corporate culture may be used to integrate an otherwise loosely coupled centrifugal system' (Heyderbrand 1989, 327). Thus a 'general, simplified profile of the typical postindustrial organization' indicates several common elements:

- small size, as firms or small sub-units of larger organizations;
- an object that is 'typically service or information, if not automated production';
- computerized technology;
- informal and flexible division of labour;
- a managerial structure that is 'functionally decentralized, eclectic and participative, overlapping in many ways with nonmanagerial functions' (327).

Again the practices and principles resonate with those of Kanter and Reed; they are also compatible with aspects of Drucker's theory of 'new' organizational forms (Drucker 1992). Also broadly consistent with these claims are those of Clegg, who focuses on the economic embeddedness of Japanese enterprises

(Clegg 1990, 176–207) and presents data that are detailed and descriptive but 'societal and macro' in orientation rather than generated at an organizational level (204).

Let us draw together some characteristics commonly associated with new forms of organization:

(i)   fragmentation or decentralization within large organizations, or small size;
(ii) increasing autonomy and self-regulation of these smaller units, 'minimization of obligation,' increased 'responsibility,' and decreased surveillance;
(iii) responsiveness to markets and to technological advances;
(iv) cultures of involvement, cooperation, and participation, of trust, of risk-taking and expression;
(v)   the turning of services into businesses, greater focus on 'core' activities, and contracting out.

What brought about these new organizational forms? A spectre of crisis is seen to loom behind both anti-modernism in general (Burrell 1990, 281–2) and the emergence of new organizational forms in particular. Reed mentions changes that forced development of non-bureaucratic organizations: the failure of Keynesianism; emergence of microelectronic information technologies; and dwindling confidence in the abilities of national governments to 'manage' an increasingly global economic system (Reed 1992, 231).

Similarly, Heyderbrand cites both 'external turbulences' and 'internal conditions.' Among the former are internationalization of capital and the increasingly global natures of markets, as well as the growth of computer-based production and service systems; among the latter, the growing complexity of organizational structures and the effects of new technologies on the social organization of work and the labour process (the latter ushering in reduced formalization and standardization) (Heyderbrand 1989, 338–9; and see also Drucker 1992, 128). Clegg points quite simply to the limits of Taylorism (Clegg 1990, 179).

These images of both crisis and change are significant. If one takes seriously the common claim by organization theorists that bureaucratic forms of organization function most 'efficiently' in 'stable and predictable' environments (Morgan 1986), then crisis or uncertainty (Keane 1992) might undermine such forms of organization.

In this speculative sketch, I am not concerned with the extent to which such organizational forms actually exist. Indeed, the above theories vary along a range of criteria. For example, some characterizations have been developed on specific empirical analyses of economic activity in districts, regions, even nation-states – typical reference points are the Emilia-Romagna region, Japan, and East Asia (see, for example, Clegg 1990; Reed 1992). Others claim that they are describing existing realities that prefigure wide-scale change of 'organization' (Heyderbrand 1989; (Kanter 1991). Yet other work is explicitly prescriptive and produced from a managerialist perspective (Drucker 1992). Moreover, there are also major ideological and political differences between the sources and perceived implications of these arguments (Bagguley 1991). Finally, these arguments vary in their adequacy. Some claims are grandiose, generalize too broadly, periodize faultily, fail to distinguish long-term trends from short-term fluctuations, and show a problematic slippage to and from description and prescription. Debates around such critical points have spawned a vast literature, as have debates within these debates, most notably around flexible specialization.

However, I wish to sidestep such issues, indeed controversies, here. My concern in this paper is with the implications for corporate crime of new organizational forms. If new structural characteristics and values are emerging, what does this mean for the incidence of safety crimes and, more important, for their prevention? There is some evidence to suggest an embracing of some elements of new organizational forms and departure from the ideal-typical bureaucratic organization; the concerns of this chapter are neither purely academic nor speculative.

CRIME, SAFETY, AND NEW ORGANIZATIONAL FORMS

In this section, I draw on some recent empirical work on the nature of safety organization in the British chemicals industry. Of course, I do not intend to imply that the British chemical industry is 'postmodern,' 'postbureaucratic,' or 'post-Fordist,' nor that new forms are of great or particular significance here. But the industry gives increasing signs of many of the elements of new organizational forms discussed above. And for that reason, it provides one empirical basis on which we can consider key elements of new forms in terms of their implications for corporate crime.

Indeed, given the arguments of some of the theorists discussed above, one might expect to find such forms developing in the British chemical industry. Knowledge and knowledge workers are crucial there, especially since many Western chemicals corporations turned increasingly towards (low-volume but high value-added) speciality chemicals in the 1980s as part of a global restructuring of corporate divisions of labour within the international chemical industry. Further, in the United Kingdom, at least, the industry has had a tradition of cooperative workplace relations, based on 'responsible' trades unions and management (Gill, Noris, and Eaton 1978). And, finally, automated production is of great, and increasing, significance.

Much of the material presented in this section has been treated in far greater detail elsewhere (Tombs 1992). I wish simply to look at the possible implications of new organizational forms for safety crimes and corporate crime in general. I gathered this material at the end of the 1980s, as part of case studies of the organization of safety in six multinational chemicals companies operating in Britian. The British chemical industry (Pettigrew 1985) and the global industry (Aftalion 1991) had undergone extensive restructuring as part of an explicit attempt to emerge from crisis. The oil shocks of the 1970s had followed postwar expansion of chemicals production (based on oil as a crucial raw material); overcapacity in 'developed' chemicals industries had followed years of attempts to exploit economies of scale in a growing world industry; and highly competitive chemicals industries had emerged in various markets. Within the West, this combination of events has led to a general shift towards specialty chemicals and less emphasis on bulk production, drastic reductions of production capacity, and significantly lower staffing levels (Aftalion 1991).

In the previous section I summarized a number of features commonly associated with new organizational forms. As we consider changes in the organization of safety in six multinational chemicals companies, it will be helpful to do so in relation to such features. Unfortunately, it is not possible to organize the following material tidily under headings taken directly from the features listed above, for the data presented here were gathered for somewhat different purposes. Nevertheless, I have developed headings within which the data can be examined and presented and which are also consistent with the features set out above. However, these headings will not be exhaustive of the features of new organizational forms outlined above.

- The category 'Decentralization, autonomy, and forms of accountability' used below relates fairly unproblematically to features (i) and (ii) above; (i) referred to fragmentation or decentralization within large organizations, or small size, and (ii), to increasing autonomy and self-regulation of these smaller units, 'minimization of obligation,' increased 'responsibility,' and decreased surveillance.
- 'Commodification of relations' encompasses category (iii), namely, responsiveness to markets and to technological advances rather than to hierarchies, and two parts of (v), turning of services into businesses and greater focus on 'core' activities.
- 'Contracting out' – the other element of (v) – is considered separately; it is

consistent with aspects of greater focus on 'core' activities – also in (v) – and involves creation of networks.
- 'Employees involvement' captures one aspect of (iv) – cultures of involvement, cooperation, and participation.

Decentralization, Autonomy, and Forms of Accountability

Each of the six companies studied had decentralized management and operating structures in the 1980s through corporate reorganization, extending the autonomy of independent business groups within these overall structures. This shift – consistent with postmodern 'diffusion of power' – had increased both the possibility of, and the incentive for, compromising safety in the face of other goals. The possibility had been created by the very nature of autonomy (particularly independent cost accounting) and by isolation from central corporate departments. Incentive existed in the form of 'career-minded' individuals at the head of independent businesses (see also Keane 1992, 4–5). It was Kanter who claimed that 'the opportunity to be essentially in business for oneself, inside or outside the large corporation, puts more control in the hands of smaller groups' (Kanter 1991, 75–6); in addition, we can see, decentralization and autonomy can make (safety) crimes both more possible and more likely.

In other words, decentralization and greater autonomy had created a structural problem of a variety of power centres – and possible conflicts of interests – within these corporations. This was exacerbated in the context of safety by the absence there of any independent, senior individual with an oversight role – that is, the absence, or removal, of 'surveillance'/normative regimes (Reed 1992, 232); and, indeed, this absence of independent oversight was (and, it must be said, traditionally has been) reproduced at the lower level of site and plant safety officers, the latter lacking executive authority within workplaces, so that their demands are frequently subsumed under those of individual plant and line managers. While safety officers could offer advice, they lacked the social capacity (or, to use Braithwaite's [1985a] term, the 'clout') to have this advice acted on. The result, as I witnessed myself, was subsumption of safety requirements under local production imperatives.

The resulting problems were exacerbated by the absence of mechanisms to make safety performance count. One – albeit sometimes rather blunt – means of monitoring safety performance is, of course, through collection and use of accident and incident data. The collection and analysis of such data were rudimentary – a situation unthinkable vis-à-vis returns on capital investment or product market analysis – but two companies had abandoned use of such data in the 'monitoring' of safety performance in the early 1980s. More generally, where such data were used, failure to meet targets was not acted on. Managers' non-compliance with internal safety standards was generally not recognized as an issue, despite general claims around 'total quality management' to the effect that if 'they can't manage safety they can't manage much else.'

Such lack of monitoring might not be a case of organizational inefficiency but could more cynically be viewed as motivated. In other words, while increasing decentralization and autonomy can make safety crimes more likely, these facts suggest 'wilful blindness' (Coffee 1981, 389, cited in Pearce 1992, 9), or constitute an element of mobilization of techniques of distancing or neutralization (Keane 1992; Pearce and Tombs 1993).

Commodification of Relations

Further marginalizing safety, and thus increasing the potential for safety crimes, all the reorganizations had either created or reconstituted central safety departments. Relations between these central departments and other business groups had been commodified – that is, safety had become an internal service to be provided at a cost determined by an internal market. These departments marketed their own safety products and 'systems' outside their own organization. Such commodification involved real or paper monetary transfers, yet there was a clear shift towards the former. And as an indication of the problems that can result, one company, experiencing severe problems in managing 'major hazards' sites, recognized the need to train managers in such locations above a certain level of competence but accepted the fact that central safety services did not have the resources to provide such training. Individual businesses simply did not recognize such training as significant enough to meet its 'market' price.

Contracting Out

Similar contracting out was to be found in the move away from retention of maintenance staff towards contracting out plant maintenance to other, specialist organizations. All six companies had reduced their maintenance staff since the early 1980s, and some were even sub-contracting out all maintenance work to external contractors. Such steps are highly problematic vis-à-vis safety management and prevention of safety crime.

First, the British Health and Safety Executive (HSE) began, through reference to the deleterious effects on safety performance of 'fragmentation' and 'contractual changes' (HSE 1987a), to state publicly that both use of sub-contract labour and the activity of maintenance work were major sources of industrial accidents (and, relatedly, violations of safety standards). The HSE has made the former point generally, the latter, both generally (HSE 1985a, 1985b) and with respect to the chemical industry (1987b). Where sub-contracting and maintenance intersect, one might reasonably expect safety problems. And safety 'problems' should not be taken to imply a series of unconnected, ad hoc 'accidents'; rather, what has been occurring are systematically/organizationally produced deaths and injuries, up to 83 per cent of which would have been prevented had managements done all that is 'reasonably practicable' (HSE 1985a, 1985b, 1987a, 1987b) – that is, they should have been prevented through adherence to sections 2 and 3 of the Health and Safety at Work Act (1974), a criminal statute.

Second, the organizational complexity introduced by the shift towards sub-contracting makes safety crimes more likely, through ever-tighter tendering, through introduction of smaller, less able (in terms of resources and safety expertise) companies into worksites, and through the 'invisibility' offered by contractual complexity. In addition, post-hoc detection of responsibility and administration of justice become difficult or impossible (a point frequently made in the United Kingdom with respect to the construction and offshore oil industries – see Carson 1982; Bergman 1991; Tombs 1990b).

The problems generated in contracting out may reflect a point made by Clegg – namely, that shifts in 'organization' may produce 'winners' (within core groups of employees), but this winning is predicated on the existence of significant groups of 'losers' (Clegg 1990, 206).

Employees' Involvement

Employees were little involved in organizing safety in the companies studied. Each firm did have structures – especially joint committees – where workers' representatives formally raised safety issues. Yet such structures were not very effective, and the involvement thereby secured was highly problematic. In one company, unions had been de-recognized in the early 1980s – hardly a sign of greater trust, though perhaps an aspect of flexibility – although no contradiction was seen between this change and employees' 'involvement' in safety organization. Moreover, in all companies, the role of the workforce in safety organization had diminished since the early 1980s (see, more generally, Grunberg 1983, 1986; Dawson et al. 1988; Tombs 1990a).

Alongside this weakening of workers' power, and the increasing view of safety committees as dealing with 'trivial' issues (see also Walters 1987), the six firms generally 'involved' workers through autonomous groups or teams, a tendency consistent with elements of the new forms of organization outlined above. But such a shift undermined employees' ability to perform an internal and localized 'regulatory' role with respect to safety. Most autonomous working groups have been introduced in ways that circumvent or render obsolete traditional forms of worker representation, such as unions and shop stewards (Marchington and Parker 1990). And a 'voice' without any formalized backing is precarious indeed (Tombs 1990b).

NEW ORGANIZATIONAL FORMS AND SAFETY CRIMES

Thus some of the elements associated with new forms of organization can make safety crimes more likely to occur and less likely to be detected. The above treatment is far from exhaustive (for example, it does not consider in detail forms of flexibility and flexible specialization). However, enough has been said to temper the more optimistic scenarios created by prescriptive and descriptive analyses of such phenomena.

Indeed, if one lays over the practical organizational changes described above some of the more general principles of new organizations – for example, risk-taking, innovation, flux – then the prognosis vis-à-vis corporate crime becomes even gloomier. (It is important to consider not simply structural forms themselves, but also the values said to help generate and be derived from them.) As Kanter acknowledges, any emergence of such 'post-entrepreneurial' forms produces 'more contingencies, more uncertainties' (Kanter 1991, 75). Keane (1992, 3) observes: 'The greater the uncertainty, the greater the incentive to reduce it through illegal means.'

When referring to Box's 1983 list, I state above that we might add elements within particular organizations. This proposal perhaps makes greater sense now but can still be expanded on. When intra-organizational relationships become decentralized and commodified, conflict between and within organizations becomes potentially significant. And this point further casts doubt on any assumptions concerning 'rationality' in unitary organizations. The sense of a unitary entity becomes even more at odds with organizational reality as changes noted above develop.

To restate a general point, while the nature of new organizations blurs the boundaries of and between organizations, it also creates myriad competitive relationships within them. Uncertainties are likely to increase, as will certain kinds of corporate crime. Moreover, while corporate crime will be more likely, there may be a greater incentive for organizations to fail to meet legal safety duties – since the regulatory structure is unlikely to be sufficiently complex and flexible to guarantee equal conditions of competition for those who might meet legal minima. Further, corporate/organizational complexity, coupled with traditional regulatory structures, might further encourage illegality through diminishing probability of detection.

To the extent that the organizations described here approximate elements of new organizations and hence depart from the modernist, bureaucratic, 'rational,' unitary entity, then these changes affect 'appropriate' forms of regulation. Certainly national states have been, and are still being, forced – often through a combination of 'crisis, struggle, and pressure group activity' (Snider 1987, 53) – to adopt more effective regulatory strategies. Yet to the extent that these assume that the organization is a rational, unitary entity, realities may be outstripping and rendering anachronistic, and therefore inappropriate, such attempts.

This analysis seems like a highly negative balance sheet in terms of elements associated with new forms of organization. These negative conclusions are related to greater organizational complexity (Vaughan 1983; Haines 1992). But the crucial issue concerns the forms of complexity and the conditions that produced them – economic crisis and the resurgence of free-market versions of enterprise, manifest in deregulatory rhetoric and, to some extent, practice.

CONCLUSION AND DISCUSSION: BEYOND PESSIMISM?

If I offer above a pessimistic scenario, let me end on some more hopeful notes. There seem to me at least three interrelated ways in which emergence of new organizational forms both presents a challenge and suggests a more positive academic and political agenda.

First, these new forms, and representations of them, contain clear contradictions. While the present 'resolution' can be related to economic and political crisis, such resolutions are in principle contingent and subject to change. Thus, for example, emphases on 'high-trust' relationships, involvement, participation, the demise of surveillance and bureaucratic control, and diffusion of power can all raise the issue of organizational democracy. While present/emerging organizational forms seem profoundly anti-democratic, elements of them clearly offer grounds on which political action is possible. Legge, for example, has pointed out contradictions within human resource management and 'flexibility' (Legge 1989). Are high-trust relationships, and development and use of employees' skills and knowledge, really consistent with functional and numerical flexibility? Is the denial of union recognition or rights consistent with participation and involvement?

In so far as new forms of organization open up corporate forms and recognize the existence and legitimacy of a plurality of voices, possibilities for democratization emerge that are worth pursuing. The blurring of divisions between organizations and indeed even perhaps between organizations and their environments creates a potential for legitimate democratic participation by groups of 'external' stakeholders. If pro-regulatory pressure groups 'are absolutely central to the regulatory process' (Snider 1991, 210–11), then any prospects for democracy in and around organizations (Clegg 1991, 208–35) might help minimize safety crimes.

Other possible contradictions within new organizational forms require critical attention. For example, what are to be the practical effects of the tensions between greater intra-organizational autonomy and less inter-organizational autonomy created by alliances or networks? Perhaps related, how can the claims of some theorists – that new forms of organization allow an abandonment of modernist 'short-termism' – be squared with simultaneous emphases upon change, flux, innovation, uncertainty, responsiveness to market and technological changes, and so on?

To the extent that elements of new forms might be emerging, or be approximated by organizations, then the contradictions that these promote in practice must be raised and highlighted. Critical questions emerge. The answers will be assessed and indeed fought out concretely and cannot be predetermined, even if balances of forces point to particular forms of resolution. Thus it is possible to capitalize on possible contradictions within the corporation (Pearce 1992), and indeed within representations of it. This 'capitalizing' can be done in academic work and in practical political terms. The exposing of contradiction, and the opening up of alternative and more progressive paths out of it, seem to me to represent important tasks, not least for those seeking to minimize the incidence and effects of corporate crime.

Second, emergence of new organizational forms also requires that current debates about 'appropriate' regulatory strategies continue and, indeed, broaden. If corporations continue to represent themselves as unitary, rational actors, then as they increasingly fail to act as such, they increase the legitimacy of more interventionist regulation. If, however, they are diverging significantly from the ideal-typical bureaucratic form, then this shift surely necessitates new development both of flexible and local forms of regulation/regulatory structures and further consideration of a range of juridical responses to corporate crimes. We need to shift from instinctive equating of 'organization' with a bureaucratic machine and, thereby, to recognize the diversity of organizational and corporate forms, if we are to understand, and thereby effectively control, corporate crime.

Third, and related, as arguments about new forms of organization illustrate the diversity of forms that capitalist corporations can take, these forms may be more or less democratic, and more or less likely to produce and obscure crime. Moreover, these forms are not predetermined, and they are certainly not exhausted by the bureaucratic organization (Burrell 1988; Power 1990). This simple point is a necessary antidote to pessimism and political passivity. Moreover, new organizational forms offer possibilities of new types of social, political, and economic relations. Reformulation and problematization of existing realities (Gergen 1992, 208) are essential elements in any revival of the search for non-reformist reforms, which prefigure a (modernist), pluralist, and socialist order.

NOTE

1 Thanks to Frank Pearce, for comments on an earlier version of this chapter, and more generally to participants at the Queen's University conference 'Corporate Crime: Ethics, Law and the State.'

8

Management, Morality, and Law: Organizational Forms and Ethical Deliberations

PETER CLEARY YEAGER

To this time,[1] most research on corporate wrongdoing has taken one or another of three forms: statistical examinations of the financial and structural correlates of offending as determined in the public record (e.g., Clinard et al. 1979; Clinard and Yeager 1980; Simpson 1986, 1987; Baucus and Near 1991); case studies of specific illegal events based largely on public records, investigative journalism, and interviewing (e.g., Geis 1967; Sonnenfeld and Lawrence 1978; Mokhiber 1988); and numerous surveys of business executives' and managers' attitudes and behaviours in respect of ethics and law (e.g., Baumhart 1961; Silk and Vogel 1976; Brenner and Molander 1977; Zey-Ferrell, Weaver, and Ferrell 1979; Zey-Ferrell and Ferrell 1982; Clinard 1983).[2] While these valuable studies have produced tentative conclusions regarding the roles of organizational culture and structure in the production of business deviance and conformity, we have neither adequately developed nor tested these arguments through fieldwork in the settings they purport to describe.[3]

One useful way to extend criminological research and paradigms therefore is to inspect the ways in which rules of morality – and of law – are socially constructed and enacted in corporate organizations. In much of the research to date, and reaching all the way back to Sutherland's (1949) foundational work, there has been an assumption that companies may maintain a law-abiding (therefore moral) ethos, a rational/calculating approach to compliance (amoral), or even an aggressively antiregulation culture (immoral). But surely views of morality (and of law) may vary considerably within complex organizations and may even be systematically structured. Indeed, morality and moral theory are themselves complexly variegated, so it would be surprising if organizational morality were not.

Of course, self-interest surely affects the use of self-justifying techniques of neutralization for deviant behaviour (Sykes and Matza 1957; Matza, 1964). But even these means should not be written off merely as hollow, post-hoc rationalizations. Instead, social constructionism directs our attention to the ways in which social organization and human interaction differentially structure the availability and viability of alternative moral reasonings.[4] My thesis here is that such an approach affords a more penetrating view of organizational deviance (including crime) and control than do approaches that assume either the moral clarity of law or law's utter corruption.

Moreover, this interpretive approach permits us to avoid the analytic weaknesses of the anthropomorphic view of the corporation as actor and of an 'over-socialized conception' of behaviour (Wong 1961). For the study of organizational offending, dynamic creation and recreation of 'moral worlds' can help explain variation in managerial behaviour relative to legal constraints. Such understanding also corrects errors associated with radical individualism, according to which managers and executives are held principally accountable for organizational crimes, quite apart from the potential effects of their social context (cf. Cressey 1988).

Analytically, both organizations and personalities are 'black boxes' into which too much explanation is packed at our peril. We can do better, I think, in unravelling the complex moral worlds in which managers negotiate the moral distinctions that commonly cross-cut the requirements of formal, written law. To borrow from Jerome Miller's (1988) discussion of parallel problems in theorizing about 'common' crime, doing otherwise may leave our theories 'filled with *fabricated aliens* made more so by those who should know better.' Ross's (1907) notion of business lawbreakers as 'criminaloids' will simply not do.[5]

In what follows, I first discuss elements of a moral conception of the corporation. Second, I present some initial evidence from our recent study of managers' perceptions and handling of moral questions in their routine responsibilities. Third, I discuss some implications of this work for social control.

A MORAL CONCEPTION OF THE CORPORATION

Moral Concerns and Two Views of the Firm

In general terms, morality involves considerations of right and wrong in behaviour affecting others. The two principal logics in such considerations often compete with each other in moral decision-making. Consequentialist reasoning is outcome-centred, requiring that actions be directed at achieving the best results overall for those affected by them. Utilitarianism is the most familiar variant in Western cultures. Utilitarian arguments are used to justify many government policies – for example, those supporting market economies on the supposition of their more efficient production of wealth (as compared to socialized economies).

In contrast, deontological arguments are action-centred and involve constraints on the means used to achieve even socially beneficent outcomes. These constraints are lodged in conceptions of individuals' rights – for example, regarding the scope of liberty and maintenance of integrity – and they resist even well-intentioned policies that threaten to compromise them (e.g., as in cases of paternalism and deception). One notable formulation is Kant's injunction that individuals are never to be used as means only, but are to be treated as moral ends in themselves. For example, child-labour laws restrict commercial exploitation of children regardless of their potential contribution to market efficiency.

In sum, the tension between these two views in moral theory is that between the concepts of right and of the good. This dichotomy corresponds closely to the tension in social theory between individual and society.[6] If anything, such moral tension is only exacerbated in the realities of practical ethics, particularly in the complex institutions of modern states and economies. Decision-making in both the public and private sectors commonly exhibits (fundamentally moral) conflict over the means and ends of action and passionate disputes about the proper moral relation between them. To approach the relevant dynamics in the corporate sector, it is helpful to distinguish between business organizations as moral agents and as moral environments (Goodpaster 1989).

In the anthropomorphic corporation-as-agent view, we attend to the effects of corporate outputs on various groups: consumers, communities, the environment, the market itself (e.g., with respect to competition). Here we distinguish between companies' socially valued production (jobs, products, wealth) and the costs that production imposes on society's members, and we ask to what extent the ends may justify the means, and under what conditions. Consider, for example, the case of plant closings. When a company decides to close a plant that provides a major share of the employment in a community, we are likely to have one view of the matter when the firm's economic survival (and the remainder of its employment) is clearly at stake,[7] and quite another when the closing is motivated simply by the desire to maximize near-term (as against long-term) financial results. In sum, the view of the firm as agent tends to be a broadly consequentialist one, concerned with the effects of policies and strategies, although deontological constraints will operate as checks on means, especially in connection with the rights of affected parties.

In the view of the corporation as a moral environment, we raise a different – though not unrelated – set of questions. Here we are interested in how companies treat their employees as human beings and how their hierarchies might shape employees' moral character, or moral vision. As instruments of production, corporate bureaucracies are inherently ends-oriented and emphasize efficiency. In the absence of any other moral and/or legal constraints, they would respect workers' rights and dignity only to the extent that such respect served their own means and ends and would seek to restrict (if not eliminate) consideration of ordinary morality in employees' decision-making. Such consideration would be seen as a source of harmful inefficiency, while restrictions on it would be justified by reference to the social goods produced by the corporate pursuit of profit and wealth in a market economy (cf. Friedman 1962).

It is in the theory of the firm as moral environment that I am principally interested, although the connection between the two views should be clear. The literature on corporate deviance and ethics has, at least implicitly, taken up both of them in various respects. It contains a differentiated perspective on the moral climates said to characterize firms, with some embracing not only legal requirements but also broader notions of social responsibility, while others appear to cultivate an amoral, calculating approach to such social limits (e.g., Sutherland 1949; Clinard and Yeager 1980). A (not incompatible) unified view posits that business hierarchies impart a characteristic moral stance to their managers, which typically minimizes many private moral concerns in the service of organizational ends (see, for example, Jackall 1988).[8]

The perspective I wish to suggest here entwines these notions of differentiated and unifed morality in large corporations. That is, I argue that what is characteristic of the environments of all such firms is a complexly differentiated set of moral concerns, which vary according to managers' responsibilities. I briefly sketch an argument for this next and then examine it with evidence on corporate managers' own accounts of their moral experience at work.

Bureaucracy and Morality

Bureaucracies do, of course, shape their participants' moral lives, in ways characteristic both of bureaucratic forms and relations generally and of their institutional settings, whether in the public or private sector. The very strengths of rational hierarchy – efficient pursuit of goals through specialization in a complex division of labour, impartiality, and universalism (e.g., in respect of meritocratic processes) – virtually assure conflicts between the obligations of managers[9] and at least some requirements of common or ordinary morality (e.g., Kant's injunction, partiality claims between friends, and so on). In the business context, for example, the 'implicit morality of the market' may conflict with such common moral requirements as the principles of mutual aid and non-maleficence, as in cases of firing unproductive employees and plant closings

(McMahon 1981, 261–2). Negation of such requirements is typically justified by reference to pursuit of the organization's socially legitimated goals. Moreover, in their very design, specialized role responsibilities in the division of labour narrow the range of appropriate considerations in decision-making. This feature of bureaucracy tends to reduce the reach (if not always the salience) of common moral principles for incumbents and, as I argue below, to segment their application as well.

It is important not to overstate the degree of conflict between common and corporate moralities. On the contrary, aspects of conventional morality are normatively required by the very nature of free-market enterprise. The requirement of telling the truth, for instance, is necessary to the free flow of information on which efficient markets depend. In addition, some consideration of the rights and interests of others is imperative if productive exchange is to occur, particularly over the long term. Thus the requirements of fair dealing with suppliers, customers, and subordinates are lodged not only in common morality but also in commerce's functional dependence on trust, loyalty, morale, and productivity.[10] Indeed, alongside the formal emphases on bureaucratic impartiality and competition in the free enterprise systems, there exists a nexus of informal relations of trust and cordiality linking managers within and between companies.[11]

But if such moral concerns and informal relations implicitly suffuse corporate hierarchies, it is plausible to suggest that a division of moral labour[12] exists in managerial ranks, according to which managers emphasize different sets of moral considerations, depending on their responsibilities. In many firms, some moral and legal requirements are placed rather uniformly on all managers, as in the case of institutionalized procedures to safeguard employees' rights in such areas as workplace safety (e.g., right-to-know laws) and civil rights (systems of disciplinary appeals, sexual-harassment and anti-discrimination procedures). But the types and weights of (potentially) competing moral demands will also vary with the hierarchical and functional divisions of labour of firms in specific industries.

To take only the simplest general case, top executives will generally concentrate on outcome-centred, utilitarian considerations for the firm as a whole; in the language of business policy, their purview is strategy and tactics. Middle and lower-level managers, however, place increasing (not to say decisive) emphasis on action-centred morality, as policies and procedures come to bear on individuals. This focus is a natural consequence of the facts of social psychology: because we tend to treat as most morally significant those individuals with whom we have sustained contact (and on whom we most concretely depend), managers overseeing the work of subordinates and relations with customers (as an example) are more likely to feel the moral weight of the rights and needs of subordinates and customers. And as I note above, such factors are also functional for the enterprise. Coercion and unfairness do not develop productive, loyal employees; short-dealing and other deceptions will not secure stable markets.

If this description of the normative requirements of corporate hierarchies is reasonable, two conclusions follow. First, moral dimensions are of the essence in managerial work. Far from being tangential, they are typically part of the core matter that all managers manage. Second, as in moral argument generally, there is great potential for ethical conflict in companies. It is likely to be commonplace, either in overt or (more likely) covert forms, and to engage legal as well as other moral rules. At times, the requirements of law may confront (arguably) other moral considerations, and managers will justify resolution of such conflicts in moral terms. In addition, managers' views of law's morality may vary as well – whether by the viewer's position, company, or industry, or by the regulation at issue. Any such negative views require analytic inspection, not only of the place of their holders but also of law itself. They may not simply be written off as immoral.

In the remainder of this chapter, I present some empirical support for these hypotheses, focusing first on a fieldwork study of ethical dilemmas that illustrates their operation and resolution, and then considering some issues in law that bear on these conflicts.

DECISIONS AND REASONS: AN EMPIRICAL STUDY

Issues and Methods

The motivating purpose of this research was to develop an understanding of the organizational forces and constraints that may routinely – but differentially – shape how corporate executives and managers act in situations that pose ethical dilemmas. We wished to explore the ways in which the structures and (sub)cultures of specific organizations affect managers' action on the ethical dimension, including the domain of law (Kram, Yeager, and Reed 1989).

This interest implied two key criteria in sampling design. First, it would be necessary systematically to sample and interview managers in crucial functional areas (e.g., finance, operations, and marketing) and at all levels of responsibility, from the chief executive office (CEO) down to first-line managers. Only such a strategy would permit careful assessment of the ethical dimension from multiple, important angles of vision within the same firm. Second, we would need to compare and contrast results from different corporate settings. A comparative case study would allow us to develop hypotheses regarding the influence of industry and organizational features on managers' behaviour. Taken together, these approaches would allow us to determine whether there were systematic differences by managerial position in the perception and handling of ethical conflicts, and which features of organizational design, environment, and culture appeared to account for the variation.

To implement this design, we chose our research sites from banking and high technology. These sectors are both central to future economic health in the United States, and during the 1980s both were experiencing substantial uncertainy, or 'turbulence,' in their markets – a condition that often highlights the regularly recurring ethical tensions in corporate management (cf. Staw and Szwajkowski 1975; Clinard and Yeager 1980). In banking, government deregulation opened up new markets and forms of competition, while financial hardships had resulted from failed loans (e.g., to Third World countries). In high technology, increasing foreign competition had taken the steam out of the high-growth period of the 1970s, and many companies recently had faced their first layoffs, including our sampled firm.

We gained access to companies in each industry: a multinational, high-technology firm with annual sales of several hundred million dollars, and a large regional bank with assets of several billion dollars.[13] We refer to the companies pseudonymously as Jaycor, Inc., and Williams National Bank. We interviewed selected managers at a number of other firms as well.

In both of our principal sites, our research teams conducted intensive, semi-structured interviews with executives and managers in major functional areas, from the CEO and top management down through first-line managers. We interviewed twenty-five individuals at Jaycor, and forty-six at Williams.

Each interview covered identical terrain and on average took three-and-a-half hours over two sittings. To build rapport prior to raising sensitive questions regarding the respondent's own moral dilemmas (and the company's role in them), the first interview began with a series of questions on the individual's work history and perceptions of the corporate culture and practices (e.g., reward systems, corporate values). Then the interview moved to detailed consideration of a difficult decision the executive or manager had recently made or implemented, in which (in his or her view) the right thing to do was not clear, not easily implemented, or contradicted by some (other) company directive or policy. Here we were concerned with the features of the situation that made it difficult and with the manager's perceptions and behaviour in resolving the matter (e.g., whom she consulted in making the decision).

The second interview began with detailed examination of a second difficult situation in the individual's recent experience and then explored the extent to which three 'typical' (to the industry) scenarios of ethical dilemmas represented matters of concern either to the respondent or to others in the organization. Finally, we asked a series of questions about the individual's personal background and influences that shaped her own values.

Dilemmas and Their Sources

Our respondents reported a variety of dilemmas involving conflicts between standard corporate purposes and relationships with employees, customers, superiors, suppliers, other groups, and the law. For example, included were questions of whether to lay off employees or invest in retraining, whether to exceed minimum safety standards in a work station, whether to insist on or to short-cut product quality standards, and whether to mislead consumers about the value of products.[14]

From our initial evidence,[15] the managers' experience of such dilemmas derives largely from two common features of corporate bureaucracies. First, the ranks of hierarchy tend systematically to segment moral views, according to responsibilites and experiences of incumbents at different levels of authority. Corporations implicitly house a division of moral labour according to which managers at different ranks are inclined to perceive dilemmas from differing moral angles. For example, many managers described conflicts between some vital business objective and concerns for the welfare of employees harmed by policies designed to achieve such objectives. But while top-level managers generally framed these decisions in terms of utilitarian concerns for the organization's ends, middle- and lower-level managers – asked to implement such policies as layoffs and increased workloads – typically experienced them as hurtful to individuals' ends, implicitly registering deontological concerns with human rights and dignity.

Second, there is conflict between competing policy objectives of the business. As promulgated by corporations' leaders and described in formal documents, these guiding values, policies, and goals appear to be both internally consistent and rationally related to the companies' legitimate purposes. But under the complex requirements of management in large organizations, managers often experience them as dictating contradictory choices, and ones often ethically (if not always legally) suspect. For example, at least some branch managers saw the bank's recent emphasis on entrepreneurial creativity and salesmanship (in the context of deregulated markets) as competing with the more traditional banking value on the provision of professional advisory services to clients. In this case, pressures to multiply investment products and increase sales through aggressive marketing may sacrifice customers' best financial interests to the bank's bottom line. This happens, for example, when bankers present customers with confusing arrays of new financial products without adequate information for judging their relative value and perhaps pressure them to purchase those most profitable to the bank but not necessarily of greatest value to the customer.

Not only was this tension between basic policy values denied by top executives,[16] but it was felt differently by bankers at various levels of responsibility. Middle managers more often construed the dilemma in terms of their conceptions of what it means to be a professional banker. The notion of 'professional banker' often remained implicit in the interviews but was revealed in such complaining comments as, 'We're not car salesmen,' and 'We're not insurance salesmen.' (This result suggests a third source of ethical dilemmas in business: potential conflict between the financial goals of the enterprise and norms of conduct in the professions with which at least some managers identify. I revisit this matter below.)

In contrast, lower-level, branch managers – those in direct contact with depositors and borrowers – responded with more expressive concern for their customers. They were more likely to complain that increased corporate pressure to 'sell them,' combined with more stringent cost controls (which, for instance, limit the time spent informing customers of options), forced them to abuse customers' trust. In sum, the respondents commonly expressed concern for customers as ends in themselves, doubtlessly having to do with their relatively close association with them. They also often complained that these corporate pressures violated their self-conceptions as professional bankers.

Excluding the Ethical

The existence of such differential perceptions already suggests that communication about ethical matters is limited in typical corporate bureaucracies, a finding also commonly made in case studies of corporate lawbreaking (e.g., Vandivier 1972; Stone 1975). But our comparative case study further suggests that such barriers to ethical communication may also operate in non-obvious ways.

In both companies, interview data strongly indicate that ethical issues as such are sublimated, both organizationally and personally. In brief, managers commonly indicated that ethical dilemmas were both not publicly discussible as matters of implicit corporate policy and privately inadmissible as matters of personal morality. Naturally, these two dynamics only mutually reinforce each other.

The non-discussibility of moral dilemmas may result from tensions between a firm's goals and its policies, as illustrated above, even when management sincerely endorses such discussion in the abstract. Of course, many top managements apparently do not, further chilling communication. But non-discussibility may also derive from other, otherwise laudable values in the corporate culture. In particular, the value placed on managerial responsibility and autonomy may prevent subordinates' communication with superiors when faced with difficult and unexpected ethical problems. In short, managers are typically evaluated and rewarded on their ability to manage problems and uncertainties without constant advice from superiors; consequently, they are more likely to consult peers than to communicate difficulties to their bosses, as indicated by one branch manager at the bank:

Ninety percent of the time if I've got a loan decision I'm not sure of, or an operations problem, instead of going to my boss I go to a branch manager and they do the same. I get calls a lot, especially from less experienced managers. There's an unwritten network out there that's used all the time. Usually you get good advice and it doesn't make you look stupid to your boss. If you call him up all the time saying, 'What do I do here?' or 'I'm not sure what to do here,' they say they are open but after a while they're gonna say, 'Geez, can't that guy make a decision out there?'

To the extent that ethically challenging situations are so screened, the ethical quality of decisions will reflect the values of managers' 'local' subcultures or 'unwritten networks.' Moreover, the non-discussibility of ethical conflicts only reinforces the general priority of utilitarian justifications regarding profit-making goals over other moral (and often legal) considerations.

Both firms have this pattern of communication, even as companies with markedly different organizational forms. The bank represents the traditional authoritarian bureaucracy, with power and basic decision-making concentrated in upper management. In contrast, the managerial hierarchy at the high-technology firm is relatively flat, and top managers stress the core values of decentralization, autonomy, and open communication. One might reasonably assume that communication barriers would be more impenetrable in the bank. But our interviews suggest that Jaycor's managers may be even less likely to discuss ethical problems with their direct superiors than are Williams National's. The value placed on decentralized management emphasizes lower-level managers' ability to solve on their own the problems that they regularly face. Indeed, this ability is taken as a measure of managerial talent. While this finding and conclusion remain preliminary,[17] the putative communication advantages of flat hierarchies may be counteracted by cultural messages, regarding individuals' autonomy, responsibility, and achievement and corporate efficiency and flexibility.

Arguably, the 'inappropriateness' of publicly discussing ethical issues encourages managers to deny the moral implications of their decisions. This inadmissibility is underscored by the specific interpretive work that managers often do when faced with ethical dilemmas. Our interviews suggested this process in a number of ways. For example, when asked if they had ever felt pressure to compromise their own values in order to meet the company's expectations, 65 per cent of respondents answered 'no.' However, when they were later asked to describe difficult decisions they had faced, most managers readily identified and reflected on situations involving a range of ethical dilemmas. But rather than use the language of morality, especially when the implications of their decisions and roles were personally troubling, managers instead commonly defined problems in terms of 'judgment calls,' 'strategic decisions,' and as matters involving 'professional norms.'

This last construction was involved when managers appeared to deflect the more straightforward moral meaning of problems in their work. Rather than expressing the dilemmas as conflicts between the requirements of ordinary morality (including legal compliance) and business values, for example, individuals often construed them as pitting their professional values against organizational requirements – an attitude seen above in bankers' concerns regarding relations with customers. A similar response occurs when engineering managers encountered conflicts between achieving assurable product quality and ensuring efficiency and on-time product delivery. When quality was risked to meet deadlines, they often appear to construe the matter as involving not honest and fair treatment of customers but their professional engineering values.[18]

One middle manager falsified the profits of his unit by large amounts under pressure from his superior, in a manner that violated standard accounting procedures and federal law (i.e., by manipulating several accounts). This individual had earlier asserted that he had never felt pressure to compromise his personal values in his work with the company. But this situation clearly gave him pause as he described it later in the interview: '[What I was asked to do] was wrong ... [I thought it was] unethical, if you will. I had to compromise my financial ethics.'

This manager clearly saw the action as wrong – and did vigorously resist it at first – but placed his struggle in terms of professional norms. Indeed, he appeared to wrestle with the concept of the ethical in his attempt to ward off the personal moral implications of the situation. Thus, while financial ethics are consequential and their breach is problematic to this individual, basic badness had nothing to do with it. This interpretation was perhaps more pronounced in his assessment of his superior's role in making the decision:

What he did was not unethical. It just ... um ... well, he knew exactly what he was doing. It's not that he did it out of ignorance or anything. What he did was not unethical. What he did was he made the best of a bad situation without having to sacrifice the company's progress. If we wouldn't have gotten the [profits increased this way], I don't know how we would have gotten the money. We might have had to cut back on some things we didn't want to sacrifice, like our marketing budget, or on people. You know, I mean the alternatives to [the decision] were probably a lot uglier.

Repetition of the assertion that 'it was not unethical' indicates a strong need to deny one implication of a deed clearly wrong in the face of law and professional norms. 'Badness' here is diluted not only by the self-distancing notion that 'only' professional standards are at stake but by his assertion that his colleague's action served higher organizational purposes – even moral ones (e.g., saving people's jobs) – in the context of real market pressures. One perspective interprets this as little more than after-the-fact rationalization by someone who should have shown more moral courage. But another sees that the situation is more complex. True, it involves illegitimate extension of the logic of moral justification from reasonable contexts of real dilemmas to what is essentially a pseudo-conflict. But the extension is facilitated not only by the existence of such logic and real conflicts but also by the difficulties entailed in separating true dilemmas[19] from their imitators (not all so pale) and heightened by (while also contributing to) the failure publicly to deliberate moral questions in organizational settings.

MANAGEMENT, MORALITY, AND LAW

If this interpretation is sensible, it suggests that even well-intentioned companies commonly fail to meet moral – and often legal – requirements in organizing productive activity. The reasons range from inadequate attention and foresight regarding ethical traps, to the deep complexities of morality itself, particularly as exhibited in the form of applied ethics in corporations.

But the failure of moral and legal constraints is also rooted in the nature of rational bureaucracy, whose operations are oriented to efficiency and ends rather than to the moral nuances of means and therefore value some (essentially moral) views over others. If, as I argue above, there is a division of moral labour in corporate organizations, not all moral views have equal weight therein. Authority relations in hierarchies and the cultural strength of utilitarian justifications for the primacy of profit-making in capitalist political economies mean that the corporation's goals and purposes (the purview of top management) tend often to override other moral considerations (e.g., as held and experienced by lower-level managers). The combination of power relations and segmented moral experiences not only emphasizes some views but too often silences other considerations.

A parallel result in legal regulation of business also rests on the rationality of bureaucratic forms. In the implementation of such law, there is commonly a basic shift in moral emphasis: from the normative, often passionately held values that motivated the legislation to a 'demoralized' focus on technical problems and solutions.[20] Part of the historical rationalization of social relations, this is Weber's 'disenchantment' of law, displacement from legal process of substantive (or moral) criteria and their replacement by 'rational' calculations of means and ends (cf. Ewing 1987).[21]

This is the case, for example, in environmental regulation, in which implementation and enforcement of law commonly give way to deliberations between governmental and corporate experts over such matters as the costs and benefits of various degrees of pollution control and levels of compliance. Here industry's technical input on such issues as technologies and feasibility takes precedence. Typically excluded are the citizens' and public-interest voices most likely to urge the broader ethical bases of regulation (such as environmental imperatives), but which often lack the money and information needed to participate in complex bureaucratic decision-making. The consequence is regulatory results well short of the law's intended (and arguably feasible) reach, as with U.S. environmental regulation (see, for example, Yeager 1991, 1993).

There is also a more subtle consequence. The process reinforces business's perception that much regulatory law itself is (at best) morally neutral or ambivalent, which in turn strengthens the limited, utilitarian moral calculus that emphasizes the 'moral' imperative of capital accumulation over other considerations.

Another difficulty obtains when regulated parties can construe law as capricious, unfair, or unsensible. This occurs when regulation is unevenly applied, whether across firms or over time. When it does, executives and managers will conclude that the law has little or no moral force.

In U.S. environmental law, for instance, regulation often falls more heavily on smaller companies, which find compliance relatively more expensive and often do not possess the resources to appeal for leniency (an avenue more commonly travelled by their larger competitors) (Yeager 1987, 1991; cf. Hawkins 1983, 1984; Lynxwiler, Shover, and Clelland 1983; Shover, Clelland, and Lynxwiler 1986). In addition, while business generally requires stable, predictable, and evenly applied regulatory constraints for its strategic planning, powerful interests within it often act to destabilize or disorganize regulation, as when large corporations or industry trade associations use court or administrative challenges to forestall controls or gain special considerations ('unevening' the playing field) (Yeager 1991).

One example of this latter process involves corporate pressure that had 'disorganized' regulation under the U.S. Clean Water Act, which result was then used in business arguments for relaxed controls. In testimony before Congress, a steel industry executive argued for delayed compliance dates as the Congress considered amendments to the law in 1977. In his words:

With the sums of money [for compliance] that are at stake here, I think that the people who assume the responsibility for the spending of that money have to have the assurance that the regulations are in fact going to fall uniformly, throughout the industry on a competitive basis, and that they're not – that an individual company is not, in fact, going to invest major funds in compliance with a rule that hasn't been tested, and subsequently be disadvantaged if that's litigated and overturned. I think that's a very real competitive problem.

But he also engaged in this exchange with Representative Harsha:

Harsha: Mr. Graham, in all honesty, one of the problems created – or creating this area of no-return, so to speak, and the failure of the Environmental Protection Agency to promulgate the necessary rules and standards so that you know where you are, is the fact that you've been fighting the proposed rules and regulations all along, isn't that true?
Graham: I think there is clearly an element of that present. (U.S. House of Representatives 1977, 324)

Whatever else its consequences, operation of this systemic contradiction can only weaken law's moral authority among regulated businesses.

Shifting political winds can also change enforcement policy, which may ultimately discredit law among business persons. One example that surfaced in our research involves the federal Bank Secrecy Act, a dead-letter law in the 1970s which the Reagan administration dusted off in the mid-1980s for some aggressive enforcement of its drug-control policies. The law requires banks to report to the federal government all cash transactions in excess of $10,000, and the administration saw it as a tool in the effort to prevent 'laundering' of drug proceeds through the banking system. During the 1980s, there were a number of high-profile prosecutions of major banks for failing to make the required reports, and the sense generated in media accounts was that the convicted banks had been hugely irresponsible and even immoral in failing to comply.

But our interviews with bankers uncovered a different perception. According to this view, until the crackdown in the mid-1980s the federal government had made little effort to communicate its expectations and standards for properly accounting cash transactions. Thus the rush of prosecutions seemed completely unexpected, unwarranted, and unfair, and many bankers appear to have taken a cynical view of the policy as a result. For example, one respondent, a senior banking official, argued that the law was not only unfair but probably ineffective, as money launderers would only find more creative ways to manage their cash (a result apparently realized by 1990, as overseas transactions replaced domestic ones). In his view, the public policy benefits hardly justified the corporate costs of compliance: 'I think we've spent a lot of money on [compliance], and I don't think it was all necessary. I think we could have afforded to take a risk of not complying to the letter of the law in some senses.' He took this position after his own bank had been fined for violations of the law.

In sum, a number of systemic and political processes marginalize the ethical content of much regulatory law.[22] But moral and legal constraints that are 'disprivileged' in the corporate context are not always eclipsed. We found lower-level officials resisting pressures from above and saving loyal employees scheduled for firing or insisting that product quality not be sacrificed to sales and profits. The problem for public policy is how to ensure that the moral impulses behind regulatory law are not only clear to corporate managers but are also given weight and voice in deliberations over ethical/legal conflicts that regularly recur within their bureaucracies.

Our respondents' references to professional ethics may offer a promising lever for the improved social control of business. In both companies, managers noted that corporate pressures towards wrongdoing often contradicted not their personal moral views but their professional identities and ethos. Some managers appear to have fought these pressures, sometimes successfully (as in quality control), on the basis of their professional ethics. This countervailing normative framework can perhaps be more safely expressed in internal corporate debates than can 'personally' held norms such as honesty and fairness. Professional standards are publicly available and legitimate frameworks for resisting and making discussible at least some pressures towards improper business behaviour. Leveraging these standards may go considerably farther than the more common establishment of formal codes of ethics, which research suggests better serves public relations than the public interest.

Indeed, these are not new conclusions; they are merely submerged in most considerations of corporate crime and control. But they were established decades ago – for example, in Richard Quinney's (1963) findings regarding the differential tendencies of professionally versus business oriented pharmacists to violate prescription laws.

Even more impressive, they were identified by Emile Durkheim, who clearly outlined the matter (see, for instance, Durkheim 1958). In his pre-eminent concern for the analysis and securing of social integration, he argued that development of modern industrial economic relations threatened to bring about social disintegration because classical (now, neoclassical) market doctrine emphasizes the 'utilitarian notion that social order is the product of each person acting *only* in his or her own interests, [thereby undermining] the whole idea of morality' (Hall 1982, 54), which idea made sense to Durkheim only when conjoined with notions of the collective good and social cohesion.[23] Furthermore, such market 'morality' was becoming dominant, displacing the morally integrating values of family, church, and even state.

As a result, he prescribed an increasingly important role for professional associations and their promise of a strengthened moral stance or collective conscience. Drawing on the examples of the ancient and medieval guilds, he noted their fundamentally moral nature and argued that professional groups both better realize fundamental human needs for association and shared meaning than does classical market utilitarianism and promise a stronger base for societal integration than does the market's radical individualism.[24]

CONCLUSIONS

In this chapter, I posit that corporate behaviour – and regulatory law – share a capitalist political economy's cultural emphases on rationality and bureaucratic organization in ways fateful for control of harmful business behaviour. Here I briefly summarize some conclusions on social control of corporate business.

One conventional response that many companies have made to the perception of an 'ethical crisis' in business is promulgation of codes of conduct. A large body of empirical work, now including our own,[25] has demonstrated that by themselves such codes are entirely insufficient for meaningful reform of corporate ethics and legal compliance. What is necessary is that ethical considerations be made the focus of a routine process of inquiry in which managers discuss with each other alternative choices.

A significant step in this direction is to identify ways in which managers' professional identities – hence their moral voices – may be strengthened. And here law may help. It does so, for example, when it incorporates professional standards in its rules (as in accounting regulation); it may also seek to recognize and promote new associations of managers, as in the licensing of specialists in marketing, sales, advertising, environmental and worker safety, and so on. But law may also more directly shape internal corporate communication, as when it requires dissemination of certain forms of information (e.g., through right-to-know laws on toxic materials). Some time ago, Christopher Stone (1975) made a sophisticated and detailed proposal for enlarging the role of law in this respect: legislating a set of organizational positions and internal and external reporting requirements covering a wide range of legal and ethical concerns. The proposal remains as important and relevant today as it was then, but it is still largely unimplemented in law because – one assumes – of corporate resistance to greater government 'intrusion' into corporate affairs. Such resistance may be overcome only to the extent that scandals continue to eviscerate the legitimacy of corporate business and/or the state.

Not only must political resistance to such legal intervention be eventually overcome, but public policy must also address the tendency for the ethical content of law to be marginalized in corporate cultures and decision-making.

Such considerations lead to an obvious if often overlooked conclusion. While legal constraint is necessary to ensure adequate consideration of the full moral requirements of corporate enterprise, it will undercut its mission if it is either fanciful (as much regulatory law was made to appear during the deregulatory thrust of the Reagan administration) or 'loaded' in favour of more organized and resource-rich interests. It need not always and immediately correspond to the corporate view of reasonable, nor should it. But it must be clear, consistent, and competent in establishing social constraints. Good public policy, like good corporate policy, must be based on wide, democratic deliberation on moral values rather than on narrowly construed technical matters or political exigency.[26] Good law will seek to reinforce crucial social values and thereby support good management, while bad law undermines these, ensuring the lowest common denominator in business ethics and corporations' social responsibility.

NOTES

1 I wish to acknowledge gratefully the contributions of my wife, colleague, and co-principal investigator in this work, Kathy E. Kram, and of our research associates: Maria-Paz Avery, Wendy Handler, James Hunt, Kathleen Jordan, Jeanne Liedtka, and Gary E. Reed. I am also grateful for the financial support of the Amsterdam Foundation and the Human Resources Policy Institute at Boston University's School of Management, without which this research would not have been possible. Finally, I owe a debt to Harvard University's Program in Ethics and the Professions for a fellowship year that permitted me to pursue more deeply the questions of organizational morality.

2 There have also been recent empirical contributions on the question of deterring corporate crime. See, for example, Braithwaite and Makkai (1991) and Simpson and Koper (1992).

3 Jackall's (1988) recent work has made a nice contribution in this regard. In addition, Fisse and Braithwaite (1983) and Braithwaite (1984) have interviewed top officials

in some U.S. corporations about business lawbreaking and social control, while Clinard (1983) interviewed retired middle managers about ethics and law. Researchers in schools of management have had more success in mounting fieldwork in corporate settings, presumably being more willing than most sociologists to contract with managers and organizations for research work of mutual benefit (i.e., for both scholarly and applied purposes). Such researchers have investigated sensitive topics, such as race relations (e.g., Alderfer and Tucker 1980; Thomas 1990), organizational conflict (e.g., Alderfer and Smith 1982; Brown 1981), and more recently business ethics (e.g., Toffler 1986; Derry 1987; Waters and Bird 1987).

However, most studies of business ethics have been conducted with samples of 'disconnected' managers from different organizations, or with a quite limited subset of managers (e.g., lower-level personnel), limiting researchers' ability to assess corporate cultures and subcultures from the range of potential viewpoints inside firms.

4 The lineage of this approach reaches back at least to the early Chicago School tradition of ethnographic research, which urged an 'appreciation' of deviance from the standpoints of those said to engage in wrongful behaviour. One conclusion was that deviants' needs, motivations, and aspirations were not so wildly different from 'our' own.

5 In this chapter, my normative stance is in the 'middle ground.' While I assume that what is done in pursuit of business goals too often constitutes moral offences of greater or lesser gravity, I bracket the larger question of the morality of our political-economic system as a whole, a question beyond the scope of this chapter. But on the morality of systems of competitive market exchange, see, for example, Sen (1985) and Buchanan (1985).

Some philosophers (e.g., Sen) have concluded that capitalist markets are justified, but only weakly, by careful consideration of moral theory. This result parallels the judgments implicit in much of the sociological and sociolegal scholarship on corporate lawbreaking. This literature more often points to increased legal (less often, professional) controls on harmful business behaviour than to alternative forms of economic organization (e.g., socialism). See, for example, Braithwaite (1985a), Clinard and Yeager (1980), Coffee (1980, 1981), and C.D. Stone (1975).

6 For a useful philosophical discussion illuminating some of these ideas and tensions, in the context of an analysis of justice and a critique of liberalism, see Sandel (1982).

7 Recall the labour leader Samuel Gompers's notable judgment: 'The worst crime against the working people is a company which fails to make a profit.' Quoted in Goodpaster (1989, 94).

8 For example, Jackall writes that 'bureaucratic work causes people to bracket, while at work, the moralities that they might hold outside the workplace or that they might adhere to privately and to follow instead the prevailing morality of their particular situation' (1988, 6). In a similar vein, he later notes: 'Work – bureaucratic work in

particular – poses a series of intractable dilemmas that often demand compromises with traditional moral beliefs' (12).

9 I am restricting the analysis to the roles and experiences of corporate executives and managers, those formally identified as part of the managerial cadres and having responsibility for organizing the work of subordinates. Aspects of the analysis may be relevant as well to blue- and pink-collar workers, but I do not take up that possibility here.

10 Such rules are of course violated in companies. But the argument here suggests that rates of corporate offences (both moral and legal) may well vary according to the importance of the rules to business's central mission, with rates increasing the more removed the rules become from profit-oriented goals, for example. Just this sort of variation is suggested in Clinard et al.'s (1979) findings that large corporations more often appear to violate environmental, product-quality, and labour laws than they do financial and market regulations (e.g., anti-trust laws). The relative centrality of rules to market functioning also connects logically to evidence that the state tends to punish market-related offences more seriously than it does the so-called social regulations; witness, for example, the prosecutorial enthusiasm of the otherwise deregulation-minded Reagan administration for the 'white-collar' crimes of defence contractor fraud and insider trading in capital markets. Business may not always perceive or enact even these moral prerequisites for success, as when companies pursue short-term gains at the expense of longer-term stability and growth (as in the marketing of shoddy goods). At any rate, these various hypotheses are deserving of more explicit research.

11 The idea that informal social relations often have more to do with the functioning of organizations than do their formal systems is, of course, a commonplace in social science. One of the more interesting and counter-intuitive findings is Stewart Macaulay's (1963) that U.S. business rivals prefer to resolve disputes informally rather than legalistically through the courts, in constrast to the image of litigiousness and bare-knuckled competition in American society.

12 I have adapted this phrase from Nagel's (1979) analysis of an 'ethical division of labor' in the public sector. The extension to morality in private-sector management owes much to McMahon's (1981, 1989) earlier efforts.

13 To protect the anonymity of the companies, we are imprecise about the corporate financial figures. On the difficult issues in gaining access for such intrusive research, and how they were managed in this case, see Yeager and Kram (1990).

14 In presenting actual situations and managers' commentary on them below, some of the details of managers' accounts have been omitted to protect further sources' anonymity. In addition, at times I do not identify whether one of our two principal companies was the site, or whether the account was given by a manager from our small secondary sample (involving other firms). In all key respects, however, the presentations offered here are accurate.

15 Analysis of these data – almost three hundred hours of taped interviews – is ongoing.

16 Indeed, the only senior manager who commented on our finding that bank managers often felt pressed to push products on customers that might not be in the latter's best interests in fact rejected it. To him, it was simply not plausible, a result that itself supports some of our other findings regarding the essential obscurity of ethical considerations in organizations.

17 This argument awaits more intensive analysis of the large database using a qualitative data-management software package, Ethnograph.

18 For example, one engineer who reported sacrificing quality to tight, new-product deadlines spoke as follows: 'In most cases in our particular environment, we're given less time than what's necessary ... When you're given a situation when you know what it takes to do the particular job and you're only allowed half that time to do that, from the beginning of the project you feel under a lot of stress and pressure that, you know, "I'm not going to be able to do this right and do it successfully. I'm not utilizing my creativity and my individual professionalism to be able to develop or create a new concept or technique."'

19 Not only do real moral dilemmas exist in business, but their seeming intractability also arguably contributes to managers' sense that they are not discussible; in turn, the latter characteristic renders dilemmas less manageable. This was the case, for example, for a manager in one company who lamented a decision by superiors to hire many new employees for work that was expected to be of limited duration; the new employees had not been made aware of the expectation: 'What am I going to tell these people when it's over? It gives me a gnawing feeling. It's going to be our problem when it's over, but what can we do about it? There was never an opportunity to discuss our concerns constructively. We are doing what we can within the division to locate other opportunities [for those who would be laid off]. The expectation is that we'll find other business, but we won't, and corporate won't. I don't think anyone else is worried about it, so I won't. The conflict is between what the corporation is [saying], and what they're actually doing. I can't answer people's questions [regarding their employment futures] so I'm misleading them, and compromising my own integrity and credibility. But still I have to keep business running and get the job done.' Here, the subtlety and complexity of the moral tension simultaneously render its public deliberation both more necessary and less likely.

20 There is therefore also an 'ethical division of labour' in government (Nagel 1979), analogous to that in corporate business. For example, the legislature and units within the executive branch often concentrate on the utilitarian consequences of broad policies, while the courts have the responsibility for securing individuals' fundamental human rights. But this division of labour may shift with political-economic circumstances. For example, in some periods conservative federal courts may 'roll back' or otherwise limit such rights while social movements experience

greater success in arguing them in legislative fora. The 1990s in the United States may be such a period.

21 Compare, for example, Garland's (1990) fine account of the history of criminal punishment in the West.

22 I have illustrated the argument largely with my own research on U.S. environmental law, but it probably applies with equal force to a number of other areas of social regulation, including product-quality and occupational-safety law. It also applies to areas of financial or economic regulation, such as tax law (where arcane technical manipulations of the corporate tax code hold sway) and the case of the Bank Secrecy Act.

23 Consider this remark of Durkheim's (1958): 'It is said that for normal economic activity there is no need of regulation. But from what source could it derive such a privilege? How should this particular social function be exempt from a condition which is the most fundamental of any social structure? Clearly, if there has been self-delusion to this degree amongst the classical economists it is because the economic functions were studied as if they were an end in themselves, without considering what further reaction they might have on the whole social order' (quoted in R. Hall 1982, 55).

24 Cf. R. Hall's reading of Durkheim (1982, 57–8): 'An individual's involvement in his or her profession or occupation is as much a moral as it is an (economically) utilitarian activity. The purpose of business is not just to make a profit; it is to carry on economic activities as a collective enterprise, and people can and should derive as much pleasure and benefit from the collective enterprise as from the strictly economic function.'

25 I have not developed the evidence here, but our respondents routinely indicated the lack of force in their companies' codes of ethics (e.g., through their vague recall of their requirements).

26 For example, governments might give greater thought and priority to policies enabling (and subsidizing) the organization and competence of citizens' groups concerned with such matters as environmental, consumer, and employee protection. Citizen-suit provisions (such as that included in the Clean Water Act) and the historic expansion of the law of standing are examples of legal developments in this direction.

9

Loosely Coupled Systems and Unlawful Behaviour: Organization Theory and Corporate Crime

CARL KEANE

Over the past two decades, researchers have paid increasing attention to corporate crime and have proposed a number of explanations of corporate criminality. At the social-psychological level, they include theories such as differential association (Sutherland 1949) and variations of strain theory, formulated at both the individual and corporate levels (Clinard 1983; Simpson 1986; Keane 1993), while recently Coleman (1989) proposed a combination of conditions such as motivation, neutralization, and opportunity. Theories developed at the corporate or industry level include those focusing on corporate culture and structure (Vaughan 1983) and on market conditions and regulatory enforcement (Geis 1967). Other organizational-level theories have considered multiple criminogenic factors, such as organizational goals, structure, and environment (Kramer 1982) as well as a compilation of both intra- and extra-corporate factors (Keane 1991). The power of the modern corporation, and the abuse of that power via exploitation, have also been well documented (Pepinsky 1974; Pearce 1976), and at the macro level are explanations informed by the writings of theorists such as Karl Marx (1973) and Bonger (1916), which focus on the criminogenic inclinations of capitalism (Michalowski 1985).

McMullan (1992, 53) has recently summarized this position, arguing that the combination of 'the process of extraction of surplus value, the competitive drive for the accumulation of capital, and the centralization and concentration of capital and wealth have a direct bearing on the evolution and character of the corporation as a criminal actor.' These theorists and others (see Snider 1993 for a review of the dominant approaches) have focused attention on the crimes of the elite (see Simon and Eitzen 1986) by adopting several perspectives. Rarely, however, are organizational theories used to explain this form of behaviour. This chapter attempts to shed some additional light on corporate corruption by looking at organizational structure.

Before examining that topic, we can begin by asking: how do organizations operate in a rapidly changing world? First, they can be seen as goal-oriented entities with attainment of those goals a priority (Finney and Lesieur 1982). (In fact, Gross [1978] argued that this commitment produces a criminogenic situation.) Further, organizations may have a number of goals, and goals will differ among them. They do not, however, operate in a vacuum. With growth and globalization of business, they face high degrees of external and internal uncertainty. Their external environment includes political, socio-cultural, economic, physical, and technological factors and, perhaps most important, other organizations. Their political environment may affect them through legislation such as changes in tax laws; the socio-cultural, through consumers' changing tastes and values; the economic, through economic changes such as a recession or rampant growth of the economy; the physical, through pollution or resource depletion; and the technological, through changes in technology used. Other organizations may have an effect through their actions as competitors, suppliers, or consumers. These elements of an organization's 'task environment' (Dill 1958) produce uncertainty and demand response. At the same time, the internal environment is becoming more complex, as evidenced by changing values of employees in the workplace and greater government involvement in corporate life through programs such as employment equity – programs that could threaten existing power relations.

This chapter suggests that rather than coping with flux by formal means, epitomized by the notion of bureaucracy, many organizations will decouple themselves from their constituent parts, be they organizational or individual. Decoupling allows them to meet their goals while operating in a highly unpredictable task environment. This notion of decoupling follows from a view of the organization as having a structure consisting of loosely coupled entities.

LOOSE COUPLING – ORGANIZATIONAL LEVEL

Systems that are loosely coupled are responsive to each other, but each preserves its own identity and independence by physical and/or logical detachment (Weick 1976). I argue below that corporations strategically adopt a loosely coupled structure as a way of dealing with the vagaries of business life. Such a structure allows the corporation to take advantage of opportunities as they arise and react quickly to threats, in and from the task environment. It also allows the organization to distance itself from illegal actions, illegal actors, and undesirable attention.

This view of organizations as open, loosely coupled systems differs markedly from the view of them as being closed, rational systems. The image of a highly formalized, rational system can be traced to Max Weber (1946) and his view of bureaucracy as the ideal type of rational authority – possessing formality, precision, clarity, regularity, reliability, and efficiency achieved through a fixed division of tasks in which roles are circumscribed by limits to authority, hierarchical supervision, and detailed rules and regulations conceivably covering every possible contingency (see Morgan 1986). Also, Weber implies movement towards increasing bureaucratization and rational authority in modern society. His approach sees modern organizations as rational systems that should operate as efficiently as machines. This theory suggests that the dimensions or parts are tightly coupled to each other; a change in one part will affect the entire system. As in a machine, if a part malfunctions, the machine stops. This view is reflected in Woodmansee's description of the General Electric (GE) Co. (cited in Clinard and Yeager 1980, 24–5) paraphrased below.

GE's employees are organized into layers of authority. The corporation is like a pyramid. The majority of its workers (over 300,000) form the base; working in groups of five to fifty people, they take orders from a supervisor on the next level. The supervisor takes orders from a department general manager. There are about 180 of the latter, each in charge of one or two thousand employees. They in turn are supervised by a division vice-president/general manager, of which there are fifty. These officers report to one of ten group vice-presidents/ group executives. At about the same level of authority are the executives of GE's corporate staff, which is concerned with accounting, planning, legal affairs, and employee relations. The next level consists of three vice-chairs of the board of directors, and at the top sits the chief executive.

This description reflects the size and complexity of the modern corporation. One way of coping with this size and complexity is decentralization. Thinking about the organization mechanistically may have been useful in the early stages of industrialization, but the idea of a parallel between mechanized production and the growth of bureaucratic organizations may no longer be valid in a post-industrial society (see Morgan 1986 for various ways to conceptualize organizations).

So, although corporations may present a public image of rationality and efficiency, in practice these goals are difficult to accomplish. As the corporation grows, it becomes harder to centrally manage thousands of employees. As it expands through mergers and acquisitions, overseeing businesses perhaps operating in a number of industries becomes a challenge. And geographical expansion means managing subsidiaries around the world (for a discussion of the increasing size, power, and scope of the corporate sector, see Snider 1993). Thus decentralization may decouple the parent company from its subsidiaries. Although this practice allows the latter to react quickly to local opportunities and threats, it also permits the parent to distance itself from the subsidiary's actions. So a loosely coupled structure may prove functional.

FUNCTIONS OF LOOSE COUPLING

Weick (1976, 6–8) lists several possible functions of such systems. First, 'loose coupling lowers the probability that the organization will have to – or be able to – respond to each little change in the environment.' The organization's existence is not threatened by individuals entering or leaving one part or minor changes affecting a subsidiary. This implies a certain amount of autonomy among departments – say, between Finance and Marketing – as well as among divisions reporting to the same parent, and finally between divisions and head office. Each unit is thus shielded from day-to-day upsets affecting other units.

Second, 'loosely coupled systems preserve many independent sensing elements and therefore 'know' their environments better than is true for more tightly coupled systems which have fewer externally constrained, independent elements.' This point is similar to Granovetter's (1973) assertion of the 'strength of weak ties,' which may provide information about unknown or unfamiliar parts of the environment. Loosely coupled organizations provide their members with access to a wider band of information/resources than do tightly coupled ones. They, more than their counterparts, are thus more likely to be exposed to novel situations.

Third, 'in loosely coupled systems where the identity, uniqueness, and separateness of elements is preserved, the system potentially can retain a greater number of mutations and novel solutions than would be the case with a tightly coupled system.' They can better adapt to change and heterogeneity and in turn are more likely to experience change and heterogeneity or diversity than are tightly coupled organizations. They perhaps preserve more diversity in responding to environmental stimuli and therefore can adapt to a considerably wider range of choices in the environment (Weick 1976, 7).

Fourth, 'efficacy might be greater in a loosely coupled system with autonomous units than it would be in a tightly coupled system where discretion is limited.' The latter type of system may have fewer options, and choice may be restricted at both the organizational and individual levels. Loose coupling provides discretionary freedom, which also increases the likelihood of mistakes or abuse of the freedom.

Fifth, 'a loosely coupled system may be a good system for localized adaptation. If all of the elements in a large system are loosely coupled to one another, then any one element can adjust to modify a local unique contingency without affecting the whole system.' In that case, a geographically dispersed subsidiary can adapt swiftly to local threats and opportunities without having to wait for directions from a head office official who may not be familiar with the local environment.

Sixth, a loosely coupled organization may be more cost-effective to manage. It takes time and money to coordinate, control, and maintain a tightly coupled system. For example, transfer of corporate functions, such as purchasing, to a subsidiary allows it to take advantage of local purchasing opportunities.

Seventh, 'if there is a breakdown in one portion of a loosely coupled system then this breakdown is sealed off and does not affect other portions of the organization.' If, for example, a subsidiary is suffering financial losses, or is subject to a large fine, it can, because of its autonomy, be sold or closed down. So parts can be subtracted or added with often relatively little disturbance to either the parts or the system (1976, 3).

In summary, a loosely coupled system may be the most effective type of form for global corporations faced with great uncertainty in a rapidly changing environment. Lawrence and Lorsch (1967), for example, found that organizations faced with extensive environmental uncertainty had a looser structure than those operating in more stable surroundings. Loose coupling results in the ability to develop a number of stances in a variety of situations (Rubenstein and Woodman 1984). Glassman (1973, 84) suggests that 'in a tightly coupled system a perturbation in any one variable would require readjustment of all the other variables of the system. In any complex system there are so many variables that readaptation would then be astronomically improbable. A system whose parts are less richly connected, one with independence or temporary independence between parts, forms local stabilities which ignore limited perturbations elsewhere in the system.' Finally, Peters and Waterman (1982) suggested that overall corporate excellence can be attained through adoption of an appropriate degree of coupling (see Orton, Weick, and Weick 1990 for a review of the literature).

DYSFUNCTIONS OF LOOSE COUPLING

Although loose coupling provides many benefits for the organization, it may have certain liabilities for the public and corporate 'stakeholders.' For example, environmental uncertainty, which may lead to a loosely coupled may be the impetus to illegal behaviour, and such a structure may facilitate disreputable acts on behalf of the corporation. Specifically, companies faced with increasing uncertainty may attempt illegally to influence elements of their task environment – through bribery of officials, violation of pollution laws, illegal use of computers, misleading advertising, and price fixing. Braithwaite (1984, 182) offers an example of reducing uncertainty when he relates a discussion with a pharmaceutical company executive, who admitted: 'Just recently we got together about 30 of us, all of the accountants and finance directors ... to sit around the table together and work out prices that we could all agree on in the submissions that we make to the Health Department.'

Collusion can thus be seen as an attempt to reduce financial and organizational uncertainty. And the greater the uncertainty, the greater the incentive to reduce it illegally. In brief, the examples of illegality cited above can be seen as attempts to reduce uncertainty in the task environment. Furthermore, a loosely coupled structure may be more conducive to corporate corruption than one more tightly coupled.

For instance, although a loosely coupled organization does not have to respond to minor environmental changes – a strength – it may as a result be less attentive to needed changes. It may be able to resist attempts to reduce the disreputable practices of a distant subsidiary. As well, a parent company may be able to ignore complaints launched against a loosely coupled subsidiary. A problem occurring with an autonomous unit may not come to the attention of the parent's management or may be ignored and/or overlooked by it.

Further, a highly divisionalized, loosely coupled system may lack internal control, which can leave it vulnerable to illegal behaviour. Freedom and discretion may be abused by those who are able to avoid detection. For example, Vaughan (1982) has suggested that if senior management's ability to control or monitor a business unit is lessened, the unit is more likely to engage in an illegal transaction.

Loosely coupled systems can decouple organizational or individual parts of the system, separating one part from another, perhaps to the disadvantage of a group such as employees. A unionized parent company may claim that one or more subsidiaries is wholly autonomous. This decoupling may prevent the union representing employees of the parent from including the subsidiary's workers under the contract held with the parent. Subsidiaries may be represented by different unions, implying weaker bargaining units, or the union may have to begin its organizing drive individually with each subsidiary. Braverman (1974) has argued that the increasing specialization and subdivision of the work process has not been done to improve efficiency but rather to fragment the workforce and maintain power in the hands of management.

Meyer and Rowan (1977, 357) suggest that decoupling enables organizations to maintain standardized, legitimating, formal structures while their activities vary in response to practical considerations. This process involves separating legitimate structures and practices from illegitimate actions in another part of the organization. Hence, decoupling may isolate an illegal act and/or an illegal member. The organization can then use 'impression management' techniques such as neutralization to restore the public image of legitimacy. For example, Elsbach and Sutton (1992) cite the case of the environmental organization Earth

First!, which was accused of driving a metal spike into a tree, ultimately injuring a lumber worker when his saw blade hit the spike. A spokesperson used the neutralization technique of 'denial of responsibility' (Sykes and Matza 1957), stating that although members may have spiked trees, they did so as individuals, not as a group. (For other examples of use of techniques of neutralization, see Keane 1991, 229–30; McMullan 1992, 67–71; and Snider 1993, 69–70.)

Similarly, as companies reduce fixed personnel costs by sub-contracting tasks such as marketing research, maintenance, and security, they replace fixed with variable costs (usually increasing profitability), and these functions become decoupled. Decoupling may change power relationships. For example, Tombs's (1992, 79–81) study of the British chemical industry describes how a move to smaller, independent operating units increases the possibility of safety violations as these units compete to maximize profitability. Further, where separate safety departments have been established, their autonomy has minimized their clout. Because of their independence and role as an advisory body, their reporting relationships to senior management are not strong. This lack of access and influence is translated into lack of power, and ultimately the safety department loses respect (Tombs 1992, 79–81). This autonomy effectively reduces corporate responsibility to, and from, the loosely coupled unit.

Barney, Edwards, and Ringleb (1992) report that in the United States, employees exposed to hazardous materials on the job, or their heirs, have the right to compensation from their employer if the exposure can be shown to have led to disease, disability, or death. Therefore firms in high-risk industries, where employees are liable to such exposure, may adopt a non-vertically integrated production system by contracting out parts of the production process. The resulting arm's-length relationship between the large company and its smaller supplier shifts legal liability to the smaller corporation. The authors cite the example of Allied Chemical, which manufactured Kepone, a product used in insecticides and pesticides. In the early 1970s, Allied decided to discontinue manufacture of Kepone. It contracted with the Life Science Products Co. to supply Allied with Kepone. Allied provided it with all the raw materials needed and agreed to receive certain shipments of the product at the smaller company's plant. Although title to all raw materials and to the Kepone produced remained with Allied, a subsequent court ruling found that Allied had acted as an independent contractor and was thus not liable for workers' injuries at the smaller firm. Thus the loosely coupled organization can use its corporate form to evade responsibility.

It has also been argued that the corporation can benefit by a claim of diffused accountability, yet when it needs to for its own purposes, it can usually achieve adequate accountability (Braithwaite 1984, 138–9). The degree of coupling can apparently be manipulated to meet the needs of the organization. But I would also argue that loose coupling makes it easier to designate a scapegoat, because of the resulting 'obfuscation as to responsibility' (Sutherland 1949, 226). An example of designating a scapegoat is the Exxon oil-spill off the coast of Alaska, in which the ship's captain was held to blame. Little or no attempt was made to identify the individual who made the decision to purchase a single-hull tanker rather than a more durable, double-hull tanker.

Another example of organizational and individual decoupling appears in Pearce and Tombs's (1993) study of the Union Carbide Corp. (UCC) disaster at Bhopal, India. In describing the response of the parent company, UCC, to the gas leak of its subsidiary, Union Carbide of India Ltd (UCIL), the authors note that UCC asserted that production of methlisocyanate in India, the siting of the plant, and the quality of the materials used were all UCIL's responsibility and that of the Indian government. Whereas actual control remained with UCC, UCIL was declared independent and responsible for its own affairs (1993, 193). These statements by UCC serve to decouple the parent from its subsidiary and thus shift accountability. The 'sabotage theory,' which Pearce and Tombs (1993, 193–5) argue plays a key role in UCC's version of events, holds that a disgruntled employee, not working at the time, intending only to spoil a batch of chemicals, created conditions that led to the disaster. This explanation appears, both logically and legally, to decouple the organization from the individual saboteur, who allegedly was acting on his own behalf, contrary to corporate policies and procedures. The organization can now join the ranks of victims.

In brief, at the organizational level, a loosely coupled structure allows the corporation to use its form to evade legal responsibility.

LOOSE COUPLING – INDIVIDUAL LEVEL

Although a loose structure may enable the corporation to react to environmental contingencies, the concept of coupling may also be used at the micro level. Glassman (1973) writes that the degree of coupling, or interaction between two systems depends on the activity of the variables that they share. To the extent that two systems either have few and/or weak variables in common, they are independent of each other. At the individual level, some employees may be loosely coupled, others tightly coupled, to the corporation. Firms may, use strategies that result in some managers being tightly coupled to the company culture and loosely coupled to the external community. This end can be accomplished through such means as promotions and transfers, which may result in both social and geographical mobility. Such increased mobility may weaken social ties outside the company and strengthen both social and corporate ties within it.

I have argued elsewhere (Keane 1991) that this process can be interpreted in relation to a variation of control theory (Hirschi 1969). Specifically, if we modify control theory to use it at a micro perspective, such as the subculture of an organization, we can hypothesize that corporate criminals may be tightly bonded/coupled to the culture of the organization. Thus the individual comes to identify strongly with the corporation and its goals, through work-related activities and social interaction with other employees, which intensify the individual's loyalty. Promotions and transfers (see J.W. Coleman 1989, 220) make it difficult for individuals to develop and maintain close long-term relationships outside the corporation. Individuals come to associate predominantly with other members of the organization for whom they come to care, and from whom they may learn the behaviour required to attain corporate goals with which they have come to strongly identify.This notion reiterates Sutherland's (1949) emphasis on differential association. Some individuals may learn not only the goals of the organization but techniques such as bid rigging, which will ensure that the company meets its goals.

The concept of coupling may also be used with R. Merton's (1957) 'anomie' theory of deviant behaviour if we conceive of the 'innovative' executive as being coupled tightly to the goals of the corporation but loosely to the legal means to achieve the goals. In this case, the executive may resort to illegal behaviour to meet personally the company's goals. Research has found a relationship between poor corporate performance and corporate crime, suggesting that an element of strain may be present, affecting those responsible for attainment of goals (Clinard and Yeager 1980; Keane 1993).

To summarize the preceding, those corporate members most tightly coupled to the organization, its members, and its goals may be the most likely to resort to illegal behaviour to meet those goals in a climate of uncertainty. The absence of senior corporate responsibility, reflected by loose control systems, may exacerbate this likelihood.

In addition, although a loosely coupled structure may be imposed by top management, it succeeds because it is readily accepted, and in fact desired, by ambitious lower-level managers. It grants autonomy, which can be translated into power. This conception is similar to Kriesberg's (1976) 'organizational process model,' which conceives of a 'constellation of loosely allied decisionmaking units, each with primary responsibility for a specific range of problems' (1976, 1,101). The less tightly coupled a department or subsidiary is, the greater its operating freedom. So, a loosely coupled structure may actually become looser over time, as middle management employees strive to expand their personal corporate responsibility.

CONCLUSION

I began this chapter with the argument that many corporations, as goal-directed organizations, adopt a structure that will allow flexibility to achieve goals in a highly uncertain task environment. Further, I argued that this form is one of loose coupling, whereby components are loosely connected, yet still responsive, to each other. This type of structure also allows the company to decouple components if that is deemed necessary. However, there are also some liabilities to such a structure. Rules may often be violated, decisions often not implemented or implemented with uncertain consequences, technologies inefficient, and evaluation and inspection systems subverted or rendered so vague as to provide little coordination (Meyer and Rowan 1977, 343). Envisioning the organization as a loosely coupled system requires discarding our views of the modern corporation as a formal, efficient, bureaucratic structure. By adopting this new perspective, however, we may gain insight into an informal structure, where the various elements, though operating within the framework of the corporate body, also have a high degree of independence. Unfortunately, this type of structure, while providing autonomy, may also create the potential for abuse of responsibility.

PART III

Financial Crimes

10

Serious Fraud in Britain: Criminal Justice versus Regulation

MICHAEL LEVI

When evaluating the objectives of governments in capitalist societies in dealing with 'serious fraud,' the initial starting point of readers may be cynicism. Particularly if governments wish to develop 'popular capitalism' and attract overseas funds into their markets, it has become conventional wisdom to assert that national and individual corporate reputation for fair dealing and for prevention of outright securities fraud is very important. However, the relation between reputation and actual action against fraud, and the precise role of the criminal justice process, remain sites for considerable conflict. The difficulties that governments have experienced in raising revenues during the late 1980s and the 1990s, combined with the deterioration in the fortunes of financial services firms, once the flagships of Britain's global prestige and employment prospects (Budd and Whimster 1992), have intensified concern about 'cost-effectiveness' in both crime prevention and criminal justice. Maximizing the symbolic effect for the minimum expenditure is the central objective of both government and the private sector: each seeks to shift the cost of policing onto the other, as manifested in the regulation of fraud.

Unlike most 'crimes of the working classes,' where, 'peace officer' role notwithstanding, prosecution routinely follows crime, business crime has never been considered a natural candidate for the criminal process. The role of ideology and political pressure in relation to 'corporate crime' is a central part of the more general debate about how conceptions of 'appropriate social order' are constructed. (See, for some Canadian illustrations, Snider 1993). At a crude level, if the police deal with it, it is crime; if other agencies deal with it, it is not crime. However, those offences by the poor and 'lesser' social groups – such as social security frauds and tax frauds by building sub-contractors – that are dealt with by non-police agencies are treated as if they were 'real' crimes.

The frauds discussed here constitute the arena of business violation that has the closest analogy to 'real crime,' being concerned largely with the extraction by deception of very large amounts of money from other capitalist organizations or from general investors and pensioners. Although some of these offences have been committed by persons who are arguably part of some finance-capitalist elite, their victims also are frequently part of this elite. For example, 'insiders' at Lloyd's of London have happily 'skimmed' profits from the nobility as well as from the *nouveaux riches* among syndicate members. Moreover, unless the nature of the activity can be redefined – for example, by representing it as an ordinary business loss (and therefore a 'misfortune' or 'accident' or 'error of judgment') rather than fraud – it is in the interests of government to be seen to do something about it, whether that 'it' be prosecution, prevention, or both. This pressure has been intensified by globalization of the financial-services industry and oversupply of staff in it, which means that nation-states are in competition for business. One of the components of comparative attractiveness is confidence that fraudsters will be dealt with, but another is the cost and speed of doing business, which may be inhibited by 'too much' regulation, civil or criminal. As in other spheres, there are key internal contradictions, the effects of whose interplay may be seen partly by looking at changes in the law and practice of regulation and criminal justice.

The past five years has seen major changes in the response of the British state to financial white-collar crime. Following the Report of the Fraud Trials Committee (Roskill, 1986) – itself established in the wake of some celebrated failed prosecutions in the early 1980s – and with strong backing from Margaret Thatcher, the Serious Fraud Office (hereafter SFO) was formed in 1988. In the interests of effectiveness, the SFO deliberately violates the principle of separating the investigation from prosecution, on which basis the Crown Prosecution Service – which prosecutes all other cases investigated by the police – was founded in 1986. Despite pressures to divert finite resources from central detective squads to uniformed 'sector policing,' and reflecting the substantial growth in serious fraud reported, the number of Fraud Squad officers in England and Wales also has grown, from 588 in 1985 to 770 (of whom 238 are in London) in 1992. Largely on cases such as real estate frauds involving professional people, but also in corruption investigations such as that into former Labour Left councillor Derek Hatton (who was acquitted in March 1993 after a two-month trial and again on further charges in 1995), an additional 210 officers who are not normally part of Fraud Squad establishments were in April 1992 employed full-time on fraud inquiries lasting longer than six months.[1]

Moreover, a relatively new regulatory apparatus has been created under the Financial Services Act, 1986, which is arguably intended to prevent fraud and thereby reduce the number of 'City frauds' with which the police and the

Department of Trade and Industry (DTI) will be required to deal in future. (If it does not reduce fraud, then the City institutions that contribute to the compensation funds of the self-regulatory organizations will have to pay heavily for their negligence, so even the most cynical have to take fraud prevention seriously, even if the desire to minimize subscriptions induces optimism in risk assessment and minimal staffing levels.)

The SFO has brought areas of formerly private commercial misconduct – or areas that, where known about, were public only in the sense of being dealt with by insolvency practitioners or by securities and banking regulators – into the arena of the criminal courts and, thereby, into greater public visibility and debate. This 'new wave' of prosecutions has brought about some criticism from those who think that some areas of commercial misconduct are not the criminal law's business and who complain that there has been a serious overreach of the criminal law as well as poor judgment of individual prosecutions on the part of the SFO. In their view, it is acceptable to harass alleged moral renegades such as the Maxwell brothers who are accused of stealing hundreds of millions of pounds from pension funds, but not to punish senior executives of major banks for 'stabilizing the market'! Some might argue (unfalsifiably) that SFO prosecutions constitute merely a symbolic morality play to trick the public into believing that something is being done about elite crime, and certainly legitimation motives loomed large in establishment of the SFO (Levi 1987).

But my interviews and observations suggest that although all the prosecution agencies are much more cautious when dealing with elite suspects and their professional advisers than they are with middle-status people, the non-prosecution of some top managers and professionals is attributable principally to the difficulty in proving guilty knowledge in the positions they hold see futher Levi 1987; Braithwaite and Fisse 1994. The SFO's annual budget was £21.2 million in 1992–3, roughly the same as the amount spent by the Department of Employment in handling unemployment-benefit fraud (£21.44 million in 1990–1). This budget is tiny compared with the size and complexity of the losses it is required to investigate (totalling some £6 billion 'at risk' in 1994) and the funds available to some of the corporations and individuals it is investigating.[2]

It was anticipated that the new SFO would deal with all of the most serious or complex frauds. However, expansion of the number and size of cases – particularly via massive insolvencies which are a by-product of the recession – has meant that since the SFO limits itself to sixty cases at any one time, multi-million–pound cases of great complexity are handled by the Fraud Divisions of Headquarters Casework, or Fraud Investigation Group (FIG),[3] of the Crown Prosecution Service (CPS) and even by CPS branch officials in the regions. Additionally, although they prosecute relatively rarely and have other methods of administrative control, DTI, the Securities and Investments Board (SIB), the Bank of England (in respect of unauthorized deposit-taking), the Stock Exchange, and the Revenue departments also deal with serious frauds.

There is no statutory definition of 'complex or serious fraud,' and precise delineation is elusive. Many frauds that are serious to their victims – such as non-supply of goods by mail order and grossly overpriced and faulty roofing and driveway-building – fall well below the FIG range and, if reported and recorded at all, are dealt with by police and local CPS, where they seldom receive high priority. This brings into focus the psychological ordering of costs of crime and their associated seriousness. In police terms, any crime involving more than a few thousand pounds is likely to be seen as 'serious.' Yet fraud occupies a different perceptual category, as if, once one passes a certain figure, the number of additional 'zeros' becomes irrelevant. The SFO's current (1994) minimum limit for acceptance is £5 million, and that of FIG is £250,000. During 1990, in the whole of England and Wales, the police recorded 'only' 123 robberies, 419 burglaries, and 819 thefts over £50,000, very few of which would have been significantly over that amount. Data from the Association of British Insurers indicate that the costs of crime in England and Wales in 1990 totalled some £432 million for theft of and from motor vehicles, £800 million for burglary, and £500 million for arson. The alleged frauds in any one of the most serious cases – those involving Bank of Commerce and Credit International (BCCI), Barlow Clowes, Guinness, Maxwell, and Polly Peck[4] – approach or exceed these figures, and in 1992, there were twenty-one SFO cases where more than £50 million is estimated to have been involved. To illustrate this starkly, Robert Maxwell (two of whose sons were tried in 1995) and others allegedly looted from pension funds alone a sum equal to the total financial losses from car crime.

SERIOUS FRAUD AND CRIMINAL JUSTICE

The investigation and adjudication of complex fraud present difficulties that are not merely the rhetoric of criminal entrepreneurs and their allies seeking immunity from criminalization. Whether in a DTI report or, often some years later, in a courtroom, reconstruction of complex corporate events is an inherently arduous and subjective exercise, even with the aid of the documentary evidence that is often lacking in other areas of criminality. In serious fraud trials, the key issues usually relate to interpretation of mental elements by the defendants (and, sometimes, prosecution witnesses). Who was party to which agreements? Was anyone actually deceived by them? Was the defendant director acting as the directing mind of the company, or was he 'on a frolic of his own'? Did each defendant have enough awareness of 'the big picture' for culpability to be clear? And if they did see the overall picture, did each one appreciate the risk that ordinary people would regard their actions as dishonest?[5] Unlike eyewitness testimony, where the principal problem since passage of the Police and Criminal Evidence Act (PACE), 1984, has been what one might term honestly believed but inaccurate evidence, many witnesses in fraud cases have a stake in portraying events in a way that minimizes their culpability – sometimes, as with professionals such as accountants and lawyers, to mitigate professional insurance liability as well as reputations or even personal criminal liability. They suffer less financial and reputational loss if others believe that they were 'conned' rather than were conspirators or wilfully blind. Even without any pressure from the police, in witness statements they may consciously or unconsciously distort what happened: these distortions may emerge in court and take the prosecution unprepared, or may never emerge at all. Moreover, by analogy with 'methodic suspicion' of some groups of the population as 'criminal types,' assumptions may be made about the character of previously 'suspect businesspeople' that unconsciously influence interpretation by investigators and prosecutors, particularly when the latter work closely with the former.

Apart from 'populist' frauds involving clearly visible harm to individuals, some of whom are people of modest means, such as the *Barlow Clowes* (a £215-million investment fraud targeted at retired people) and *Maxwell* (pension-fund fraud) cases, media treatment of fraud is by no means as hysterical as that which accompanies terrorism and adds to the pressure to charge suspects there. However, media and political pressure during the late 1980s and early 1990s has acted to bring more people and more complex cases into the prosecutorial net. The growing number of financial journalists with an interest in exposure of fraud has been influential in this shift, with intensified competitive pressure to find not only new victims and 'scams' but also to reveal (or, as seen by some regulators, to invent) new examples of regulatory incompetence in allowing frauds to occur or continue. This interest is allied to broadening of the proportion of people who hold investments and therefore are vulnerable to, and interested in, such misconduct. Where the suspect is a 'famous name,' media interest increases, as seen in the many more journalists than SFO staff members who were investigating the background to the collapse of the Maxwell empire, at least until the arrests created a ban on publication of related criminal issues.

We should look at these developments within the more general (and often internally contradictory) context of alarm about 'miscarriages of justice' and about the effectiveness of police/criminal justice which led to establishment in 1993 of the Royal Commission on Criminal Justice. The rights of white-collar suspects are not a socially attractive cause for most civil libertarians. One would expect most violations of rights to occur when the crime under investigation is viewed seriously, encouraging investigators to feel that they must 'do justice' (the 'Dirty Harry' syndrome); great organizational pressure is exerted towards obtaining 'a quick result,' perhaps to reassure the public that 'crime' (or a particular sort of crime) is under control; and the individual under suspicion has a tainted character, in the eyes of the investigators. Traditionally, whatever the inherent seriousness of white-collar crime, little active pressure has been exerted by the public or government to do much about it – especially not to do much about it immediately – and the kind of people who commit it are not normally those whom the police (and prosecutors) feel it is important to 'put away,' however much they may envy their affluence.

However, the portrait of the regulation of fraud painted in the mid-1980s (see Levi 1987) may be somewhat dated. First, setting up organizations whose *raison d'être* is control of a particular form of crime – be it fraud or drugs – requires these organizations to justify their staffing in relation to that crime. Even in the United Kingdom, which lacks the sort of political/careerist motivation shown by some American prosecutors, this problem leads investigators to 'play up' the seriousness of the offences, which tendency is assisted when the accused either have previously been involved in major (non-fraud) crime or are personally or corporately famous.

Investigative Powers

One of the intriguing paradoxes in the sociology of social control is that in England, which, unlike Canada and the United States, has no constitutional protection for suspects' rights, far greater powers are available to investigate white-collar than any other type of crime, even terrorism. Nevertheless, white-collar investigative agencies differ enormously in powers available, degree of judicial scrutiny of those powers, and conditions under which the results of the exercise of power are admissible as evidence in subsequent criminal trials. It is not my object here to set out those powers systematically: for such more detailed reviews, see Levi (1987, 1991a, 1993).

These agencies perceive the overriding purpose of investigations very differently. The Bank of England, and the Self-Regulatory Organisations that are under the general supervision of the DTI and the Securities and Investments Board, see their essential role as being prudential or preventive; Her Majesty's Customs and Excise (in the area of value-added tax, or VAT) and Inland Revenue conceive their task as being maximization of revenue; it is only the police and associated prosecutorial agencies (i.e., the SFO and CPS) that focus on criminal prosecution. This does not mean that non-police agencies are always mild in their approach to those they investigate: the desire to maximize revenue can lead to heavy-handed treatment of taxpayers, particularly since the new 'incentivization' approach in the public sector means that the personal income of tax inspectors is boosted by the amount of money they bring in. (Their organizations are also under pressure to reach their financial targets.)

By contrast to their increasingly critical approach to the use of powers by the police, in recent years the courts have consistently held that there is no right to silence or privilege against self-incrimination in white-collar cases, except in those investigated only by the police. Indeed, white-collar crime has been at the 'cutting edge' of well-funded jurisprudence, almost all of which has been lost by the suspects and enhances investigative powers to require suspects and those actually charged with fraud to answer the questions of bankruptcy examiners and company liquidators, even though their answers to these civil-law bodies can be used as evidence against them at subsequent criminal trials (Levi 1993). Most SFO cases likewise have yielded enhanced powers.

Apart from the admissibility in its prosecutions of statements made under compulsion to DTI inspectors and liquidators (as in Guinness and Maxwell, both discussed below), the SFO's most controversial power is its right under section 2 of the Criminal Justice Act, 1987, to require suspects to answer questions even if answers might tend to incriminate them (although they can only be used in evidence only if the person making them later gives evidence that contradicts what he or she said in interview). The SFO can even require defendants to answer questions after charge.[6] Of enormous importance also, section 2 allows the SFO to require witnesses to answer questions and to provide documents. The increase in use of these powers may be seen from the following statistics concerning notices issued by the director and senior staff under section 2, without the need to obtain further authority from any court: 1988–9, 233; 1989–90, 574; 1990–1, 765; 1991–2, 793; 1992–3, 931; and 1993–4, 657. Thus both bank secrecy and the right to silence are dead in SFO and DTI cases, although, somewhat bizarrely, the same case dealt with by the CPS would have to be handled with ordinary police powers, with no ability to require answers from suspects and with any seizure of confidential material having to be authorized by a Circuit Court judge.

In England, as in the United States (Stewart 1992), some controversy has been caused by the 'coincidence' of the police making highly publicized arrests when there is no serious likelihood of anyone either fleeing (if summoned to appear for questioning) or being tricked into admissions when tired. The most famous recent example was the arrest in 1992 of Kevin Maxwell, whose wife, Pandora, told the plain-clothes officers who rang the bell at 6:40 a.m. to 'fuck off or I'll call the police,' producing the classic response that 'we are the police.' By good fortune, an ITN camera crew and legions of journalists were there to report this, and it got headlines in every 'quality' and tabloid newspaper! Most lawyers, businesspeople, and police whom I interviewed believed that the arrests of senior executives in County NatWest Merchant Bank and UBS Phillips & Drew (the *Blue Arrow* case) were carried out to make a symbolic statement to the City and general public: in which respect it was highly successful and did achieve its objectives.[7] Such behaviour is common enough in non–white-collar crime investigations, where it normally passes uncommented on (although media tip-offs are rarer). However, where 'famous names' or any professional people are subjected to a milder version of the same status-degradation ceremony, this leads to protests.

Prosecution Policies

The debate between utilitarians and 'just-desserts' theorists (Braithwaite and Pettit 1990) also relates to financial fraud. Sophisticated questions may be asked about the equity of prosecutions, especially different treatment of similar cases (or more lenient treatment of 'worse' cases than of 'better' ones) by any given agency and disparities of prosecution levels. For example, in 1991–2, H.M. Customs and Excise (VAT fraud), Inland Revenue, the Department of Social Security (DSS) (income-support fraud), the Department of Employment (DOE) (unemployment-benefit fraud), and the police prosecuted respectively 153, 257, 8,932, 2,260, and about 1.9 million people.[8] No department prosecutes everyone against whom it has *prima facie* evidence, but my interviews as well as the data show the Revenue departments to be by far the most selective of the non-police agencies, prosecuting only when they deem this strategically necessary (Levi 1993: see also D. Cook 1989).

The judgment of what is or is not 'in the public interest' is essentially subjective and can be political (with a small or a large *p*). British examples in which it has been alleged that pressure has been exerted *not* to prosecute in fraud cases include the *House of Fraser* case (involving the take-over of Harrods department store by the Fayed brothers, allegedly supported by the Sultan of Brunei); the *Peter Cameron-Webb* case (involving alleged 'baby syndicates' given preferential treatment at Lloyd's of London); and the decision by the Department of Public Prosecution (DPP) in 1978 not to prosecute companies that broke sanctions imposed at the time of Rhodesia's Unilateral Declaration of Independence on the grounds that 'no good would be served by raking over these almost dead coals.' (The last is the only example in which policy rather than that usually unfalsifiable category 'insufficient evidence' was given as the reason for non-prosecution.) Yet in some other cases when there has been a risk of political problems for the government – the most notable being the Matrix-Churchill directors (wrongly) prosecuted in 1992 for deceiving the government to the effect that arms components for Iraq had a peaceful purpose – prosecutions have taken place, indicating a certain level of political autonomy.[9]

Ironically, given their own conservative political affiliations, a number of formerly high-status white-collar defendants stated to me that they were the victims of politically motivated prosecutions – for example, Guinness, where it is alleged that the government needed prior to the 1987 election to demonstrate that it was getting tough on white-collar criminals, and *Blue Arrow*, where the government was embarrassed by revelations in the *Economist* magazine,[10] and – as in *Guinness* – was concerned about its reputation in the international marketplace. Other prosecutions that might never have taken place had it not been politically important to do so include those relatively minor defendants in *BCCI* who remained within the jurisdiction of the English courts.

However, to show that a prosecution had (or was intended to produce) a political benefit to a country and/or a party reveals nothing about whether or not it was legally justified. Moreover, none of these examples provides an adequate, grounded explanation, for there is no evidence that any governmental official 'instructed' the police to arrest Guinness's chief executive, Ernest Saunders, or the *Blue Arrow* defendants. Nevertheless, they do highlight the incestuous constitutional and financial accountability to the attorney-general of the DPP and of the SFO's director. Frequent consultation with the attorney-general and dependence on his support for organizational resources may induce second guessing of what would please the government, even if no actual instructions are given. Despite the occasional judicial inquiry – such as that into the Bank of England's handling of *BCCI* (Bingham 1992) and into arms for Iraq (by Lord Justice Scott) – there is no British equivalent of the U.S. Special Prosecutor to challenge alleged cover-ups by the 'Establishment.'

It may be that 'justifications' of *raisons d'état* apply to the prosecutions in *Blue Arrow* and *Guinness*, whatever the eventual results; businesspeople readily appreciate that 'the process is the punishment.' Likewise, with the prosecution of commodities brokers DPR Futures and LHW in 1990 for allegedly deceiving investors, to demarcate the new line between acceptable and unacceptable commercial behaviour. Some white-collar prosecutions raise the hackles of those in the City who complain about the unfairness of 'trial by ordeal' as a method of social crime prevention in commerce. In their perception, the SFO (and the revenue departments) are adopting the role of the police in the nineteenth century[11] – 'domestic missionaries' (Storch 1976) cleaning up the loose *mores* of 'the City.' But *this* City has rather greater resources in the 'class struggle' than did the working-class city under threat from the nineteenth-century police.

REGULATORY OPTIONS

The SFO enjoyed a brief honeymoon with the conviction of the 'Guinness Four' (Levi 1991b). However, several events – its abandonment of *Guinness 2* (because of the certified suicidal condition of banker Roger Seelig, since seen driving his Porsche around Oxfordshire antique shops and now advising multinationals on take-over strategy) and of *Guinness 3* (with Seelig and elite stockbroker David Mayhew, whose solicitors magically produced some private evidence that led the SFO to withdraw its prosecution); the jury acquittal in *Guinness 4* (during which the defendant – American lawyer Thomas Ward, whose defence included the claim that he did not know how to open a Swiss bank account – dramatically produced details of a bank account that the prosecution later showed could not have existed at that time); the directed acquittal of five defendants (including three corporates) in *Blue Arrow*, with all four convictions being overturned by the Court of Appeal; plus major problems with other cases – have led to a storm of protest about the competence of the SFO in particular and the criminal justice process in complex fraud cases. Politically, the option of abolishing jury trial is not plausible at present, and there has been much discussion of whether the difficulties could be avoided by greater use of self-regulatory disciplinary tribunals. Such recommendations have occurred at the same time as widespread (politically and media-inspired) criticism that diversion of juveniles from criminal courts has led to a massive explosion of crime.

The police and government bodies are by no means the only 'official' agencies that investigate serious fraud: such investigations are also sub-contracted to the Securities and Investments Board (SIB), Self-Regulatory Organisations (SROs) and Recognised Professional Bodies (such as the Law Society and Institute of Chartered Accountants). During 1991–2, there were 298 cases of intervention to restrict or stop investment business under the Financial Services Act, 1986 (FSA), of which only one was the result of action by SIB itself, and there were eight statutory investigations by SIB under section 105 of the FSA, of which three were passed to the police or SFO for fraud investigation and one to the DTI for further investigation. These powers are given by contract,[12] and the need for those disciplined to be members is a generic brake on the scope of such regulation, compounded by the substantial (though declining) number of regulatory bodies – a factor that undoubtedly leads to postponed action because each self-regulatory body has to consult others, each of which may take time to consult its legal advisers, and many hope that one of the others will take (costly) action. In one case, a regulator decided that it could not obtain a restraint order to freeze the assets of a suspected firm because it was not sure whether it was an investment company or an unauthorized deposit-taking institution and considered that it might be either DTI or Bank of England business. In other cases, assets of suspended companies can be put into trust, but the bill for professional trustees is often greater than the assets to be preserved.

One alleged fraud took three years to develop from being suspected by regulators to a full criminal investigation. Following compliance visits, the case was reported to the Bank of England as suspected unauthorized deposit-taking. The Bank decided that it was not a deposit-taking scheme in the United Kingdom, although it might well be overseas.[13] The regulator carried out further compliance visits and then closed down the operation. SIB (with the regulator) carried out an investigation under section 105 of the FSA and reported the matter to the DTI, which passed it to the SFO for further, lengthy investigation (the scheme's operator was later imprisoned). This is a classic, if extreme, illustration of the problems generated by multi-agency investigations. As many as twelve self-regulatory and statutory bodies have been involved in case conferences on what should be done and – more critical after financial crisis in the regulatory body had reduced the number of investigators in one SRO to one – *who* should do it. Cynics might view this fragmentation as '*lex imperfecta*' (Reisman's memorable phrase); however, obligations to pay compensation to victims produce a pragmatic incentive for greater effectiveness.

Most regulatory action does not involve the criminal process. In the four years since SIB was established, it has prosecuted one case for the conduct of unauthorized investment business under section 4 of the FSA, although it claims that its investigations have resulted in detection of fifty cases of fraud, which have been passed onto the police or the SFO, resulting in twenty-two convictions to date. There are, however, indications of a markedly more aggressive stance by SIB and by some of the other regulators, particularly over mis-selling of pensions and other products important to our society.

In a number of examples relayed to me, some regulators had been kept uninvolved deliberately, in order to get some kind of action. One regulator who was something of a moral entrepreneur for more vigorous action against white-collar crime justified this evasive tactic by quoting one senior enforcement official, who allegedly had stated to him: 'The purpose of SIB is to detect breaches of the [FSA], not to put people in prison.'

Setting aside early cases, when overloading of the system can explain late action by regulators, eventual closure of BCCI and action against Maxwell for looting pension funds have reinforced general concerns about both banking and self-regulation, whether via official organizations or via corporate governance. During the period from April 1991 to April 1992, the Securities and Futures Authority – which was generally rated a very professional one – prosecuted twenty-five cases (including eleven individuals), who were fined on average over £50,000. (The most common fine was £70,000.) Other regulators fined companies similar sums – for example, large insurance firms that made investments in companies to influence their sales of their insurance products, even though the investee held itself out to be giving independent advice. The number of very large fines has been increasing, and firms involved – knowingly or not – in cases where salespeople on commission have sold investments to people without taking care to discover their financial position and 'needs,' have been required to make restitution. The bad publicity has an unknown further effect on profits and organizational morale.

Those who advocate the regulatory alternative do so largely on the grounds of lower cost, speed, and greater 'rationality of judgment' than is offered by trial by jury.[14] The cynical may suspect that they want greater control over results so that they can acquit insiders, but this is not self-evident: the political 'spin' may be for the practitioners who sit as assessors to 'hang 'em high' to satisfy the public's desire for vengeance (and, perhaps, to eliminate competition from firms undercutting on prices). Many of the most serious fraud offenders are not members of any regulatory body, making it rather difficult for the latter to discipline them – a challenge for enforced self-regulation in the sphere of fraud, whatever its merits in health and safety control. Moreover, whatever the *formal* standard of proof, the practical standard generally applied by such tribunals allegedly is not far different from the criminal one.[15]

The most common view among those I interviewed was that no substantial disciplinary action would have ensued against senior personnel involved in Blue Arrow's alleged share manipulation had the DTI's report not been commissioned and published. However, in advance of prosecution, albeit late in the procedure, the Bank of England effectively ensured that four of those subsequently prosecuted, were not 'fit and proper' to be senior executives in banks (at least in the near future).[16] Those defendants and non-defendants who are members of the Stock Exchange remain liable (at the time of writing) to be disciplined for breaches of the Stock Exchange rules as they existed at that time. Had the case happened after the FSA came into force, the Securities and Futures Association could easily have taken action against three defendants whose prosecutions were dropped following quashing of the convictions of co-defendants and against the other defendants, except for the solicitor, Keat, who in theory might have been disciplined by the Law Society. Since Clark and Keat were acquitted (at the direction of the judge), and those who were convicted in *Blue Arrow 1* were given suspended prison sentences (before their convictions were quashed), the difference in formal sanctions between the criminal and disciplinary processes is negligible: if anything, the disciplinary process would probably have imposed much tougher sanctions. Whether the political symbolism of the prosecution (and any general deterrent effect it had) would have been achievable by dispensing with prosecution is, however, more questionable.

Unlike many defendants who come before the courts, those charged with 'up-market' white-collar crimes are extremely conscious of the economic as well as penal consequences for them of particular adjudications: they carefully analyse every stage of the process, usually in concert with legal advisers. The consequences of conviction or disciplinary action (or, even, of acquittal) vary greatly, depending on the individual's role and institutional support for him or her. Keat, a partner in Travers Smith Braithwaite, and Mayhew, a partner in Cazenove – no evidence was offered against Mayhew in the abandoned *Guinness 3* – were supported financially and socially by their partners despite being charged. In contrast, Saunders was ostracized by Guinness and cut off from legal support, and Parnes was unemployed pending the outcome of his trial.[17] After conviction in *Guinness 1*, Parnes was 'barred' by the Stock Exchange from trading securities, probably forever, while Ronson – like those convicted initially in *Blue Arrow* – was not disqualified from acting as a director.[18] It is rumoured that during his spell as an accused, before the extreme stress and *nolle prosequi* that put an end to his trial, *Guinness 2* defendant Seelig earned £1 million a year from consultancy – which does not require registration and might have continued even had he been convicted – while *Blue Arrow* defendant Brimelow was unemployed and lived on family hand-outs for years pending her trial, whose delay was no fault of hers. For most individual and corporate defendants, the opportunity cost (in career terms) of being prosecuted is enormous, almost irrespective of the outcome, and this fact should focus our attention on use of discretion to prosecute, although such sensitivity will normally favour people of previous 'good character' and thereby produce an unintended social bias. Nevertheless, the semi-privatization of justice is an important element in the set of sanctions that are applied in the non-carceral archipelago within which white-collar offenders are 'warehoused.'

CONCLUSION

When socially prominent businesspeople are to be prosecuted or imprisoned, they and others in their social group raise questions about the purpose of 'the system': is it essentially fraud prevention or is it 'justice' (as defined in bourgeois conceptions of just desserts)? If the criminal justice process became more 'efficient' and/or if more fraudsters were prosecuted, would this situation help to prevent fraud or even assist social equity? The mode in which we deal with crime is legitimately a site for struggle. If large cases are handled by the SFO from the beginning, rather than being subject to a DTI investigation into corporate governance, this should speed up the criminal process, but issues of public importance – whether the same person should be both chairman and chief executive of a major public corporation; whether the risks of transaction banking outweigh the benefits; the appropriate role of pension-fund trustees – may not be aired to the same extent unless, like *Maxwell*, they raise essential questions of public interest. (In the latter sort of case, defendants then face problems of multiple jeopardy from civil, regulatory, and crime investigation agencies.)

The way in which these tensions will be played out remains unresolved. Although conflicts remain over whether certain forms of securities misconduct are 'real crime,' some expensive acquittals have led even the SFO's director to agree that some cases would best be diverted from the criminal process into the regulatory one, particularly for suspects on the margins of major frauds whose presence as criminal defendants makes cases unmanageably large (Staple 1993). Yet the symbolic issues loom large in public debate: granted that *some* forms of securities and insurance misconduct can be dealt with more expeditiously (and at no expense to the taxpayer, since legal aid is not available) by the appropriate regulatory bodies, is this (or, for that matter, the present) form of diversion for adult offenders really fair on people prosecuted for minor offences in the 'blue-collar' field? And, more sociologically, what would be the effect of such an explicit policy on the ideology of equality before the law (assuming that the public got to hear about it)? The contrast between treatment of tax fraudsters (who can repay their debts and fines) and social-security fraudsters (who cannot do so) is part ideological, part pragmatic. Simultaneously, there is an enormous push to toughen up the English criminal process to require greater pre-trial disclosure of its case by the defence and to tie defendants to that case, making the fraud trial like a civil trial conducted before a jury. This move is being resisted by defence lawyers, who see it as a slippery slope to erosion of the accusatorial system: in serious fraud cases, not only does the defendant have to answer questions truthfully; he or she must also supply the detailed defence case so that the prosecutor can alter the indictment to cover what he or she actually did!

The need to be seen to be doing something about vast and visible crimes – given considerable publicity by the media – versus the desire to minimize costs and risk incrimination of 'respectable entrepreneurs' involves structural balances more delicate than those caused by regulation of the poor. What I have sought to throw some light on is how these contradictions are worked out in practice and what are the consequences of them. White-collar crime causes policy problems that have been neglected by 'left realists' who imply that local accountability is the primary solution to crime (Matthews and Young 1986). How would such a policy deal with international crime? Would a left realist want white-collar prosecutions to be independent of any political influence (and if so, how?) or to be accountable (and if so, to whom and for what sorts of policy decisions?).

King Lear observes in his 'madness': 'See yonder justice railing at yon thief? Change places and handy, dandy, Which is the justice and which the thief?' Whether the justice's 'accidental' underdeclaration of income would be detected and whether it would, if handled criminally, reach the attention of the Lord Chancellor's Department are matters for speculation. If (assuming differential gender-based fraud risks) he were merely found out but not prosecuted, would he be fired or reform 'his' sentencing practice towards the poor? *Pace* Braithwaite and Pettit's (1990) utilitarian logic, perceptions of seriousness of crime are often conflated with actual use of criminal justice and penal consequences of the act in question. Should we then applaud the symbolic reintegration implied by the Queen Mother's shaking hands with *Guinness* convict and multimillionaire Gerald Ronson at a Covent Garden charity function while he was still on parole (Levi 1991b)?[19] It is hard to believe that she would knowingly have shaken hands with a thief!

NOTES

1 The Department of Employment (DOE) has 820 inspectors to investigate unemployment-benefit fraud, while the Department of Social Security (DSS) has some 3,000 staff to deal with income-support fraud.

2 The defence in one case alone – the *Blue Arrow* market manipulation in 1991–2, paid for initially by the banks that had employed those charged and that were also themselves defendants – cost about as much as the SFO's annual budget. Following the quashing of their convictions by the Court of Appeal on the grounds, inter alia, that the trial had become unmanageable, the taxpayer will now have to reimburse costs.

3 The Fraud Investigation Group was the Office of the DPP's precursor to the SFO and, until recently, continued with this full title. Its staff, however does not have the power to direct investigation or to investigate, though the police may (and increasingly do) accept its influence. From 1995, the SFO will take over most of its cases.

4 The SFO's four-part *Guinness* saga began with the 1990 convictions of four leading players in the company's take-over battle for Distillers. Ernest Saunders, Gerald Ronson, and stockbroker Anthony Parnes were jailed. Jack Lyons was fined £3 million for theft, false accounting, and conspiracy. The convictions were seen as vindication of the decision to form the SFO to tackle complex commercial crimes. The organization's reputation suffered with the collapse of the *Guinness 2* trial. Roger Seelig,

former director of Morgan Grenfell, suffered exhaustion conducting his own defence and was deemed too ill to continue. His co-defendant, Lord Spens, was later acquitted. *Guinness 3* never happened. Charges against take-over consultant David Mayhew were dropped before his case reached court in February 1992. In February 1994, Thomas Ward was acquitted of theft.

Within days of the collapse of *Guinness 2* in February 1992, four financial advisers were convicted for their part in the *Blue Arrow* fraud. Six out of ten charged were found guilty of conspiracy to mislead the Stock Exchange over a plan by Blue Arrow to raise funds for a take-over bid. In July 1992, four City advisers had their convictions overturned. Appeal judges said that the case was unfair because of its complexity. The case is estimated to have cost more than £35 million.

Although London was at the heart of the world's biggest bank fraud (*BCCI*), SFO investigators were hindered because many of the central figures were beyond the reach of the British courts. Syed Akbar, former head of the treasury at the collapsed bank, was charged with 16 counts of false accounting relating to £117 million in 1982 and £646 million between 1983 and 1986. He was charged in April after he was deported from France. An estimated £10 billion in undisclosed transfers was made form London. The SFO formed a special, sixty-strong unit to investigate those responsible for the bank's collapse in 1991. The liquidator, Touche Ross, has estimated the value of its own expertise at £85 million. Only £311 million has so far been recovered.

Peter Clowes was jailed for ten years in 1992 after he was found guilty of fraud and stealing investors' money in the £109 million collapse of his company. Peter Naylor was also jailed for his part in the affair. (Michael Levi, 'Paying the Price for Macho Posturing,' *Observer*, 4 July 1992, 13.)

In 1990, Asil Nadir's company Polly Peck collapsed with £1.3 billion of debt. Nadir was arrested and charged first with 18 accounts of theft and false accounting of £18 million, and subsequently with theft involving £155 million. Nadir was later declared bankrupt after creditors claimed £80 million, and an injunction froze £278 million of his assets. He had contributed £360,00 to the Conservative party. In May 1993, he jumped bail and fled to Cyprus. (Michael Gillard, 'Hook, Line and Stinker,' *Observer*, 4 July 1993, 13).

5 Including did they have grounds for believing that what they were doing would be publicly tolerated?

6 *Smith v. Director of Serious Fraud Office*, [1992] 3 All ER 456.

7 (Almost) everyone agrees that the looting of corporate assets, particularly from 'widows and orphans,' is a serious crime, so the pragmatic justification that high-profile arrests are needed to teach 'the business community' the proper norms of conduct before the trial gets under way was inapplicable to the allegations made against the Maxwells. This argument was more contentious in *Blue Arrow*, which involved an

alleged attempt to trick the market into believing that a rights issue to fund the take-over of the American Manpower Inc. was more succcessful than it was: this eventually resulted in the Court of Appeal's quashing the convictions of the four people (out of eleven charged) who had been convicted by the jury.

8 The DSS operates a selective prosecution policy focusing on what it describes as 'serious fraud': in 1989–90 – the last year for which these data are available – its 13,577 prosecutees were overpaid by £39 million, a modest sum by comparison with cases handled by fraud squads. The DOE's 820 inspectors investigated 335,678 cases and prosecuted 3,456 persons during 1990–1. In 1991–2, 2,260 individuals (including 49 employers) were prosecuted, and – an alternative assessment of impact – 50,000 claims for benefit were withdrawn. Some of the DSS and DOE cases, and all of the police cases, are prosecuted by the CPS, but since the annual criminal statistics in England and Wales only patchily cover non-police prosecutions, I have obtained these data directly from the non-police departments.

9 Presumably in order to satisfy the British and American public that the United Kingdom had never supplied the arms that had been turned on the allied troops and, perhaps more salient, to reassure Arab oil interests. After the prosecution failed to suppress the secret government files, and a former minister admitted that he had encouraged the trade, the prosecution was finally dropped: had the files not been disclosed, a miscarriage of justice might have occurred, which some suggest would have been a deliberate malicious prosecution of persons known not to have deceived the DTI (D. Leigh 1993). The prosecution was undertaken by HM Customs and Excise, and when it charged the directors, it probably did not know about the prior history of contacts among them, DTI, and MI5. If it had known, it is doubtful that it would have prosecuted (Levi 1995).

10 As it had done almost a century earlier, when observing that 'while Parliament is leisurely enquiring into the working of the Companies Acts and discussing their amendment, investors are being fleeced, and the worst types of company promoters are flourishing' (31 July 1897).

11 Though the police controlled primarily the public leisure habits of the poor.

12 Except in the case of SIB, whose powers to investigate persons who are not members of SROs are granted by statute.

13 The delineation of whether something is deposit-taking, an investment within the terms of the FSA, or something not covered by either act is often difficult. For some analysis of the meaning of deposit-taking, see *SCF Finance Company Limited v. Masri* [1987] 1 All ER 175.

14 In England, unlike in Canada and the United States, defendants cannot elect trial by judge without a jury, except by seeking trial before magistrates.

15 Indeed at Lloyd's of London's insurance market, for reasons that are obscure, the standard (like that in police disciplinary hearings) is the criminal one. In the United

States, the burden of proof is the preponderance of evidence rather than beyond all reasonable doubt, and my U.S. sources state that this does make a substantial difference there.

16 The way that powers are exercised under the Banking Act, 1987, is more complicated than for SROs as the Securities and Futures Authority. The Bank of England has power to impose conditions on authorization of any bank such that the bank itself will risk being deauthorized if it employs people in specified positions whom the Bank considers not to be fit and proper. Normally, this extends to people who exert substantial control over the financial institution and excludes, for example, compliance officers, who may be 'sanctioned' informally.

17 Or – somewhat academically, and so that the appearance of equal treatment of Parnes and Mayhew would be sustained – subject to Parnes's acceptability to a 'pukka' broking firm under the same conditions of close supervision as was Mayhew, who was authorized to deal in investments after the SFO decided to offer no evidence against him and aborted *Guinness 3*.

18 Though unlike those convicted in *Blue Arrow*, he was not subjected to any regulatory action, since he was not engaged in banking, investment, or insurance business, the only areas in which such 'fit and proper person' requirements apply.

19 The irony is that the subsequent collapse in the profitability of his Heron corporation means that he now has few funds left to donate.

11

Saving the Savings and Loans? U.S. Government Response to Financial Crime

KITTY CALAVITA AND HENRY N. PONTELL

In early 1988, the mass media began to report signs of extensive fraud in the U.S. savings and loan (S&L) industry.[1] After his election as president, George Bush announced a major effort to bail out the crippled industry and investigate and prosecute thrift crime. Several months later, Congress passed the Financial Institutions Reform, Recovery and Enforcement Act of 1989 (FIRREA). This law authorized $225 million over three years to finance the Justice Department's prosecution of financial fraud. The FBI's budget for these cases went from less than $60 million for fiscal year 1990 to over $125 million in 1991, and its personnel dedicated to financial fraud almost doubled (U.S. Congress, Senate, 1992, 45). By 1992, over eight hundred S&L offenders had been convicted, with 77 per cent receiving prison terms (U.S. Department of Justice 1992b, 66).

This chapter attempts to explain two related paradoxes regarding the state's response to the S&L loan debacle. First, the government's aggressive reaction to these crimes and the relatively high rate of imprisonment of those convicted seem to contradict extensive evidence in the white-collar crime literature relating to legal favouritism towards elite offenders and the state's general reluctance to take corporate crime seriously. Since Edwin Sutherland's (1949) study of the leniency received by corporate offenders compared to perpetrators of more traditional street crimes, a vast literature has attested to this differential treatment (Geis 1967; W.G. Carson 1970a, 1982; Clinard 1979; Clinard and Yeager 1980; Ermann and Lundman 1978, 1980; Barnett 1982; Levi 1984; Pearce and Tombs 1988; Snider 1978, 1991).

The government's aggressive effort seems inconsistent with that literature. We suggest below that the way the state responds to corporate crime depends in large part on the nature of the offences and their relationship to the broader financial and economic structure. We argue that the government's response to

S&L fraud was related to the perceived need to contain damage to the financial system and avert a potentially crippling economic crisis. Unlike corporate crimes hurting workers (e.g., violations of safety and health codes) or consumers (e.g., product-safety violations), these crimes can undermine the financial system itself. Washington is likely to react more vigorously than it would to the traditional manufacturing-sector crimes addressed in much of the literature on white-collar crime.

The government's unprecedented response has none the less been sharply criticized as under-funded, inefficient, and plagued by overwhelming backlogs (US General Accounting Office [GAO] 1992a, 1993). Here, then, is the second paradox. While the state has funnelled hundreds of millions of dollars to enforcement and has launched unprecedented efforts to prosecute and imprison the elite offenders, substantial evidence suggests that the response remains inadequate. In an attempt to explain its limitations, we use the concept of 'system capacity' (Pontell 1982, 1984). We show that despite the best intentions of Congress and law enforcement agencies, the system possesses an intrinsic limitation on its capacity to respond. This situation highlights the importance of such systemic factors and their utility in explaining limitations to law enforcement, despite the urgency of deterring such crimes.

We offer, first, an overview of the scholarship addressing the relatively lenient treatment of white-collar crime. Second, we trace law-enforcement strategies in the investigation and prosecution of thrift (or S&L) crime, and explore the possibility that these crimes differ from those traditionally focused on by students of white-collar crime. Citing the strategies used vis-à-vis thrift fraud, we argue that the vigourous response is less a reflection of a new emphasis on control of white-collar crime than it is a belated and desperate attempt at damage control in a decimated financial sector. Third, we discuss the system's limited capacity as a potential explanation for the inadequacies of this effort, using as illustrations statements from enforcement officials involved in the clean-up.

Our data come from a variety of sources, including government documents, Congressional Hearings and Reports, and interviews with key policy-makers, investigators, and regulators. We tape-recorded our open-ended interviews with FBI investigators and officials in the Federal Deposit Insurance Corp. (since 1989, the thrifts' insurance agency), the Office of Thrift Supervision (the federal regulatory agency for thrifts since 1989), and the Resolution Trust Corp. (the agency charged with managing and selling insolvent thrifts' assets). They took place in Washington, D.C., and in field offices in California, Texas, and Florida, and generally lasted between one and two hours, with some crucial respondents being interviewed several times over the course of two-and-a-half years. Secondary sources and journalistic accounts of specific cases supplement the primary and archival material.

'WHITE-COLLAR CRIME' REVISITED

Sutherland (1949, 2) defined white-collar crime as 'crime committed by a person of respectability and high social status in the course of his occupation.' Recognizing that this concept encompasses many types of behaviour and motivation, subsequent scholars have attempted further classification. The most widely accepted distinction is that between 'corporate,' or 'organizational' crime, which is committed by executives acting as representatives of their institutions, and 'occupational' crime, perpetrated by white-collar individuals acting independently of their organization and victimizing it for personal gain (Clinard and Quinney 1973; Schrager and Short 1978; Shapiro 1980; Wheeler and Rothman 1982); and J. Coleman 1985). It was the former variety that Sutherland (1949) addressed in his landmark study of seventy large corporations, and it is this type that has been the focus of much subsequent research on white-collar crime.

Within this tradition, it has generally been found that corporate or business crimes are treated differently by law enforcers than are common street crimes. Clinard and Yeager's (1980) comprehensive study of legal actions taken against 582 of the largest U.S. corporations supports Sutherland's contention not only that corporate crime is extensive but that the law enforcement and regulatory system tends not to take it very seriously. Case studies of specific industries and/or specific corporate violations corroborate these findings. Whether the subject is the great electrical-company conspiracy (Geis 1967), occupational safety-and-health violations (Carson 1970a, 1970b; 1982b; Berman 1978; Calavita 1983), environmental crimes (Gunningham 1974; Barnett 1992), or antitrust infringements (McCormick 1977), a vast literature documents the anaemic legal response.

Some scholars have explained this lenient response as a product of the greater identification of judges with business defendants, whose class backgrounds, education, and occupational prestige are similar to their own (Clinard and Yeager 1980, 286–94). Others have looked at offenders' financial ability to secure the highest-quality, most expensive legal counsel (Mann 1985; J.W. Coleman 1989, 190). Some scholars (Yeager 1988; Snider 1991) have addressed the structural limitations on the state in prosecuting business offenders whose enterprises provide the employment and tax revenues on which the state depends.

A handful of researchers have contested this depiction of relative leniency. Katz (1980), for example, has argued that, beginning in the 1970s, public officials and prosecutors increasingly took the initiative in prosecuting white-collar crime. Hagan and Nagel (1982), in their study of the Southern District of New York from 1963 to 1976, point to 'proactive' policies, which included an increase in resources for prosecution of white-collar crime and an 'activist' approach to successful completion of these cases. Wheeler, Weisburd, and Bode (1982), concluding their study of eight types of white-collar crime in seven federal districts in the late 1970s, speculate that the assumed favourable treatment has always been a myth.

Despite these periodic challenges, most studies continue to point to the difficulties of prosecuting corporate crime. Indeed, not only are disparities in prosecution and sentencing widely, if not 'universally recognized' (Clinard and Yeager 1980, 286), but an extensive research tradition has developed documenting the difficulties of regulating corporate behaviour with the criminal-justice model. Many now suggest abandoning that approach for a more 'cooperative' model (Thomas 1982; Fisse and Braithwaite 1983; Braithwaite 1985a). Thus, while some recent research may show decreasing tolerance for white-collar and corporate crime, Sutherland's primary thesis remains well entrenched.

'THROW THE CROOKS IN JAIL': CRIME CONTROL OR DAMAGE CONTROL?

Attorney-General Richard Thornburgh (U.S. Department of Justice 1990, 1) prefaced a Department of Justice report on S&L fraud with the promise, 'The American public can be assured ... that prosecution of white collar crime – "crime in the suites" – and particularly savings and loan crimes, will remain a top priority of the Department of Justice.' In a speech to U.S. attorneys in June 1990, President Bush swore, 'We will not rest until the cheats and the chiselers and the charlatans [responsible for the S&L disaster] spend a large chunk of their lives behind the bars of a federal prison' (quoted in U.S. Department of Justice 1990, 1). The president was unequivocal: 'We aim for a simple, uncompromising position. Throw the crooks in jail' (quoted in U.S. Congress, House, 1990a, 128).

Undoubtedly, Bush hoped to gain political mileage from an emphatic response to the worst financial fraud epidemic in U.S. history. However, this was not empty political rhetoric – at least not entirely. By 1989, both the legislative and executive branches were devoting considerable attention to the investigation and prosecution of S&L fraud. FIRREA allocated $225 million to the Justice Department's financial fraud efforts. Almost immediately, the number of FBI personnel assigned to financial fraud investigations climbed from 822 to 1,525. The Department of Justice's total budget for financial fraud went from $80.8 million to $212.2 million (U.S. Congress, Senate, 1992, 45). The 1989 law also provided for increased penalties for financial-institution crimes and extended the statute of limitations for such crimes from five to ten years.

The Comprehensive Thrift and Bank Fraud Prosecution and Taxpayer Recovery Act of 1990 focused on law enforcement efforts and enhanced sanctions against thrift fraud. It increased penalties for concealing assets from government agencies, obstructing their functions, and placing assets beyond their reach, as well as obstructing examination of a financial institution. The law also raised maximum statutory penalties from twenty to thirty years' imprisonment for a range of violations, including false entries or reports, bribery, and intentional misapplication of thrift funds, reserving the most severe sanctions for 'financial crime kingpins.'

Special working groups and task forces to cope with the S&L crisis had been drawn up in the law enforcement and regulatory communities during the early and mid-1980s. The Bank Fraud Working Group in Washington, DC, brought together high-echelon officials from the Office of the Comptroller of the Currency, the Department of Justice, and the Treasury Department to improve communication, provide an arena for policy discussions, and generally coordinate enforcement. In late 1983, a special task force ('Texcon') was established in Dallas, Texas, to deal with the overload of criminal referrals involving S&L fraud related to land purchases and condominium development along Route I-30 east of Dallas. While Texcon processed the I-30 cases, the Dallas Bank Fraud Task Force ('Thriftcon') was launched to deal with the numerous other S&L cases still being referred to the FBI in that city. The Department of Justice increased the Dallas FBI staff by 19 special agents and added support personnel and equipment. More prosecutors were assigned to assist the U.S. Attorney in the Northern District of Texas. When the Thriftcon Task Force began operations in 1987, it included twenty-seven FBI agents, twenty-one Department of Justice and Northern District of Texas attorneys, four officials from the Office of Thrift Supervision (OTS, the thrift regulatory agency), and seventeen Internal Revenue Service (IRS) agents. By 1990, Thriftcon had 94 full-time agents. By the spring of 1992, it included 150 law-enforcement personnel from four Justice Department sections or agencies and two Treasury Department divisions (U.S. Attorney, Northern District of Texas, 1990; U.S. Congress, House, 1990b, 4–5; U.S. Department of Justice 1992b). While the Dallas Bank Fraud Task Force is the nation's largest and most active, the attorney-general has set up similar task forces in twenty other major cities.

With this infusion of resources and personnel, the number of prosecuted S&L offenders grew quickly. Investigations of fraud involving major financial institutions increased by 54 per cent from 1987 to 1991. The FBI opened over

260 major investigations every month and in 1992 had over 4,300 under way, of which about 1,000 involved S&Ls (U.S. GAO 1992a). From October 1988 to April 1992, over 1,100 defendants were formally charged in 'major' S&L cases,[2] and 839 were convicted (for completed prosecutions, the conviction rate was 92.6 per cent). Of the 667 offenders sentenced by the spring of 1992, 77 per cent received a prison sentence (U.S. Department of Justice 1992b, 64).

Clearly, the U.S. government had begun an unprecedented attack on fraud in financial institutions. At no time in its history has it allocated so many resources and concentrated so much of its law enforcement effort on pursuing white-collar criminals and sending them to prison. Why? Two obvious explanations come to mind. The first is simply that the epidemic of thrift fraud has required a corresponding response. The second is that this assault is an indication of the erosion of the official tolerance for white-collar crime postulated by the scholars cited above. There is a common flaw in both of these explanations, however: the 'crackdown' is highly selective. While Congress, Justice, and the thrift regulatory agencies take a 'get-tough' approach to such fraud, corporate and business crime in other sectors is virtually ignored. Since the Reagan administration began dismantling the Occupational Safety and Health Administration in the early 1980s (Calavita 1983), sanctions against employers who violate safety and health standards have plummeted. Even though hundreds of thousands of U.S. workers are killed or disabled annually in work-related accidents and illnesses, convictions of employers almost never result in criminal prosecution, much less imprisonment. (Production of asbestos will result in 170,000 deaths from lung cancer and other related diseases, yet none of the corporate executives who deliberately concealed the dangers have been criminally charged.) The U.S. Food and Drug Administration continues to be reluctant to recommend criminal prosecution of corporate executives who conceal the hazards of their products or deliberately fabricate data to attest to their safety (J. Coleman 1985, 44–5). Indeed, for traditional forms of corporate crime in the manufacturing sector, there is no evidence of any crackdown.

In order to understand the relatively vigorous response to thrift fraud, we should examine the details of that response. Priority is placed on financial institutions that are on the verge of failure or are already insolvent and in which fraud played a significant role in the collapse. The official definition of 'major cases' – those that receive top priority – refers to dollar losses, the role of insiders, and so on (as discussed above), yet government officials consistently specify another factor as among the most important ingredients: whether or not the alleged fraud contributes to insolvency. Ira Raphaelson, special counsel for Financial Fraud in the Deputy Attorney General's Office, was questioned by the Senate subcommittee recently:

Senator Dixon: 'How do you define a major case?'

Mr. Raphaelson: 'If it involves an alleged loss of more than $100,000 or involves a failed institution.'

Senator Dixon: 'There are at least 4300 cases over $100,000?'

Mr. Raphaelson: 'Or involving a failed institution, it might be less than $100,000. But because it is linked to a failure, we still consider it a major case.' (U.S. Congress, Senate, 1992, 10–11)

At the same hearing, the GAO (U.S. GAO 1992a, 1) defined such cases as 'those involving failed institutions or alleged losses of $100,000 or more.' One FBI agent in Florida gave us an example: 'If you steal over 5 million dollars and you make a bank fail, you've popped the bubble on the thermometer there!' The same agent tied the influx of federal resources to the economic importance of these cases. A few years ago, 'We as financial crimes or financial institution fraud investigators were vying for manpower in this office along with [drugs and public corruption] squads. We had to share the white collar crime staffing ... with these people. *Now that we've had such dramatic increases in the number of failed institutions in the last year and a half, they're being investigated here and Congress has appropriated huge amounts of funds to target that.*'

In June 1990, the Office of Thrift Supervision, the Resolution Trust Corp., and the Federal Deposit Insurance Corp. developed a matrix with which to 'prioritize' investigations and used it to draw up a list of the 'Top 100' thrift institutions for investigative purposes. Among the most important ingredients were financial health, whether fraud had contributed to insolvency, and the economic effect on the larger community.

Even a cursory look at enforcement policies and statistics suggests that these priorities have shaped responses. A report from the GAO (U.S. GAO 1992a, 8) reveals that of the approximately 1,000 major thrift cases under investigation in fiscal 1991, one-third involved failed institutions, and two-thirds, fraud that contributed to major losses. Thriftcon in Dallas handles only failed institutions. Indeed, the task force was established in 1987 when officials in Dallas learned that eighteen area thrifts were on the verge of collapse. In answering to a query from Congress about criminal referrals made in connection with Silverado Savings and Loan, the Department of Justice (quoted in U.S. Congress, House, 1990a, 121) explained that one of the referrals in question was dropped: 'This matter involved no demonstrable loss; prosecution was declined in the United States Attorney's Office, District of Colorado.'

The regulatory and law enforcement community thus concentrates on fraud in failed or failing, 'problem' institutions, in which the alleged fraud undermines the thrift's financial health. The focus is reminiscent of Patricia Ewick's (1985) study of 'redundant regulation.' Ewick found that Securities and Exchange Commission (SEC) sanctioning varies according to a firm's 'operational viability,' with the most severe administrative sanctions applied to those that are already bankrupt. She concluded that this is 'redundant regulation,' in that it is too late to reform the organization through deterrent sanctions, and in any case administrative sanctions are largely irrelevant once the firm has failed. Ewick suggests that this selectivity may be related to reluctance to sanction viable offenders for fear of harming innocent employees and/or clients.

This interpretation may be partially accurate, but it does not tell the whole story. Financial regulators have long been reluctant to punish wrongdoers and publicize fraud lest it undermine public confidence and trigger a 'run' on the bank. The House Committee on Government Operations (U.S. Congress, House, 1988, 17) has pointed out: 'Although every other federal regulatory agency discloses final enforcement actions, the banking agencies continue to refuse to ... disclose the existence or a summary of final ... enforcement orders taken against individuals or institutions.' The U.S. Attorney for the Southern District of Texas testified before the House Subcommittee on Commerce, Consumer, and Monetary Affairs (U.S. Congress, House, 1987, 126): 'The public's faith in the security and integrity of their banking institutions is considered so vital to the continued viability of the banking system that Congress has promulgated laws to prevent people from even starting rumors about a bank's solvency or insolvency.'

However, that officials have targeted failing institutions – and investigate only frauds leading to significant losses – suggests that they intend precisely to shore up investors' confidence and protect the economy. In other words, the crackdown on financial fraud represents less crime control than damage control, designed to salvage a fraud-ridden and ailing industry. Rep. Henry Gonzalez, chair of the House Committee on Banking, warned FBI Director William Sessions about thrift crime: 'The issue is very, very serious. We cannot allow ... a loss of faith in the deposit insurance system ... Confidence is at the root of everything because if we lose the confidence of the people, no system will stand up to that' (U.S. Congress, House, 1990b, 15). GAO Director Harold Valentine (U.S. GAO 1992a, 19) called bank and thrift fraud and the financial collapse to which they contributed 'perhaps the most significant financial crisis in this nation's history.' The U.S. Department of Justice (1990, 2) referred to it as 'the unconscionable plundering of America's financial institutions.' A senior staff member of the Senate Banking Committee explained the attention being given to thrift fraud: 'This industry is very close to the heart of the American economy! We teetered on the edge of a major, major problem here. Well ... we got a major problem, but we teetered on the edge of a major collapse ... You know, all these [financial] industries could bring down the whole economy' (personal interview).[3]

Bank and thrift fraud is of course not new. Investigators and regulators report that abuse by thrift insiders was frequent in the 1960s and 1970s, but that it attracted little attention, since the institutions were generally thriving (personal interview). One regulator who said that fraud has always existed in thrifts claimed that '[hot prices in real estate are] the only thing that pulled everybody's asses out for years' (personal interview). A staff member of the Senate Banking Committee explained it this way, 'People basically bet on the come. If the market goes up, we all win. And if the market goes down, you begin to look back and see what corners were cut. *But you don't look back if the market goes up*' (personal interview). The current response to thrift fraud thus has little to do with punishing crime per se; instead, it is crisis avoidance, aimed at preventing further damage to financial institutions that lie 'close to the heart of the American economy.'

A number of studies have recently noted the role of certain regulatory agencies in shoring up investor's faith, minimizing uncertainty and risk, and generally stabilizing the financial system. Shapiro's (1984) study of the SEC is exemplary. As she reports, SEC officials see their function as protecting the securities and exchange system, rather than as being its adversaries. Similarly, Reichman (1992, 2) underlines the stabilizing effect of regulating risks in the stock market: 'Regulations introduce hierarchies into the market that stabilize the environment so that individuals can continue to pursue profits.' Abolafia (1984) observes a similar dynamic in the commodities futures market, where regulations 'structure anarchy.' And Yeager (1986) points out that the Reagan administration, while virtually dismantling the worker safety-and-health system and eroding environmental protection, was relatively aggressive in attacking insider trading and stock-market fraud in an effort to restore confidence in the integrity of the market and encourage investment. As Snider (1991, 224) explains, 'Controlling this type of corporate crime turns out to be in the interests of the corporate sector overall, as well as being compatible with state objectives. Such laws protect the sanctity of the investment market, which is central to the ability of corporations to raise money by issuing shares.'

Much as this regulatory literature emphasizes the role of federal agencies in preserving faith in the financial system and stimulating investment, the U.S. government has begun a massive effort to salvage the thrift and banking industries directed less at penalizing wrongdoers than at limiting damage to the thrift industry and preventing comparable damage in other financial sectors. An upper-echelon official in Washington, when asked to comment on this interpretation, said simply, 'You hit the nail right on the head' (personal interview).

DAMAGE CONTROL: THE STATE'S LIMITED CAPACITY TO RESPOND

Despite the urgency of the government's efforts, there are signs that even this unprecedented blitz is inadequate. The *Public Citizen's Congress Watch* notes, 'There is a growing enforcement gap between galloping S&L fraud, and the government's slow-starting efforts to catch up with the criminals' (reprinted in U.S. Congress, House, 1990a, 98). The report disclosed that by 1990, close to seven thousand criminal referrals relating to possible S&L crime remained unaddressed by the Justice Department.[4] Although the backlog has been reduced since the influx of resources subsequent to passage of FIRREA (U.S. Congress, Senate, 1992, 4), unworked referrals continue to be a problem (see, for example, U.S. GAO 1992a).

The GAO's latest evaluation (U.S. GAO 1993) of the Justice Department's role is cautiously critical. The report concludes: 'GAO believes that Justice did not do all it could with the authority it has to strengthen the government's financial institution fraud program' (1993, 2). It cites, among other things, an extremely high rate of declination (formal refusal to take on a case): 'For example, the percentage of FBI investigations [that were] closed following U.S. Attorney declinations ... increased from 64 percent to 76 percent between fiscal years 1987 and 1991' (1993, 6).

Congress itself regularly questions the job that the Justice Department is doing. Introducing a House hearing entitled 'When Are the Savings and Loan Crooks Going to Jail?,' Rep. Frank Annunzio, chair of the Subcommittee on Financial Institutions Supervision, Regulation and Insurance of the House Committee on Banking, charged: 'Frankly I don't think the administration has the interest in pursuing Gucci-clad, white-collar criminals ... It is far easier putting away a sneaker-clad high school dropout who tries to rob a bank of a thousand dollars with a stick-up note, than a smooth talking S&L executive who steals a million dollars with a fraudulent note' (U.S. Congress, House, 1990a, 1). Rep. Joseph Kennedy complained, 'Over 21,000 referrals and complaints regarding S&L fraud, 7000 of which involved losses of more than $100,000, are currently gathering dust at the Department of Justice ... The swindlers are getting off easy. The few convicted have received less than 2 years jail time. Five times less than the 9.4 years the average bank robber gets' (1990a, 9).

We argued above that the government is interested in prosecuting these 'Gucci-clad' offenders. As we see here, however, systemic forces limit its ability to respond effectively. Pontell (1978, 1982, 1984) has demonstrated the importance of 'system capacity' in determining the limits of law enforcement; similarly, others have discussed 'system overload' (Geerken and Gove 1977), 'resource saturation' (Nagin 1978), and 'caseload controversy' (Nardulli 1979).

Two dimensions of the concept are most relevant to the S&L context. The first has to do with the difficulty of detecting and ferreting out financial fraud this complex and the related demand for vast resources. The second is the unprecedented scale of this fraud.

Given the high workload in criminal justice agencies, institutional limits affect all areas of crime control, especially complex corporate crime. As Katz (1979) has noted, white-collar crimes are woven into ordinary business routines and are often well hidden by intricate and misleading paper trails; crimes of the S&L sort are perhaps the most complex of all. One FBI agent observed:

When it comes to these insider, conspiratorial things, they are extremely complex, they are disguised ... The problem is figuring out what the crime is. What did they do, how did they do it, and then can I explain it to a court of law, to people who are high school graduates or less. You know, I spent I think about five and a half months where all day, everyday, I sat in a room with boxes and boxes of records. You look through these things to see where the money went ... It's difficult. To figure out what's happened in these things is really tough.

Some perpetrators deliberately used this complexity to disguise their offences as normal business transactions and put off wary regulators. One investigator described his experience: 'I have got a little financial background. I have been here for a while. It took the regulators a while to explain to me what they were doing, and the regulators said it took them a while to figure it out too. You have a Keating. [Charles] Keating said, "You don't understand my land deals and my junk bond deals." [David] Paul said, "You don't understand my junk bonds. You're too stupid"' (personal interview).

Each case may take several years and millions of dollars to investigate and prosecute. One FBI agent estimates the time expended on investigations: 'The FBI investigation from the time we open the investigation until we get it to the indictment stage ... I don't know any case that has taken less than six months, and some have taken three years. The really big cases – two or three years' (personal interview). Other investigators repeated the same concern: 'You have to subpoena massive amounts of documents, attempt to locate witnesses, attempt to put together things that were disguised ... That takes a lot of time ... Typical things – land flips, straw borrowers, money being diverted, in this case, laundered along the way – that took quite a bit of paperwork and review just to find out where it all went. This was a heck of a lot of work right here, just in this one case' (personal interview).

Prosecutors find it difficult to present these cases persuasively to a jury. As one investigator described it, 'These things get so convoluted and complicated that you really have a hard time discerning the end of the investigation. You have a hard time convincing the prosecutor that they ought to prosecute this case and then you have a virtually impossible time with the jury' (personal interview).

In response to the time and budget constraints posed by the complexity of these cases,[5] and in order to simplify them for presentation to lay juries, investigators and prosecutors have developed a streamlined 'rifle-shot' approach. They focus on one or two clear violations of the law that will be relatively easy to document and explain rather than attempting to piece together the whole fabric of complex illegal transactions, which could take many years and be far too complicated to follow. One investigator explained: 'The theory is not meant to prove a global picture in which these people caused the downfall of the institution. The theory is to pick out the best and most egregious case that has jury appeal, that has hard facts, that can be proven and understood by a jury ... So, you may have a myriad of ten or fifteen things, and you focus your investigation on those prime areas that you think are going to take you into the courtroom and get the guilty pleas' (personal interview).

An FBI agent related the rifle-shot approach to the complexity and expense of these cases:

The Bureau, I think, is very much up front on this, that you could stay in there with a bevy of agents ... and investigate every criminal allegation because many of these places were such rats' nests. You could investigate them for a decade and still not be sure that you got everything that they were involved in. So, you have to, with the resources you have say, all right, this guy's a bad actor, we want to be able to go in and get to the meat of the problem and we want to be able ... to see that he gets a substantial criminal sentence without having spent an inordinately long amount of time because we've got these other cases that are backing up over here. (Personal interview)

The rifle-shot approach has won accolades from the financial-fraud law-enforcement community. However, it leaves much criminal activity undetected and is likely to result in less prison time for offenders. One official explained this disadvantage: 'We started out originally with the strategy that was much more global and we found it consumed way too many resources ... Now what we've tried to do is the much more focused stategy ... The problem with not putting together the entire story is if he only pleads guilty to one or two counts he may not get significant jail time' (personal interview). An official at the Resolution Trust Corp. expressed dismay over the crimes that go unprocessed:

What I'm hoping to be able to do ... is to go back to these hot, smoldering ashes – because they are by no means cold, they are still very active – sift through them deeper, get into what I think are the very sophisticated convoluted fraud schemes that I believe are there, and pull together the network of fraudulent schemes between these incestuous relationships of these various institutions that I believe are there, but unfortunately resources and time constraints have let us take a big chunk and look at only pieces of it. But I still think that there is more there to be found. (Personal interview)

Frustrated officials repeatedly spoke of the impossibility of investigating and processing the thousands of offenders involved in the thrift disaster. A top federal law-enforcement official expressed it succinctly: 'There was a time [when] ... we were having trouble keeping people from giving us too much to deter, the groundswell ... Did we clean it up? Are we cleaning it up? No. We are addressing it. Are we addressing it quickly enough? Probably not' (personal interview).

Another official commented: 'I feel like it's the Alaskan oil-spill. I feel like I'm out there with a roll of paper towels. That's as close as I can come to it. The task is so huge, and what I'm worrying about is where can I get some more paper towels? ... I stand out there with my roll and I look at this sea of oil coming at me, and it is so colossal and at the same time people are yelling at me, 'The birds and fish are dying! Do something! Do it faster!' I'm going as fast as I can' (personal interview).

An enforcement official in Washington, D.C., explained that, while their efforts had received funding increases, the volume has created bottlenecks. Not only are funding increases still inadequate, but more general limitations exist: 'The greatest stumbling block is the lack of resources ... It's not just the lack of agents investigating. It's lack of prosecutors, lack of judges, lack of places to book' (personal interview).

An FBI agent expressed his frustration: 'There's so much of it going on ... And a lot of these people are very bright, exceedingly bright people. You easily catch the dumb ones and some of the bright ones, but the exceedingly bright ones ... I have to believe it continues. They out-fund us. They have more money to do it, to out-strategize us, and it continues. I know they're there' (personal interview). Another FBI agent was equally straightforward: 'I guess it's the old iceberg theory ... We probably see more of the stupid people, and by definition we're gonna catch a whole lot less of the smarter people. I don't have any way of knowing how much of the actual crime we are uncovering and prosecuting, but ... it's probably a very minuscule amount' (personal interview).

These statements suggest that, despite the unprecedented federal response, there are limits to the system's capacity. While these limitations help explain constraints on crime control in general, they are crucial in the S&L situation. While the imperatives of shoring up the financial system make the endeavour urgent, the complexity and unprecedented scale virtually ensure overload and limit the response.

DISCUSSION

We began by noting two apparent paradoxes relating to the state's response to S&L fraud. First, contrary to what much white-collar crime literature would predict, the U.S. government has undertaken a massive effort to investigate, prosecute, and imprison these elite offenders. In an attempt to explain this reaction, we suggest distinguishing among types of white-collar crime, according to the relationship between those offences and the broader economic system.

One distinction is vital here. The literature generally defines corporate crime as committed by corporate offenders on behalf of the organization; but thrift fraud undermines the institution and ultimately the industry itself. Thus there is a distinction between corporate crimes that increase profits and institutions' viability and those that may do long-term and far-reaching damage to the economic system. The state is likely to tolerate the former, taking action primarily in response to grassroots political demands and to salvage its own legitimacy. In contrast, the reaction to financial fraud is likely to be more rigorous, motivated by the need to preserve the economic system itself.

Here, then, is the second anomaly. For, despite the urgency and the resources, the response has been sharply criticized as inadequate. We borrow from the literature on system capacity to explore the underlying causes of this deficiency. The complexity and the almost unlimited volume of potential cases necessitate a kind of investigatory and prosecutorial triage. The inevitable result is, as the FBI agent quoted above put it, 'the old iceberg theory.'

In untangling these two apparent paradoxes, two general points find support here. First, studies of corporate crime must go beyond monolithic treatments of the state's response to elite offenders. Most important, they must specify not just the precise nature of those offences but their relationship to a variety of state interests. We have argued that the vigorous response here, relative to other sorts of corporate crime, can be explained at least in part by the potential for these crimes to decimate a whole financial sector and damage the larger economy. Unlike occupational health-and-safety violations, for example, which follow the logic of capital and increase corporate profits while undermining workers' health, these crimes violate that logic and undermine economic stability.

Second, this case underscores system-capacity arguments. For, despite urgent intervention, successes are at best partial. Overwhelmed by the complexity and the unprecedented volume, officials can only 'clean up the oil-spill with paper towels.'

NOTES

1 For a description of the types of savings-and-loan fraud and the factors that facilitated it, see Calavita and Pontell (1990, 1991).
2 'Major' cases are those in which '(a) the amount of fraud or loss was $100,000 or more, or (b) the defendant was an officer, director, or owner [of the S&L] ... , or (c) the schemes involved multiple borrowers in the same institution, or (d) involves [*sic*] other major factors' (U.S. Department of Justice 1992a, 9).
3 One official spoke of the 'havoc ratio' – the amount of havoc that a given thrift crime wreaks on the institution, the community, and the general economy. The reason these crimes are so serious, she said, is that they can do damage far beyond the millions of dollars that the offender actually steals. She explained, 'Using a thrift to go on a shopping spree is a lot like a fellow who wants to rob a teller at a bank ... In order to get the twenty thousand dollar cash drawer, he blows up the entire building' (personal interview).
4 As Justice Department officials are quick to point out, a 'referral' is not synonymous with a 'case' (which often involves several defendants but one set of crimes). Criminal referrals are formal complaints against an institution or individual, forwarded by the thrift regulatory agencies, or, more commonly, the institution itself. Several referrals often involve the same incident, and some percentage do not involve criminal violations or prosecutable cases. Thus, even if all referrals were acted on, the number of cases or even individual defendants would not be likely to approach the number of original referrals.
5 Most of these frauds were committed in the mid-1980s, so in addition to facing the statute of limitations, investigators must deal with the dampening effects of witnesses' fading memories and spotty documentation.

12

Public Policy towards Individuals Involved in Competition-Law Offences in Canada

W.T. STANBURY

Given the great rewards and low risks of detection, why do so many business people adopt the 'economically irrational' course of obeying the law? (Braithwaite 1985b, 7)

Since 1889, Canada has made certain restraints of trade (notably conspiracies to fix prices and/or divide up markets) criminal offences.[1] Thus Canada preceded the much more famous U.S. Sherman Act (1890) in attempting to prevent agreements among competitors designed to lessen competition because such agreements strike at the heart of what constitutes a competitive market economy. From the beginning, both countries have made both individuals and corporations subject to virtually all of the criminal offences in their respective competition/anti-trust law.

Even though all organizations operate through the directing minds of men and women, Canadian competition law has, until very recently, treated corporations as if they were sentient beings capable of reasoning and even of forming the necessary mental element associated with the commission of a criminal offence (*mens rea*). Thus judges have never questioned the idea of convicting several corporations for conspiring to fix prices and lessen competition unduly, even though no executives were charged. A review of conspiracy and bid-rigging cases suggests that the Crown believes that corporations do evil things – but the people employed by them do not!

The role of individuals in criminal offences under the Competition Act and its predecessors might be described as a little like *Hamlet* without the Prince of Denmark. First, until 1991, the Crown rarely charged individuals in such cases, except where firms involved were unincorporated (sole proprietorships or partnerships), and so the owner(s) and/or managers had to be charged and where the head of a trade association had been the central figure in organizing firms into a price-fixing conspiracy. Second, in conspiracy cases, the crown often named managers/executives as unindicted co-conspirators and used their testimony to secure convictions against the corporation for which they worked or other firms. In a few cases, the crown charged such executives (and their firms) but dropped the charges if their testimony helped convict their employer or other firms. Third, outside of three misleading advertising cases, the crown almost never requested imprisonment as a penalty – only a fine.[2] (This is in sharp contrast to the United States, particularly since the advent of the guidelines of the U.S. Sentencing Commission (1991). Fourth, until the compressed-gases and *Cormie* cases in 1991 and 1992, the crown has never sought large fines against the (few) individuals convicted of criminal offences under the Competition Act or its predecessors. However, in recent policy statements, the Director of Investigation and Research at the Bureau of Competition Policy has said that he will regularly recommend that individuals be charged – see below.

My purpose in this chapter is to examine the crown's policy with respect to the role of individuals in criminal offences under Canadian competition law and to provide an empirical analysis of the subject. The paper is organized as follows. The next section argues that individuals should be held accountable for their illegal anti-competitive acts, despite the problems of adopting a policy of almost always charging individuals directly involved in competition law offences. The following section reviews the historical record relating to the prosecution of individuals in conspiracy, price-maintenance, and misleading-advertising cases. The section after that examines the Director of Investigation and Research's policy statements concerning treatment of individuals involved in competition-law offences. The final section summarizes the important findings and offers some conclusions.

HOLDING INDIVIDUALS ACCOUNTABLE

The purpose of this section is to discuss the case for consistently prosecuting individuals directly involved in competition-law offences. From 1950–1 to 1991–2, in only 29 of 121 conspiracy and bid-rigging cases were individuals charged or subject to an application for a Prohibition Order without Conviction. The positive and normative bases for regularly prosecuting individuals can be summarized as follows:

• Only people are capable of forming mens rea and have the capacity to commit crimes. While corporations are often convicted of criminal offences, they can only act through individuals (employees, officers, or at the behest of directors).[3]

- Since individuals make the decisions that result in offences, they should be held accountable for their actions.
- Failure to hold individuals accountable for their unlawful acts in the context of their role as an employee of a corporation brings the law into disrepute because perpetrators, enforcers, judges, and ordinary citizens are aware that specific individuals 'made the crime happen' and are 'getting away with it,' usually because the crown has failed to indict them. A *Financial Post* editorial (27 August 1983, 9) noted that 'it's not a simple matter to pierce the corporate veil and root out the individuals who directed the corporation's unlawful activity. But it has to be done. And if the practice became more common, it's likely the need for elaborate new *corporate* sanctions would lessen as corporate officials faced the possibility of jail sentences and personal fines.'
- White-collar individuals are more likely to be deterred from committing illegal acts by suitable fines and/or imprisonment than are corporations. Only individuals can suffer stigma. They usually depend heavily on employment income, and fairly modest fines are more likely to deter illegal behaviour than much larger ones imposed on corporations. More important, 'corporate behaviour' is a polite fiction that blurs the reality that corporations do what their employees, officers, and directors have them do. The crown should not be party to continuation of this fiction.

Models of Defendant Behaviour

To alter an individual's behaviour, one ought to understand its determinants. The design of effective (and efficient) penalties and remedies must begin with at least an implicit 'model' of defendants' behaviour. Which one of these very simple models best describes the men (and women) who engage in competition-policy offences?

- *Crimes of impulse.* Emotional, short-term–horizon, non-economic motivation is usually associated with lower-class, blue-collar criminals for whom opportunity and immediate gratification of needs are paramount.
- *Economic man (or woman).* This model assumes maximization of the expected economic value of alternatives, including illegal ones, in light of one's risk preferences; no moral stigma is involved. (This person takes a benefit-cost approach to crime; 'moral costs' are assumed to be absent unless they translate into economic costs.) Violations of Canada's Competition Act (or the U.S. Sherman Act) are economic crimes rather than 'crimes of passion' or those resulting from moral lapses.
- *Economic man (or woman) subject to moral constraints of varying elasticity.*

Under most circumstances economic considerations will be paramount; however, moral concerns may prevent certain types of behaviour.

- *'Moral man' (or woman).* Such people are *not* influenced by economic gains or losses associated with violating the law; they always obey the law as a matter of principle or perhaps out of a belief that they will burn in hell if they do not.
- *Crime as learned behaviour.* If you grow up in an organization (or family) where the leading authority figures (or role models) condone or engage in corporate crime, the odds are that you will 'learn' similar behaviour (see Sutherland 1949).
- *Crime as product of environmental forces.* The individual here has almost no free will; economic and social forces combine to determine how the individual will behave in specified circumstances.
- *Crime committed as a result of ignorance or misunderstanding of the law.* Canada's Bureau of Competition Policy states, 'While we would hope that citizens generally understand that price-fixing is illegal, genuine ignorance of matters such as the price maintenance, or promotional contest provisions is probably not uncommon, particularly among people in the small business sector. There are numerous other situations where certainty about the aplication of the law requires a fairly sophisticated understanding. The *Guidelines* issued by the Bureau seek to address this reality'.[4]

I believe, based on two decades of study of hundreds of competition-law cases in Canada, that the economic man (or woman) model best describes the behaviour of those who are likely to violate the criminal law in this area. In a speech in 1974, U.S. Attorney-General William Saxbe put the matter this way: 'Anti-trust violations are not casual crimes. Business tycoons are not seized by a fit of passion that compels them to rig bids. Corporate executives do not gather in the boardroom to fix prices because they are in the throes of a joint, irresistible impulse. They violate the anti-trust laws deliberately because they want to and because they feel it's good for business.'

At the same time, it appears that some business executives and owners of small businesses fall into the third category. That is, their behaviour is influenced in some degree by moral and legal constraints – other than those that translate into economic costs or benefits. For them, the social stigma of being convicted of a criminal offence (even being charged) is substantial, perhaps very great.

The (alleged) perpetrators in competition-law offences are in the middle-to-upper level of socio-economic status. The heads of the largest business enterprises have high status and often have access to economic and political resources to defend themselves. In some cases, they may be able to insulate themselves ('plausible deniability') from subordinates who 'take the rap' (but whose illegal behaviour they have strongly influenced). During the merger boom in the late 1980s, the executives who initiated the largest and most daring take-overs (and restructurings) were heroes – for a short time, at least.

Connell (1977, 263) describes the defendants in U.S. price-fixing cases as follows:

As a class, individual defendants in price fixing conspiracy indictments are better edu-cated, more affluent and better informed than the average person who finds himself a defendant in a criminal case in a federal court. They have had the benefit of a college education, they are boy scout troop leaders, trustees of their churches, chairmen of the UGF drives, and veterans of combat in World War II. They are the kind of people who would probably not commit a violent crime. But they do commit a crime – price fixing – that in most cases entails a wilful, deliberate commitment to an illegal course of conduct over an extended period of time.

As a practical matter, it seems reasonable to take as the working hypothesis the 'economic man' (or woman) approach to competition-law offences. However, judges should continue to have sufficient discretion in sentencing to be able to modify the penalties where a 'moral considerations' defendant stands before them.

Problems/Issues with Individual Accountability

Even if public policy seeks to hold individuals responsible for their anti-com-petitive behaviour and seeks to ensure that corporations do not obtain any eco-nomic benefit from their 'ill-gotten gains' through an economic approach to fines (see Stanbury 1992), there are a number of problems or concerns with try-ing to hold individuals accountable for competition-law offences.

How can the crown identify the individuals who are the directing minds of the offence in the context of large corporate organizations in which decision-making responsibility is shared? It may be impossible to ascertain the different degrees of culpability of the executives involved in the decisions to commit the offence and in carrying it out.[5] Some individuals may have resisted contributing to the offence but had to 'go along' in order to retain their job and continue to be able to support their family. 'Whistle-blowers' are usually punished directly or indirectly for their efforts ('no good deed will go unpunished'). Even if the executive 'leaves quietly,' he or she may find it extremely difficult to obtain employment in the industry. In other industries, he may be feared as a potential 'fink' rather than as an honourable man who refused to violate the law.

There is often an evidentiary problem. The crown often needs the testimony of executives to convict the firm for which they work and/or other firms. Two trials could be required if individuals exercise their right to trial by jury.

Virtually all the benefits of the crime may have accrued to others – namely, shareholders (higher profits, dividends, share prices) and/or employees (higher wages/benefits, greater job security).[6] Of course, where the executive's compensation depends heavily on incremental profits (or reduced variability of profits), they may benefit directly.

While corporations may have indefinite economic lives and be little affected by a conviction for price fixing, individuals face a different situation. The greatest penalty may be the 'informal penalty' exacted by being charged with a criminal offence. Such informal, but very real, penalties include

- the stigma of a high-status, white-collar person being charged with a criminal offence;
- the costs of mounting a defence (while legal fees are tax deductible for a corporation, this is not the case for an individual);
- the possibility of being fired by their corporate employer – top management may feel that it can protect itself or the firm by being seen to cast out the evil-doers; and
- the potential loss of future income because of reduced career prospects.

Should we alter the criteria for conviction of individuals in competition-policy cases? For example, should we make mere knowledge of any violation within a company an offence? Should we presume that the firm's officer authorized and ordered the act? Should we bring within the scope of the legislation all corporate executives who had knowledge of the illegal acts or who had reason to know of a violation and authority to stop it but failed to do so?

What is the deterrent effect of imprisonment of such white-collar defendants as business executives in terms of deterrence against repetition by the defendant and as a 'lesson' to other potential violators? Do such executives experience particular shame or humiliation in being branded a 'common criminal,' i.e., a low-status person convicted of morally reprehensible acts such as theft, arson, or rape? Is deterrence reduced if executives do 'soft time,' i.e., a short sentence in a 'country club' prison for higher-status criminals? What are their future prospects *after* imprisonment, e.g., will they be hired back by the old firm or in the same industry?

There can be a conflict between efficiency and equity. The latter requires perpetrators of crimes to bear the punishment. Corporations are mere legal entities; as such they cannot commit crimes. Only natural persons can commit crimes.

They are the logical target for enforcement and penalties. Recall Woodrow Wilson's words in support of the Clayton and FTC acts in 1914:

We ought to see to it ... that penalties and punishments should not fall upon the business itself, to its confusion and interruption, but upon the individuals who use the instrumentalities of business to do things which public policy and sound business practice condemn. Every act of business is done at the command or upon the initiative of some ascertainable person or group of persons. These should be held individually responsible, and the punishment should fall upon them, not upon the business organization of which they make illegal use.

Should a company be allowed to compensate officers convicted and imprisoned for anti-trust violations? This is the moral-hazard issue: shareholders get the higher profits from, say, collusion, but executives 'take the fall.' In fact, the firm could offer its executives an 'insurance contract,' agreeing to compensate them for 'doing time' quietly.

Some more practical problems. How do we apprehend executives who flee jurisdiction?[7] What if the directing minds normally reside outside Canada, as in the case of the multinational enterprise.

Should there be minimum-sentencing provisions for individuals so judges cannot 'defeat' the purposes of the statute by being lenient with white-collar offenders? See the U.S. Sentencing Commission (1991), whose guidelines indicate minimum and maximum sentences.

REVIEW OF THE HISTORICAL RECORD

The purpose of this section is to review the penalties imposed on individuals in three types of competition policy offences: conspiracy and bid-rigging; price maintenance; and misleading advertising. While Canada's Competition Act contains a number of other criminal offences (see Table 1), very few cases have been prosecuted under these sections.

Conspiracy and Bid-Rigging

Between 1889 and 1991–2, some 146 conspiracy or bid-rigging cases were completed in Canada. Of these, 95 resulted in a conviction (Table 2), while 19 resulted in a Prohibition Order without Conviction (POWC) (Stanbury 1992, Table 2).

Of the 95 cases that resulted in conviction, only corporations were convicted in 69, corporations and individuals in 18, and only individuals in 8. In other words, only 26.3 per cent saw one or more individuals convicted. With very few

TABLE 1

Origins of the substantive provisions in Canadian competition legislation

Type of offence	Date
CRIMINAL OFFENCES	
Conspiracy (horizontal combinations)[a]	1889
Agreements among banks[b]	1986
Bid-rigging	1976
Mergers (horizontal or vertical)[c]	1910–86
Monopoly (and monopolization)[d]	1935–86
Predatory pricing	1935
Price discrimination	1935
Resale-price maintenance and refusal to supply	1951
Discriminatory advertising or promotion allowances	1960
Misleading price advertising[e]	1960
Misleading advertising re deceptive or misleading statements of fact or of guarantees/warrantees	1969
Misleading tests or testimonials	1976
Marketing practices	1976
Secondary boycotts	
Pyramid selling	
Referral selling	
'Bait and switch' selling	
Multiple ticketing	
Disclosure in promotional contests	
Sales above advertised prices	
CIVIL REVIEWABLE MATTERS	
Refusal to supply (domestic suppliers)	1976
Refusal to supply (foreign supplier)	1976
Consignment selling	1976
Exclusive dealing	1976
Tied sales	1976
Geographic market restrictions	1976
Foreign judgments	1976
Foreign laws and directives	1976
Abuse of dominant position (replaced monopoly in criminal law provisions)	1986
Delivered pricing	1986
Specialization agreements	1986
Mergers (replaced criminal law provisions)	1986

[a]The original conspiracy section had no force until 'unlawfully' was removed in 1900. Conspiracies relating to professional sports and foreign directives to Canadian firms to enter a conspiracy were made illegal in 1976.

[b]Transferred from section of the Bank Act.

[c]The Competition Act of 1986 replaced these offences by civil-reviewable-merger and abuse-of-dominant-position provisions.

[d]While the word 'monopoly' was in the definition of a combine in the Combines Investigation Acts of 1910 and 1923, it was not defined until 1935.

[e]There were forerunners of this povision in the Criminal Code.

Note re dates: 1976 = 1 January 1976; 1986 = 19 June 1986.

TABLE 2
Convictions of individuals and fines in conspiracy and bid-rigging cases (excluding POWC cases), 1889–1992

Period (fiscal year ending 31 March)	No. of cases resulting in conviction	Firms only	Firms and individuals	Individuals only	Total no. of individuals conficted	Average fine[a] per individual convicted
1889–1910	7	1	2	4	49+	360[b]
1911–25	0[c]	0	0	0	0	0
1926–42 (to May)	11[d]	3	5	3	61[d]	851[e]
1943–9	0[f]	0	0	0	0	0
1950–9	17	11	6	0	30[g]	408
1960–9	20	18	1	1	5[h]	1,540
1970–4[i]	7	6	1	0	4[j]	200
1975–9[k]	11	10	1	0	3	500
1980–4	7	6	1	0	1	2,000[l]
1985–9	13	13	0	0	0	0
1990–2	2	1	1	0	4	68,750[m]
Total	95	69	18	8	157+	n.a.

SOURCE: Tabulated from the annual reports of the Directors of Investigation and Research.
[a]In nominal dollars.
[b]Includes *R. v. Elliott* in which, according to the Court of Appeal, the trial judge 'directed that the defendant should enter into a recognizance for $4,000 to appear and receive sentence when called upon' (1905) 9 CCC 505 at 507. Note that $4,000 was then the maximum under the Criminal Code.
[c]Only one prosecution, but it resulted in an acquittal.
[d]Excludes *R. v. Simington et al.* in which some 50 defendants were convicted under other section of the Criminal Code after conspiracy charges were dropped. See (1926) 45 CCC 249.
[e]In Singer, five individuals were fined a total of $17,600, including $8,000 for one person. However, in the Basket Pool case, 15 individuals were each fined $100.
[f]Only one prosecution, but it resulted in an acquittal.
[g]Three partnerships involving 10 individuals counted as 10 individuals.
[h]Includes *R. v. C.W. Dent* which an individual was fined $7,500; he was tried separately but was part of Electrical Contractors case.
[i]Dated by date of final proceedings; in earlier periods, dated by trial judgment or date of sentence.
[j]Four individuals each fined $200 in NB meatpacking case.
[k]Between 1970 and 1979, seven POWCs were obtained; five were against a total of more than 30 individuals.
[l]Travelways bid-rigging case; firm fined $50,000.
[m]Two executives of Liquid Carbonic Inc. were each fined $75,000. Two executives of Canadian Liquid Air were fined $75,000 and $50,000.

exceptions, the individuals convicted were small businessmen operating as unincorporated businesses. For example, in *R. v. McGuire* (1903), 38 plumbing and heating dealers and contractors were convicted, all individuals. Of the 157 men[8] convicted in conspiracy and bid-rigging cases between 1889 and 1991–2, at least 49 were in cases completed between 1889 and 1910, and 59 in cases between 1926 and 1942. In the 60 conspiracy cases resulting in convictions since 1960, a total of only 17 individuals have been convicted in only six cases. In each of those cases, the individual(s) involved took an active part in the conspiracy to fix prices[9] or in bid-rigging, along with one or more corporations.

The fines imposed on individuals in cases completed since 1960 have generally been small – $50 (for four individuals in the *Linen Supply* case); $200 (for each of from individuals in the New Brunswick meat-packing case); $500 (for each of three bakers in 1975–6); and $2,000 for an individual in the *Charterways* bid-rigging case in May 1982. The only fines of note were imposed on C.W. Dent in 1961 ($7,500) and on four executives in the compressed-gases case (three at $75,000 and one at $50,000).[10]

As noted in Table 2, the average fine between 1889 and 1910 was $360 (or about $6,300 in 1992 dollars) for over 49 individuals (but this figure includes the fine of $4,000 imposed on the president of the Ontario Coal Association in 1903, which was the first conviction under the original legislation). Between 1926 and 1942 (there were no convictions between 1911 and 1925), the average fine imposed on 61 individuals was $851 in nominal terms (about $8,900 in 1992 dollars) (see also Table 3). Between 1950 and 1959, some 30 individuals were fined an average of $408 (or about $2,500 in 1992 dollars).

In Canada, no business executive has been imprisoned for violating the Competition Act or its predecessors over the past century with respect to price fixing, bid-rigging, price maintenance, predatory pricing, price discrimination, or monopoly.[11] Indeed, it was less common in the 1970s and 1980s to even charge a business executive with a violation of these provisions. In earlier times, the crown sometimes charged the individual believed to have organized the conspiracy. For example, in 1905 the president of the Ontario Coal Association was convicted of organizing an extensive price-fixing conspiracy. According to the Court of Appeal, the trial judge 'directed that the defendant should enter into a recognizance for $4000 to appear and receive sentence when called upon.'[12] The maximum fine for an individual was then $4,000 (equivalent to about $68,500 in 1992 dollars). In 1908, the president of the Alberta Retail Lumber Dealers Association was convicted of conspiracy, but he was fined only $500.[13] In one of the plumbing conspiracy cases in the 1930s, the crown charged only executives, even when corporate entities could have been charged.[14] In this case, a record fine of $8,000 was imposed in 1931 (equal to $83,600 in 1992). In contrast, 11 plumbing contractors were convicted as individuals, fined $100 each, and given a one year's suspended sentence in *R. v. White* in 1932.

In 1940, H.J. Badden, who helped organize the cartel in the *Container Materials* case, was convicted and fined $4,000, then the maximum. In 1942, Badden

TABLE 3
Fines imposed on corporations and individuals in conspiracy cases in Canada, 1923–42

	Individuals		Corporations	
	Number	Amount ($) per individual	Number	Amount ($) per corporation
1 Western Canada Fruit and Vegetable Wholesalers (1926)	4	$25,000[a]	4	$25,000[a]
2 Amalgamated Builders' Council (plumbers) (1930)	1	3,000	1	10,000
	2	2,000		
	9	1,000		
	1	500		
3 *R. v. White* (1931)	1	8,000	0	–
	2	4,000		
	2	800		
	11	100		
4 *Toronto Electrical contractors/R. v. Alexander* (1932)	8	1,000	7	2,500
	7	100		
5 Canadian Basket Pool (1933)	15	100	0	–
6 *Anthracite Coal Importers, Quebec/R. v. Canadian Import* (1933)	0	–	2	7,000
			1	6,000
			2	5,000
7 *Anthracite Coal Importers, Quebec/R. v. Hartt & Adair Co.* (1935)	0	–	2	5,000
			1	2,000
			1	1,000
			1	500
8 *Container Materials,* including Badden (1940, 1942)	1	4,000	13	10,000
			4	5,000
			2	2,500
9 Tobacco manufacturers and wholesalers (1941)	0	–	1	15,000
10 *R. v. Bathurst Power & Paper* (incl. Badden)	1	2,500	2	5,000
			2	2,500

SOURCE: Bureau of Competition Policy, memorandum 'Combines Investigation Act, 1923 to March 31, 1942' (Ottawa, typescript copy).
[a]These fines were imposed in *R. v. Simington et al.* (1926) 45 CCC 249 for fraud and offences under the Secret Commissions Act after charges under competition law statutes were dropped.

was convicted again, this time in *R. v. Bathurst Power and Paper et al.*, but fined only $2,500. Nine individuals were charged in *Imperial Tobacco*, not because they were owners of unincorporated businesses. Their conviction was overturned by the Court of Appeal. Two individuals were each fined $4000 in the *Howard Smith* case in the mid-1950s (then the maximum under the relevant Criminal Code section). Both were described as active in the conspiracy by the trial judge. Even though one individual was said to be 'the single most active person in furthering the conspiracy,' Mr Justice Spence, in his reasons for sentence, noted that 'Counsel for the Crown expressly refrained from asking for any sentence of imprisonment as to the latter two [individuals] and with that view the Court agrees.'[15] In 1961, C.W. Dent, head of the Electrical Contractors Association of Ontario, whose members he organized into a conspiracy, was charged separately from the association, convicted, and fined $7,500 after the association was convicted of price fixing.[16]

In the *Mandarin Orange* case in 1967, an executive was charged, but the crown entered a *nolle prosequi*. The same thing occurred in the *Alberta Plumbing Supplies* case, with respect to six executives in 1968, and to one individual in the *Montreal Plumbing Supplies* case in 1968.[17] It is not clear why this was done, but in every case the crown obtained a conviction against the companies involved.

From the 1950s through the 1980s, it was apparently the crown's practice to charge individuals only if they were the owners of unincorporated enterprises.[18] Individuals were frequently named as unindicted co-conspirators and used by the crown to provide evidence to convict corporations.

The crown's unwillingness to indict individuals – even those who had initiated and maintained the conspiracy – can be seen in the following excerpt from the director's annual report for 1968–9 (see Canada, Director of Investigations and Research):

In the latter part of 1961 senior officials of Burns and Company Limited (now Burns Foods Limited), Canada Packers Limited and Swift Canadian Company, Limited disclosed to the Minister of Defence Production that evidence had been brought to their attention of collusion over a period of five years among the managers of their respective branches in Saint John, New Brunswick to fix prices in respect of meat sold to Department of National Defence establishments in the area. At the same time they offered to make full restitution to the Government. A settlement in restitution acceptable to the Government was subsequently made ...

Informations subsequently laid against the three corporations and four individuals under section 32(1)(c) of the [Combines Investigation] Act for having conspired between January 1, 1957, and December 31, 1961, to prevent or lessen competition unduly in [the supply of beef to the Department of National Defence and to retail stores in New Brunswick] ...

On September 24, 1968, Magistrate H.S. Prince in the Magistrate's Court for the

County of Saint John ruled that all the co-conspirators named in the Information were to be considered charged with the offence. Crown Counsel objected and the case was adjourned pending adjudication by a higher court. An application for a Writ of Mandamus to compel Magistrate Prince to hear the Information against Burns Foods Limited, Edward R. Coughlan and L.W. MacLeod without the co-conspirators being joined was dismissed on December 3, 1968, by Mr. Justice Pichette of the Supreme Court of New Brunswick. On February 4, 1969, the Informations were withdrawn. Following the preferring of indictments against the above corporations and individuals there was a plea of guilty by all the accused in the Supreme Court of New Brunswick on June 3, 1969. The corporations were fined $5,000 each and the individuals $200 each. (1968–9, 38–9)

Several points should be noted. First, the crown sought to prevent the magistrate from treating the individuals named as unindicted co-conspirators as being indicted. When it was overruled by the appeal court, it apparently reluctantly charged the two individuals. Second, the individuals who organized the cartel were each fined only $200. At the time, the maximum fine was potentially unlimited (at the discretion of the court). Third, the case took almost eight years to complete. Surely this greatly attenuates the idea that penalties for offences are more effective if they are both sure and swift. Finally, in this as in most other conspiracy cases, the logic of convicting a number of corporations while failing to charge the individuals who are the directing minds of these legal, but inanimate, entities is hard to fathom.

Price Maintenance

Resale price-maintenance and refusal to deal became offences in the Combines Investigation Act (predecessor to the Competition Act) on 29 December 1951.[19]

Between 1951 and 31 March 1992, some 127 price-maintenance cases resulted in a conviction and a fine – see Table 4. In ten of these cases, an individual was convicted and fined, and in six of them an individual was the only defendant. In fact, the first prosecution for price maintenance was of an individual, and it resulted in a fine of $5 in 1954. (With a fine like this, it must have been hard for the accused to keep a straight face.) The second such conviction did not occur until 1964, when Mr Cooper-Campbell was fined $300 in the lengthy surgical supplies case in which the crown's costs of prosecution amounted to $11,484 (Stanbury 1976, 628). In the latter half of the 1970s, five individuals (in five cases) were fined between $1,000 and $3,000 each. During the first half of the 1980s, three individuals were fined $500, $5,000 and $10,000. The record fine occurred in the *Acme Signalisation* case in Montreal on 1 October 1982. This fine was larger than any imposed on an individual in a

TABLE 4

Fines in price-maintenance cases in Canada, from 1950–51 to 1991–2

Period ending 31 March	No. of cases in which a fine was imposed[a]	Average fine ($) per case[b]	No. of cases in which individuals were convicted	Fine ($) per individual
1951[c]–55	2	503	1[d]	5
1956–60	1	500	0	–
1961–5	2	900	1[d]	300
1966–70	7	2,179	0	–
1971–5	11	4,750	0	–
1976–80	30	17,233	5[e]	1,000 (2), 2,500, 3,000 (2)
1981–5	36	23,361	3[f]	500; 5,000; 10,000
1986–1990	35	36,610	0	–
1991	2	57,500	0	–
1992	1	190,000	0	–

SOURCE: Derived from the Director of Investigation and Research's annual report
[a]Omits POWC cases.
[b]In nominal dollars; includes all firms and individuals in each case.
[c]Legislation enacted 29 December 1951.
[d]The individual was the sole defendant.
[e]In four cases the individual was the only one convicted; in one case, a firm was also convicted.
[f]In all three instances, a firm was also convicted in the same case.

price-fixing or bid-rigging case prior to 1991, when two individuals were each fined $75,000.

In none of the 127 price-maintenance cases resulting in a conviction has any individual gone to jail. Indeed, it appears that the crown never sought imprisonment for any of the ten individuals convicted of this offence between 1951 and 31 March 1992.

Misleading Advertising

The number of prosecutions for misleading advertising and deceptive marketing has exceeded that for all other offences under Canadian competition law since the early 1970s. However, the summary data provided by the Bureau of Competition Policy does not indicate the number of individuals and corporations charged or convicted.[20] However, research by two of my students covering the 39 months and 159 cases between October 1988 and December 1991 provides some indication of the frequency with which individuals have been convicted (Jensen and Parker 1992). Table 5 indicates that 45 individuals and 157 corporations were convicted in 159 cases between October 1988 and December 1991. The individ-

TABLE 5
Fines for misleading advertising under the Competition Act, from October 1988 to December 1991

| Period | Convictions | | | Number of counts | | Average fine per case (nominal$) | | | Range of fine ($) per count | | | |
| | | | | | | | | | Individuals | | Corporations | |
	Total cases	Indiv.	Corp.	Indiv.	Corp.	Indiv.	Corp.	Total	Low	High	Low	High
Oct.–Dec.												
1988	18	3	16	11	40	$4,333	$6,517	$7,239	$600	$833	$500	$10,000
1989	42	7	45	8	149	9,357	18,939	21,851	500	25,000	125	10,000
1990	47	17	45	125	207	7,921	19,557	21,589	300	20,000	200	150,000
1991	52	18	49	51	110	4,230	19,321	19,671	500	1,460	500	150,000
Total	159	45	157	195	506	7,763	17,811	17,807				

SOURCE: Derived from Jensen and Parker (1992, Appendices)

uals were convicted on 195 counts (average 4.3 counts per person), and the corporations, on 506 counts (average 3.2 counts per corporation).

We cannot be sure why individuals were, on average, convicted with 1.1 counts more than were corporations. It may be because there are often instances where two or three individuals are charged together with only one company for a particular offence.

In terms of the total fine imposed in cases completed between October 1988 and December 1991, individuals got off much more lightly than did corporations. They were fined an average of $7,763 per case versus $17,811 for corporations. Moreover, the difference appears to be growing: in 1989, the average fine paid by individuals was 49 per cent of that paid by corporations. In 1990, the ratio was 41 per cent, and in 1991 it was 22 per cent – see Table 4. Over the period from October 1988 to December 1991, the range of fines per count for individuals ranged from $300 to $25,000, and for corporations, from were $125 to $150,000.

During the 1970s and the 1980s, the courts made a practice of imposing smaller fines on individuals convicted of misleading advertising. For the period from 1980–1 to 1988–9, the average fine per conviction (all sections combined) for individuals ranged from 18 per cent (1983–4) to 92 per cent (1988–9) of the average fine imposed on corporations in the same year (Table 6). Typically, the average fines imposed on individuals were 26 per cent to 44 per cent of those imposed on corporations.

There may be several plausible explanations for the generally large differences. First, when individuals are charged as owners of unincorporated businesses, their firms may be much smaller, on average, than the corporations convicted of misleading advertising, and the amount of commerce adversely affected was also correspondingly much smaller. Second, most of the individuals convicted may have been employees of corporations that were also convicted. Judges may feel that the firm should be hit harder than the individual(s) involved, as this will more effectively deter such illegal behaviour. Or judges may impose fines on an 'ability-to-pay' basis and conclude that, on average, individuals are less able to pay the sorts of fines imposed on corporations.

Although publicly available data for the 1970s are for the average fine on the first charge only, the average fine imposed on individuals was clearly less than that imposed on corporations.[21] For each year between 1973 and 1976, the average fine imposed on individuals under section 37 (the indictable offence) was 56 per cent, 30 per cent, 15 per cent, and 32 per cent, respectively, of the average fine imposed on corporations.

The record fine for an individual in a misleading-advertising case ($500,000) was imposed on Donald Cormie on 22 January 1992: Mr. Cormie was convicted

TABLE 6
Average fine per accused convicted in misleading-advertising cases, from 1980–1 to 1988–9[a]

	For corporations[b]	For corporations[b]	Average fine per case	No. of corporations and individuals convicted
1980–1	$3,487	$1,301 37%[c]	$3,457	123
1981–2	2,424	1,058 44	2,395	103
1982–3	5,541	1,531 28	5,047	136
1983–4	13,435	2,424 18	11,679	156
1984–5	4,369	3,145 72	5,679	130
1985–6	7,454	1,929 26	6,384	128
1986–7	6,717	2,853 42	7,120	131
1987–8	7,004	2,211 23	10,430	125
1988–9	9,001	8,261 92	12,406	99

SOURCE: Bureau of Competition Policy, *Misleading Advertising Bulletin*, no. 3, 1983; no. 1, 1985; nos. 1, 4, 1986; no. 1, 1989; no. 1, 1990. I am indebted to Chris Martin of the Bureau of Competition Policy for assistance in finding some of these figures.
[a]In nominal dollars.
[b]Average fine per conviction, all sections.
[c]Fines for individuals as a percentage of fines for corporations.

on a charge related to the 'Chairman's Message' in the Principal Group's Annual Review for 1985, which represented in a false or misleading manner that the Group had been successful in moving out of the real estate market in advance of that market's subsequent collapse. Investors relied on this representation when deciding whether to invest in products offered by the Principal Group.'[22] By comparison, the largest fine on a corporation was $1 million, imposed on Simpsons-Sears in 1985.[23]

The practice of initially charging individuals and then dropping the charges after negotiations to get a guilty plea and 'agreement' to a particular fine against the corporation also occurs in cases of misleading advertising. For example, 'In October 1990, the President of Remington Products (Canada) Inc., Victor Kiam, was charged along with the company under the misleading advertising provisions of the Act for a representation made in television advertisements. However, the charges against Mr. Kiam were apparently dropped upon the company pleading guilty and being fined $75,000' (Goldman 1992, 37).

As observed in note 11, in two misleading-advertising cases, individuals have been sentenced to one day in prison. In another case, a term of one year was imposed,[24] and in another a term of six months was imposed for failure to pay a fine of $30,000.[25]

POLICY STATEMENTS CONCERNING PROSECUTION OF INDIVIDUALS

A non-exhaustive review of the director's annual report (Canada, Director of Investigation and Research, various years) and other public documents suggests that there have been very few official statements of the crown's policy with respect to the prosecution of individuals in criminal competition-law offences. However, it is the attorney-general, not the Director of Investigation, who decides which individuals and/or firms will be charged. The historical record suggests great reluctance to indict individuals directly involved in the offences unless their businesses are unincorporated enterprises or they were very actively involved in organizing a conspiracy through a trade association (i.e., Elliott, Clarke, Badden, Dent).

There has apparently been less reluctance to charge individuals with misleading advertising than with either conspiracy/bid-rigging or price maintenance. However, only additional research can ascertain if the crown is charging individuals largely because the firms involved are not incorporated and therefore only individuals could be charged.

The 1975–6 Statement

In the past two decades, the director has made policy statements regarding prosecution of individuals. In his annual report for 1975–6 (p. 15), he stated

Until recently, only corporations and not the individual directors or officers have been charged with violations of the Act.[26] The present policy is to recommend the prosecution of the individuals as well.

One very important basis for this policy is that the personal liability of individuals is as important if not more important than the financial penalties imposed on a corporation in terms of effective enforcement of the Act.

Therefore, it will also be recommended that individual directors and officers who breach the Act be sentenced to jail terms as well as fines. The then Minister of Consumer and Corporate Affairs, the Honourable André Ouellet quoted with approval the former U.S. Attorney-General William Saxbe who stated the rationale very succinctly: 'Price fixers should go to prison ... they are no better than the car thief or the burglar or the robber ...'.

Unlike the situation in the United States where courts have sent presidents and directors of corporations to jail, Canadians are not yet accustomed to seeing large fines or jail sentences for combines offences. However, it is hoped that the courts will apply this policy and rationale in their sentencing in future prosecutions under the Act.

This was fine rhetoric, but what is the evidence that either more individuals

TABLE 7

Disposition of conspiracy and bid-rigging cases involving individuals and those involving only corporations, 1889 to 1991–2

Outcome/ disposition	1889 to 1949–50 Corp. only[a]	Indiv. involved	1950–1 to 1964–5 Corp. only[a]	Indiv. involved	1965–6 to 1975–6 Corp. only[a]	Indiv. involved	1976–7 to 1991–2 Corp. only[a]	Indiv. involved
Conviction and fine (and possibly a POWC)[b]	4	15[c]	18	7[d]	21	3	21	2
POWC	n.a.	n.a.	1	0	6	1	5	6
Acquited/discharged	2	4	0	0	5	1	12	7[e]
Charges dropped	0	0	0	0	0	0	0	1
Stay of proceedings	0	0	0	0	0	1[f]	3	0
Total	6	19	19	7	32	6	41	16

SOURCE: Derived from Stanbury (1992, Tables 1–3)

[a]Includes trade associations.

[b]At least one defendant was convicted and fined. Thus it is possible in a case involving individuals and corporations that only one *or* the other is convicted and fined. Where this occurs, almost always the charges against individuals were dropped or they were acquitted.

[c]Includes one case in which the trial judge 'directed that the defendant should enter into a recognizance for $4000 to appear and receive sentence when called upon' (*R. v. Elliott* [1905] 9 CCC 505 at 507); one case in which 11 individuals were sentenced to one year's imprisonment but it was suspended; and one case (Simington) in which the accused were convicted under the Secret Commissions Act after the charges under competition law were dropped.

[d]Includes *R. v. Morrey* in which the individuals were acquitted but the trade association was convicted and fined $1.

[e]In one case, four other individuals had the charges dropped.

[f]Two of the six individuals were later made subject to a POWC in 1968–9.

were charged or that the crown (the attorney-general of Canada) ever sought a term of imprisonment? In some cases in ethe 1970s and early 1980s, the crown demurred when requested by judges to make representations regarding sentencing of corporations convicted of competition-law offences. This is hardly consistent with the idea of getting fines that would deter such behaviour. See Stanbury (1976, 1992).

Between 1976–7 and 1991–2, the crown completed 57 conspiracy or bid-rigging cases. In 16 (or 28 per cent) of those cases, individuals were involved, in that they were charged or were the subject of an application for a POWC. But in only two of the 16 cases did the crown obtain a conviction and fine. In six cases, it obtained the 'softer' remedy of a POWC. These cases typically involved five to 17 individuals operating small business (i.e., gasoline retailing, taxi cabs). The outcomes (and the numbers of individuals involved) are summarized in Table 7.

The overall 'success rate' (fine and/or POWC) was only 8 out of 16 cases or 50 per cent. By comparison, in cases involving only corporations (or trade associations), it was 63.4 per cent (26 of 41 cases). In 28 per cent (16 of 41) of the conspiracy and bid-rigging cases completed after the 1975–6 policy statement, individuals were charged, as compared to 16 per cent (6 of 37) in the previous decade. However, during the period from 1950–1 to 1964–5, in 27 per cent (7 of 26) of completed conspiracy cases, some one or more individuals had been charged. The rate was even higher between 1889 and 1949–50 (76 per cent, or 19 of 25) – largely because the firms involved were unincorporated businesses and thus it was necessary to indict individuals if a prosecution was to be undertaken. Of the 19 cases in which individuals were charged during this period, 7 involved only individuals.

During the four periods covering more than a century, the crown's 'success' rate (conviction and fine or POWC) for cases where individuals were charged was 79 per cent, 100 per cent, 67 per cent and 50 per cent, respectively. The comparable figures for cases in which only corporations were charged are 67 per cent, 100 per cent, 84 per cent, and 63 per cent, respectively. 'Success' includes cases in which all the individuals charged were acquitted or discharged but one or more corporations was convicted and fined.

An analysis of the disposition of conspiracy and bid-rigging cases in which individuals were charged is provided in Table 8. In almost all the cases where only one or more corporations were convicted, the crown dropped the charges against the individual. Of the seven POWCs between 1889 and 1991–2, five were obtained in cases involving only individuals. The data in Table 8 indicate that of the 29 cases in which individuals were charged[27] along with one or more corporations, they suffered the same fate as did the corporations in 22. That is, both were convicted and fined or acquitted. In almost one-quarter of the conspiracy cases between 1889 and 1991–2 in which both individuals and corporations were charged, the individuals were either not convicted or had their charges dropped or prosecution stayed while the corporations were subsequently convicted and fined.

The Latest Policy Statements

In November 1990 and August 1991, Howard Wetston, who was Director of Investigation and Research from November 1989 to 1993, made speeches indicating the bureau's policy with respect to prosecuting individuals. He stated that

TABLE 8

Analysis of the disposition of conspiracy and bid-rigging cases in which individuals were involved,[a] from 1889 to 1991–2

Disposition	1889 to 1949–50	1950–1 to 1964–5	1965–6 to 1975–6	1976–7 to 1991–2
Conviction and fine				
Individuals only	7	1	3	0
Corporations only	1	1	2[b]	3[b]
Both	7	5	0	2
POWC	n.a.	0	1[c]	6[d]
Acquitted/discharged				
Individuals only	0	0	0	1
Corporations only	0	0	0	0
Both	4	0	0	4
Total	19	7	6	16

SOURCE: Derived from Stanbury (1992, Tables 1–3).
[a]Individuals were charged or subject to an order for a POWC.
[b]In one case, the individuals were acquitted; in the other the crown used the *nolle prosequi* procedure (terminated proceedings).
[c]Both individuals and corporations.
[d]Five cases involving *only* individuals; one case involving both.

'the Bureau is now conducting its investigations with a view to identifying cases where individual charges would be appropriate, and gathering evidence which would support such action' (Wetston 1990, 10). Deterrence requires that individuals be charged, according to the director: 'Our review of cases over the past several years has led me to conclude that more charges against individuals will be necessary to strengthen deterrence incentives. Among the factors that we take into account in making such a recommendation are the individual's position in the organization, his or her role in initiating, implementing or enforcing the conduct in question, and his or her knowledge of the illegality of the conduct' (Wetston 1991, 3).

In August 1991, Wetston announced a policy designed to provide incentives for individuals who may have committed criminal offences to assist the crown in prosecuting other individuals and corporations. The director stated that the bureau had

recently begun to develop a program aimed at providing greater incentives for corpora-

tions and individuals to voluntarily report their participation in conspiracy and bid-rigging activities before they have come to our attention. Given the covert nature of these offences, they are often difficult to discover or prove without the co-operation of persons who are themselves implicated in the commission of the offence ... to encourage firms to come forward as soon as possible after it has come to the attention of senior management that the firm has been involved in collusive conduct contrary to the Act. (Wetston 1991, 4).

Of course, the director pointed out that the bureau investigates cases under the Competition Act,[28] but the attorney-general decides who is charged and who will be granted immunity.

Mr. Wetston has outlined the factors that could be relevant in determining whether to recommend immunity from prosecution to the attorney-general in such 'first-in' situations: The firm must be the first to approach the bureau with evidence of an offence and ... must provide frank and full disclosure of facts at its disposal. It must fully cooperate fully with the bureau's investigation and with any legal proceedings. Its evidence must be important and valuable. The company must be prepared to make restitution that is commensurate with the facts and with its responsibility in the matter. The evidence must confirm that the company immediately terminated the activity and reported it to the director as soon as it came to light. A prior record of anti-trust violations will affect any decision as to whether to recommend immunity to the attorney-general. The firm should, as a rule, be prepared to agree to issuance of a POWC an of fixed duration under the Competition Act, section 34(2), pursuant to which commission of an offence is admitted. The firm's role in the conduct in question will also be considered (Wetston 1991, 4–5).

The previous director (now in private practice) points out: 'The Director's immunity policy is similar to the amnesty policy of the Antitrust Division of the U.S. Department of Justice, which has been in effect since 1978. In essence, the U.S. amnesty policy provides immunity to the first person or organization that brings an antitrust violation to the attention of the Department of Justice and assists the Department in the prosecution of the antitrust case' (Goldman 1992, 38).

An example of application of the new policy occurred on 3 November 1992, when the Director of Investigation and Research announced that Abbott Laboratories was granted immunity from prosecution for conspiracy and bid-rigging while Chemagro Ltd was charged with these offences. Promptly after top executives discovered that a lower-level employee had engaged in an agreement to share the Canadian market for the biological insecticide Bt with Chemagro, they voluntarily reported it to the director, who did not know of the agreement. The conduct was contrary to Abbott's written policies, and the firm cooperated fully with the director in his inquiry. Further, Abbott agreed to make restitution of $2.122 million to the provinces of Ontario and Quebec, which had purchased Bt.[29] It appears that Abbott met all the criteria established by the director to obtain immunity from prosecution in a 'first-in' situation.

CONCLUSIONS

For individuals involved in competition-law offences in Canada, the evidence strongly suggests that 'crime pays' – but probably less well than it has in the past.

From 1951 to 1991–2, in only 24 per cent of 121 conspiracy or bid-rigging cases has the crown charged an individual or sought to make him or her subject to a POWC. Prior to 1991, no individual convicted of conspiracy or bid-rigging paid a fine greater than $8,000 (although this fine was imposed in 1931 and is the equivalent of $83,600 in 1992). In 1991 and 1992, three executives were each fined $75,000 and one was fined $50,000 in the compressed-gases case (while five firms were fined a total of $6 million – both record amounts).

Since 1951, in only 10 of 127 (8 per cent) price-maintenance cases that resulted in a conviction and fine was an individual involved either as sole defendant or along with a corporation. The fines imposed on individuals ranged from $5 to $10,000, but in only two cases was the fine over $3,000 ($5,000 in one case and $10,000 in the other). Between October 1988 and December 1991, individuals were convicted in 28 per cent of the 701 counts in 159 misleading-advertising cases involving convictions. Individuals were involved in about one-quarter of the cases during the thirty-nine-month period. From the mid-1970s to date, the courts have almost always imposed substantially lower fines on individuals in misleading-advertising cases. Typically, the average fine imposed on individuals has been one-third to one-half that imposed on corporations convicted of violating the same section of the Competition Act (or its predecessors). In the past two years, the Director of Investigation and Research has adopted a new policy of recommending to the attorney-general that individuals be charged in conspiracy cases, depending on their role in initiating, implementing, or enforcing the agreement and their degree of knowledge of illegality.

There is a strong normative and positive case for holding individuals account-able for their anti-competitive behaviour by routinely charging them (as well as corporations) with violation of the criminal offences in the Competition Act and seeking substantial fines and short terms (say, 3 to 6 months) of imprisonment.[30] Except for three individuals convicted of misleading advertising, no business executive (or owner) has ever served a day in jail for violating the Competition Act or its predecessors.

It is impossible to say, however, how much competition-law crime has not been detected in Canada. As John Braithwaite (1985b, 7) has observed, 'Given the great rewards and low risks of detection,' it is hard to understand why 'so many business people adopt the "economically irrational" course of obeying the law.' The fact that – misleading advertising aside – there have been so few prosecutions for violating the Competition Act does not mean that those who have not been subject to investigation are as pure as driven snow. Canadians should probably be concerned about the fact that over the past few years the number of prosecutions for competition-law offences has dropped somewhat, particularly in misleading advertising and price mainte-nance.[31] However, the crown has obtained record fines in conspiracy, bid-rigging and misleading-advertising cases in this period. These may have some deferrence effect.

This largely empirical study of white-collar crime does not give much indication of the larger and broader forces at work in Canada that strongly shape the statute that defines the crimes being studied and provides the means for enforcement. The real power of business interests in Canada goes far beyond the modest fines in competition-law cases prior to 1990 ('crime pays'). It is much more pervasive and subtle and takes a variety of forms.

First, it has included the ability to prevent elimination of 'unduly' from the basic-conspiracy section; this word was responsible for half the acquittals in such cases between 1889 and 1990–1.

Second, business interests have been able to delay and weaken proposed reforms to competition law that began in 1969 but were enacted in two stages effective 1 January 1976 and 19 June 1986. The reform efforts can be traced through the Economic Council's report in 1969, Bill C-256 in 1971, Bills C-42 and C-13 in 1977, and Bill C-29 in 1984. Along the way, severally potentially significant legislative initiatives were lost in the hard bargaining and shifting priorities that marked the lengthy process that resulted in Bill C-91. These include the following:

- class actions (introduced in Bills C-42 and C-13);
- substitute actions brought by the official responsible for enforcing competition legislation (in Bill C-42);
- interlocking management (in Bills C-256, C-42, and C-13);
- civil provisions regarding abuse of intellectual property (in Bills C-256, C-42, and C-13);
- a civil provision regarding price differentiation (in Bills C-42 and C-13);

- criminal provisions regarding international conspiracies (in Bills C-42 and C-13);
- civil provisions regarding agreements to restrict imports or exports (in Bills C-42 and C-13);
- making certain horizontal agreements illegal per se (in Bill C-256 and the Minister's Proposals in 1981);
- registration of export agreements and franchise arrangements by the tribunal (in Bill C-256);
- reciprocal buying (in Bill C-256);
- initiation of proceedings before the tribunal by 'any person who is materially affected' by the impugned practice (in Bill C-256);
- awarding of costs by the tribunal against respondents (in Bill C-256);
- criminal provisions regarding foreign directives (in Bills C-42 and C-13);
- amendments to the price-discrimination section (in Bills C-42 and C-13);
- civil provisions regarding agreements to limit imports or exports (in Bills C-42 and C-13); and
- written interpretive opinions by the official responsible for enforcing competition legislation (in Bill C-13) (see Stanbury 1986).

Third, the business community has successfully promulgated the idea that it would be unthinkable to create new/amended competition law that was not negotiated on a line-by-line basis by representatives of leading trade associations, large firms, and their legal advisers (see Stanbury 1986).[32]

Fourth, the same interests have created a climate of opinion hostile to charging individuals (except owners of unincorporated businesses) responsible for criminal offences under the Competition Act and its predecessor. The same climate has effectively deterred the crown from requesting jail sentences for the few individuals convicted. The Bureau of Competition Policy states that 'the Director's recent pronouncements and actions in high profile conspiracy and misleading advertising cases show that individuals are now being charged when warranted.'[33]

Fifth, business interests have also helped to establish public opinion that favours a compliance-oriented approach[34] with softer penalties/remedies – except in the most egregious cases.[35] Further, the same climate would produce adverse effects for the reputation of any Director of Investigation and Research who failed to be sufficiently accommodating to the entreaties of senior corporate executives and their legal counsel.

Sixth, business interests have been able to create an atmosphere in which most judges are reluctant to infer existence of illegal conspiracies from circumstantial evidence in price-fixing cases. In contrast, in conspiracies involving drugs, the same judges often find it easy to infer existence of a conspiracy among the accused. Is this difference the result of the vastly different socio-economic status of the two groups of defendants? It is too early to say whether the director's new (1991) policy with respect to charging individuals in conspiracy cases will move Canada's enforcement efforts closer to those in the United States.[36]

NOTES

1 See Table 1, which lists the year in which various offences or civilly reviewable matters became part of the Competition Act or its predecessors (Criminal Code, 1889 – 1960; Combines Investigation Act, 1910 – 1986). Detailed analysis of the conspiracy provisions and its enforcement can be found in Stanbury (1991, 1992). A description of the amendments resulting in the Competition Act effective 19 June 1986 can be found in Stanbury (1986). A non-technical description of the act can be found in Sanderson and Stanbury (1989).
2 There are two exceptions. In *R. v. White* (Unreported Ontario Supreme Court decision, 1 April 1932), eleven individuals were convicted and each fined $100 and given 'one year's suspended sentence.' In the Imperial Tobacco case (Unreported Supreme Court of Ontario decision, 28 July 1941), nine individuals (along with 27 corporations) were convicted and fined from $250 to $10,000 or 60 days in prison (four months in the case of the $10,000 fine). All individuals were acquitted upon appeal.
3 See Drew Fagan 'Getting Off with a Nod and a Wink,' *Globe and Mail*, 17 December 1990, B1, B2.
4 Personal communication, 11 February 1993.
5 Braithwaite (1985b, 7) contends that 'it is not difficult for powerful actors to structure their affairs so that all of the pressures to break the law surface at a lower level of their own organization or in a subordinate organization' (e.g., a contractor). Further, organizations are able to 'manufacture an impression of confused accountability for wrongdoing' (7).
6 Fining corporations (or imposing other economic penalties on them) raises the question of the true 'incidence' of such fines. In theory, such fines – like corporate income tax – may be borne by three sets of individuals: shareholders, customers (in the form of higher prices), and/or employees (in the form of lower wages and/or benefits).
7 Bench warrants can and have been issued against individuals that would result in arrest if they attempted to re-enter Canada (e.g., the case of Remington's misleading advertising, involving Victor Kiam). Extradition is possible for certain indictable offences, one of which is conspiracy.
8 No women have ever been convicted of a conspiracy or bid-rigging or price-mainte-

nance offence under the Competition Act. The figure of 157 omits two early cases in which the number of individuals convicted was not reported.

9 Although C.W. Dent was tried separately from the firms in the *Ontario Electrical Contractors* cases, he was the president of the trade association and helped to organize the conspiracy.

10 In mid-October 1991 each of the two top executives of Liquid Carbonic Inc. was fined $75,000 after pleading guilty to assisting in a price-fixing scheme among companies supplying 97 per cent of the compressed gases sold in Canada. The Bureau of Competition Policy concluded that the firms had conspired to rig bids for six months. The crown's lawyer said 'We think it's important for individuals to know they can't hide behind corporate coal tails.' See 'Pair Fined $75,000 Each for Price-fixing Role,' *Globe and Mail*, 19 October 1991, B3; 'Big Fine Warns Executives Not to Fix Prices,' *Vancouver Sun*, 19 October 1991, C4. In July 1992, two senior executives of Canadian Liquid Air Ltd were fined $75,000 and $50,000 each.

11 In *R. v. Simington* (1926) 45 CCC 249, which began as a combines case, charges were dropped in favour of prosecution for fraud under the Criminal Code and the Secret Commissions Act, the four individuals were each fined $25,000 and sentenced to one day in prison. In December 1974, an individual was imprisoned for two years with respect to a charge of misleading advertising. The accused had a criminal record. The sentence was later reduced to one year. See the director's annual report for 1974–5, 40–1, and the annual report for 1975–6, 67. In two other misleading-advertising cases, a prison sentence of only one day was imposed.

12 *R. v. Elliott* (1905) 9 OLR 648 (Trial); CCC 507 (Appeal).

13 *R. v. Clarke* (1907) ALR 358 (Trial); (1907) ALR 368 (Appeal).

14 *R. v. Singer et al.* (1931) OR 202 (Trial); (1931) OR 699 (Appeal); (1932) 2 DLR 866 (SCC).

15 (1954) 109 CCC 214.

16 See the director's annual report for 1960–1, 15, and for 1961–2, 13. Both Dent and the association were also made subject to a POWC.

17 Information obtained from the Bureau of Competition Policy.

18 An obvious exception occurred in the *Barton Tubes* case. The executive who was charged was discharged at the preliminary hearing. See the director's annual report for 1978–9, 98. Also, a vice-president of a firm under investigation was prosecuted for destroying documents left by a bureau officer in a sealed package in the firm's offices. Upon conviction for impeding an inquiry, the individual was fined $1,750 plus costs 'rather than imprisonment, [because] the magistrate who tried the case stated that he was taking into consideration the poor health and age of the convicted man' (director's annual report for 1954–5, 35).

19 Resale price maintenance, now called price maintenance, was common at the time

the original anti-combines legislation was enacted in 1889 and was widespread in certain sectors of the economy until it was made illegal per se in 1951.

20 Until 1990–1, it was possible to ascertain this from a case-by-case review of the summaries in the director's annual report and Bureau of Competition Policy, *Misleading Advertising Bulletin* published quarterly.

21 Derived from Bureau of Competition Policy, *Misleading Advertising Bulletin*, (July–Sept. 1977), 4–5; (July–Sept. 1978), 5.

22 Consumer and Corporate Affairs Canada, 'Donald Cormie Fined Record $500,000 for Misleading Advertising in Principal Group Case,' News Release, NR-10610/92-01, 1992.

23 *R. v. Simpson-Sears Ltd.* [1985] CCL 11437 (Ontario County Court).

24 See *R. v. O'Brien* (1975) NSR (2d) 629; 25 CPR (2d) 143.

25 See Addy (1991, 463). It is common to impose jail sentences in default of payment of a fine.

26 As data in Table 2 and discussion make clear, this statement is not true, strictly speaking.

27 Thus the twenty-nine cases exclude POWC's and those in which only individuals were charged.

28 In criminal cases, the director submits a 'Summary of Evidence' to the attorney-general in which he or she recommends prosecution and suggests which corporations and/or individuals should be charged. If the director believes that prosecution is not warranted, he or she discontinues the inquiry and reports this fact to the minister of consumer and corporate affairs. See sections 22 and 23 of the Competition Act.

29 Consumer and Corporate Affairs Canada, 'News Release,' NR-10898/93–32, 3 November 1992, and 'Agreed Statement of Facts,' Federal Court of Canada (Trial Division), 27 October 1992.

30 See for example, Baker (1981), Block and Sidak (1980), Geis (1972), Werden and Simon (1987), and U.S. Sentencing Commission (1991).

31 For example, between 1986–7 and 1990–1 the Bureau of Competition Policy completed 571 misleading-advertising cases and won two-thirds of them. During the period from 1981–2 to 1985–6, it completed 806 and won 74.4 per cent. Between 1980–1 and 1984–5 it completed 61 price-maintenance cases and won 61 per cent. Between 1985–6 and 1989–90, it completed 47 and won 72 per cent. The bureau indicates that 'the compliance approach also explains some of the decline in prosecution statistics in areas such as misleading advertising and price maintenance. The Bureau's approach has been to focus prosecution resources on high priority cases. Alternative case resolutions are being used more frequently in these areas in particular. They nonetheless represent enforcement action and need to be factored into the equation. As with advisory opinions we believe they are valuable tools in appropriate circumstances' (personal communication, 11 February 1993).

32 Efforts to redesign competition law are quite different in that it is deemed to be acceptable for potential offenders to lobby government to shape laws intended to constrain their activities. Indeed, both the Liberal and Progressive Conservative federal governments believed that it was important to negotiate details with major trade associations through which many firms and their senior executives funnelled their comments, suggestions, and 'demands.' Perhaps the highest-status and most sophisticated association, the Business Council on National Issues (BCNI), spent at least $200,000 to have an entire new statute drafted in 1981 to replace the aged Combines Investigation Act. It is hard to imagine drug dealers and users or car thieves and break-in artists being invited to submit their views during revision of the relevant sections of the Criminal Code. It is harder still to imagine them and their advisers meeting with the minister revising the legislation.

33 Personal communication, 11 February 1993.

34 The Bureau of Competition Policy states: 'Although a greater emphasis was put on the program post-1986, it was not adopted as a result of public pressure from businesses but rather as a means of [compliance] allowing the Bureau to make more effective use of its resources in the face of financial restraints. We believe it is clearly cost-effective and beneficial for the investigators to provide advice on the application of the law given that it is better to prevent the commission of an offence than to punish it after the fact. This compliance approach is part of an overall trend in government in relation particularly to "regulatory offences" which the Supreme Court of Canada has described (in cases such as *City National Leasing* and *Wholesale Travel*) as offences which prohibit conduct as the means to a particular end, rather than because it is inherently morally wrong' (personal communication, 11 February 1993).

35 It is also hard to imagine the police offering confidential (albeit non-binding) advice to potential offenders (or their counsel) concerning actions that might well violate the Criminal Code. Yet the director's 'Program of Compliance' provides several mechanisms through which this is done under the Competition Act. See the director's annual reports since 1986.

36 The U.S. Sentencing Commission's guidelines of 1 November 1987 provided for a minimum jail term of eight months for individuals convicted of price-fixing, market allocation, or bid-rigging. In addition, effective 1 November 1991, a mandatory minimum fine of $20,000 is to be imposed on these individuals. See CCH, Trade Regulation Reports, 15 November 1991, 13, 041–3, 13,036.

PART IV

Crimes against Occupational Health and Safety

13

And Defeat Goes On: An Assessment of Third-Wave Health and Safety Regulation

ERIC TUCKER

Reform of occupational health-and-safety regulation tends to occur in waves which sweep over much of the industrialized capitalist world, leaving behind a more-or-less common model. The first wave, dating roughly from the 1830s to the 1880s, resulted in a regime of market regulation. The second, dating roughly from the 1880s to the 1970s, instituted a weak 'command and control' model of direct state regulation. The third and current wave began in the 1970s and combined participatory rights for workers with reforms to external enforcement to create a regime of mandated partial self-regulation.[1] With each reform, there is renewed hope that the toll of work on the lives and health of workers will be reduced to more 'acceptable' levels. With passage of time, that hope is dampened by continuing carnage.

Although by historical standards the current regulatory regime is young, it is not too soon to begin to evaluate its effectiveness. The results in Ontario and in other jurisdictions have been, on the whole, disappointing, as is documented in the first part of the chapter. In the remainder, I analyse the reasons for this poor performance, using Ontario as a case study. I employ a dialectical model which locates class struggles over health-and-safety within the broader political-economy and ideological environment in which they are conducted. I will argue that although workers' struggles have produced some amelioration and have improved the material and ideological conditions under which future struggles can be carried on, the continuing imbalance of power between labour and capital and the strength of the dominant ideology constrain, but do not determine, the likelihood of significant change and improvement.[2]

As a preliminary matter, it will be useful to identify two interrelated major premises of this dominant ideology, sketch their place in the first two stages of health-and-safety regulation, and put into historical context the third wave.

There are two major premisses.[3] First, risk is a natural and unavoidable consequence of productive activity because any technology carries with it an irreducible level of risk and because people are wont to be careless. It follows from this that, to a significant extent, the level of risk is independent of any particular set of social relations and that only a part of the burden of work-induced death, disease, and injury is preventable through health-and-safety regulation. Second, occupational health-and-safety are an area in which workers and employers share a common set of interests and objectives constructed around the acceptance of reasonable risk. Reasonable risks are ones that, given current economic conditions and technological developments, employers must create if they are to operate profitably. Unless these risks are egregious when compared to the range of risks to which workers are currently exposed, rational workers should be willing to incur them. Any disputes between workers and employers that arise within these parameters can be resolved through joint problem-solving rather than through adversarial confrontation.

These two premisses are interrelated because reasonable risks come to be defined as unavoidable ones, which cannot be eliminated by state regulation. Thus not only is the social construction of the limits of state regulation obscured but, to the extent that a social process is acknowledged to be involved, conflict is banished from it. Rather, its workings are seen through the distorting lens of consensus theory.

These ideas are deeply rooted in the historical development and practice of health-and-safety regulation.[4] When workers first sought redress from their employers through legal actions, the courts imposed a regime of market regulation. They insisted that terms and conditions of employment, including hazard levels, were to be negotiated between workers and their employers through the individual contract of employment. In the absence of express agreements, courts presumed, as a matter of law, that workers voluntarily assumed the risk of injury from hazardous conditions present in the workplace. Thus, not only did courts refuse to impose a duty of care on employers, but they also placed workers in an unfavourable initial bargaining position.

By the last quarter of the nineteenth century (earlier in some countries such as Great Britain), workers and social reformers pressured the state to become directly involved in regulation of workplace safety through establishment of minimum standards enforced by specially appointed inspectors. The standards, however, were set at levels that respected the 'natural and necessary' risks presumed to be inherent in production. Translated into statutory language, workers were entitled to protection that was reasonably practicable in the circumstances.

Implementation of these 'command and control'–type statutes also followed a pattern. Inspectors constructed the meaning of compliance in ways that did not significantly impair profitability or interfere with managerial prerogative. They also relied primarily on persuasion to achieve compliance. Prosecution was a last resort. This stance was defended on the basis that no reasonable employer had any incentive to defy the law. Safety, as defined by the inspectors, paid. Most violations were seen to be the result of ignorance or incompetence, not wilful wrongdoing, and therefore did not warrant sanctions.[5] Moreover, because workers and employers had a common interest in health-and-safety, there was no need to give workers an independent role in the regulatory process. Of course, workers could complain that health-and-safety conditions violated the law, but the response of inspectors was conditioned by the premiss of a common interest; it was presumed that the worker complained because of a conflict with the employer over an issue unrelated to health-and-safety.

In sum, the persistence of these ideological presumptions, and workers' limited influence over the legislation and, even more so, implementation, shaped the way in which direct state regulation replaced direct market regulation. Self(market)-regulation by default, rather than direct state control-best characterized the result. Thus the danger inherent in such a shift – that state power will be exercised to alter significantly the outcomes that exercise of economic power in the market might otherwise achieve – was avoided. Moreover, creation of a distinct regulatory regime separated health-and-safety issues from normal industrial relations. This was beneficial to employers because the killing and maiming of workers were one of the least acceptable features of capitalist relations of production and always carried with them the potential to call into question the legitimacy of those relations. A separate and ineffective health-and-safety regime reduced the risk of confrontation at little cost. Also, enactment of no-fault workers'-compensation statutes helped stabilize the regulatory structure, by providing injured workers with some replacement income.

In the late 1960s, the model was challenged. Worker unrest and renewed concern about the social cost of work-induced disability led to a third wave of regulatory reform.[6] These reforms, which are the principal subject of this chapter, focused on two aspects of the regulatory system. The first object was to alter the internal-responsibility system (IRS) at the workplace. Workers were to receive some legal rights to participate in local decision-making about health-and-safety. The strength of these rights varied with jurisdiction, but they almost always included rights to know, to be consulted, and to refuse unsafe work. The second target of reform was the external-responsibility system (ERS). General health-and-safety statutes replaced by a multiplicity of statutes that dealt with particular sectors or problems, emphasized more the control of health hazards, and rationalized the enforcement bureaucracy by centralizing all activity in ministries of labour. Moreover, workers gained rights to participate in enforcement.

Thus one can see tensions and potential contradictions within the emerging model. The ideology of common interest provided the foundation for mandated partial self-regulation while there was recognition that employers' self-regulation by default had failed. Some countervailing powers were needed, and these were to be possessed by the workers at risk and the state. The precise response to the self-regulatory dilemma varied substantially from jurisdiction to jurisdiction, depending in large measure on the relative economic and political strength of workers and employers and their ideological commitments. For example, the United States opted for the weakest version of worker rights, remaining more firmly within the liberal model, in which the state bore primary responsibility for health-and-safety regulation. The United Kingdom is an example of a weak corporatist regime, in which a serious attempt was made to shift responsibility to employers and workers through a reformed IRS system; workers, however, enjoyed rather weak participatory rights. Sweden represents a social-democratic alternative, with substantial delegation of authority to the labour-market parties accompanied by strong participatory rights for workers. But, whatever the framework, the law could not determine how the regime would operate.

THE IMPACT OF THIRD-WAVE REFORMS

Any attempt to measure the effectiveness of occupational health-and-safety regulation by its effect on the incidence of death, injury, and disease is fraught with difficulty. For example, most data on occupational injury and disease come from workers' compensation claims. Numerous distortions are introduced as a result. Some studies suggest that unreported injuries and diseases outnumber reported ones by a 3 to 1, while others suggest that an unknown percentage of compensation claims are fraudulent.[7] Also, changes in law, policy, and administration may affect both the definition of compensable injuries and the likelihood that workers will make claims in the system. Finally, because the incidence of injury and disease is a function of many variables, it is almost impossible to isolate the affect of changes. Yet, despite such limitations, both quantitative and qualitative assessments of effects have been attempted in numerous jurisdictions that have adopted third-wave reforms, and the data provide some indication of their impact across a range of models, including the United States, the United Kingdom, Sweden, and Ontario.

The United States

American workers enjoy relatively few and generally weak rights to partici-pate in decision-making at the plant level.[8] Joint health-and-safety committees are not required by statute, and although the act permits an authorized employee representative to accompany the inspector, it does not entitle that worker to be paid for the time spent. No other powers are given to the worker representative – for example, to conduct periodic inspections on their own. Regulations promulgated under the act have strengthened workers' legal rights and, not surprising, were fiercely resisted by employers. In 1973, work-ers obtained an individual right to refuse work that they reasonably believe poses an imminent danger, and, since 1988, all workers enjoy a right to know about hazardous substances in their workplaces.[9] A ruling that would have entitled employees who accompany agency staff on inspections to receive their normal pay was rescinded shortly after it was made in 1981.

Law primarily strengthened workers' participatory rights in the ERS, not the IRS. Thus workers were given a right to call an inspector, to accompany an inspector, to participate in opening and closing conferences between the inspec-tor and the employer, to contest abatement periods set out in citations, to obtain party status in enforcement actions contested by the employer, and so on. Finally, workers were protected against employer retaliation for exercising their rights under the act.[10]

The emphasis on worker rights in the ERS reflected the primacy of enforce-ment by state governments. A general review of U.S. enforcement practices is beyond the scope of this chapter, but in general there was a brief period of increased toughness during the Carter administration (1977–81), followed by a decline in the extent and vigour of enforcement in favour of voluntarism (self-compliance). This shift occurred even though that the act provides workers with few rights and little power in the IRS of the employer.[11]

In the absence of either strong rights for workers or vigorous enforcement, most assessments of the effectiveness of the Occupational Safety and Health Administration (OSHA) are negative. After considering the results of a number of studies, Noble concluded: 'It is unlikely that OSHA had a major effect on the safety of American workers between 1971 and 1984. The agency seems to have reduced the risks of occupational disease for workers in a few industries, such as textiles, and helped prevent some kinds of accidents, such as explosions. Overall, however, OSHA's standard-setting and enforcement activities must be judged a failure, in relation both to the hazards that workers face and the goals of the OSH Act' (Noble 1986, 205) .

Studies by other researchers using different theoretical models have reached similar conclusions. Moreover, recent data suggest that injury rates have been increasing since 1984.[12]

The United Kingdom

Unlike in the United States, the major aim of British health-and-safety reform in the 1970s was to encourage creation of institutional mechanisms for self-regulation by industry. A condition of self-regulation was that workers would have the right to be involved in local decision-making. Thus, the Health-and-safety at Work Act (HSWA), 1974, empowered the secretary of state to make provision for appointment of health-and-safety representatives. Such a regulation was promulgated in 1977, for unionized firms. Safety representatives have the right to be consulted by and to make representations to employers with respect to health-and-safety, to conduct investigations and inspections, and to obtain information from employers and inspectors. They are entitled to time off work with pay for time spent performing and being trained to perform their duties. When asked by two safety representatives, an employer must set up a safety committee. Such committees keep under review measures taken for the health-and-safety of workers and make recommendations. They do not possess any power of decision and have no authority to shut down unsafe operations pending an inspection.

In addition to provisions for worker representation, there is a specific statutory duty to provide workers with information, instruction, and training. The content of this right to know, however, is not more clearly defined by regulation, as it is in the United States. There is no statutory right to refuse unsafe work, but an employee who is disciplined or discharged for this reason may have a remedy under common law or general employment-protection legislation.[13]

Numerous studies have attempted to measure the effect of these changes. There appears to be general agreement that fatality and injury rates dropped in the years immediately following enactment of the legislation but that since 1981 the situation has been deteriorating.[14] Moreover, at least one researcher has argued that the improvement in the second half of the 1970s cannot be attributed to the act.[15] At the very least, the data suggest that the success or failure of this particular version of third-wave regulation may depend on changing external conditions. Not only do injury rates respond to the business cycle, but, more important, they react to the shifting balance of power between workers and employers, especially in a regulatory regime that depends so directly on workers' acting as a countervailing power to their employers. Moreover, the decline of labour's political power has led to a diminution in the number of inspectors at a time when the number of workplaces in increasing. Reduction of the state's presence makes the workforce even more dependent on its own resources for protection against unsafe conditions.[16]

Sweden

Swedish workers enjoy the strongest participatory rights in the Western world. The history of these rights can be traced back to legislation enacted in the early part of this century that recognized the right of elected worker-safety delegates to be consulted by the inspector. The next landmark was the 1949 act, which required appointment of safety delegates, made joint health-and-safety committees mandatory in large workplaces, and allowed trade unions to appoint regional safety delegates to represent workers in small workplaces. A statutory right to refuse unsafe work was also enacted. Subsequent agreement between trade-union and employers' organizations increased workers' rights in this scheme. These included a right to training and to information, paid time off to accompany the inspector, and a right to call the inspector. In brief, the third wave was firmly established in Sweden twenty years before it reached most other countries, the result of victories achieved by workers during the 1920s and 1930s, when working-class movements in most other countries were suffering setbacks.

Thus when workers renewed the struggle over health-and-safety in the late 1960s, they began from a higher plateau. Reform in the 1970s was premissed on an expanded notion of the appropriate domain of health-and-safety regulation. While in most countries the focus was broadened to include physical health in addition to traditional safety concerns, in Sweden, psychological well-being also became an object of health-and-safety regulation. A central tenet of this approach was that a healthy work environment was one in which workers exercised some control over their work situation. More specifically, safety delegates were given the right to shut down unsafe operations pending investigation by an inspector and the right to participate in the planning of new premises and working methods. In addition, peak labour-market organizations negotiated an agreement that gave workers a majority on joint health-and-safety committees and gave those committees limited decision-making power.[17]

These reforms, however, have not had the impact their proponents expected. The average annual injury rate during the seven years preceding the Work Environment Act of 1977 was actually lower than the average rate for the following six years.[18] The accident rate over the 1980s remained relatively constant, while the rate of reported occupational diseases increased. Fatality rates decreased, but more slowly than during the preceding thirty years.[19]

Disappointment led trade-union and government officials to recommend changes, and in 1991 the act was amended. A major aim of reform was to impose more direct responsibility for health-and-safety on employers; management was abdicating its responsibilities while maintaining control over production decisions that affected the work environment. Since the political will and power further to democratize decision-making in the enterprise were lacking, the alternative was to make health-and-safety central to management's agenda.[20]

Ontario

Ontario's version of third-wave reforms provided workers with moderately strong participatory rights. The first reforms were introduced in 1976, by a minority Conservative government that needed more labour support than usual. Workers obtained a statutory right to refuse unsafe work, a right to accompany and be consulted by the inspector, and protection against retaliation, while the minister of labour was empowered to require establishment of joint health-and-safety committees (JHSC's) and/or appointment of worker safety representatives.[21] In 1978, another minority conservative government enacted an omnibus statute substantially overhauling the province's health-and-safety system, including the participatory rights of workers. The act made JHSCs mandatory in workplaces with twenty or more employees and gave them the power to investigate and make recommendations regarding health-and-safety to the employer. No power of decision was granted. A designated worker-member could conduct periodic inspections of the workplace, and workers were given a right to know of hazards in the workplace and to receive appropriate instruction on how to handle them safely.[22]

The province's continuing commitment to this model was reflected in amendments enacted in the 1980s. The two most significant changes extended and strengthened the role of the IRS. First, in 1987, as part of a coordinated effort to create a national right-to-know system, the act was amended to introduce the Workplace Hazardous Material Information System (WHMIS), designed to ensure that information about hazardous materials in the workplace flowed from the supplier or manufacturer to the end-user and the worker. It also required that workers be trained in safe use of hazardous materials to which they were exposed.[23] Second, in 1990, the legislative passed Bill 208, which required JHSCs in more kinds of workplaces and imposed certain procedural requirements. For example, employers must respond in writing to recommendations made by the JHSC. To strengthen the JHSC's technical capacity, of the committee at least one worker-member and one employer-member have to be specially trained and certified. Moreover, a new bipartite body, the Workplace Health-

Figure 1
Frequency of LTI (per million person-hours), total, all industries, Ontario, 1969–86

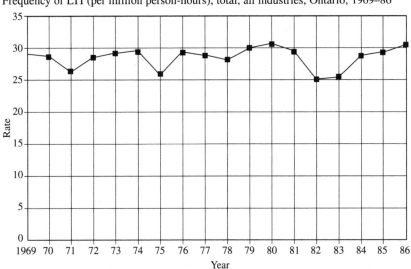

SOURCE: Advisory Council on Occupational Health and Occupational Safety
(ACOHOS), fourth and tenth annual reports (1982 and 1988).

and-safety Agency, was set up to oversee health-and-safety training in the province and to establish criteria for certification of JHSC representatives. A unilateral right for workers to shut down unsafe operations pending inspection was
considered but rejected in face of intense opposition from employers. In its
place, a formal mechanism was created through which work could be stopped if
certified worker and employer representatives agreed that this was required.

Bill 208 also strengthened the ERS. In particular, directors and officers of a
corporation were made directly responsible for securing compliance with the
act in their workplaces and liable to prosecution if they failed to do so. Conviction could lead to a fine of up to $25,000 or a prison term of up to one year.
Penalties and fines for corporations convicted of violating the act were also
increased from a maximum of $25,000 to $500,000.[24] The effect of these
changes on injury rates is difficult to measure. Constructing a time-series is
difficult because of changes in how data are collected. The first time-series
(Figure 1) presents lost-time injuries (LTI) from 1969 to 1986 and allows for
comparison of pre- and post-reform statistics. Clearly, the rate remained fairly
constant; indeed, if there is any movement, it is upward. The average annual
LTI rate for all industry for the seven years prior to the first reforms is 28,

Figure 2

Frequency of LTI (per 100 workers), total, all industries, Ontario, 1980–91

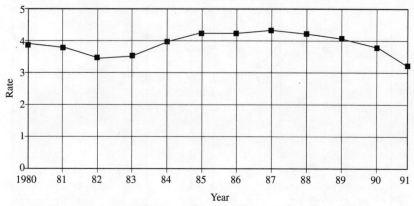

SOURCE: Workers' Compensation Board, annual reports, and Statistics Canada, *The Labour Force*, cat. 71-001.

whereas for the eight years after enactment of the OHSA in 1978, it is 28.7.

This time-series could not be extended past 1986 because the Workers' Compensation Board (WCB) stopped collecting the payroll data on which it was based. In order to get a better view of the 1980s, a second time-series was used, based on LTIs per 100 employed workers (Figure 2). After a slight decline at the beginning of the decade, the injury rate rose until 1987, when it began to decrease. For particular sectors, the pattern varies somewhat, although there is a general decline in the injury rate in all sectors in recent years.[25]

The severity of injuries is another significant measure of regulatory performance. Typically, it is measured by the average number of days of temporary total disability per LTI. Like other indicators, this one has severe problems in measurement, but it is still of interest. Severity increased through the first half of the 1980s and levelled off afterwards.[26] With respect to fatalities, one time-series from 1977 to 1986 indicates a mild decrease in the rate per one million person-hours, while a second shows an increase in the rate per 100,000 employed workers from 1985 to 1988 followed by a decrease to the end of the decade and an increase in 1991.[27]

Summary

The point of this discussion is not to prove that third-wave regulation have failed to reduce work-induced death, disease, and injury; the data cannot support such a stark conclusion, given their limitations. Nevertheless, the data, when looked at cumulatively, raise serious questions about the efficacy of mandated partial self-regulation, especially when workers' political and economic position is under strong attack in the emerging 'new world order.'

WHAT WENT WRONG?

Change in a regulatory regime sets in motion a chain of events whose dynamics and outcome depend not only on the intent of the reformers but also on the responses of workers, employers, and government officials. In short, reforms create opportunities and impose constraints. The ability to effect change is conditioned by many factors, including the power and ideology of the parties involved. The interaction between regime design, including its underlying assumptions, and the affected parties substantially determines how the regime will operate. Applying this approach to operation of the two principal components of the new regime – the ERS and the IRS – illuminates the reasons for the disappointing results achieved to date.

The IRS

As noted above, reforms to the IRS aimed at allowing workers a more active voice in local health-and-safety decision-making. This was to be achieved by giving them rights to know, participate, and refuse unsafe work. Employers and employees would work cooperatively to find acceptable solutions to workplace problems, thereby reducing injury rates and dependence on the state to establish and enforce health-and-safety standards. This goal was considered achievable because of workers' and employers' common interest in eliminating unreasonable risk.

The right of workers to know the hazards they are exposed to is a precondition for any effective participation. For that reason, it is often one of the best-developed rights in the IRS regime. Certainly, this is the case in Canada, where WHMIS was adopted nationally in the late 1980s. But there are problems. There is still no positive obligation to test products to determine their hazardous properties, if any, before introducing them into the workplace. As a result, workers will still be used as guinea pigs to determine the hazardous effects of exposure to many substances and agents. Moreover, the quality of the training received by workers exposed to hazardous materials or physical agents varies enormously. Unionized workers are much more likely to get decent training than their non-union brothers and sisters.

Having knowledge is one thing; acting on it to improve health-and-safety is another. One American study, for example, found that while workers were reasonably familiar with the risk of injury at work, their dissatisfaction was manifested in a number of ways, only some of which were likely to improve health-and-safety.[28] One factor that encourages positive action is workers' knowledge of their legal rights, as shown by the research of Vivienne Walters and her colleagues. Yet they discovered that almost one-third of respondents knew nothing about their legal rights. Moreover, the workers most likely to know their rights were unionized, were male, and had higher levels of education. The most disadvantaged workers were the least likely to have this elementary information.[29]

Architects of the system hoped that if workers were given information and an opportunity to communicate with their employers, acceptable solutions would be produced. Unequal power did not figure prominently in their analysis. But, it seems, power may be a precondition for acquisition of knowledge, let alone for its use.

JHSCs are the central institution through which workers can participate in the IRS. Ontario's faith in the efficacy of this institution is evidenced by Bill 208, but is this faith justified? A growing literature suggests that, under some conditions, they can improve health-and-safety but that their mere existence does nothing towards that end.[30] Some of the conditions that affect their performance might be characterized as 'micro' and tend to cluster around organizational issues – number of members, location within the management hierarchy or involvement with a trade union, frequency of meetings, procedures at meetings, amount of paid time and training received by worker-members and requirements for management to respond formally to recommendations. These kinds of matters are most amenable to legal reform and, not surprisingly, have been addressed in that way. Bill 208 tackled just these issues.

Another set of factors relates to the 'macro,' or structural and ideological environment – distribution of power and political-economic and ideological circumstances. Management guards its control over basic investment decisions, including what, when, where, and how to produce, JHSCs have been unable to change these prerogatives and are unlikely to be able to do so unless there are dramatic and unexpected changes in the direction of more economic democracy. The case of Sweden is telling in this regard. A strong social-democratic government supported by a powerful trade-union organization was unable to advance significantly the cause of economic democracy. The unwillingness of Ontario's government to grant certified worker representatives the unilateral right to shut down unsafe operations pending inspection or to give the JHSC any power of decision is indicative of how difficult it is to obtain such rights. Governments contemplating legislation that infringes managerial prerogative to an unacceptable extent will face vociferous opposition from employers.

The fact that unionization is positively correlated with JHSC's functioning also is indicative of the importance of the distribution of power in the workplace. But the amount of power that workers gain through unionization varies enormously. In part, this is related to the economic environment of the firm and industry. Firms operating in highly competitive environments with low profit margins are unlikely to be willing to invest in the health-and-safety of their workforces unless compelled to do so, and workers in those industries, even if unionized, will probably lack the clout necessary to achieve this end. Similarly, neither management nor workers in declining industries that are shedding workers are likely to be emphasizing on health-and-safety. Even in better circumstances, JHSCs are more likely to resolve easy cases, where there is agreement about what the problem is and how to fix it, and where the costs of eliminating the risk are not substantial. Changes that require more fundamental and expensive changes are less likely to be achieved.[31]

In sum, many studies have identified management's commitment to good health-and-safety as a key factor in JHSC's performance. The process through which that commitment is built is less well understood. Liberal pluralists, both in academe and in government, tend to focus on micro-organizational factors. Their ideological premises encourage them to do so. Consensus theory supports the belief that partial mandated self-regulation should work. By ignoring or playing down conflict and power differentials, however, they may be overlooking some of the more powerful determinants of JHSC's effectiveness. It is arguable that the flatness of the injury rate after third-wave reforms is related to this failure in regulatory design.

The right to refuse unsafe work, unlike the rights examined above, is rooted in recognition that there is scope for conflict between workers and employers over health-and-safety. Although settlement mechanisms are provided to reduce the level of unnecessary conflict, it is the refusal of a worker to obey that triggers them, and the right to refuse is clearly intended to empower workers. As such, it fits badly with consensus theory. Not surprisingly, the right to refuse has always been carefully circumscribed by grievance arbitrators and labour-relations boards. Adjudicators have been careful to emphasize that the right to refuse does not give workers the right to strike during the life of a collective agreement. Only workers who perceive themselves to be at risk can refuse, and others cannot join them in solidarity. Risks that are ordinarily present will generally not be seen to be sufficiently hazardous to justify a refusal. Also, adjudicators worry that the right to refuse may be abused by shop-floor activists. For example, Walters's recent study found that the Ontario Labour Relations Board is more likely to believe a 'good, respectful worker' than one who challenges managerial authority.[32] Generally, there is solicitude for management rights, which colours decision-making.[33] As a result, workers who refuse unsafe work can never be sure whether they will be vindicated.

In addition, while the statute intends to be empowering, only workers who are already empowered independently of the statute will exercise their legal rights; the right is exercised overwhelmingly by unionized workers. Clearly, in this area as in others, most non-unionized workers understand that the law cannot protect them, given the precariousness of their employment. Figure 3 plots the number of work refusals in Ontario against the provincial unemployment rate. While there has been a general increase in workers' willingness to exercise the right to refuse, at any given level refusals seem sensitive to changes in the unemployment rate. Even unionized employees recognize that in slack times they lack the security to confront their employers. High unemployment is disempowering.

In sum, a fundamental weakness of North American IRSs is that they deny the salience of unequal power relations. Unionized workers in large workplace enter the IRS with some power and may be able to make some gains. Unfortunately, this sector is declining rapidly. Most workers are therefore dependent on the performance of the ERS.

The ERS

Reforms of the 1970s rationalized the enforcement apparatus and gave more emphasis to health hazards but did not change fundamentally the strategy of inspectors. Gentle persuasion remains the basic approach to enforcement, and prosecution is still a last resort, but because workers have rights in the IRS, the legitimacy of self-compliance is more easily defended, even though it has done little to improve health-and-safety for workers. This situation has obvious advantages for governments, which need to explain from time to time why they are not doing more to protect workers. There are, however, conflicts within the system which produce marginal changes to enforcement practices. The dynamics of enforcement in third-wave regulatory models can best be understood in relation to the influence of the dominant health-and-safety ideology, the unfavourable balance of power between labour and capital, and the struggles *which are* conducted within these parameters.

Resources allocated by the state to enforcement of health-and-safety are inadequate and have not increased substantially as a result of third-wave reforms. In Ontario, for example, the budget of the Occupational Health-and-safety Division (OHSD) of the Ministry of Labour (MOL) has grown only slightly when measured in constant dollars or in relation to dollars per employed person, and most of this growth has taken place since 1986, for reasons to be examined below (see Figure 4).[34] Thus the ideology of cooperative enforcement relieves

Figure 3
Work refusals and employment rates, Ontario, 1977–90

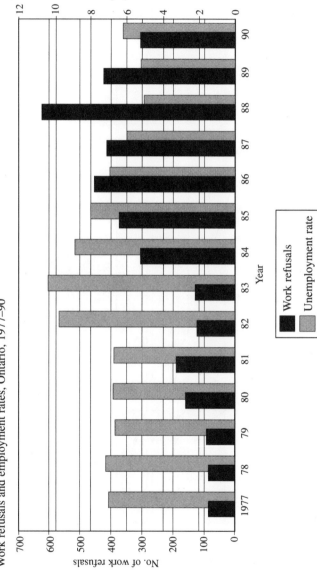

SOURCE: Ontario, MOL, annual reports, and Statistics Canada Canadian Economic Observer, *Historical Statistics Supplement 1990–91*, cat. 11-210, Table 12.5

Figure 4
Health and Safety Budget, OHSD, 1972–90

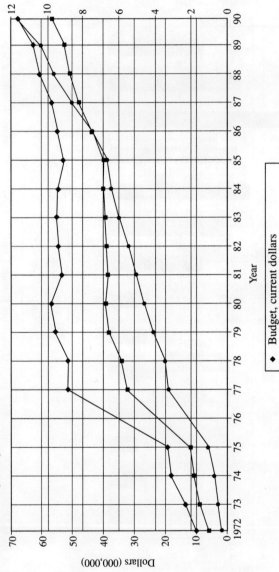

SOURCE: MOL, annual reports, Canadian Economic Observer Statistics Canada, cat. 11-210, 1991/1992, 3.2 and 12.3.

Note: Mine Safety Division was added in 1976–7.

Figure 5

Field activities of inspectors, ISHB, 1970–90

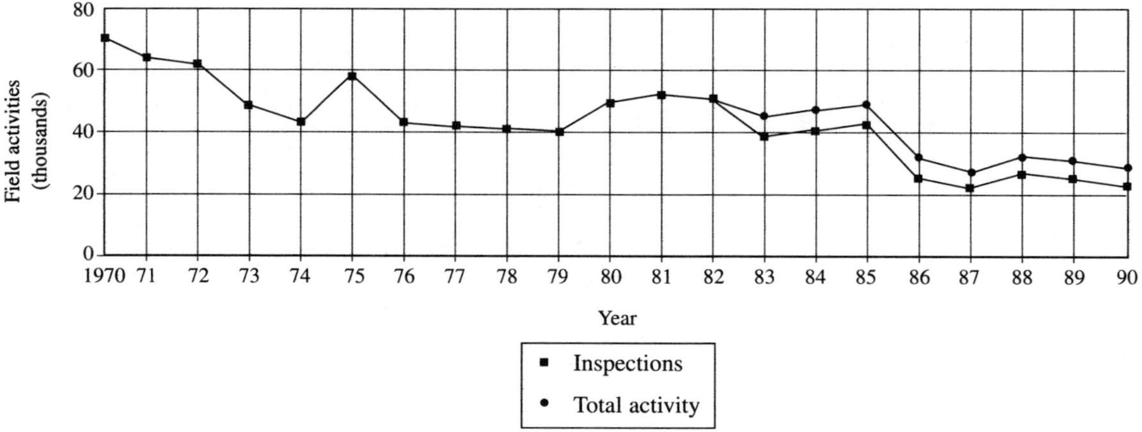

SOURCES: Ontario, MOL, annual reports, and Industrial Health and Safety Program, Operations Division.

political pressure on the state to put fiscal resources behind its rhetorical commitment to occupational health-and-safety.

Limited resources constrain enforcement but do not determine how resources will be spent. In Ontario, there has been a long-term decline in the number of inspections and other inspection-related field activities conducted by the industrial health-and-safety branch (IHSB), the largest by far of the OHSD's three sectoral branches (see Figure 5). In 1991–2, about 7 per cent of all establishments under its jurisdiction were inspected – troubling, because many analysts have suggested that frequency of inspection affects safety performance.[35] The decline in field activities is rationalized on the basis that resources are targeted to establishments where internal responsibility functions least well, but this may not be the case. For example, from 1988 to 1992, nearly 35 per cent of all inspections were conducted at unionized workplaces.[36] This rate is higher than the percentage of unionized establishments under the IHSB's jurisdiction. One reason for this skewing is that resource allocation is partly driven by demand.[37] Employees' complaints and work refusals, for example, require some response, and because unionized workers are more likely to take these actions, a larger share of enforcement resources will be directed towards them. More vulnerable, non-unionized workers may be doubly disadvantaged; because of their powerlessness, the IRS works less well for them, and the ERS is less likely to be present.

A second rationale for the decline in field activities is the alleged shift towards better-quality inspections and enforcement. We have relatively few ways of measuring the intensity with which compliance strategies involving persuasion, bargaining, and provision of information and advice are pursued. How can we tell whether gentle persuasion has become vigorous persuasion? What we can quantify is the frequency with which coercive powers are exercised, including orders, stop-work orders, and prosecutions. Admittedly, this measure provides only a partial view of intensity, but it is useful, especially since punishment complements persuasion.[38]

The frequency and stringency of enforcement actions have increased at the margin in Ontario. The average number of directions issued per inspection doubled, from 0.6 in 1970 to 1.2 in 1990. Use of stop-work orders has also been increasing, both absolutely and as a percentage of all orders issued, since they became available in 1979. Finally, except for the period 1986–88, the number of cases prosecuted has grown only slightly.

Whatever toughening of enforcement has occurred is attributable primarily to struggles conducted by workers and their political allies. In opposition, Ontario's New Democratic Party (NDP) regularly embarrassed governments over failures of the MOL to enforce the law. In 1985, the Conservative government was defeated, and the Liberals came to power on the basis of an accord with the NDP. Shortly thereafter, a new, stricter enforcement policy was issued, and the budget of the OHSD grew. Also, there has been a steady increase in average fines, even when calculated in constant dollars. This is a result partly of a series of legislative changes that increased the maximum fines. As well, from the early 1980s, the courts began to take employers' violations of health-and-safety laws more seriously. The decision of the Ontario Court of Appeal in the *Cotton Felts* case sent a clear signal to the lower courts that fines should be set at levels that have deterrent effect.[39]

These change must be kept in perspective, however. For example, from 1984 to 1990, prosecutions amounted to a little less than one-third of one percent of all orders issued. The average fine of an employer in 1990 was only $5,626, an amount not likely to have much of a deterrent effect on medium-sized and large employers.[40] Finally, it is unclear whether the coercive power of the ERS is being exercised more vigorously on behalf of less powerful workers who are more dependent on it.[41] For example, the IHSB issued orders at the same rate on inspections at unionized and non-unionized plants.[42]

The relation between the IRS and the ERS brings us back to a basic ambiguity in third-wave regulation. Reformers spoke of the common interests of workers and employers in health-and-safety, but they also recognized that the old system of employer self-regulation by default was inadequate. They hoped that institutional reform that brought workers into the IRS and rationalized the ERS would be sufficient. Blinded by their own ideology, they ignored or played down conflicts between workers and employers and the imbalance of power between them. But the ideology is not fully hegemonic. Workers in third-wave systems of regulation have fought to increase their power, both by strengthening their position in the IRS and by demanding stronger external enforcement. They have made slight progress – they have not obtained joint decision-making power with their employers over health-and-safety, and persuasion is still the dominant strategy.

WHERE DO WE GO FROM HERE?

So far, I have argued that a dialectic of struggle and reform drives development of occupational health-and-safety regulation but that this struggle occurs within a broader political-economic and ideological context that shapes both the reforms and their implementation. The imbalance of power between labour and capital, and between capital and state regulators, and the dominant ideology that constructs workers and their employers as voluntary partners in a mutually beneficial, but inherently risky, enterprise create powerful obstacles to control of corporate misconduct. Reforms that ignore or accept, rather than acknowledge and challenge, these constraints may not produce much amelioration.

Yet these reforms have created institutional arrangements and lent rhetorical support to claims that can be used as a platform from which to carry on the struggle for more fundamental change to the system. These possibilities, considered briefly below, build on the dual nature of third-wave reforms, which have enhanced the potential for direct state regulation and built a base of worker rights.

With regard to direct state regulation, Ontario's experience is instructive. A concerted campaign by workers to politicize the problem of unsafe and unhealthy workplaces can put pressure on the state to expand its regulatory power and to exercise it more forcefully. When this is accompanied by election of a government that feels itself to be at least somewhat dependent on labour support, a tougher approach may be implemented. In short, making health-and-safety at work the object of public regulation sets up a foundation for further political struggles over how public power is exercised and whether it is expanded. Moreover, by making health-and-safety at work a public rather than a private issue, workers can attack the ideology of voluntarism that is so inimical to their long-term interests. If it is recognized that risks are not assumed but imposed and that the state sets limits on the extent to which employers can impose risks on workers, then the seriousness of kiling and maiming at work might be better appreciated. Prosecution strategies that emphasize this reality, and, in particular, use of criminal prosecutions in appropriate cases, could reshape popular perceptions. In addition, the threat of serious sanctions, including jail terms for officers and directors, might influence corporate decision-making, which otherwise tends to place profits over safety.[43] While undoubtedly the decline in Ontario's accident rate since 1987 is attributable to a number of influences, especially the slowdown in economic growth after 1989, it is worth considering whether the shift to somewhat tougher enforcement had a marginal impact as well.

The second branch of a strategy for change is to build on the principle of internal responsibility. If the starting premises of regulation is changed so that risk is seen to be imposed by profit-seeking employers on workers whose job options are constrained, the logic of redelegating responsibility for health-and-safety to the parties, subject only to a duty on the employer to share information and consult with workers, loses some of its appeal. The achievement of internal responsibility will require more. In particular, arguments in favour of workers' empowerment become easier to justify. Workers as the primary, and largely involuntary, risk-bearers should be able to exercise greater control over decisions that affect levels of risk.

Whatever the strategy, progress will be difficult. Changes in the global economy do not bode well for workers. Increased competition on a global scale weakens their bargaining position. Even if more economic democracy is achieved at the firm level, the costs to workers of insisting on safer and healthier conditions may be prohibitive.[44] As well, internationalization of capital increases its leverage in dealings with government, thereby diminishing the regulatory capacity and will of nation-states. Yet it is clear that there can be much more amelioration before the structural limits of change are reached. The challenge is to find appropriate responses to the reality of unequal power, and that cannot be done by ignoring it.

NOTES

1 The term is found in Rees (1988, 9).
2 Similar approaches can be found in W.G. Carson (1979); Pearce and Tombs (1990); Snider (1990); Curran (1993).
3 This draws from Glasbeek and Tucker (1992).
4 I have discussed this at much greater length in Tucker (1990).
5 On development of this approach in England, see Carson (1979). Also for its more modern application see Carson (1970b).
6 For Ontario, see V. Walters (1983); for the United States, Donnelly (1982) and Noble (1985); for the United Kingdom, Nichols and Armstrong (1973); and for Sweden, Asard (1980).
7 For reports of under-reporting, see Brickey and Grant (1992); Ontario, Legislative Assembly, Standing Committee on Resources Development, 'Report on Accidents and Fatalities in Ontario Mines' (1st sess., 34th Parl., 1987); and Stevens (1992). For over-reporting, see Leslie Papp, 'Workers Bilking Injury-Pay Plan, Companies Say,' Toronto Star, 9 January 1992, A10.
8 Generally, see Noble in this volume and Rothstein (1990).
9 Drapkin (1980), Robinson (1991).
10 On workers' rights to participate in the ERS, see 'Employee Participation in Occupational Safety and Health Review Commission Proceedings,' Columbia Law Review 85 (1985), 1,317.
11 For recent data, see Donahue (1991). Earlier studies include Noble (1986). See also, Calavita (1983) and Szasz (1984, 1986). For a more positive assessment of cooperative or voluntary compliance, see Scholz (1991) and Rees (1988).
12 For example, Viscusi (1986). He concludes: 'The overall impact remains relatively modest, however, as job risks continue to be largely dictated by forces other than government regulation' (263). On recent trends, see The Rising Wave: Death and Injury among High Risk Workers in the 1980s (Chicago: National Safe Workplace

Institute 1987); AFL-CIO, Department of Occupational Health-and-safety, *Death on the Job: The Toll of Neglect* (Washington, D.C.: April 1992) and Beckwith (1992). For a more positive assessment, see Scholz and Gray (1990).

13 For an overview, see Selwyn (1982, 46–58). On employment law remedies, see Hepple, Hepple, and O'Higgins (1981).

14 For example, Dawson et al. (1988); Nichols (1990); Codrington and Henley (1981).

15 Nichols (1990).

16 Tombs (1990a).

17 See Navarro (1983); Tucker (1992).

18 Tucker (1992, 110).

19 See Frick (1990); Malker (1991). The increase in occupational injuries reflects at least in part changes in the criteria for establishing work-relatedness and greater public awareness of the adverse health effects of work.

20 For a description of these changes, see *NBOSH Newsletter* (March 1991).

21 Employees' Health and Safety Act, 1976, SO 1976, c. 79.

22 Occupational Health and Safety Act, SO 1978, c. 83.

23 SO 1987, c. 79.

24 SO 1990, c. 7.

25 The aggregate rate, however, disguises the much greater variation in accident rates in particular industries. Injury rates in mining and construction seem to have declined over this period while rates in manufacturing and services increased, suggesting that regulatory reforms affected sectors differently. Further studies are needed, however, to determine whether this was the case and, if so, why.

26 Ontario, Workers' Compensation Board, *Annual Report* (1987); Lewycky (1986). Also, the changing mix of injuries affects the severity rate. For example, an increase in the proportion of sprains and strains will result in more time off per LTI because these injuries take longer to heal. See MOL, *Injuries and Illnesses in Ontario's Workplaces: Statistics and Analysis* (Toronto: Policy and Analysis Unit, Health-and-safety Policy Branch, MOL, October 1991) 20–1.

27 The first time-series is derived from Ontario, Advisory Council on Occupational Health and Occupational Safety, *Annual Report* (1981–8), while the second is from Ontario, Ministry of Labour, Health-and-safety Policy Branch, *Occupational Health-and-safety: Facts and Figures* (June 1990 and December 1992).

28 Robinson (1987, 665; 1991, 14–39).

29 Walters and Haines (1988); Walters and Denton (1990).

30 For Ontario, see V. Walters (1985) and Tuohy and Simard (1993); for Sweden, Tucker (1992); and for the United Kingdom, Dawson et al. (1988, 50–8).

31 For example, Rees (1988, 154–72) notes that even successful JHSCs were able to resolve only the easy cases involving momentary hazards and behavioural problems. Similar observations have been made about Sweden's JHSCs (Liukkonen 1987).

32 Walters (1991, 722).

33 Gross and Greenfield (1985, 647–61).

34 The difference between what governments are prepared to spend on treatment and what they will spend on prevention is striking. For example, in 1986, Ontario spent $9.57 per employed person on occupational health-and-safety regulation. By comparison, health-care expenditures per person in 1986 were $1,831. See *National Health Expenditures in Canada 1975–87*, Cat. H21-99/1990E (Ottawa: Ministry of Supply and Services 1990), 30. The problem of inadequate enforcement resources in the United States is documented in Noble (1986, 178) and his piece in this volume.

35 For Canada, see Cindy Moser, 'What's New with You?,' *OH&S Canada* (July/ August 1992), 54 (health-and-safety professionals indicating status tied to frequency of inspections). For the United States, see Graye and Scholz (1991, 185); Robertson and Keeve (1983, 581); and Viscusi (1986, 262) where he notes, 'What was particularly striking is that the OSHA policy variable that seemed most instrumental was the rate of OSHA inspections rather than the penalty level.'

36 Data provided by Ontario, MOL, Policy and Analysis Unit, Health and Safety Policy Branch.

37 Clearly, other factors, expecially injury rate, affect allocation. See Tuohy and Simard (1993, 10–11). For comparable U.S. results, see Weil (1991, 20).

38 On the connection between punishment and persuasioin, see Keith Hawkins, 'Bargain and Bluff: Compliance Strategy and Deterrence in Enforcement Regulation,' *Law and Policy Quarterly* 5 (1983), 48–50, and John T. Scholz, 'Voluntary Compliance and Regulatory Enforcement,' *Law and Policy* 6 (1984), 385. Recently, the British Health-and-safety Executive recognized this. 'HSE Plans to Toughen Up on Enforcement,' *Health and Safety at Work* (August 1992), 11.

39 *R. v. Cotton Felts Ltd.* (1982), 2 CCC (3d) 287.

40 In 1991, the maximum permissible fine was raised twentyfold, to $500,000. Since then, the courts have imposed, on average, higher fines, including some in excess of $100,000.

41 A number of writers have suggested that the crucial issue in enforcement is not whether to use persuasion or punishment, but to recognize when it is appropriate to use each. For example, see Braithewaite (1985a) and Rees (1988, 175–218).

42 Data provided by MOL. The study by Tuohy and Simard found that among unionized establishments, orders were issued more frequently where there were antagonistic relations on the JHSC. In the United States, unions were found to increase OSHA enforcement in the manufacturing sector. See Weil (1991).

43 Glasbeek (1988b); Bergman (1991); Bixby (1991).

44 Grunberg et al. (1984, 413).

14

Regulating Work in a Capitalist Society

CHARLES NOBLE

In modern capitalist societies, governments that attempt to protect workers from occupational hazards face a formidable political problem: to be effective, they must force corporate actors to change their behaviour. In most cases, to improve occupational safety-and-health, employers will face increased costs and, in those instances where worker protection requires it, even share power at 'the point of production' with well-trained and informed employees. As a result, when governments attempt to exercise state power in defence of workers' interests in occupational safety-and-health, they usually runs into concerted business opposition.

Typically, corporate managers argue that worker protection costs too much, interferes with the always-necessary managerial prerogatives to organize production in the most efficient manner, gives workers and unions too much power to disrupt the workplace, and undermines the process of capital accumulation. True or not, these objections are quite compelling, particularly when made by legions of lobbyists and backed up by the not-inconsiderable threat to disinvest in industries, regions, and even entire national economies that do not take the needs of capital seriously.

None of this should be theoretically surprising. Students of the capitalist state have long argued that governments that seek to redistribute power and wealth from capital to labour should expect employers to object and to mobilize their vast economic and political resources to make sure that their objections are heard and heeded by legislators, executives, and judges. Moreover, all other things being equal, employers' objections will win out; even if reformers make some headway in periods of crisis, corporate counter-mobilization will eventually dilute and 'rationalize' those gains, making them more compatible with profits and managerial prerogatives.[1]

That literature also suggests, however, that progress is not impossible. Indeed, recent research indicates that earlier accounts exaggerated the inherent 'structural' limits to reform in capitalist societies – that more depends on politics, and the choice of political and reform strategies, than once imagined (Przeworski 1990). Indeed, there are any number of political factors that might push governments to act in the name of social change, from working-class struggle, through the demands of middle-class reformers, to pressure by capitalists who calculate that government-sponsored reforms can, if properly organized, work in their interests.

The history of workplace safety-and-health reform confirms these expectations. Since the late nineteenth century, in the face of political pressure, governments everywhere in the West have struggled to reform work, imposing new obligations on employers and wrestling with opposition to those changes. Government inspectorates were first established in the nineteenth century to investigate the most serious instances of death and injury in the mines and factories. Workers compensation systems were set up in the late nineteenth and early twentieth centuries both to provide injured employees with some compensation and to relieve employers of the uncertainty of tort suits. Both came at the end of long and bitter struggles to improve working conditions, and neither fully lived up to reformers' expectations. The new regulatory agencies were weak; the new workers' compensation systems failed to provide real income maintenance. In the 1960s and 1970s, workplace safety-and-health regulation was again transformed. Governments adopted stronger legislation, strengthened regulatory agencies, and increased workers' rights to participate in decisions that affected their exposure to health risks at work.

In historical perspective, workers have made substantial gains. Today, all democratic governments recognize that occupational health-and-safety constitutes a social problem to be dealt with through exercise of public power. No longer does the law assume, as it did in the nineteenth century, that workers accept the 'inherent' risks of work. Everywhere among the rich capitalist societies, states seek to force managers to rethink the impact of work on the labour-force and society.

But capital and labour also continue to struggle over workplace safety-and-health, and everywhere periods of reform have been followed by retrenchment. In response, reformers continue to search for regulatory strategies that might more effectively regulate work. Which are the most effective tools for protecting workers from occupational safety-and-health hazards in modern capitalist societies? And which of these are politically feasible?

OPTIONS

In the United States, the debate about regulatory strategies has focused on the relative merits of five basic approaches. In this section, I consider each in some detail, identifying what we know about their efficacy and speculating on their political appeal.

Command and Control

Liberal states entered the modern world by exercising their traditional police powers. In the case of occupational safety-and-health, that meant sending investigators into the factories and punishing employers who broke the factory laws. As the modern bureaucratic state developed, this police approach was transformed into something more administrative and less judicial – what is now called 'command-and-control' regulation.

With command and control, regulators, typically a government agency housed within the executive branch, set health-and-safety standards. These standards in turn are enforced by either the executive or the judicial branch, through administrative fines or, where courts enforce standards, civil penalties. Where employers wilfully endanger their employees, they are also subject to criminal sanctions.

The command-and-control strategy is the foundation of nearly all occupational safety-and-health regulatory systems, and a strong case can be made for it. In principle, it provides an ideal way to resolve the inevitable conflicts that arise in all environmental matters between science and political accountability. Typically, administrative regulatory agencies are run by political appointees who oversee and are counselled by experts in the subject area in question. Thus, the agency can balance two sorts of messages – the politically determined goals of the regime in power and the less-partisan ones of the permanent staff. In the best of all possible worlds, experts tell regulators about the economic and health implications of their choices, while politics determines the pace and direction of change – deciding how much worker protection society wants.

Enforcement under this scheme relies mostly on the size, training, and effectiveness of the inspectorate. Inspectors examine working conditions and penalize employers who fail to protect workers. While there are many potential conflicts over exactly what 'protection' might mean – for example, do employers have a 'general duty' to protect employees from all known hazards or only an obligation to comply with existing standards? – the strategy is relatively straightforward. Indeed, it is for this reason that governments turn to it. Moreover, depending on how they are instructed, and the resources at their disposal, inspectors can also play dual roles – giving advice to managers who seek it and, by levying fines, deterring non-compliance from those who flaunt governmental authority.

There are, however, several problems with the strategy. To begin with, it only appears to resolve rationally the conflict between science and politics. Everywhere, politically appointed regulators enjoy administrative discretion. Indeed, discretion is an essential component of this approach, and it is easily abused. Dissenting experts can be silenced, sound policies can be rejected, and shifting political and economic winds too often determine the agency's direction. The abrupt *voltes-face* in health-and-safety policy in Great Britain in the Thatcher era and the United States during the Reagan administration make this quite clear.

If command-and-control regulation is to be consistent, capital and labour must have already reached some agreement on the scientific and political issues, including how much attention to pay to workers' health-and-safety, and how to pay the costs of protection. If workers' interests are to be effectively represented in that agreement, unions must be strong and privileged participants in policymaking. Both these conditions are rarely met. When they are not, administrative regulation too easily becomes a way for government to legitimate rather than reform the status quo.

It is also difficult to mount sufficient enforcement using only a factory inspectorate. The size and diversity of every modern capitalist economy make it almost impossible for inspectors to cover the field. It is also politically difficult for government to levy fines sufficiently high to force employers to change their behaviour. And unless fines really do hurt, employers are likely to treat them as a cost of doing business, particularly if the likelihood of being inspected is small, as when the inspectorate is small.

Conversely, when it is working, command-and-control regulation is inherently conflictual. Government uses the power at its disposal to force employers to change their behaviour. As a result, employers are likely to resist; those most affected usually mount major campaigns against regulation. In this sort of highly politicized atmosphere, science is likely to succumb completely to politics.

Cooperation

In the last two decades, some countries have moved towards more 'cooperative' forms of regulation, which now supplement and in some instances replace more traditional forms of command and control. Here the goal is to replace conflict with negotiations among workers, employers, and government. Rather than punishing employers, the state uses its power to encourage all affected parties to reach agreement on workplace safety-and-health.

Cooperation can occur on three levels. General policies to protect workers can be determined within a broader, corporatist framework, with the associations of labour and capital bargaining over occupational safety-and-health as part of wider negotiations about employment, wages, and working conditions. This kind of bargaining is restricted to those capitalist states where tripartite bargaining is already a routine means of containing and coopting class conflict.[2]

Bargaining can also occur over specific standards. Called 'regneg' (regulatory negotiation) in the American debates, it allows affected workers and employers to negotiate how they will deal with specific hazards (Bacow 1980; Mendeloff 1988). For example, employees and employers in the textile industry would bargain over the level of cotton dust to which workers would be exposed, compliance methods (e.g., engineering controls versus respirators), and compliance schedules. Presumably, the two groups would find some middle ground between maximal protection (protecting workers to the extent technically feasible regardless of cost) and the 'economic feasibility' standard preferred by employers.

Finally, government can bargain with employers over enforcement. It can encourage compliance by using carrots (including subsidies) to supplement traditional reliance on sticks (including fines). Here, government takes a more benign view of employers' intentions than is sometimes taken by inspectors in the command-and-control modality.

Advocates of cooperation argue that it is inherently more flexible and less adversarial than command and control. Because government does not set hard and fast rules that must be obeyed at all costs, public and private actors can respond flexibly to their changing environment; no one is encouraged to regulate 'to rule' or to fight to the death. Because employers get regular access to standard-setters and policy-makers, they are more likely to be reasonable. And their cooperation is rational: their interests are likely to be taken into account.

Advocates of cooperative strategies also suggest that bargained solutions will be more market-efficient (in welfare economists' terms) because players will probably choose levels of protection that reflect their own cost-benefit calculations, rather than the judgments and values of experts. Finally, supportors argue that these agreements are more likely to be implemented with a minimum of resistance than are traditional policies, because they already enjoy widespread support.

There are several objections to this approach. First, peak bargaining over health-and-safety could easily become an elitist alternative to democratic deliberation. As in corporatist arrangements generally, only the most powerful and best-organized employers and employees may be heard. Moreover, cooperation could easily increase the power of capitalists beyond what they enjoy under command and control. In bargaining environments, employers would have dual access, first informally through government authorities who are already sensitive to their concerns, and, second, through their representatives at the bargaining table. In this system, the potential check on capital provided by the nonpartisan expert is all but eliminated, leaving workers even more vulnerable to pressure to reconcile protection with profits.

That pressure may be especially dangerous and politically explosive in bargaining over standards. While corporatism in setting general health-and-safety policy makes some sense, government would be hard-pressed to justify explicit policy trade-offs in which workers agreed to take a much-enhanced risk of death and injury to hold onto their jobs or wages. Clearly, these decisions occur daily, but in private; now government would be asked to give its imprimatur to them in public. Imagine the scandal when, in the midst of a deep recession, government announced that workers in the coal industry had agreed to forgo protection from coal dust in return for an agreement by the operators' association to keep the mines open for another year.

Finally, bargaining over occupational safety-and-health is likely to develop only in certain, highly restrictive settings. In general, corporatism develops where private actors are well-organized, governments work along parliamentary rather than separation-of-power lines, and the political culture supports cooperative rather than adversarial modes of conflict resolution. Thus, whatever their virtues, cooperative regulatory strategies may be little tried beyond northern Europe.[3]

Worker Participation

It is also possible to design protection that relies for its force on workers' participation in workplace governance – workers' involvement with management in identifying and abating hazards, and, at a maximum, participation in making investment and personnel decisions that directly affect the design and organization of the workplace itself.[4]

The participatory approach is the product of the labour left and has taken root where social democrats have enjoyed influence within the labour movement and politics. Participatory schemes in occupational safety and health have been adopted in some Canadian provinces and in several northern European nations, including Sweden and Germany.[5] As a creation of organized labour and rank-and-file worker movements, the approach builds on the idea that empowering workers is both just and efficient – just, because it gives to those most affected by workplace hazards a privileged role in making decisions about protection, and efficient, because it allows government to take advantage of workers' interest, knowledge, and expertise about hazards, thus reducing its own reliance on a paid factory inspectorate.

This model is like command and control in that government continues to set standards and enforce them, but here workers become the inspectorate. Like corporatism, it institutionalizes workers' participation in decision-making, but here government does not seek to balance capital and labour. This approach is clearly intended to empower workers, not employers.

In theory, the approach reflects the wider social-democratic strategy of reforming capitalism by redistributing income and power downward. It also reflects rank-and-file criticisms of the tendency of organized labour to be coopted by capital and the state. In practice, workers' participation requires a legislated 'right to act,' mandating safety-and-health committees with the power to investigate accidents, conduct inspections, perform routine health monitoring, settle disputes, respond to imminent danger, and even abate hazardous situations when needed. Members of the committees in turn would be selected by employees and trained in government-approved programs. In the more ambitious schemes, government would also mandate workers' participation on corporate boards to ensure that health-and-safety concerns are taken into account in strategic investment decisions.

The appeal of worker participation is obvious. Workers would exercise much greater control over the conditions that endanger them, and government would benefit from the input of informed and active workers. But there are also problems with this approach. First, involvement still rests on workers' willingness to press their demands and leaves open the possibility that workers will restrain themselves when they believe that aggressive action might cost them their jobs. As with corporatism, unless workers are protected from the economic hazards of capitalism, they remain vulnerable to cooptation. Second, while participation might increase the efficiency of the government's regulatory effort by lowering the costs of the inspectorate, mobilizing those directly affected by hazards could easily lead to heightened conflict at the workplace. Unless empowered workers could easily reach settlements with employers, industrial conflict would mushroom. Unless government were prepared to deal with this conflict, either by repressing it or by moving even more aggressively towards new forms of production, stalemate would ensue. Finally, unless workers were given rights to participate in basic decisions about corporate investment, committees would still be constrained by the economic implications of decisions taken elsewhere. It is hard to reconstruct the firm, or the labour-capital relationship, from the shop-floor up.

Markets and Torts

A fourth approach to workplace regulation rests on the principle that individual choice in markets, not government decisions, is the most fair and effective way to resolve conflicts over health-and-safety. Most often associated with the right rather than the left, and with opposition to government intervention, this approach has attracted some liberals in recent years, and it is worth considering.

In such a model, government lets employers and employees bargain over working conditions as they do over wages and hours, with employers offering and workers 'choosing' among jobs that offer different combinations of protection and income. Advocates argue that as long as information about hazards is readily available, and labour markets are reasonably competitive, the economically 'optimal' amount of health-and-safety will be supplied – the amount of protection that employees at risk want, given how else they might spend their money, and the real costs to employers of providing protection. Moreover, because it reflects individual preferences, the results are just: they represent what workers want, not the preferences of bureaucrats and experts.[6]

In one respect, this is not regulation at all. Advocates say that this approach minimizes the heavy hand of government. Indeed, its claim to base the distribution of worker health-and-safety on classical liberal ideals of individual responsibility and autonomy is its principal appeal. But this claim is disingenuous. To work, market-based systems must be policed, and government must set some limits on what employers and employees can do, just as government today prohibits slavery, even when those enslaved agree to it.

In this case, information must be made available, employers must be prevented from conspiring to control access to jobs, and certain 'egregious' acts would have to be banned. Presumably, occupations that placed workers at enormous risk but still found takers (for whatever reason) would fall outside the pale. Most important, workers would still retain the right to sue employers who violated the terms of their contract – who placed workers at risk in unexpected, unannounced, or unfair ways. Tort suits would be the remedy and would obviously be adjudicated in the courts on the basis of legal norms established by the state, including the legislature and, in common-law systems, the courts themselves.

Government might also reform the workers' compensation system to change the incentives facing employers, by more severely experience-rating firms with high accident rates. In this way, riskier workplaces would be forced to internalize more of the costs of accidents and injuries through substantially higher insurance premiums. In any case, government would remain involved. Alhough its role would be limited, it would still structure the market to achieve certain socially desireable outcomes.[7]

Critics suggest that this approach would return occupational health-and-safety to the nineteenth century, when workers had to hold capitalists individually accountable for their actions. This is not quite true. Workers would be better off as long as government did not allow employers to recover their traditional common-law defences against employees' suits. Still, forcing individual workers to protect themselves is likely to degrade occupational health-and-safety. Many workers would not sue their employers, and, because of the uncertain etiology of many occupational diseases, many of those who did so would lose. Unless courts and juries routinely found for plaintiffs and the sums awarded were huge, many employers would calculate that they stood a rather decent chance of evading the true costs of their actions. The workers' compensation system does not give much cause for hope in this regard. Even in those places where costs of compliance have soared, workers remain ill-treated and occupational diseases remain underreported.

Criminal Sanctions

The fifth approach to workplace safety-and-health uses the court system in a different way, by criminalizing employers' misdeeds and punishing corporate managers who endanger workers. This is not really a full alternative to other approaches; it would coexist with other methods of rule-making and only supplement command and control by adding criminal sanctions to existing civil fines. Nonetheless, because it seeks to change enforcement, it is worth considering separately.

This approach would add criminal penalties for wilfully endangering workers to the civil fines that regulators now impose on corporate entities. These penalties could be imposed on individual managers both as representatives of corporations and as individuals acting in their own right. Presumably, stiff prison terms would dissuade employers from putting workers at risk.

The case for criminal sanctions is appealing. They are highly visible and they personalize the conflict between labour and management and make individuals responsible for corporate acts. In these ways, they could prove effective in the ideological struggle to make workers' health-and-safety a test of the state and capital's class commitments. By criminalizing the conduct of corporate managers, government would also make clear that it takes workers' health-and-safety seriously and that endangering workers is unacceptable.

This model also has the advantage of making use of the existing judicial apparatus. Imposition of criminal sanctions would not require construction of a new form of state power, and, because courts are decentralized, enforcement would also be decentralized and, presumably, more efficient. Reliance on criminal sanctions in the place of administrative fines would also make enforcement less dependent on the power of labour unions. In traditional command and control, regulators respond to political pressure and are most likely to act aggressively when organized constituencies can apply that pressure. Courts are different. Presumably, judges and juries would act, especially where workers are weak; indeed, they might define their role precisely in this way, as advocates of the 'little man,' helping individuals fight corporate organizations.

But there are also several disadvantages to this strategy. Even as they make corporate conduct more visible, criminal sanctions may cede important ideological ground. By attempting to blame one or more persons for the actions of an organization, this strategy may valorize the classical liberal view that only individuals are responsible for social outcomes. Moreover, employers could defend themselves as they once did, by arguing that workers themselves were responsible for accidents. In the nineteenth century, workers almost always failed to surmount the common-law defences available to employers. Recently, the Texas legislature raised the spectre of those defences again protecting employers from criminal negligence in environmental and occupational safety-and-health cases. According to a newly enacted 'shield' law, employers who knowingly or intentionally commit violations of pollution-control laws can still avoid criminal prosecution if they can show that employees 'freely consented' to be endangered, that the 'danger and conduct charged were reasonably foreseeable hazards of the person's occupation,' and that the person at risk 'had been made aware of the risks involved before giving consent' (Bureau of National Affairs 1991, 349).

Criminal sanctions might also complicate enforcement. Information about workplace accidents will take on special significance with greater possibility of criminal prosecution. It is hard to imagine that employers will not resist government and union investigations into working conditions and related issues.

Finally, the purported institutional advantages of criminal sanctions – decentralization, delinking of regulatory effort from union pressure, the sympathy that juries might show injured workers – may prove illusory. Enforcement will still depend on political will, not the willingness of prosecutors to pursue cases. Administrative discretion will remain alive and well. And here organized labour, lacking institutional clout in the judicial system, may find it harder, not easier, to force the government to act. In addition, because the court system is decentralized, rulings will probably vary widely, heightening uncertainty about what is and is not a corporate crime. Finally, workers' advocates will have to confront the ignorance of judges and juries about the workplace and the scientific and technical issues surrounding occupational health-and-safety.

THE OCCUPATIONAL SAFETY AND HEALTH ACT OF 1970

Until 1970, workplace safety-and-health regulation in the United States was largely ineffective. Except for select categories, most employees were protected by state-level agencies that were, at best, reluctant regulators. The state-level workers' compensation system, established in the early twentieth century, provided few economic incentives to employers to change their behaviour. Moreover, the system all but ignored occupational diseases.

The system was changed significantly in 1970 with passage by Congress of the Occupational Safety-and-Health Act (OSHA). Its passage reflected a shift away from the bread-and-butter issues that had dominated postwar labour-management politics towards new, 'quality of life' issues, ranging from environmentalism to workplace democracy. Reform regarding workers' health-and-safety also reflected the confluence of several distinct and often competitive social movements – organized labour, radical rank-and-file labour activists, the environmental movement, and the public-interest movement. All were, to varying degrees, involved in the struggle for OSHA.

The vision behind the act reflected the goals of these diverse forces. Advocates talked of bringing a new, environmental awareness to the workplace and giving the grassroots, in this case individual workers, the kinds of rights and powers once reserved to labour unions and management. In practice, the act, and the new agency created by it, represented both old and new views of state power by blending command and control with a bit of worker participation, labour-management cooperation, and criminal sanctions.

Command and control took pride of place. The OSHA gave the Department of Labour (in practice, its newly created Occupational Safety-and-Health Administration) discretionary power to set and enforce standards on regulated firms (with the proviso that health standards were to protect workers 'to the extent feasible'). It was also empowered to enforce these standards by inspecting workplaces and imposing penalties on employers who failed to comply. The act further imposed a 'general duty' on all covered employers to provide healthy and safe workplaces.

Reflecting the ideas of the public-interest movement, the act also gave workers some innovative rights to participate in rule-making and enforcement. Such rights were novel in 1970 and reflected the movement's belief that corporate power over government could be limited only by empowering citizens to participate more directly in the making of administrative decisions. The OSHA gave workers rights to participate in standard-setting, workplace inspections, and monitoring of hazards; to have access to information about hazards and agency findings; to appeal agency rulings to the courts; and to be protected from discrimination against them by employers for exercising these rights.

The act also allowed labour-management bargaining over standards. OSHA could create Standards Advisory Committees representing organized labour, employers, and the wider public-health community to develop rules. Finally, the act included limited criminal sanctions, authorizing prosecution of an employer whose wilful violation of an OSHA standard resulted in a worker's death and providing for a misdemeanour prosecution with a maximum fine of $10,000 and/or six months in jail.

OSHA

To date, OSHA as an agency has relied almost exclusively on the command-and-control strategy. It sets standards and fields an inspectorate to police employers. The agency has wavered between more and less aggressive postures, depending on the political winds. When Republican administrations were in power – eighteen of the agency's first twenty-two years – OSHA was fairly passive, responding more to White House efforts to contain its regulatory zeal than to unions' and workers' demands for more standards and enforcement.

There was one brief period of regulatory activism during the Carter administration, when agency head Eula Bingham attempted to set standards and enforce them, resulting in the benzene, lead, and cotton-dust rules, among others; the number and size of fines also went up. Bingham tried to use the agency's rules and resources to promote workers' participation, protecting them where it could from employers' reprisals for complaining about health-and-safety at work, and channelling 'New Direction' education and training grants to rank-and-file Committees on Occupational Safety-and-Health (COSHs).

Neither the standards advisory committees nor criminal sanctions have been used extensively in either Republican or Democratic administrations. The agency did bring the steelworkers' union and steel-company executives together to negotiate compliance with the coke-oven standard, but that episode was exceptional, and bargaining has not been pursued aggressively. Nor has the agency made much use of the act's criminal sanctions. In its first eighteen years, OSHA recommended only fifty-seven cases to the Department of Justice for prosecution (U.S. GAO 1988, 30, 37). OSHA picked up the pace somewhat in 1989, but the agency remains slow to pursue criminal cases.

OSHA's overall impact on workers' health-and-safety has been quite limited. The agency has been particularly cautious in setting standards, especially for levels of exposure to toxic substances. There are only thirty comprehensive health rules setting permissible exposure levels and requiring employers to monitor workers' exposure and its effect on their health. Other, less comprehensive rules do exist, but the vast majority of toxic substances used in the workplace are unregulated by OSHA. As of 1992, the agency had set control levels for less than one-fourth of the 526 identified as carcinogens by the International

Agency for Research on Cancer, the National Toxicology Program, the American Council of Governmental Industrial Hygienists (ACGIH), and the NTP/ National Cancer Institute Cancer Bioassay Program (Oleinick, Fodor, and Susrelman 1988, 57–8). There are also significant gaps in the setting of safety standards. Many known hazards, such as repetitive-motion injuries, are only partially regulated (U.S. GAO 1988, 21), or completely unaddressed.

Enforcement is anaemic. There are simply far too few inspectors – approximately 2,150 to cover 5.9 million employers[8] – to make command and control work. With this size of inspectorate, OSHA can inspect only 3 per cent of the nation's workplaces annually (Bolle 1988). OSHA has conducted almost all of its investigations in the most dangerous industries and the most dangerous establishments in the manufacturing sector – in practice, exempting many workplaces from regularly scheduled visits. And in response to employers' pressure, Congress has excluded other categories of workers – farmhands on small farms, for example. Consequently, only 11 per cent of U.S. employees are currently covered by general-schedule safety inspections (1988, 1). Even with targeting and legislative exemptions, the agency is spread too thin, checking less than one in ten high, safety-hazard worksites (U.S. GAO 1988, 28). Only one in five workers in high-hazard establishments sees an OSHA inspector in any given year (1988, 1). Thus the potential to deter violations is diluted; few employers are likely to be cited for job hazards.[9]

OSHA's civil penalty structure is also too limited to be very effective. Until Congress revised it in 1991, the act prescribed a maximum fine of only $1,000 for serious violations likely to result in physical harm, and $10,000 for wilful or repeated violations. But in practice, the penalties have been much lower: in 1986, the average fine for a serious violation was $208.[10]

After OSHA began more aggressive enforcement in the mid-1980s, both the number of cited violations and the total amount of penalties rose significantly. The average fine for a serious violation also climbed, though less precipitously, to $261 in 1988 (U.S. GAO 1988, 31). More important, however, in 'egregious cases' – where the agency adjudged employers' actions to be reckless and irresponsible – OSHA began to cite each instance of a hazardous condition as a separate, wilful violation. Very large, headline-grabbing 'megafines' ensued. After an October 1989 explosion in its Pasedena, Texas, refinery, Phillips 66 was fined $5.7 million (National Safe Workplace Institute 1989, 12). But these megafines remain the exception, reserved for the very worst offenders. From 1986, when the egregious-cases policy was initiated, through March 1991, only 100 of 300,000 citations were handled in this way (Bureau of National Affairs 1991, 1, 495). Moreover, the proposed fines were regularly reduced in settlement negotiations with employers.[11] As a result, while the average fine for serious penalties rose – to $365 in 1990 – penalties have remained far below statutory ceilings. Even after the Omnibus Budget Reconciliation Act of 1990 increased most maximum fines sevenfold and established a $5,000 minimum for wilful violations, the agency remained reluctant to use these new powers.

As a result, there are major gaps in industry compliance. For example, available research indicates that from one-third to one-half of the companies inspected still exceed OSHA standards for maximum levels of lead and silica, two commonly recognized hazards for which companies routinely test. The record is probably worse for the hundreds of substances for which OSHA issues standards but does not effectively monitor workplace exposures (Ochsner 1977, 25).

BEYOND OSHA?

Given this rather sorry record, the call for reform of OSHA has been something of a Washington perennial. Worried that OSHA might rediscover its activist face and one day fulfil its mandate, critics on the right have argued that command and control should be jettisoned in favour of market-based approaches. Neo-liberals, affirming their belief in OSHA's goals but not its 'counterproductive' and 'economically-inefficient' methods, have called on the agency to build on the coke-oven experiment and institutionalize bargaining in standard-setting and compliance.

Health-and-safety activists have looked elsewhere. Some have taken heart from state and local use of criminal sanctions. In the face of OSHA's inaction, some state and local prosecutors have charged employers with battery, reckless homicide, and involuntary manslaughter. In one notorious case, *People v. Film Recovery Systems, Inc.*, Cook County, Illinois, successfully prosecuted the president, plant manager, and foreman of a firm that had knowingly exposed its employees to acute cyanide poisoning. All three officers were convicted of murder and received twenty-five-year jail sentences (Magnuson and Leviton 1987). In California, more than 280 cases were prosecuted between 1973 and 1988 (Bureau of National Affairs 1988, 1, 877). Recently, that state passed a law that allows local prosecutors to file felony charges against managers who expose their employees to a 'serious concealed hazard.'[12] Success at the state and local level has led some reformers to press Congress to give the federal government the authority to seek felony charges against any employer who knowingly and wilfully exposes a worker to the risk of serious bodily injury.

The left continues for the most part, however, to rely on command and control and workers' participation, calling on the agency to set and enforce standards more aggressively and on Congress to force agency action and to strengthen provisions on workers' rights in the law, including adopting the 'right-to-act' committee system. The Oil, Chemical, and Atomic Workers union has been particularly effective in this campaign. The decision to press for more aggressive regulation within the conventional command-and-control approach and to supplement that with strengthened workers' rights makes sense. A lot more could be done within command and control, as the brief experience under Bingham makes clear. But that experience also shows that politics will always help determine just how far the agency goes. Under President Carter, OSHA was constantly hounded by White House economic advisers to rein in the regulators, and White House review agencies, especially the Office of Management and Budget, forced OSHA to slow its pace and reconsider its standards. As the theory of the capitalist state suggests, even under a Democratic administration, cost considerations and capitalist pressure weigh heavily in policymaking. When organized labour is weak, as it is today, the agency is unlikely to be able to defend itself against those pressures.

Given organized labour's weakness, it would also make sense to press for stiffer criminal sanctions, or even to reform workers'-compensation laws to make it easier for individuals to sue their employers in cases of negligence. Ultimately, however, the future of workplace reform probably rests on workers' ability to protect themselves through aggressive exploitation of any and all rights to know and to act and through pressure to strengthen those rights. Here, too, there are severe obstacles, including concerted opposition by employers to strengthening workers' organizations at the workplace and the government's reluctance to do anything that might increase business costs in an increasingly competitive international economy. Nonetheless, participatory modes probably offer the best hope for protecting workers in capitalist economies.

NOTES

1 See, for example, Lindblom (1977); Block (1977).

2 For the classic statement, see Schmitter (1974). Also see the essays in Goldthorpe (1984); Katzenstein (1985); Freeman (1989).

3 For one argument about the impossibility of corporatism in the United States, see Salisbury (1979); Schmitter and Lehmbruch (1979).

4 See, for example, Ruttenberg (1989).

5 See, for example, Sass (1991); Tucker (1992).

6 See, for example, Viscusi (1983).

7 On the role of workers' compensation reform in a market and tort system, see R. Smith (1976).

8 This number includes 300 federal supervisors and trainees. U.S. GAO (1988, 2).

9 U.S. GAO (1988, 2). Even in manufacturing, where enforcement is concentrated, the average employer can expect an inspection only once every six years.

10 The 1986 figure is from U.S. Department of Labour (1988).

11 The megafines have been reduced on average by 66 per cent. U.S. GAO (1988, 36).

12 'Employers Adjust to Tough Work Safety Standards,' *Los Angeles Times*, 26 April 1991.

15

Judgments of Legitimacy regarding Occupational Health and Safety

VIVIENNE WALTERS, WAYNE LEWCHUK,
R. JACK RICHARDSON, LEA ANNE MORAN,
TED HAINES, AND DAVE VERMA

Risk and definitions of pathology are socially constructed, emerging from complex social and political relationships (Nelkin and Brown 1984). Occupational hazards are not determined through scientific investigation alone, and neither is the distinction between normal and pathological reliant solely on medical evidence. Studies of the social construction of occupational health-and-safety have highlighted the processes involved in definition of hazards, shifts in definitions of acceptable and unacceptable working conditions, linking of symptoms with workplace exposure, and the recognition of 'new' diseases. The importance of changes in the balance of social relations of production (in labour's position vis-à-vis capital), the role of the state, and the part played by medicine have all been outlined.

In the case of black lung (B.E. Smith 1981) and repetitive-strain injury (Meekosha and Jakubowicz 1986; Reid and Reynolds 1990), for example, we see the conflicts preceding recognition of the diseases as work-related and eligible for compensation. Debates continue over the risks associated with exposure to age-old substances such as asbestos (T.H. Murray 1988) and more recent technology such as VDTs (Schrecker and Tremblay 1986). These constructions in turn legitimize occupational health-and-safety policies – whether a substance is controlled in the workplace, whether the pace of work or level of staffing is changed, whether compensation is awarded, what types of training are provided, or whether no action is taken to change working conditions. Prevailing definitions – judgments of legitimacy – contribute to social production of illness, for they help to shape workers' exposure to risk and their chances of experiencing work-related illness and injury.

While we have increasing documentation of how such changes occur at a societal level, we know much less about the social construction of hazards in the workplace itself. Partly, perhaps, because of the difficulty in gaining access to a range of workplaces, we have limited understanding of how occupational health-and-safety problems are defined, how definitions change over time, and how 'new' problems are recognized. This chapter draws on recent interviews with managers, workers' representatives, and nurses and explores elements of the social construction of hazards in the workplace. Judgments of legitimacy permeated the interviews; respondents questioned whether injuries were real and whether real injuries were work-related. Here, we explore their views about what is a legitimate claim for compensation, what constitutes a 'real' work-related accident, and what is a hazard. In the following sections – after outlining our method – we look at three aspects of occupational health-and-safety – interpretation of Workers' Compensation Board (WCB) lost-time frequency rates; whether or not accidents are seen to be 'genuinely' work related; and the process whereby hazards are defined, involving distinctions between 'acceptable' and 'unacceptable' conditions of work. We argue that such definitions are generally phrased in negative terms, limiting what is considered occupational risk and work-related illness or injury. At the same time, the ideology of individual responsibility continues to be strong, with little emphasis being placed on the importance of the labour process and social relations of production. Such narrow definitions, together with the pattern of individual attribution, deflect attention away from control of risk in the workplace. We also comment on the possibility of development of a symbiotic relationship between management and workers' representatives, which may inhibit the dispute of prevailing definitions of risk and pathology.

METHOD

The data are drawn primarily from face-to-face interviews conducted as part of a larger research project.[1] Managers and workers' representatives in over five hundred workplaces in Ontario had already replied to a mailed questionnaire concerning occupational health-and-safety. In the subsequent, qualitative phase of research, we selected a sub-set of seventeen companies employing two hundred or more workers, with the aim of visiting these and interviewing people in key positions among management, labour, and medical staff.

We sought to approach both workers and management independently. But in the absence of a union, no independent route was available, and even when workers were unionized information on the union local was not always available to us. Our first approach then was to the senior manager at each workplace. In some cases, we were able to contact union or workers' representatives independently in order to explain the research and, if possible, arrange to interview them away from the workplace, so that they might feel less constrained.

TABLE 1 Interviews

Workplace	Interviews with:		
	Managers	Workers' respresentatives	Nurses
I	2	1	1
II	2	2	
III	4	1	1
IV	5	3	1
V	3		
VI	4	2	
VII	3	2	
Total	23	11	3

But our efforts were far from successful. Only seven of the workplaces agreed to participate, and all of them were unionized.[2] Moreover, while we did interview workers, they were in the minority, the interviews were arranged by management, and they took place on company time. In an effort to broaden our data base, we also cite comments that respondents were invited to write on the mail questionnaires in the main project.

The interviews, which took place in June and July 1991, were unstructured, and we encouraged people to talk to us at length about what they considered important with respect to health-and-safety. We interviewed a total of thirty-seven people and these were distributed as shown in Table 1. Managers included top levels of management such as director of manufacturing, director of operations, and personnel manager, as well as the management co-chair of the Joint Health-and-safety Committee (JHSC) and supervisors. Workers' representatives included the worker co-chair of the JHSC, other worker health-and-safety representatives, and the president of the union or the business agent for the union.

LOST-TIME FREQUENCY RATES

WCB claim rates are typically used as an index of the frequency and severity/duration of illness and injury. Yet both managers and workers' representatives acknowledged that they are not necessarily an accurate index. In their opinion, the rates do not reflect the 'real' magnitude of occupational injury and illness. They argued that rates are influenced by a number of factors that have little to do with safety in the workplace. As managers, workers, and nurses spoke of these influences, common strands in their arguments became apparent, as well as their differing interpretations.

Some managers outlined what they saw as financial incentives for workers on compensation, particularly before lay-offs or plant closures. Several noted that 'when lay-offs are pending the accident rate seems to increase accordingly.' Even a 'rumour of a lay-off would be enough to send people to the health centre with aching backs and stubbed toes.' One described the jump in lost-time accidents just before his plant was due to close down. Others suggested that fluctuations in claim rates were a more general problem experienced across companies, reflecting the state of the economy. A manager described the perceived relationship: 'I spoke to the clinic just last week. I said we were experiencing a high rate all of a sudden of injury claims and I asked whether this was common. "Are you getting that from all companies?" And she said it goes in cycles, "You're not the only one," she says. You wonder what other factors are affecting people, that more claims are being filed. Does the economy have anything to do with it? Does it have anything to do with recession? Are their husbands out of work?'

Doctors and the WCB were sometimes seen by managers as the allies of workers – if not encouraging them, then at least allowing them to make dubious claims. Some doctors were seen as being too willing to recommend time off work: 'Abuse can become commonplace when doctors write slips that don't say anything except your employee can't come back to work for two weeks.' The WCB was also criticized for being too sympathetic to workers, accepting 'bogus' claims and no longer being 'an unbiassed tribunal' – it was a frequent theme in the comments added to the mail questionnaires. One manager wrote: 'I feel the WCB system is heavily stacked against management and in favour of the worker. Most of our workers are honest but occasionally we encounter a bad one who will try to milk the system for everything he can. There is no mechanism for a balanced consideration of whether he might be faking and whether his "accident," to which there are mysteriously no witnesses, really occurred.'

These arguments that claims are a result of factors other than occupational health-and-safety emphasize the ways in which management viewed claim rates as an overestimate of the 'real' incidence of work-related illness and injury. In turn, this perspective helps to legitimize 'claims management' (as opposed to 'risk management') in response to high claim rates. The challenge, in the eyes of managers, is to minimize illegitimate absenteeism through control of claims.[3] Provision of modified work, or light duties, was one way in which they sought to avoid any lost time or to return workers to the job as soon as possible. As we noted above, one of the obstacles they perceived was the greater willingness of family doctors to advise time off work: 'It's interesting because their family doctors and the clinic doctors don't always agree on the types of diagnosis as well as what treatment to follow. You know, I'm sure the clinic here would be a lot quicker to say "You could do this type of work" and they'll encourage us to find it. Whereas the family doctor would say "Well, you stay home and rest for two weeks, then we'll see you again, check you again."'

The response of managers was not necessarily to approach the physicians concerned but rather to talk over the problem with the worker. In this way, he or she would be encouraged to return to modified duties: 'I always go after the employee themselves and say, "Well, how do you feel about it? Do you think you could do this and this and this?" If they say that they're at least willing to try, then I tell them "Go back to your doctor and tell him this is what you're going to do and this is what you'd like to try."'

Nurses also monitored 'spurious' claims, shouldering much of the responsibility for checking claims and other forms of absenteeism. Their records of absences were detailed, and each worker's history could be readily summarized. An important component of their role was to assess whether an employee had a 'legitimate' work-related problem that was sufficiently severe to warrant time off. If not, their powers of persuasion were engaged. In this respect, they can help to legitimize and enforce corporate definitions of 'real' problems. One nurse recalled:

She came in and we talked and I shared with her that our program is important to us, our safety program is important. And to have a lost-time accident – you know she just wanted to have the time off because she had other things going on – and I said 'This would be considered a lost-time accident for a [minor injury]. We can't accept that, we have – require – modified work. I'll call your doctor' – because she had sent in a doctor's note and he had advised her to be off work. I spoke with the doctor and ... so anyway, she ended up she's on modified work. But she didn't want to work. I said 'Well, we don't want this to be a lost time, that's important to us.'

According to both managers and nurses, workers also pressed each other to return to work earlier than they might otherwise have done. It was suggested that if workers feel that a co-worker is malingering, that their absence is unnecessary, or that they do not deserve light duties, they will hassle the person concerned. One manager suggested that he had to be attuned to potential conflicts between workers:

You have to be sensitive that people don't take a negative attitude towards the person that's on modified duties ... 'Mary's doing that, I mean I have a sore shoulder too, why shouldn't I be doing that type of work too?' ... There's jealousy ... It's very frustrating because, you know, there's Betty on the other line working very hard and, you know, she's hurting, for whatever reason she's pulled a muscle of some kind. But she's there because she wants to work and doesn't want any problems and doesn't complain.

With safety incentive schemes, there was even greater reason for workers to monitor each other and sanction those who 'don't want to work.' A nurse commented: 'Yesterday was the day her crew was going to have [a reward] because they didn't have any accidents last month ... The manager today was telling me that all the ladies are, I guess, giving her a hard time. All the other ladies saying hey, what are you trying to do, being off for something like that ... I've had lots of cuts and I don't even say anything, type of thing, or don't think it's a big deal.' However, such regulation of workers by colleagues did not emerge as a theme in interviews with worker co-chairs of JHSCs, worker health-and-safety representatives, union officials, or business agents.

The comments of workers' representatives had a somewhat different emphasis. They, too, recognized fluctuations in claims along with the threat of layoffs, a worker's penchant for a fishing holiday, or other such distractions. But the tone was sometimes different, more accepting – with a wry smile or shrug of the shoulders – and more likely to place this in context, showing why workers were so motivated. In this respect at least, blame was less likely to be placed on workers. Many of those we interviewed suggested subtle links between the organization of work and propensity to file claims.

When you got a lot of guys out there that work lines and it's a mundane job and repetitious, to break the monotony of that job, what they do is whine ... You know, all of a sudden – I'm not saying a lot of these injuries that happen aren't legit – but if you're feeling down and stuff like that and you're doing that same job day after day, all of a sudden that arm does start to ache ... But if you were doing something you enjoyed that wouldn't happen so much.

You know if you work here 15 years and you work at all the jobs in this plant and they shut down, you don't have any qualifications to go anywhere ... You know, your morale drops, you don't feel too hot about yourself, so all of a sudden you develop comp. [Workers' Compensation] cases. 'Oh my back! Oh my this! Oh my that!' You know, just to get out of there for a while ... It's like getting drunk – it's a solution – at least I'm out of there for a while, I can go home. Maybe they really are legitimate injuries, but some of them aren't you know, they're bogus injuries.

Yet the tone of the comments was not always so sympathetic, and at times there were undertones of racism: 'We get a lot of the back sprains and shoulder strains and I think a lot of it is almost suggestive, the power of suggestion kinda thing, you know. We've got a lot of immigrants and, you know, maybe I shouldn't be saying this, but I sometimes think it's just an easy way for people to get money.'

Workers' representatives also commented on the ways in which claim rates may underestimate problems. For them, claims management was distorting the 'real' magnitude of occupational illness and injury by deterring 'legitimate' claims. Workers might be dissuaded from filing claims that are justified,[4] or they might be encouraged to return to work despite continuing health problems. One listed problems associated with claims management: 'due to injury.'

Such pressures did not come from management alone. Some worker co-chairs of JHSCs appeared to work closely with management and strongly identified with its concerns about unnecessary claims. It is one of the ways in which they can reinforce the power of management. For example, one warned workers that if they had accidents because of their own carelessness, they would get no compensation (which is not true)! But this was not a common observation. Worker representatives were more likely to speak of pressures on workers from management, although even this was not a prominent theme in the interviews.

While there is evidence of workers being hassled (see, for example, Berman 1978; Clement 1981; Elling 1986; Walters and Haines 1988), we did not generally hear such accounts, perhaps because we interviewed relatively few workers and because management arranged most of the interviews. As well, JHSC co-chairs and health-and-safety representatives may be less likely to be aware of such problems than are workers on the shop-floor and more likely to be coopted by management. Workers' representatives such as those interviewed here can spend a lot of time with management and can end up sharing more interests with managers than with those they represent.[5]

In sum, both workers' representatives and managers recognized many influences on claim rates and that these can produce both an over- and an underestimation of work-related illness and injury. Overreporting is attributed to workers who claim benefits when their jobs are threatened, when they want relief from boredom, or when they just want to take it easy. Underreporting is attributed to workers being misinformed or hassled by management or other workers for filing a claim. Workers may also be pressured to return to the job earlier than they might otherwise have done. In all these respects, WCB claim rates are seen as distorting the 'real' incidence of occupational illness and injury. Claim rates being seen as overestimates can legitimize a view that the workplace is not hazardous and justify policies that emphasize management of claims rather than reduction of risk.

CAUSES OF ACCIDENTS

So what is a 'real' occupational injury or illness, if it is not that which is captured by WCB claim rates? The concept is elusive, and the interviews are more helpful in identifying what it is **not**. Workers and managers implied that whenever there is an element of employee culpability, then it is not a 'real' work-related injury, not a 'genuine' health-and-safety problem. Workers were often blamed for accidents. Both managers and workers emphasized the effects of carelessness, horsing around, lack of attention to safety procedures, older workers who are set in their ways, and the effects of drugs and alcohol.

One senior manager felt that the company had reduced its accident rate almost as much as it could and was concerned about the life-styles and physical health of workers who were described as 'couch potatoes.' In interviews and in comments added to the mail questionnaires, it was often remarked that 'workers appear to have little concern for their own health.' Older workers were often blamed for being set in their ways, resisting attempts to educate them to work safely.[6] Some managers spoke of 'human error,' implying that the problem lay with the worker rather than the work process itself. Another manager tended to invalidate workers' concerns by commenting that 'there will always be complainers.'

Such themes did not always imply negative images of workers. For example, in describing workers' attitudes to health-and-safety, one manager suggested that only a minority are a problem, but he was still explaining good safety performance in terms of individual attitudes.

[Workers have] a very positive attitude. The majority of your people out there are genuinely concerned and do not want to get injured ... Generally, the people realize that safety is here and it's here to stay and it's just part of the culture for the majority of people. There's a minority that – again, it's always that small percentage of bad apples in a cart – and their attitude towards safety is that 'it's not going to happen to me.' But that attitude probably carries over to production, quality, cost, and everything else involved – and probably goes into their home life.

This emphasis helps to legitimize occupational health-and-safety policies that are worker- rather than workplace-oriented. A different understanding (and different strategies) would derive from a focus on the workplace itself – on the organization and intensity of work and social relations of production. It might be expected that employees would be more likely to adopt a workplace-oriented perspective, if only because it would deflect blame. Yet this was not a common theme; the ideology of individual responsibility was pervasive.[7] Workers' representatives also blamed workers for unsafe practices – failing to wear personal protective equipment, poor housekeeping, for generally treating health-and-safety too lightly. Some were frustrated with lack of support from the workforce:[8]

[The worker co-chair] is in a tough position as a safety man because he's tried to enforce the rules that stand ... He cares about your sight, he cares about your safety, and he works really hard. But no one takes that into consideration. They just feel he's on a power trip trying to make a point. 'Put your glasses on or you might get your eye put out.' 'Aw, get lost!' All they think is he's out there trying to push them around ... sort of like a policeman. A guy [had an accident] out there, horsing around and [the worker rep.] seen them horsing around and [get injured]. So by law he has to report it and sign an accident sheet saying this is how it happened. And all these guys climb all over him for being a rat on this guy. 'What are you doing, you rat, you rat?' It's his job, you idiot ... Some of the times you can't do them both. You gonna be a bad guy sooner or later and that time he was a bad guy ... He did what he was supposed to do, but you have these guys jumping on you.

This attitude sometimes is translated into mutual mistrust. Workers' representatives were seen as having been coopted by management, helping to discipline workers. They had become 'the policeman,' 'the bad guy.' For their part, the representatives expressed frustration with workers. The links between them were not always strong and supportive.

They call you 'company'. Because you're right and they're wrong, then they call you 'company' and you get a lot of names called ... That's the biggest problem in this place right now, name calling – and through safety most times. Most of the times it's alright 'cos I look up in my book and legislation states this and this, right, and you just can't change the law of the government. Trying to explain this to these people is like banging against that wall ... Sometimes these guys are like – I'd like to have 500 five-year-olds, at least you can teach them something. These guys are like adults and they all act like five-year-olds – they go backwards.

[Workers] don't do no wrong, but all we do is wrong, right? ... I got to do it for these people because that's what my job is to help these people, and sometimes it gets frustrating that I gotta help these people ... They don't want to help themselves ... I can't explain why people are like this, you know. I get so frustrated, I says why do people have to act like this? Why?

Yet the blame of workers was sometimes qualified. For example, the workers' representatives we interviewed were more likely than managers to draw attention to the role of supervisors and other levels of management in encouraging workers to cut corners and neglecting to enforce safe working practices.

We have a safety-hazard report book and [workers] are supposed to write down their hazard, take it to the supervisor. But to get people to write in that book is almost impossible ... If they feel the supervisor don't care, then why should they? ... I had one incident where I came in one night and found out that – there's this door, 2 ft by 3 ft, it's a guard door, ok? It was completely off, and they had run the thing for two hours with a piece of plastic board stuck on the limit switch so the thing would run. (It's got a safety switch – you open the door, it will shut off, right?) Now, do you report hazards to a supervisor who does things like that? No.

Managers saw the role of supervisors as problematic but were more likely to stress their importance in monitoring workers and encouraging safe practices – a difference of emphasis.

Workers' representatives, managers, and nurses put relatively little emphasis on the nature of the work itself and social relations of production. The dominant themes echoed traditional approaches – unsafe acts and individual responsibility. Yet there was some recognition of the importance of the work environment. One manager was starting to doubt the conventional wisdom that the vast majority of accidents are a result of unsafe acts:

They talk about safety as, basically, ninety-six per cent of the accidents are caused by unsafe acts and ... when you start looking at this your first impression is that, yeah, it's the people. And you work on that for a while and when you do, you get better results. And then after a while it tapers off or goes the other way. It starts getting worse again. And when we took that concept and reviewed it a second time, we came to the conclusion it wasn't entirely true ... I think it's because the environment is creating a situation where you can have a lot of unsafe acts.

This manager was starting to focus on problems such as fatigue and production rates, but such comments were very rare. When we heard other accounts of the ways in which increased production and an intensification of labour contributed to higher claim rates, they were voiced by nurses.[9]

Our production has dramatically increased over the last 3 years ... increase in sales, increase in production ... like they want everything yesterday ... Production requirements are higher, hours are longer. We went to 12 hour shifts ... We're getting busier, lines are faster, the work is heavier. They're lifting repetitively ... They're doing the same thing over and over again.

No one should stand for 12 hours, nobody. You're gonna have problems with your feet, your back, fatigue, you know. It's a terrible thing to have people do ... but [management's] theory is that if you give them somewhere to sit down, the job won't get done properly ...

Nevertheless, there was relatively little mention of the workplace itself, on aspects of the social organization of work and social relations of production. The culture of individual responsibility was strong – among workers' representatives as well as managers. Just as workers were blamed for inflating claim rates, so too they were faulted for causing accidents. Insofar as foolishness or human error was involved in injuries and illnesses, then these were not viewed as 'real' health-and-safety problems. They were problems of education and control. The definition of 'real' hazards is, then, further limited. What then of the process of redefining hazards? What evidence is there that such definitions are contested and that they might expand?

REDEFINING HAZARDS

A central premises of the political economy of occupational health-and-safety is that workers can improve conditions of work through identifying hazards, pressing new definitions, and enlarging the concept of unacceptable conditions of work (B.E. Smith 1981; Elling 1986; Grunberg 1983; Navarro 1983; Sass 1986). Managers initiate change in response to pressures from workers from the state or in the face of the rising cost of industrial illness and injury. But we still have few detailed studies of the different perspectives that workers and managers bring to the social construction of hazards. In what ways is there conflict over the expansion of definitions of hazards? How do workers introduce new issues to the corporate world? In what respects do managers influence the process of redefinition?

While it would be unwise to generalize from our small sample, the interviews do provide examples of perceptions of hazards, including variations within management and labour. In neither camp were hazards readily identified. Yet there were differences in the ways in which workers' representatives and managers talked about identification of hazards and what influenced their perceptions. Managers spoke most often about the problems of balancing occupational health-and-safety with productivity and profitability. Workers' representatives spoke of workers' fears regarding job security and plant closures and of being labelled as a troublemaker. The insecurity of workers in secondary labour markets was most pronounced. According to these accounts, many rank and file appeared to have a weak sense of entitlement; their expectations were low. In these respects, 'real' hazards remained relatively narrowly defined, and there was little contestation of prevailing definitions.[10]

Managers have often bemoaned politicization of occupational health-and-safety. In their eyes, unions have 'used' the matter to achieve other goals. But some of the managers we interviewed emphasized that the company – including both management and labour – was dealing with the 'real' issues. One top manager said that health-and-safety had been depoliticized and that management was now 'treating every issue as a pure health-and-safety issue and getting on with it. So we've got the right kind of attitude.' He added that once the structure is in place for a system of internal responsibility, 'then you start to deal with the real issues on a straightforward basis, not imaginary issues.'

What this means in practice is not easy to decipher, but such claims appear to signify cooperation between management and labour. Both come to share an understanding of what are acceptable and what are unacceptable hazards. What is 'real' is the outcome of a shared definition. This sense of a common view was expressed by one worker representative who described at some length how he enjoyed a measure of autonomy and how he handled different types of health-and-safety issues, defining them as more or less pressing, more or less important. The scope of his authority to correct problems and the strength of the pressure he put on management varied accordingly. He had developed a sense of what might 'reasonably' be expected from the company and what position the Ministry of Labour might take in adjudicating any conflicts: 'Most of the time, like, I pretty well know how the inspectors will operate whenever there's a safety aspect. 'Cause I know ... inspectors will say "Look, this has to be done today" or "This has to be done in two weeks." I have a pretty good judgment about what an inspector would say about the job. So I go with that flow myself.'

A similar pattern emerged in the comments that worker co-chairs wrote on the mail questionnaires. They often noted that relations with management were placid and that they worked in a spirit of co-operation. They were addressing 'the issues.' What this appears to represent is development of a series of shared understandings about the dimensions of health-and-safety problems – common understandings of what is a 'real' problem.[11] It does not necessarily signify any given level of safety performance.

A key issue is whose 'understanding' gets shared. The claim that the 'real' issues were being addressed did not preclude an emphasis on productivity and profitability. Managers often linked definitions of hazards with the firm's financial health; they were 'realistic'. They qualified their emphasis on safety: 'You may get the impression that sales and profits are more important than health-and-safety issues. But remember, without a sale and without profit, there is no company and there are no jobs and health-and-safety becomes a non-issue. We meet the spirit, if not the intent of the legislation. We're not that altruistic, you've got to make a buck somewhere.'

Moreover, recognition of problems can shift, depending on the company's financial position and the broader economic climate. One nurse noted that constraints had become more severe with the recession: 'We need labour-saving devices. Something that's going to make work easier for people. If most of our accidents are strains and sprains, then we've got to reduce the workload for employees. But now the thing is money. There was $100,000 in the budget for this year for just that ... but that has gone by the wayside, we don't have the money.' Hazards are redefined, and this legitimates a different response. The issue was rephrased as an attitude problem (with a focus on workers) rather than one of heavy workload (a workplace problem).

There were variations not only among companies, but also within companies in managers' propensity to acknowledge health-and-safety problems. Lower levels of management might be frustrated at the lack of financial support from the top: 'Our president has said "Your safety record is atrocious, but you can't have the money, come up with other ways of improving it." I guess I find that a challenge, but managers are disillusioned and angry and saying "If safety is a priority, if it's that important, why don't they have the money for it?"' At other times, top managers voiced concerns that lower levels – especially supervisors – were not paying enough attention to safety.

Managers also competed for corporate funds, and departments jostled for their share. Introduction of experience rating (NEER – a scheme wherein WCB assessments are made on the basis of performance, with the possibility that companies receive rebates or surcharges) increased the bargaining power of managers responsible for safety. This also helped to change the way in which the line was drawn between acceptable and unacceptable conditions of work.[12]

I handed him a cheque for [a couple of hundred thousand dollars] and I said, 'See, all these years, it does pay off!' Every year since then we've had substantial cheques ... I don't think [NEER] has changed the way we do business, but it accentuates certain aspects of it. You always knew safety paid, and it was, sort of – if you had anybody in management, you wanted a good defence, you could always go by and wave a NEER cheque in front of them.

Where [NEER] pays is with the doubting Thomases ... the number-crunchers, the pencil-pushers, the people that may not be married to safety within the corporation. It's very hard to go to an accountant who's doing your books and get safety on his – his or her – mind. It's very difficult ... A typical accountant's view would be 'Why are you spending $10,000 to do this? We can't afford time off the line for a safety meeting. Do you know that you're taking 20 people for an hour?' You know, you get these types of stereotyped attitudes and sometimes, if you have a NEER rebate, it just gives you the ammunition you need to say, 'Don't bother me, it's paying for itself.'

As already noted, workers' representatives often spoke of cooperative relationships with management, although in some cases conflicts had been very severe in the past. Voices of dissatisfaction and impatience with management were in the minority. This may be because of the way in which the workers' representatives we interviewed were selected, but even in the broader survey the level of conflict between management and labour was rated as relatively low. It did not seem that workers were pressing hard for recognition of hazards. The reasons may be several. Perhaps the most obvious is that workers' fears for their jobs stopped them from raising issues. The conflict between health and the need for a wage was expressed in various forms. At the level of the individual, it might be fear of being labelled a trouble-maker, with the threat of losing one's job. One worker JHSC co-chair wrote:

The right to refuse unsafe work was a big step for workers' rights but because of intimidation and the subsequent threat to job security most workers prefer to work around the problem or live with it (unless the hazard is so blatantly obvious and immediately health threatening). Once a worker has drawn attention to him or herself via a work refusal or the reporting of a hazard, the worker's high profile sets him up for constant scrutiny by supervisors who will use any deficiency in production, performance, attendance, etc. to their advantage in order to put them in their place. Once a worker has experienced this, he is very reluctant to speak up in the future which is exactly what the company wants.

The demands of mortgage payments and other responsibilities meant that older workers might 'think twice about refusing to work.' One worker representative suggested that the workforce had mellowed and become less militant as it had aged. But insecurity appeared to be particularly strong among workers who were more marginal – recent immigrants, for example: 'It's new people coming into this country now. There's a lot of immigrants and they need to work. They are afraid a little bit ... The old immigrants they know what to do, they no afraid. But the new immigrants coming in ... they need money, they need work. They think twice before they start say anything.'

At a collective level, workers also feared redundancy. We heard many accounts of the effects of the recession and of the Canada–United States Free Trade Agreement on the companies we visited, and some were in a particularly precarious position. According to workers' representatives, our unexplained appearance on the shop-floor could start a rash of rumours. Workers were reluctant to pursue health-and-safety issues – they could not afford to be 'unrealistic' and push the company too far. One union official said that health-and-safety had a lower priority after a number of plants had closed during the past year. Workers feared for their jobs. The possibility seemed strong that plants might close or relocate.

One union business agent commented that there was not much he could say to workers other than that he would help them to collect unemployment insurance benefits:

But the response from the people is 'OK, I go on unemployment insurance now, but 6 or 7 months from now, what am I gonna do? I work for this company for 30 years. What am I gonna do? I got a family, I got a mortgage to pay, I got rent to pay. Even on unemployment insurance, what am I ... The money is not enough to cover all these things.' And you know, when you hold a meeting, you have a group of 50 people in front of you and half of them, you can see that they're real frustrated, they don't know what to do. Especially people at the age of 50, 55, 60. What goes on in their mind is 'Where am I going to find a job at my age?'

Apart from such pressures, there was evidence that workers had low expectations with respect to their conditions of work and that they did not link their health problems with work. For example, repetitive-strain injury or bad backs were not necessarily linked with work, even though it seemed reasonable to suppose a connection. One union representative said that workers brought with them the expectations of the 'old country,' and these were not high. They were grateful for relatively little. But the pattern was not limited to immigrants. From the comments of workers' representatives, we had a more general impression of workers' weak sense of entitlement, of 'realistic' acceptance of what was.

Neither were many unions proactive in identifying problems. One worker JHSC co-chair said: 'Unions seem loath to take anything to arbitration unless they are virtually guaranteed to win.' Asked about ergonomic problems, one official commented: 'Nobody say anything. Nobody complain about it. If they don't tell me – if they have something and don't tell the union – we can do nothing about it. I mean we don't know. We don't know.'

Unions, particularly smaller ones, did not have time to be proactive. Business agents and other officials spent their time reacting to other critical issues. Some spoke at length about the problems associated with plant closures, negotiating wage rates, and fighting contracting out, use of outside workers, and attempts to get rid of unions. Monitoring implementation of the recent legislation on pay equity had also been especially time-consuming. Health-and-safety were sacrificed in favour of these other immediate demands on their time. In these respects, unions lacked the resources to define issues, heighten workers' consciousness, and place them on the corporate agenda.

These are familiar themes. Redefinition of hazards is influenced by, for example, the state of the economy, the economic performance of a company, the strength of workers' position in labour markets (depending, in part, on individual characteristics such as age, sex, and ethnicity), and the bargaining power of managers responsible for occupational health-and-safety. Particularly in times of recession, pressures force an even narrower definition of health-and-safety. Managers' claims that occupational health-and-safety are depoliticized do not necessarily denote a more inclusive approach. They refer to the extent to which definitions of the situation are shared.

CONCLUDING COMMENTS

One manager we interviewed commented 'It's not what is, it's what's perceived.' Definitions of the situation shape actions and legitimize corporate and union policies regarding occupational health-and-safety. One of the more enduring impressions from the interview transcripts is that the emphasis on individual culpability is still strong. 'Blame the victim' themes have a long history (Sass and Crook 1981), and despite a burgeoning literature and provincial policies that draw attention to the workplace and social relations of production, they continue to legitimize worker-oriented explanations. They can reinforce claims management and control of 'accident-prone' workers and others who, it is claimed, use health-and-safety provisions to gain advantage. At the same time, they limit the range of problems seen as 'real.' One manager said that management had done everything to minimize accidents. The same was implied by others – hazards had been anticipated regarding the work itself, and it was the workers who were less amenable to control. The problems that remained were seen as the result of poor industrial relations, difficult or unrealistic unions, and selfish or careless workers.

Throughout this second phase of our research, we were well aware of the imbalance in our sample: no non-unionized workplaces; many workers' representatives selected by management; and lack of access to any workers' representatives in one workplace. We cannot claim to portray a spectrum of workers', managers,' or nurses' concerns. This study reflects a limited range of social relations of production. Yet this does not invalidate our observations. They still reveal features of relationships surrounding occupational health-and-safety in workplaces. Given the composition of our sample, we see elements of a symbiotic relationship between management and workers' representatives – shared understandings regarding occupational health-and-safety, representatives who identify with the concerns of management and who can reinforce its authority. Often management has helped select representatives. Such patterns prompt questions about the ways in which legislation is translated into the workplace: to what extent does it allow representation of an alternative view and to what extent does it coopt workers and legitimize management's approaches? Do the emphases on internal responsibility and on bipartism embodied in provincial policy strengthen the hand of management?

A further observation concerns our understanding of the ways in which definitions of hazards are negotiated or socially constructed. Here, too, there are policy implications. Past research has tended to emphasize change at the macro level, and it has often focused on conflicts that have brought issues into the sphere of public debate, the most recent of these being repetitive-strain injury. We have paid much less attention to the workplace with no major overt conflicts – a situation that would typify the provincial norm. What might such a focus add to our understanding? that workers play no part in defining hazards? that they have accepted the dominant ideology of individual responsibility? that workers' representatives have been coopted? that there is no form of resistance other than at the individual level, through absenteeism, for example? Maybe.

But even our small sample sensitized us to variations, not only among companies but also within both management and labour. There seem to be slow processes of 'negotiation,' wherein definitions of hazards and what constitutes a 'real' accident gradually change. When workers are in a particularly weak position in the labour market, definitions may become even more limited. In other cases, they may broaden or simply change in character. We have a poor understanding of what and how change occurs where conflicts are much less obvious. Such questions are especially relevant as we move towards institutionalization of health-and-safety conflicts through representation of labour in all public bodies concerned with regulation of hazards in the workplace.

NOTES

1 The method and the results of the research are reported in Shannon et al. (1992).
2 The workplaces varied in terms of safety performance: three were classified as bad, one as average, and three as good. Our measure of safety performance relied on claim rates and should be interpreted with caution, in the light of the discussion in the following section. 'Good' performance was defined as a claim rate in 1986–8 less than or equal to 50 per cent of the group's average. 'Poor' performance refers to a claim rate in 1986–8 that was higher than that.
3 At its most extreme, this has led to collusion between union and management, allowing injured workers to be laid off so that they could draw government unemployment

benefits in addition to 'under the table' benefits from the company. The firm was able to avoid inspections by recording low levels of injury and illness (Wokutch 1992, 7).

4 It was more often nurses who told us that – out of either pride or fear – workers did not report problems they experienced; management would be unhappy when records of no lost time were broken by people being injured.

5 The worker co-chairs in two workplaces had been picked by management and were closely identified with management. In another company, the JHSC had no worker co-chair. There were other departures from what we had anticipated: the membership of the committee in one workplace was not clear, and it had an informal quality; in another company, the union president had selected the worker co-chair. In such cases, it might be expected that ties with the workforce would not be strong and that ties with management might be favoured. In the broader survey, well over 40 per cent of worker co-chairs said that management had some influence on selection of worker-members of JHSCs (Shannon et al. 1992, 117).

6 Our survey did not confirm this; companies with better safety performance tended to employ proportionately more workers over the age of fifty.

7 In this respect, the views of workers' representatives mirror the dominant ideology with respect to health and illness. An emphasis on individual responsibility is a major component of lay concepts of health and illness (Crawford 1984).

8 In two workplaces, there were also conflicts between the worker health-and-safety representatives and the union, with the latter being viewed as unsupportive because it did not appear to assign a high priority to occupational health-and-safety.

9 It is difficult to draw conclusions about the role of nurses because there were only three in this sample. However, it is interesting to note the diversity in their responses. At the same time as they played a role in the management of claims and the monitoring of absenteeism, they focused on hazards arising from the labour process and acknowledged the constraints that workers faced.

10 These interviews were conducted at a time of recession, with shrinking job opportunities and many plant closings. We would expect to see, if anything, even narrower definitions of health-and-safety problems.

11 In contrast, some workplaces had experienced very high levels of conflict, which had prompted reappraisal of how health-and-safety, as well as other aspects of labour relations, were handled. Managers told us that health-and-safety had been 'used' by labour to gain advantage in conflicts, that the 'real' issue was one of leverage, and occupational health-and-safety was a convenient tool. Management defined the issue as political, claiming that the union had focused on hazards because of their strategic value. When the label of politicization is attached to conflicts over occupational health-and-safety, the source of workers' discontent is invalidated.

12 However, in light of our discussion above, this can also lead to greater emphasis on claims management.

PART V

Crimes against the Environment

16

Environmental Harm and Corporate Crime

ROBERT PAEHLKE

Determining the extent to which environmental harm is corporate in origin and the exact sense in which this damage is criminal is important. This chapter addresses, largely indirectly, both aspects of this task but emphasizes the political and policy means of reducing environmental harm. It identifies some of the limits and uses of a corporate-crime approach to environmental policy and protection. It explains why the notion of corporate crime should not be ignored in a rush to find methods that are more politically acceptable in the present climate.

There is little doubt that in a moral, as distinct from a strictly legal, sense, crimes against nature and the environment have been everyday events for centuries. It is useful to divide this harm into three categories – *ecological damage*, direct assaults on non-human forms of life, especially on nature's ability to sustain and reproduce itself; *environmental threats to human health* – a concern that distinguishes environmentalism today from the earlier conservation movement; and *non-sustainability*, or intergenerational non-equity, where resources used today are not available in future. Each of these types of harm can be imposed in ways that can reasonably be characterized as criminal and involve activities and results for which corporations are at least in part responsible.

Acts that are difficult to see as other than corporate crimes abound in the extractive industries, such as mining and forestry. Destruction of the tropical rain forests is now known and is taken by many to be criminal. Less widely known, but no less horrendous, are the activities, especially within poorer nations, of multinational mining firms. One spectacular example is the Panguna copper mine on Bougainville in Papua New Guinea, which dumped 130,000 tons per day of tailings – 600 million tons in total – into the Kawerong/Jaba river system. The tailings contain metals and leach acids; virtually no life survives in the river system, and damage has spread for more than thirty kilometres. This mine and the damage that it inflicted helped to provoke a civil war, and it was eventually closed (Young 1992). Many other mines and smelters continue to operate with utter disregard for the environment in Brazil, Chile, Peru, the Philippines, and Russia.

Damage of this sort has occurred in what are now thought of as developed nations. Hundreds of thousands of hectares of agricultural land have been lost to metal smelting in the United Kingdom since the time of the Roman conquest. More recently and locally, Sudbury, Ontario, and Trail, British Columbia, offered dramatic instances. These activities were not treated as criminal when they were at their worst. Effects there are now less than they were and are much less damaging than they typically are in comparable operations within poorer nations. As Young (1992, 107–8) notes: 'Smelters in industrial countries are now often required by law to have pollution control equipment, but few in developing countries or the former socialist nations have any such controls. For each kilogram of copper produced, 12.5 times more sulfur dioxide is released to the air from Chilean smelters than from those in the United States.' As well, few open-pit hard-rock mines even today, anywhere, restore the nature they disrupt.

Harm to human health is also widespread, although it is more difficult to define and attribute. Wholesale decimation of an ecosystem of the sort identified above is usually obvious, both in fact and in attribution. But effects on human health are often less obvious or visible, largely because disease and death do nicely without human help. It was not until quite recently that epidemiology became able to confirm suspicions and allow attribution in multiple and complex causation. Most environmentally induced diseases would also exist in the absence of pollution. Most pollutants, whether exposures occur within workplaces or are mediated through the wider environment, cause only an incremental increase in damage to health. Multiple environmental assaults on health still make attribution enormously difficult.

Nonetheless, there are cases where there is no doubt that environmental harm to human health has been and is being imposed knowingly. The two most noted examples are perhaps asbestos and tobacco, for which the epidemiological evidence is overwhelming. Concerning asbestos, there have been strong suspicions of harm for some 2,000 years. Some, more scientific, evidence was developed in the 1930s, and clear demonstration can be dated to the studies of Selikoff and others published in 1963 and thereafter. In the 1990s, the governments of Canada and Quebec continue to use tax dollars to lobby the U.S. Environmental Protection Agency and trade officials in several countries to permit continued and unimpeded imports of Canadian asbestos. The case against tobacco is equally overwhelming, in terms of its addictive properties and its health effects, for both users and anyone consistently near to them. One can at least loosely use the word 'criminal' about many people involved in production, sale, use of, and profit from these two commodities.

Here, however, we begin to see problems in practical application of the concept of corporate crime to environmental harm. With asbestos, miners and production workers are the first victims. But they are also parties to exposure of others – those living near facilities, those who work with products produced from the material, and those exposed through use of those products. Are workers who made asbestos brake-linings in part responsible for the health of the millions of urban dwellers who now have asbestos particles from those brakes lodged in their lungs? Probably not. But what of the cigarette smokers who knowingly expose their co-workers and families to cigarette smoke? What of store owners who earn a living in part from sale of tobacco? These questions are not easily answered.

This problem is compounded when one turns to the harm associated with lessened sustainability. Corporations and individuals extract resources to the detriment of our collective ability to extract those resources in the future. This would presumably include fishing workers and loggers. The latter often knowingly expend political effort to gain the opportunity to eliminate the last models of particular types of forests. Cutting old-growth remnants will make it difficult, if not impossible, to even approximate those forests in the future. Beyond this concern, the consumers of declining resources are also potentially implicated.

Let us consider but one example of this type of environmental harm. Most future fossil-fuel options are likely to be even more problematic than our present supplies of oil and natural gas. Eventually all fossil-fuel reserves will be exhausted. Is it, then, criminal behaviour to drive to the store to get milk when one could almost as easily have walked? Has one in doing so assured that someone in the future will freeze? Obviously this is an altogether too simple-minded view of the world. Harm involving sustainability is real and serious but cannot reasonably be characterized as crime in any ordinary sense. Not all environmental harm is a crime.

Indeed, the above discussion hints at the central political tension within the environmental movement. Who is at fault as regards environmental harm? If there are environmental crimes, are they corporate in origin, or are we 'all' complicitous? How should one proceed in terms of policy and politics. Should the emphasis be on changing the behaviour of all or most individuals in the marketplace? Or should one focus on those who impose on nature with atypical severity? Is the problem overconsumption (possibly linked with human population levels), or is it primarily wrong-headed extraction and production?

In actuality, there are at least four causes of environmental harm. All contribute and all must be altered for the better if the future of human and non-human nature is to be as abundant and pleasant as in the past. Without such changes, most humans will probably never live as well as some people do now. Human economic activities, environmentalists argue, are destroying the ecological underpinnings of all life forms. The causes of environmental damage are human population levels; the affluence of some humans; the amount and character of the natural resources imbedded within each unit of human consumption; and the choice of technologies associated with each production activity. Only to the last-named case can the term 'crime' be sensibly attached. Even regulation is not easily applied other than in the latter two causes.

The tension within environmentalism regarding attribution of blame is, of course, politically significant. It distinguishes environmental politics from a politics of self-interest as ordinarily understood. Environmentalism as an ideology allows at least the possibility that we are all to blame. Divisions between left and right and between genders and among regions, sectors, and ethnic groups are all oriented to external blame and economic self-interest; someone *else* is primarily at fault for the condition of one's group.

That does not necessarily place non-environmental politics on a lower moral ground. The self-interestedness of human groups is often essential to moral and social progress. As well, environmental divisions in some instances reflect economically self-interested conflict (as between often-prosperous wilderness advocates and loggers). Nonetheless, environmental politics is often argued on behalf of non-humans, as-yet-unborn generations, or principles not easily translated into economic values. It does not have a constituency so automatic as that of economically interested, everyday politics.

The tension within environmentalism between 'we are all at fault' and 'we are all imposed upon by a few environmental despoilers' is not likely to be resolved. There is too much truth on each side. An irony, however, may attend on this tension. The view that we are, all of us, the problem would seem appropriate to a right-of-centre version, and a focus on corporate despoilers, to a left-of-centre variety. The former would seem to urge mild collective impositions on all, the latter to call for more stringent impositions on economic elites – regulations and criminalization, for example. However, capitalism as an institutional structure could be more profoundly affected by a widespread conclusion that the environment can be protected effectively only if we – all of us – make do with less by way of material possessions and/or find ways to reduce human numbers.

The political significance of environmentalism is bound up in considerations of this sort. Is it a movement that will make common cause with the right? Is it a political movement that will make common cause with the left (or even supplant it as the leading threat to the hegemony of corporate capitalism)? Or is environmentalism more likely to remain so purist and sectarian that it has no more than a passing influence on partisan politics as we know it? These questions require further consideration of environmental harm and a look at corporate environmental crime in a context of contemporary environmental politics within advanced political economies.

UNDERSTANDING ENVIRONMENTAL HARM AND VARIETIES OF ENVIRONMENTALISM

One can distinguish three distinct environmentalist views – right, centrist, and left. Their differences turn in large part on adherents' understanding of the socio-economic and institutional roots of environmental harm. The difficulties associated with linking environmental ideas to the political spectrum have been considerable and widely discussed (Paehlke 1991). The irony regarding the threat posed to corporate capitalism by a we-are-all-to-blame perspective speaks to this point. Nonetheless, the lines are not utterly blurred.

Right environmentalism has gained considerable visibility. Previously, the political right was content to dismiss or ignore environmental problems. The strength of the second wave of environmentalism (1985–present) has been too great to forgo attempts at accommodation and integration (Paehlke 1992). Right environmentalism can be seen as having four principal tenets: (1) human population levels require continued increases in wealth and economic development, although they must now take environmental constraints into account; (2) the blame for environmental harm is universal; (3) unconstrained markets can and will lessen that harm; and, implicitly at least, (4) environmental harm is not so serious as claimed by environmental 'extremists.' The preferred policy options of right environmentalism are multi-'stakeholder' consensus-seeking forums, removal of governmental subsidies from environmentally damaging activities, and voluntary initiatives of all kinds.

Left environmentalism would concur with the right on the need for continued economic growth but would disagree on how this might be achieved. Few on the left have recently had much distinctive to say, however, about how to achieve growth. Left environmentalism is, however, more consistent than the right in allowing that environmental problems are indeed serious: multinational corporations are to blame for most, if not virtually all, such problems. Parallel to the old Marxist notion of 'false consciousness,' left environmentalism believes that marketing and advertising determine and control the material desires of individuals. Only elimination or control of market forces and corporations can, in this view, lessen environmental harm.

Centrist environmentalism is often more purely, or militantly, environmentalist. Damage is not only serious but may determine the future existence of humans and all other species. Such views can drift into millennialist lunacy in some cases. But in political and policy terms, this view is potentially more pragmatic and moderate than the other two. Human population levels are a problem but are not so all-determining as they tend to be for the right. All are to blame, but some are perhaps more guilty than others – the views of left and right are thus compromised and balanced. As a result, market-based policy tools are essential, but so too is regulation. The market can be useful, but so can governmental intervention. Economic growth and environmental protection can be achieved concurrently, but often they are in conflict; when this is the case, environmental values should prevail. Both the left and the right, for opposite distributive reasons, would have difficulty with this assertion.

In the real world, each perspective exists only rarely in relatively pure form. But each view is internally consistent, and each has a familiar ring within debates on environmental issues. Two variants are particularly common – centre/left environmentalism and eco-entrepreneurialism. The former (hereafter called progressive environmentalism) would balance blame for harm between corporations and individuals. Eco-entrepeneurialism would not wait for the market to, for example, ease resource shortages through higher prices for raw materials. It actively produces environmental ('green') products. How might these variants view application of a corporate-crime perspective to environmental politics?

Progressive environmentalism might take a diversified, pragmatic approach to policy even more than might an environmentalism of the centre. It would be less likely to drift towards the anti-left ideological mainstream. It might, for example, look to 'left' tools, including criminalization of some forms of anti-environmental behaviour. It might also attempt, for example, to draw labour and the left towards alternative, pro-environmental (anti-growth) approaches to high unemployment. In contrast, an eco-entrepreneurialist approach would be aggressive about actual use of the market as a tool than might a more run-of-the-mill right environmentalism. The right imbues the market with its own moral power, rather than being inclined to harness its powers through modest intervention. Implicitly, then, eco-entrepreneurs might see the market as necessary, but not sufficient. Many policy options open up once that possibility is granted.

All these perspectives make more sense if one dispenses with a conventional (one might say, pre–post-Marxist) view of left and right. Politics might be seen rather as having three poles: environment, equity, and economy. The economy is defended by capitalists, conservatives, and economists. Equity is advanced in various, and sometimes conflictual, ways by labour, minorities, feminists, and the left. The environment is defended by environmental organizations, environmental scientists, and environmentalists. Few individuals operate exclusively within one of these perspectives, although some may try hard to do so. Most of the political terrain remains open to views that are combinations of these three perspectives or that shift among them, depending on the issue at hand.

Post–Cold War ideology could come to be dominated by shifting coalitions that combine two of these three poles – eco-entrepreneurs, progressive greens, and the growth coalition. Eco-entrepreneurs occupy the ground between capitalism and environmentalism; progressive greens, that between the left (equity advocates) and environmentalists. The growth coalition – and many examples have been visible over the past several decades – links labour and capital in opposition to environmental protection. Its political potential is obviously formidable; it has easy access to governments of all partisan styles.

The politics of the future may belong to this growth coalition. As resource stocks decline and/or human population continues to grow, scarcity will occur more frequently. Conflicts will intensify over uncut forest lands, as-yet untapped (environmentally risky) energy supplies, and land use. In a context of high unemployment (a result of globalization and automation), the growth coalition and a politics of environmental denial may become strong. Many people might accept the somewhat ascetic alternatives of environmentalism, but it is harder to imagine a majority actively pursuing of what might be characterized by opponents as shared poverty.

If and when political contests come to a straight fight between advocates of growth and environmentalists, even assuming an eco-entrepreneurial – progressive green alliance, the outcome would seem doubtful for environmental protection. The best prospect for pro-environmental politics within this plausible scenario hinges, in my view, on two issues. First, it depends on the development by greens of a broadly acceptable means of resolving, at least partially, the problem of 'jobless growth.' High unemployment almost guarantees formation of, and the ascent to power by, a growth coalition of some stripe. Many environmentalists understand this already; they are at pains to find alternatives for displaced forest workers, for example.

Second, a balanced view regarding blame for environmental harm must be maintained. Unequivocal attacks on capital are problematic in an age of maximized capital mobility. (This is to say not that such attacks should not be raised but rather that they will not easily succeed.) Equally, any undue emphasis on 'we-are-all-to-blame' themes opens environmentalists to labels of 'elitism' by defenders of capital. These accusations are already commonplace, and the profound ironies of their origins are all too frequently missed. Thus it might be hoped by greens that there is enough political space to expand the definition of corporate crime to include more frequently some forms of environmental harm.

This may be possible only as a very careful undertaking within the present polit-ical context.

ENVIRONMENTAL HARM, CORPORATE CRIME, AND
THE TOOLS AVAILABLE TO ENVIRONMENTAL POLICY-MAKERS

Environmental harm should be considered also within a policy context. Histori-cally, the favoured tool here has been regulation (Paehlke 1990a). More recently, many have argued for use of a wider range of policy tools. Some of these stances are unabashedly the view of either right environmentalists or the right. But many others simply see limits to the effectiveness of past approaches and are open to options. The line between right environmentalists and right anti-environmentalists might be the extent to which the proponents of the new, most often market-oriented, tools would deny the need for continued regulation. That is, some would take it that regulation is necessary, but not sufficient. Others would say that it is too draconian and that the environment would be better served by market-based tools, which are more flexible and, they would assert, more effective.

The range of tools that can lessen environmental harm is impressive. In other publications (Paehlke 1990b), I have identified twelve including taxes, subsi-dies, removal of subsidies, governmental procurement, suasion (including alter-native dispute resolution, ADR), bans on certain substances, nationalization (and privatization), and criminalization of environmental harm. The first four are market-oriented, the fifth is even less interventionist, and the final three (excluding privatization) are perhaps more interventionist than is regulation. This range I take to be further evidence of how difficult it is to characterize environmentalism.

A few examples of how some of these tools have been, or might be, applied will suffice here. Governmental procurement has been used to establish new markets for recycled paper and other pro-environmental products. Some U. S. state governments have also required that private firms, such as newspapers, use products manufactured with recycled materials. Such initiatives can create mar-kets to ensure additional investment and, eventually, adequate savings of scale. Environmental taxes, such as carbon taxes, can also counter climate warming through promotion of investments in energy efficiency.

More radical, though still in keeping with neo-conservative presuppositions (as distinct from practice), is removing subsidies. Governments now subsidize more heavily corporations in the most environmentally harmful sectors – for example, extraction and transportation. Thus creation of a 'level playing-field' might in this instance lessen environmental harm. Needless to say, neo-conservatives in power have not levelled their supporters in the resource industries downwards on many occasions. Canadian governments have long provided subsidies to these sectors. The recent U.S.-Canadian trade dispute regarding softwood lumber suggests that Canadian subsidy levels to forest removal may well be higher than those in the United States.

The least interventionist policy tools are perhaps those that emphasize dispute resolution – that is, which seek to resolve tensions between the corporate world and environmental organizations. Mediation, round tables, and other techniques have been attempted; only rarely have environmental organizations been satisfied with the results. Much time is expended, but in the end the environmental groups have no leverage – they cannot go on strike. Only when the corporations involved need some sort of governmental or public approval that would not be forthcoming without an agreement are such efforts likely to be successful. The fact that corporations are involved at all is, however, a recognition that environmental bodies have gained credibility recently. The challenge remains for these groups to create enough pressure to force real concessions.

Privatization of public utilities has been advocated by some environmental organizations, on the grounds that subsidies to new energy-supply options would be less forthcoming if utilities were privately owned. It is noted that Ontario Hydro, a public utility, is one of the most nuclear-oriented systems in the world. Would this be the case, it is asked, if nuclear power had had to pay its own way? In fact, the record of U.S. private utilities in increasing energy efficiency is better than that of U.S. or Canadian public utilities. However, U.S. state regulatory agencies, and environmental organizations, have forced this reorientation from increased electricity supply to reduction of electricity demand. More creative use of regulation might be a better route to that goal.

Overall, the environmental movement has tended to advocate an array of tools that is less interventionist than a policy regime dependent largely on regulation. The economic tools may be more effective in some contexts than is regulation, especially if the latter remains in place as a potential sanction should other methods prove ineffective. Regulation may be effective for some sources or types of environmental harm and less so for others. This possibility will be elaborated below by way of conclusion.

A decline in the level of intervention could be offset (if it results in less effective control) through selective use of tools that are more interventionist than regulation. One option here is the substance ban, an option strongly advocated in recent years by Barry Commoner, a left environmentalist (Commoner 1989). Regulations normally seek to control the amounts of a substance that are present within workplace air or are released into the air and water outside. Commoner argues that such efforts have often failed. Others have noted as well that the greater risks to health come from consumer-based sources rather than industrial releases. For example, second-hand tobacco smoke and exposure to dry-cleaning chemicals may result in more, and more serious toxic exposures than do toxic releases from industrial sites. The conclusion might be that it is better to ban particular substances, or to control types of exposures as completely as possible, than to attempt to regulate amounts of toxic chemicals in the air or water. Regulation has been misdirected, in this view, more than it has been excessive.

Another option is more frequent application of the notion of corporate crime to environmental harm of corporate origin. Those aspects of environmental harm that involve the majority's complicity, assuming there are some, do not of course lend themselves to criminalization. One might exclude here environmental harm deriving from the reduced sustainability of non-renewable resources. One might include, however, knowing damage to the future viability of renewable resources (or to ecosystems without 'resource' value). The damage imposed on Papua New Guinea noted above is a classic example. One might also criminalize those threats to human health that could be labelled as a crime akin to 'environmental manslaughter.'

I return below, by way of conclusion, to the kinds of environmental harm that might be criminalized. Before doing so, I briefly set the preceding discussion of environmental politics and policy in a context of economic globalization.

GLOBALIZATION AND PROSPECTS FOR A PROGRESSIVE ENVIRONMENTALIST POLITICS

A progressive environmentalist politics would have several major characteristics. The effects of environmental protection on levels of employment and on distribution would be first-order concerns for it. For example, it would pay attention to the uneven effects of energy taxes. The poor spend a higher proportion of their income on energy than do the rich; therefore increased energy taxes are potentially regressive. Another example arises in careful consideration of recycling, where initiatives produce more jobs than are lost, but those new jobs are less likely to be unionized. Employment is often created within urban regions and lost in poorer, hinterland regions, where there are fewer, if any, employment options. The environmental movement has given insufficient attention to considerations of this sort.

A progressive environmental politics might well also be open to applying the notion of corporate crime to more kinds of environmental harm. However, the present trend to economic globalization poses a real threat to the prospects for this or any other related initiatives. One cannot criminalize institutions that are both perceived to be essential and in actuality globally mobile. Further, globalization, without corresponding expansion of environmental organizations and political power, produces a variety of more subtle threats.

One daunting threat is international levelling of environmental policy, including regulations, combined with non-enforcement in some jurisdictions. That is the principal environmental threat implicit in the North American Free Trade Agreement (NAFTA). Just as the Soviet Union had impressive environmental and occupational health statutes on the books, so too in many areas does Mexico. But there is only minimal enforcement and less interest. This situation, combined with low wages supported by an anti-union government, places continuous pressure on Canadian firms to press for lower standards and enforcement here, even if individual managers would prefer not to do so. But their operations will continue only if their costs are lower than equivalents in Mexico and elsewhere.

The existence of comparable legislation and standards in Mexico makes it difficult to challenge the situation on the grounds of unfair trade practices. The non-level playing-field can be demonstrated only through continuous and detailed observations within another quasi-sovereign nation. Making an effective legal case against polluters is difficult enough within one's own state, as other authors in this volume make clear. It is all but impossible elsewhere. Anecdotal evidence and impressions will not suffice with trade panels. Both Canada and Mexico opposed US attempts to strengthen and internationalize enforcement of environmental standards.

Globalization in general, independent of comprehensive trade agreements, threatens to eviscerate environmental protection in other ways. The first is through acceleration of jobless growth, which in turn affects control of environmental harm. First, high unemployment creates political pressures to allow economic activities that are patently destructive. Second, it undermines efforts at mitigation, planning, and regulatory enforcement by placing other demands on a declining pool of public funds. Third, the more stringent and interventionist public-policy tools, such as criminalization, become off-limits for a single nation. There can be no environmentalism-in-one-nation within a globalized world.

Over the past two centuries, Canada has cut an astonishing proportion of a forest more than 8,000 kilometres long and hundreds of kilometres wide. There is now increasing evidence that the biodiversity of this forest is lost even where the forest as timber has been replaced effectively. How much of the remaining old-growth forest will be preserved? In a world of jobless growth, how much stronger are the pressures to cut if and when it becomes clear that the Canadian forest industry must otherwise shrink significantly for the several decades before sufficient second growth is available? Even at the local level, when there are hundreds or thousands of people out of work, how valuable is a particular wetland which could be a supermarket? How many will oppose a new mine in a pristine wilderness or risky offshore drilling in the Beaufort Sea?

Jobless growth is the result of globalization combined with both the removal of management layers made more technically feasible by computers and the automation of manufacturing processes. The latter processes are accelerated within the wealthy nations by globalization. If a firm has a higher wage structure than a competitor in a poor nation, it must make do with fewer employees. The growing incidence of this combination of factors in recent years has put massive pressure on the leading source of employment over the past 40 years: the public sector. Layers of public-sector management will now also be eliminated and operations increasingly automated (e.g., with driver's-licence–issuing machines).

Government deficits also prevent effective oversight of local planning at the same time as pressure on local governments to approve all development proposals intensifies. These local forces stem from the need to protect employment and to generate the additional tax base necessary to cover shortfalls in local government revenue. Pollution abatement is also less effectively enforced because there are fewer inspectors.

Finally, innovative and distinctive initiatives on environmental protection are all but foreclosed. No jurisdiction is likely to further criminalize pollution when the polluter is a model citizen compared to his competition in other nations. As well, tax and subsidy regimes must be harmonized, thus lessening the prospects for innovative use of market-based tools. The decision on softwood lumber in favour of Canada suggests that subsidies to extraction may somehow be more acceptable than export restraints (which are explicitly disallowed in energy in both the FTA and NAFTA). What of product bans? Canada was instrumental in blocking the attempt by the U.S. Environmental Protection Agency to block import, sale, and use of asbestos. Such gumption may be politically possible only when a hazardous material or product is being imported. Internationalized trade regimes foreclose even this opening.

Indeed, internationalized trade institutions may themselves prove the single greatest threat to reduction of corporate environmental harm. Environmentalism historically has attempted to force more open governmental decision-making against the ordinary inclinations of the administrative state and corporate capitalism. (Schrecker 1984). That is what environmental assessment, for example, is all about. In addition, most major environmental legislation in both the United States and Canada allows public participation.

In fact, the distinction between the conservation and environmental movements turns on this point (Paehlke and Torgerson 1990). Conservationists trusted the state to recognize and protect the public interest. Environmentalists argued that the environmental bureaucracies must be forced to make decisions in public. Trade panels are for the most part closed operations, as is the whole process whereby they are established.

Globalization has undermined both the power and legitimacy of the nation-state and democracy itself. Invisible, appointed panels make the most important environmental decisions, either directly or indirectly. How can this reality be altered?

There are possibilities not yet advanced by environmental organizations. One assures a falling-out between them and the left, and indeed the overwhelming majority of North Americans, but it needs mention. Globalization depresses wages in the rich nations, and that may have some positive environmental effects – the bad economic news is at least in part good news environmentally. If North Americans cannot consume as much, there will be, for example, less waste to manage. But the price, of course, is more joblessness- and deficit-based risks to the environment, as identified above. There are also, however, four other possibilities for breaking out of this vicious circle.

Environmentalists could more aggressively pursue removal of all anti-environmental subsidies: to nuclear power, indeed all energy supply, automobiles, air travel, mining, forest extraction, and elsewhere. Second, they could, in alliance with labour, seek reductions in worktime and thereby nearer-to-full employment; they could also push for revisions of trade agreements to permit pro-environmental subsidies. Alternatively, third, they could explicitly seek international subsidies for renewable energy, recycled materials, and non-toxic replacements for toxic products. They might also pursue multinational shifts in tax patterns from income to energy and materials throughputs. If made in awareness of the equity effects of tax patterns, this change too could gain popular support. Fourth, to offset globalization's tendency to weaken protection against corporate environmental harm, environmentalists could work for agreements on corporate environmental crime anywhere within a trading zone.

Obviously, none of these goals would be achieved easily; all would require greater international cooperation. Without such action, environmental harm will accelerate. The range of policy options will contract, and political options will be restricted, at best, to those to which right environmentalism is inclined. Labour would be more and more propelled towards the growth coalition.

CONCLUSION

The newer, non-regulatory approaches to environmental protection have typically rejected or ignored the notion of corporate crime. Indeed, regulation itself is several steps short of treating environmental harm as criminal. Some environmental damage is part and parcel of the everyday fabric of human life – but much is not. The newer models largely ignore harm that is not relatively innocent. Non-regulatory approaches are put forward, rather, as a less coercive, less state-centred replacement for regulation. Market-based versions are offered as the exclusive alternative to regulation.

There is, however, another possible understanding of non-regulatory approaches. Progressive environmentalist can consider greater use of market-based methods, but as a complement to regulation, not a replacement. Regulation is seen as necessary, but not sufficient. It is seen as sometimes appropriate and sometimes not. It assumes that all tools of government are available to lessen harm to the environment. A balanced and diverse array of weapons is thought of as essential.

Regulation most often fails, in this view, because enforcement is too complex and expensive. Right-oriented environmentalists make this point constantly, but they forget that bans on substances require few monitoring stations and few inspectors and that occasional criminal prosecutions, with rather stringent penalties attached, might be cheaper than continuously monitoring many facilities.

I have argued elsewhere (Paehlke 1990a, 1992) that the best approach to environmental protection is at all levels, in all sectors, with all tools. Local, state and provincial, national, and international governments and institutions should be involved. Effective protection is not easily achieved by dependence on a single bureaucratic agency, such as Environment Canada, but must find its way into the central agencies of government – cabinet executive committees (or, in the case of the United States, into cabinet in the first place). In these two dimensions, shifts have proceeded in recent years.

But an all tools approach, while being adopted in some jurisdictions, has not been widely articulated within administrative theory or the political realm. Use of criminal law in matters environmental is crucial here; it provides a valuable counterpoint to increased use of methods less coercive than regulation. Market-based tools are not inevitably less coercive, or less effective, than regulation or criminal law. Economic instruments do not expressly require or forbid any particular behaviour. However, if stringent and/or imaginatively designed, they will rapidly alter the behaviour of individuals, profit-seeking firms, and even governments.

Cigarette taxes, to the extent that they are not criminally avoided, even slow or stop powerfully addictive behaviours. The deliberate procurement of products from environmentally responsible firms provides a powerful incentive to conform. It might also counter non-enforcement of environmental regulations if independent environmental audits became a condition of receiving supply contracts. But none of this lessens the need to apply criminal sanctions to some kinds of environmental harm in some circumstances.

Canada has experienced some movement towards criminalization of pollution. As Kernaghan Webb (1988) put it, there was, from 1986 to 1988;

a flurry of legislative activity in several jurisdictions which will significantly strengthen the penal and sentencing powers available to the courts in those jurisdictions. This new legislation includes higher maximum fines, and in some cases the introduction of minimum fines, different penalties for corporate and individual offenders, the ability to directly convict officials within corporations responsible for offenses, jail terms, and the ability to factor into the penalty imposed the profit accrued as a result of the violation.

Additional steps have followed, even at the federal level. As well, the courts have shown 'signs of growing impatience with recalcitrant industrial operations' (despite a record wherein the courts 'have rarely imposed the full possible penalties available to them').

Most dramatically, on 3 September 1992, Severin Argenton, president of Varnicolor Chemical Ltd of Elmira, Ontario, was sentenced to eight months in jail, the longest sentence yet imposed in Canada in an environmental case (Hess 1992). The case involves the illegal storage and leaking (into soil and groundwater) of more than five thousand barrels of liquid toxic waste. This was the fifth case in Canada in which jail sentences have been imposed for environmental damage. At least to some extent, then, pollution has been 'criminalized' in some Canadian provinces.

Webb (1988) also makes the following observations:

Although regulatory pollution offenses are in substance 'civil', they are enforced as penal laws 'through the machinery of the criminal law.' Because the courts responsible for adjudication of pollution offenses spend most of their time dealing with charges under the Criminal Code, it is easy to see why judges in these courts might be inclined to treat pollution offenses as criminal as well.

But there are definite dangers associated with having criminal and regulatory offenses adjudicated by the same courts. After a day of more traditional types of criminal cases, pollution offenses might not seem so serious. Most pollution incidents are not deliberate, intentional acts, there is usually no evidence of harm, and the accused in pollution cases are frequently upstanding corporate citizens. Sentences imposed by courts in pollution cases often reflect these factors.

As well, Ontario's proposed Bill of Rights would permit any two residents to request that the government investigate alleged environmental harm, so long as it occurred as a result of some person or company failing to comply with existing legal requirements (Ontario, Ministry of Environment, 1992). Employees of corporations already have some 'whistle-blower' protection, which was enforced during the above-mentioned case. These provisions, though strengthened within the proposed new legislation, are still not all they might be. Nonetheless, citizens can instigate actions that could lead to criminal proceedings.

Much U.S. legislation allows groups of citizens to bring suit to cause bureaucracies to implement regulatory proceedings. This might be sufficient in itself. Even under Ontario's proposed Bill of Rights, it will be government that will decide whether or not to prosecute. Citizen-initiated civil proceedings, or requirements that corporations carry insurance against environmental damage, might be equally effective. In most cases, there is a market-based option for each application of criminal law. The latter will be more easily enacted and enforced if the former have been first tried and found wanting.

Application of criminal law to environmental harm must be selective. Indeed, unless selection is thoughtful, such initiatives will not be easily achieved, even when environmental concerns are paramount. In summary, sustainability concerns are generally best advanced by means of economic instruments rather than through the use of criminal law. However, a combination of instruments, including criminal law, may well be appropriate in the protection of human health. The third dimension of environmentalism, ecological protection, is a more complicated matter. These distinctions are politically important, as is willingness to use all instruments – those seen as essentially 'left' and those seen as essentially 'right.' Non-interventionist instruments are effective only when strong intervention is not precluded.

To date, criminal law has, to my knowledge, been used only when human lives have been put at increased risk. However, the logic of deep ecology and the rights of non-human species have become far more widely accepted. Protection of non-human habitat and biodiversity is seen as inseparable from the well-being of humans, and we see other species as intrinsically valuable. Environmentally sensitive lands are being defined and protected ever more stringently. In some European jurisdictions, no tree can be cut anywhere without permission of public authorities. Controls on land use are the key tool in protection of ecosystems, but criminalization of some actions may come soon.

One is left with an appreciation of why an all-tools approach may be the most sensible way to proceed. Near-to-universal behaviour cannot be treated as criminal, nor can any but the most horrendous of threats to non-human species, unless and until human attitudes evolve further. But use of criminal law is necessary. In difficult economic times, in the midst of job losses, collapsing markets, and the possible demise of one's corporate existence, executives' attention is not easily gained. The possibility of criminal sanctions (or perhaps revocation of incorporation itself, as recently suggested in one environmental publication) focuses the mind. A decisive end-point to environmental protection, national and international, may be critical in the present business climate.

17

Can Confrontation, Negotiation, or Socialization Solve the Superfund Enforcement Dilemma?

HAROLD C. BARNETT

Superfund enforcement represents a unique application of federal powers to induce major U.S. industrial corporations to pay for their historic crimes against the environment. A primary goal is cleanup at hazardous-waste sites that pose threats to public health and the environment. To date, some $15.2 billion of federal money has been authorized to fund an effort estimated to cost between $100 and $300 billion. The U.S. Environmental Protection Agency (EPA) believes that cleanup at as many as 60 per cent of some 1,200 top-priority sites can be financed in this way. To this end, it has recently adopted an aggressive enforcement strategy.

Superfund enforcement exemplifies a classic conflict between the state's promotion of equity and its promotion of efficiency. Equity demands that those responsible for conditions at hazardous-waste sites bear their fair share of cleanup costs and that cleanup protect public health and the environment. However, 'making polluters pay' for expensive, permanent cleanup generates substantial transaction costs, cleanup delays, and a sacrifice of cleanup goals to settlement strategy. As a result, aggregate cost rises, speed and efficacy falter, and efficiency suffers. Conflict over who pays the toxic debt produces a program that is neither equitable nor efficient.

More complete socialization of cleanup costs and systematic emphasis on negotiated settlements have been proposed as solutions to this dilemma. I consider below whether the structural realities that have constrained the program to date will also slow adoption and implementation of these alternatives.

The chapter first examines the equity and efficiency conflicts that define Superfund's failure and summarizes instrumental and structural perspectives on the source and resolution of these conflicts. I argue that failure is consistent with the predictions of a structuralist model. In the body of the chapter, I review EPA's current enforcement strategy and evaluate socialization and negotiation as alternatives. I conclude that negotiation has the most potential to overcome the structural roots of failure to date.[1]

A BRIEF OVERVIEW

Superfund was created in 1980 to address the threat that uncontrolled hazard-ous-waste sites pose to human health and the environment, as exemplified by the horrors of Love Canal.[2] The 1980 act taxed oil and chemical feedstocks pro-duced by the petrochemical industry and provided $1.6 billion over five years to fund cleanup when financially viable responsible private parties could not be identified. The compromise required to pass the act on the eve of Ronald Reagan's election left a number of major issues unresolved, among them: 'how clean is clean?' The debate over that question encompassed diverse positions regarding the acceptable degree of public exposure to the risks posed by hazard-ous-waste sites and the priority of cost in choosing remedies. Liability for site problems was made strict, joint, and several. Strict liability results in parties being held responsible for their contributions to Superfund problems, whether or not they were negligent in their disposal practices. Joint and several liability results in any responsible party being held accountable for the total cost of cleanup when responsibility is not divisible. EPA was granted strong enforce-ment powers to induce responsible private parties to finance and/or undertake cleanup.

From its inception to mid-1983, Superfund was dominated by the Reagan administration's deregulatory 'agenda.' Under EPA Administrator Ann Burford, cleanup decisions were guided by the goal of fund conservation and a desire to rule out a more costly, reauthorized 'son of Superfund.' The potential for aggressive enforcement was sacrificed to industrial accommodation. Following the Sewergate scandal[3] and replacement of Burford with William Ruckelshaus (who was replaced by Lee Thomas in 1984), EPA adopted a 'fund first' strategy that built on its unique ability to clean-up sites with public money and then sue responsible parties for the cost of cleanup. Although cleanup and enforcement accelerated, environmentalists and many in Congress remained highly critical.

When it reauthorized the fund in 1986, Congress added another $8.6 billion to the cleanup fund, imposed statutory deadlines on EPA to forestall further administration intransigence, and provided that decisions should emphasize long-term, permanent-cleanup technologies. The new mandate raised the aver-age cost of cleanup from about $8 million per site to $25–30 million. The pro-gram remained mired in controversy: Superfund's supporters claimed that EPA was sacrificing cleanup goals to mandated schedules and fund conservation; industry claimed that EPA was concerned more with impressing Congress with confrontational enforcement than with reaching settlement through meaningful negotiation and use of settlement incentives contained in its 1980 and 1986 legislation.

With the election of George Bush in 1988 and his selection of William Reilly as EPA administrator, the agency adopted an 'enforcement-first' strategy. As EPA became more aggressive and confrontational, it was increasingly faced with the political ramifications of its enforcement targets pursuing third-party claims against municipalities, the fear that lenders would be held liable for the toxic debt, and a related increase in the cost of settling liability claims.

Equity and Efficiency

Superfund in general, and its enforcement in particular, have failed to promote an equitable or efficient solution to problems of cleaning up hazardous-waste sites. Parties to Superfund-engendered conflict agree that an equitable program is one that distributes the burden in proportion to responsibility for conditions demanding cleanup. Environmentalists, many state officials, and some members of Congress interpret this to mean making polluters pay. The Superfund Act supports this proposition through strong liability standards and enforcement powers. These parties also believe that cleanup should substantially reduce the risk faced by communities with hazardous-waste sites and that weak enforcement promotes inequitable outcomes.

In contrast, the petrochemical industry and other major generations of hazardous wastes believe that Superfund's liability standards and EPA's enforcement strategy impose an unfair burden on them. They argue that society has chosen to embrace the gains from petrochemical and industrial production and therefore should share in the cost of environmental cleanup. They advocate funding of cleanup through a broad-based tax that shifts cleanup costs to society in general. They also believe that EPA targets them as 'deep pockets' and allows other polluters to avoid responsibility. They object to the transaction costs imposed on them when they choose to reject EPA's demands for excessive cleanup expenditures and when they attempt to shift the burden to responsible third parties that EPA has failed to pursue.

Their protests are joined by the insurance industry. Insurers consider it highly inequitable that they must pay for cleanup under policies they had neither written nor priced to include these responsibilities. They object to bearing high transaction costs associated with litigating their clients' suits. Conflict over who will pay the toxic debt pervades all areas of Superfund decision-making and contributes to delay and to high settlement and litigation costs.

Parties to Superfund-engendered conflict also agree that Superfund should promote an efficient program, in which cost is justified by risk to public health and the environment. Disagreement centres on the definition of how clean is clean and the procedure for incorporating risk and cost into decisions. Environmentalists and their allies argue that cleanup should eliminate risk through selection of permanent, long-term remedies; efficiency is promoted when a least-cost remedy is chosen to attain this risk-minimization goal. They have criticized EPA for sacrificing risk to cost-minimization and settlement accomplishments in an effort to conserve the Superfund.

In contrast, generator industries and their insurers argue that efficiency demands emphasis on a cost-benefit approach. They assert that EPA prefers cleanups that yield minimal reduction of marginal risk at excessively high marginal cost. Further, they claim that they must bear high transaction costs in an effort to oppose EPA's preference for inequitable distribution of the toxic debt. Confrontational enforcement thus raises the overall cost of cleanup and promotes inefficiency.

Superfund's Failure and the State

Structuralist and instrumentalist theories of the state provide alternative conceptualizations of conflict over equity and efficiency and thus of Superfund's failure. I posit that the structuralist theory is superior. A key question is whether the structural constraints that currently promote failure also negate proposals for change that build on an instrumentalist perspective.

Instrumentalists recognize powerful competing interests involved in the program and assume that no single interest or coalition can dominate all decisions.[4] Confrontation among interests results in high transaction costs and increases substantially the total cost of cleanup and settlement; inefficiency is promoted. Inefficient outcomes are characterized by inferior environmental results and higher-than-necessary costs. The gains in environmental quality and the reduction in cost associated with a more efficient outcome encourage compromise; there is the potential for all to come out ahead.

Instrumentalists acknowledge that although no one interest can consistently dominate decision-making, results may still favour a relatively stronger party. However, efforts by the more powerful to secure all gains will simply sustain confrontation and make everyone worse off. Instrumentalists disagree as to whether environmental or industrial interests are better served by Superfund legislation and EPA implementation. They agree that both sets of interests have had their victories.

Structuralists recognize an inherent contradiction between pursuit of equity and pursuit of efficiency. They expect the state to promote the former in the interest of social harmony and the latter in the interest of economic development and capital accumulation. Structuralists argue that the state typically attempts to resolve this contradiction through such stratagems as symbolic action, socialization, and mystification of policy. When these strategies are not feasible, unresolvable contradictions become built into a program. This can happen when there is no dominant party and when competing interests cannot reach a compromise. Further, when a program contains many decision-points and decision-makers, design elements that benefit one party can be offset by elements that benefit another. Each party has some limited victories that partially offset the opposition's. The resulting system embodies contractions, and that fact promotes neither efficiency nor equity.

My analysis of Superfund over its first decade suggests that this structuralist model captures the essential roots of Superfund's failure, which emerged from several major contradictions. First, the program is not guided by definition of how clean is clean. Failure to resolve conflict over this issue has resulted in costly and impermanent remedies. Congress emphasized cleanup standards and permanent remedies in 1986 but failed to distinguish between cleanup objectives as the starting-point and cost as a secondary factor. Responsibility for balancing criteria was passed on to EPA. EPA thus became the locus of conflict among White House, state, community, environmental, and industrial interests. Unable to resolve this conflict, EPA often sacrificed effective cleanup to cost considerations and settlement goals and rationalized this in questionable evaluations of risk.

Second, inability to resolve conflict over equitable distribution of the toxic debt has severely compromised efficiency. Confronted with budgetary problems, real and perceived economic dislocation, and pressure to make polluters pay, Congress left distribution of cleanup costs to EPA and its enforcement program. EPA in turn could not resolve the basic contradiction between this expectation and its willingness and ability to demand industrial compliance.

Third, EPA's staff resources have been and remain insufficient relative to its mandate. Staff limitations have generally constrained selection of remedies, productivity of enforcement, and oversight of cleanup contractors. Blunting agency action through budgetary constraint is a hallmark of inability to resolve regulatory conflict. In such situations, strong legislation satisfies public demands for action while inadequate funding restricts action and diminishes economic burden.

Fourth and finally, failure to resolve conflict between federal funding and federal responsibilities has left elements of the program dependent on entities that cannot or do not meet Superfund's expectations. The demands of the New Federalism have imposed a cleanup and enforcement burden on the states that often exceeds their fiscal capacity. The desire to privatize much of the cleanup process has left EPA dependent on for-profit contractors. Contractors' decisions are often driven by goals that diverge substantially from the agency's.[5]

Proposals to Address the Roots of Failure

Critics have proposed greater socialization of the cleanup burden and fuller reliance on negotiated settlements as alternatives to current Superfund strategy. Both proposals are based on the presumption that aggressive enforcement has failed to promote efficient or equitable outcomes. A brief discussion of EPA's current enforcement-first strategy helps to place these alternatives in perspective.

Enforcement First

EPA Administrator William Reilly adopted enforcement-first as the agency's strategy soon after taking office in 1989.[6] Noting that the fund-first strategy applied by his predecessors was likely to exhaust cleanup resources, he predicted that the threat of publicly financed cleanup would soon become ineffective as an incentive to settlement. Under the new strategy, EPA accelerated its use of unilateral cleanup orders to compel responsible parties to act. Non-compliance with unilateral orders can result in treble damage penalties (i.e., penalties equal to three times EPA's cost of site remediation). The 1986 reauthorization had ruled out several industrial strategies for delaying compliance with EPA orders. Targets of EPA enforcement could comply with EPA requests, pursue responsible third parties in subsequent legal actions, and/or seek reimbursement from the cleanup fund; the alternative was to refuse to comply and face treble damage penalties later.

Enforcement-first was supported by an increase in EPA staff resources. The 1986 reauthorization also encouraged EPA to make fuller use of existing incentives to settlement, including mixed-funding agreements, in which the Superfund would cover the so-called orphan share that was not attributable to those willing to settle, and de-minimus settlements, in which the agency would allow minor contributors to pay for a portion of cleanup costs and avoid more costly negotiation or litigation. EPA also stated its intention to use a structured-settlement technique developed and applied with some success by one of its regional offices: those who refused to settle would be ordered to pay for a designated portion of cleanup and would be informed that recalcitrance would result in a far greater financial burden than would compliance.

By 1991, the new strategy was producing the promised increase in unilateral orders and cleanup action. Corporate compliance led EPA to believe that responsible parties could be induced to cover a far greater percentage of cleanup costs than previously expected.

Corporations targeted by EPA do not share the agency's enthusiasm. They object to their lack of options and point to an increasing ratio of unilateral orders to voluntary settlements as indicative of EPA's reliance on confrontation. They argue that EPA has not taken swift or effective action against non-settlers, thus leaving those who do settle to pursue third parties in the courts. Major corporations have sued municipalities, pointing out that they are simply applying the same liability standard that allows EPA to single out corporate 'deep pockets.' Lending institutions that have acquired contaminated property through foreclosure fear that they too might be held liable for cleanup costs.[7] The insurance industry also opposes EPA's new aggressiveness and the related cleanup and litigation costs it must bear. A 1992 study by RAND Corp. discussed below has reinforced insurers' argument that transaction costs have gotten out of control.

Socialization of Cleanup Costs

Socialization of cleanup costs has two dimensions: finance and expenditure. The former refers to whether the cleanup tax burden is imposed on society at large; the latter, to whether the fund serves as a substitute for private expenditures.

Polluting industries have consistently advocated socialization of Superfund's finance. Superfund taxes were drafted with this end in mind. In early legislative debate, key members of Congress emphasized the expectation that taxes on the petrochemical industry would be passed through to users of chemical feedstocks and petroleum. These expectations have been fulfilled to a large extent, and, consequently, cleanup costs for hazardous-waste sites have been substantially socialized. The chemical industry probably pays at most 33 per cent of the taxes imposed on its feedstock production and passes the remainder forward to customers and backwards to the Internal Revenue Service as corporate profit tax deductions. The oil industry most probably passes all of its tax burden forward to customers. Most public discussion of industry's Superfund tax burden fails to acknowledge these facts. I consider this a clear effort to mystify policy and overstate the distributive equity of the program.

Industrial efforts to socialize expenditures have been less successful than those to socialize finance. The Superfund's mandate and EPA's guidelines allow use of the fund for mixed-funding settlements, which finance cleanup out of both public and private revenues. In these arrangements, responsible parties that have contributed only a fraction of the hazardous waste requiring cleanup pay for their 'fair share,' and the fund pays for the remainder, or orphan share. EPA has been somewhat reluctant to promote mixed funding, in part out of a desire to conserve the fund.[8] Instead it has emphasized joint and several liability, which allows it to hold a 'deep pocket' liable for the total cost of cleanup. Corporations in generator industries argue that greater reliance on mixed funding would reduce transaction costs and promote efficiency and equity.

Fuller socialization of both finance and expenditures has been high on the legislative agenda of generator industries. During the 1984–6 debate on Superfund's reauthorization, Atlantic Richfield pushed for a tax on corporate revenues to finance a major expansion of the cleanup program. The Reagan administration objected to introduction of a new tax concept that could then be expanded to finance other federal programs. Service industries argued that they had not directly produced hazardous waste and objected to paying for cleanup. Conflict over who would pay for a five-year, $8.6-billion increase in the Superfund delayed reauthorization for some nine months and threatened to shut down the cleanup program. The eventual compromise created a $2.5-billion environmental tax,[9] left the chemical industry's feedstock tax unchanged at $1.38 billion, raised the total tax on petroleum to $2.76 billion, and claimed $1.25 billion in general revenues. The petrochemical industry objected to its continuing tax burden and the fact that this increase in public funding was not intended to diminish EPA's reliance on enforcement.

The insurance industry also has strongly advocated increased socialization. Expecting an increase in indemnification claims by insured responsible parties to cover both cleanup and litigation, insurers have proposed that funding come through taxation rather than enforcement. The industry has criticized the inequity and retroactive application of Superfund's liability standards. Liability applies to actions that were not illegal at the time of disposal. During the 1984–6 legislative debate, insurers proposed that liability attach only to cleanup problems resulting from hazardous wastes disposed of after 1977, the year in which the Resource Conservation and Recovery Act established a cradle-to-grave regulatory system for hazardous waste.

More recently, the American International Group (AIG), an insurance giant, has proposed a tax on environmental insurance premiums as a mechanism to convert transaction costs into cleanup expenditures (See American International Group 1989). Such conversion would allow more extensive cleanup to be financed out of a given aggregate corporate burden vis-à-vis Superfund.[10] As in earlier proposals from the insurance industry, liability would be limited to cleanup in relationship to hazardous wastes disposed of after 1977.

The AIG's proposal has mixed implications for equity and efficiency. A tax on environmental insurance premiums shifts some of the cost of cleanup and confrontation from insurers to major corporations and industries that degrade the environment. A RAND Corp. study found a steep increase in claims and insurance payments related to cleanup of hazardous-waste sites between 1986 and 1989. RAND estimated that the nation's insurers spent $470 million in 1989 on indemnification of policyholders and on transaction costs. Transaction costs arose from disputes as to whether or not insurance policies cover claims brought by policyholders (coverage disputes) and from the obligation to defend the policyholder against claims by EPA and third parties. Some 88 per cent of the insurance industry's total outlays ($410 million) were for transaction costs.[11]

The AIG's proposal makes the valid assumption that transaction costs are ultimately passed forward to policyholders as higher premiums; were publicly funded cleanup to replace enforcement, they would decrease. The cost to policyholders could remain the same while the extent and pace of cleanup accelerate.

The proposal has generally positive equity implications if there are no constraints on projected efficiency gains. An insurance-premium tax will tighten links between pollution and cleanup finance more than is likely under an environmental tax on all industry. It will increase public resources for cleanup and reduce delays associated with enforcement. The threats that waste sites pose to public health will diminish at a faster rate. Further, since cleanups by EPA have been more likely than those by responsible parties to involve permanent remedies (U.S. General Accounting Office 1992b), there is an equity gain in the form of fuller protection from hazardous-waste sites. There will, however, be a perceived loss in equity for those who want polluters to pay. Those responsible for cleanup problems caused by pre-1977 disposal will pay only a premium tax.

The proposal will encourage waste reduction and help convert transaction costs into cleanup expenditures. Enforcement is expected to deter environmentally dangerous behavior through imposition of liability on those who have acted this way in the past. Some analysts argue that polluters often do not internalize expected future costs associated with current disposal practices (Menell 1991), and so enforcement cannot induce them to reduce waste or to choose more expensive and environmentally sound disposal. If insurance premiums are priced to reflect the potential for future damages and the premium tax is proportionate or progressive, expected costs are internalized and waste reduction and sound disposal are more likely.

Whether these efficiency gains are realized depends in large part on establishment of a procedure to link waste by date of disposal to generators and to the problems demanding cleanup. In the absence of complete and accurate disposal records, dating of disposed waste will bedevil assignment of liability. Further, even with accurate dating, linking waste to cleanup may be impossible. Techno-logical developments allow scientists to detect contaminants in groundwater in minute parts per billion. However, tracing contamination back to specific wastes disposed of at a particular site poses substantial problems that contribute to litigation between EPA and responsible parties as well as among the latter. The need to date waste can only exacerbate conflict and litigation. If this hurdle cannot be overcome, transaction costs will not in fact decline and efficiency will not increase.

The predictability of revenues derived from an insurance-premium tax is also problematic. If the tax encourages waste reduction, premiums and therefore tax revenues will fall. Further, if large firms self-insure, they will avoid paying the tax and will cut into revenues.

Finally, efficiency may suffer if reduced reliance on enforcement is accompa-nied by less incentive to monitor costs of EPA's contractors. Responsible parties have a clear incentive to monitor these costs when they expect that they will have eventually to pay the bill. However, when the cost is spread over all gener-ators via taxation, the incentive will diminish.

It thus appears unlikely that a tax on insurance premiums will resolve the conflicts that contribute to Superfund's failure and to garner sufficient political support from major stakeholders. Disagreement over the size of the premium tax, its distributive burden, and whether it should substitute for existing Super-fund taxes is likely to divide industrial interests and complicate acceptance of this alternative.[12] Advocates of making polluters pay may be willing to compro-mise on this goal in exchange for broader, faster cleanup. However, if the dating issue can not be resolved, such compromise is unlikely. Conflict over distribu-tion of the toxic debt will not diminish as responsible parties focus on the date of disposal in addition to current issues that determine liability. EPA will object to any proposal that may increase confusion and uncertainty.

Congressional supporters of Superfund will reject any proposal that will probably reduce the private share of cleanup costs without providing predictable funding from non-federal budgetary sources. Congress has yet to accept a waste-end tax, which would reduce waste, because of uncertainty about its reve-nue-raising potential.

Negotiation
The case for socialization rests on the presumption that environmental enforce-ment is inherently inefficient and inequitable. In contrast, some who reject this assessment believe that enforcement can be made consistent with both effi-

ciency and equity if based on explicit objectives and negotiation and settlement that reward compromise and punish recalcitrance. The fact that no one clearly gains from failures of Superfund enforcement can support development of a program that minimizes collective loss and more equitably shares the corresponding gains.[13] The current situation is ripe for compromise.

Many critics of EPA's enforcement strategy have long argued for more use of negotiation. EPA's initial excessively accommodative stance fuelled congressional criticism during the 1982–3 Sewergate scandal, and EPA then shied away from negotiation. During the 1984–6 debate on reauthorization, industrial critics of Superfund advocated greater reliance on negotiation. A study by law professor Frederick Anderson supported this position (Anderson 1985). Anderson had concluded that EPA's reliance on threats rather than on incentives was inconsistent with its goals. Drawing on experience with alternative dispute-resolution practices and techniques, he outlined an approach that stressed negotiation and compromise. EPA also sought congressional approval for fuller use of settlement incentives. Congress provided these. However, having mandated a far more costly program, Congress also clearly expected EPA to redouble its enforcement efforts. EPA eventually adopted its confrontational enforcement-first strategy in part to satisfy these expectations.

Recent proposals from the non-profit corporation Clean Sites[14] build on failed attempts to promote negotiation.[15] In 1989, Clean Sites began a project to develop a common understanding of the tensions and difficulties involved in selecting remedies (Clean Sites 1990, Sarno 1991), building on participation by major public and private interests. It found that the ambiguous and implicit selection process was central to its failure and proposed a four-step, explicit and interactive process.

First, EPA should involve affected parties in defining the scope of remedial investigations and in selecting site objectives. To achieve this goal, it would provide detailed information on risk to human health and the environment and on problems requiring remediation.

Second, and most critical, EPA should establish site-specific objectives, through consideration of such factors as future use of the site and its environs, proximity of residents, level of contamination of surrounding properties, environmental issues, and the views of the state, responsible parties, and directly affected citizens. Making this decision at the outset facilitates resolution of conflicts that typically emerge later.

Third, there should be full development of alternative remedies, which must at least meet site objectives and incorporate permanence, treatment, and long-term effectiveness. The last-named serves as a next-best option to permanence when the latter is not feasible.

Fourth, an alternative is selected that provides the greatest long-term effectiveness at lowest cost. Cost is compared to primary benefits in the selection.

In a related document, Clean Sites proposes an enforcement strategy to reinforce responsible-party incentives to help select a remedy and to accept compromise (Clean Sites 1989). As in EPA's enforcement-first strategy, the goal is to increase the number of site cleanups while conserving the fund. To this end, EPA initiates a significant number of administrative and judicial enforcement actions to punish the recalcitrant and impel their participation in cleanup. It also undertakes more and timely cost-recovery actions. To demonstrate visibly its will to enforce, EPA pursues vigorously a limited number of 'good' cases and then aggressively pursues non-settlers. Regional offices are held accountable for meeting realistically high responsible party cleanup goals. Finally, EPA more fully uses incentives for cooperation, such as mixed-funding and minor-party settlements, and penalizes non-settlers in litigation by forcing them to pay more than if they had settled, and by targeting non-settlers first to cover subsequent cleanup. EPA has already made some progress in building an enforcement program along these lines.

To facilitate consistency in remedy selection and enforcement, Clean Sites also proposes making regional offices more accountable.[16] To facilitate implementation of all these proposals, Clean Sites advocates an upgrading of project manager positions and provision of staff training. Finally, to hold EPA accountable, it proposes that the agency track program outcomes rather than inputs. Recent EPA initiatives are in accord with these proposals.

The Clean Sites program may assist victims of hazardous-waste sites as well as major polluting corporations. If host communities can participate on an equal footing with other interests, they can be involved in remedy selection and gain quicker implementation. Establishing objectives at the outset reduces the chance that their interests will be sacrificed to fund-conservation or to settlement goals. Major polluters benefit from the fund's financing of orphan shares (e.g., mixed-funding settlements) and targeting of non-settlers. Both measures reduce their cleanup burden and the transaction costs associated with shifting a portion of this burden onto third parties, and rationalized selection of remedies and more oversight of contractors may reduce cleanup costs.

These outcomes enhance the program's efficiency and equity and, in so doing, satisfy industry's demands for greater socialization of the toxic debt. As discussed above, protests from polluting industries against paying the Superfund tax have been based on four propositions. First, society has created the problem and should therefore help pay for the solution. Second, payment of the tax does not reduce enforcement-related cleanup costs to the extent that the fund does not cover the orphan share and EPA allows the recalcitrant to take a free ride. Third, efforts to shift the burden onto third parties imposes a transaction cost on major targets of EPA enforcement and reduces any gain secured through so shifting the burden. Fourth, absence of EPA control over cleanup produces unnecessarily large costs that squander the fund and raise the cost of complying with settlement terms.

Continued development of Superfund along lines consistent with the Clean Sites proposals and enforcement-first addresses directly three out of four of industry's propositions. I believe that the ultimate goal of the socialization argument is to create a public impression that polluting industries are contributing more than their fair share to cleanup and hence to demand other concessions.[17] Although the proposal does not promote direct socialization of finance, it does encourage fuller socialization. Industry may well be willing to drop its call for more extensive socialization of finance in exchange for socialization of expenditure via enforcement.

These optimistic conclusions may place the cart before the horse. The Clean Sites process of remedy selection requires a decision on how clean is clean. Setting objectives requires agreement on a site's danger to human health and the environment as well as on the extent to which risk reduction justifies costs. Comparing cost to primary benefits retains an element of cost-benefit analysis. Polluting industries are likely to support objectives that are sensitive to the greater cost of permanence versus long-term effectiveness. In contrast, environmentalists and exposed communities will probably favour objectives that are more sensitive to risk, regardless of cost. Given the substantial uncertainties surrounding identification of the risks posed by hazardous-waste sites, disagreement here may preclude meaningful negotiation.

The most recent round of debate over the dangers posed by dioxin reminds us how self-interest has dominated science in evaluating risk. The pulp-and-paper industries, highly sensitive to the costs of dioxin disposal and cleanup, have manipulated scientific findings in a public-relations campaign intended to convince EPA and the public that the risks have been overstated. Examination of new evidence and subsequent reexamination of existing evidence suggest that the dangers may in fact be understated (Bailey 1992).

Resolution of these conflicts within the Clean Sites model requires simultaneous change in EPA's resources and major stakeholders' expectations. If EPA's staff funding expands to allow more time and effort for negotiation, it may obtain settlements without excessive accommodation or confrontation. If 'deep-pocket' generators believe that they will not have to bear the major burden of costly cleanups, they will find it more in their interest to accept more permanent remedies and to satisfy the agency's demands. If environmentalists expect that any concessions on their preferred goals will be minimal in contrast to the gains from speedier cleanup, they too would support the Clean Sites approach. Minor parties involved may not be as pleased with outcomes that satisfy the major players. However, they may possess only limited political and economic ability to short-circuit this program.

The above resolution dynamic evokes an image of three groups siting around a table to forge acceptable compromise. Each group has 'prioritized' its objectives and resolved internal disagreements. EPA represents the interests of the government; major generators, the interests of the universe of potentially responsible parties; and environmentalists, exposed communities, and, like the Lorax, they speak for the trees. This situation stands in stark contrast to the historic realities that are central to the structural analysis of failure – substantial differences within and among manufacturing and non-manufacturing industries over risk, cost, and acceptable distribution of the toxic debt, and environmentalists and exposed communities disagreeing on the acceptability of any risk at all. Uncertainties over risk and disagreement over acceptable balancing of risk and cost promote ambiguous guidelines as means to reach compromise and retain flexibility. The federal budget deficit continues to constrain EPA staff funding. Finally, the decision-making process remains decentralized, allowing each group to push for a preferred outcome through constraint on program elements that serve an opposing group.

CONCLUSION

The pessimistic conclusion of this analysis is that the structural constraints that have contributed to Superfund's failure will prevent implementation of the solutions discussed above. Socialization must contend with support for making polluters pay as an essential equity component and with resistance to inequitable taxation. Perhaps of equal significance, the logic of the AIG's proposal is contradicted by the fact that technical problems in dating waste will simply reproduce the transaction costs that socialization is to eliminate. The negotiation approach assumes that major interests are collectively able to eliminate the ambiguities and implicit guidelines that have resulted from their inability to resolve how clean is clean, to agree on distribution of the toxic debt, and to guarantee an enforcement budget and strategy consistent with self-interested compliance. In other words, it assumes that the structural constraints that are central to Superfund's failure embody the key to its success. To date, self-interested parties have chosen to contend with these constraints through a multiplication of contradictions.

The hopeful conclusion is that the mounting cost of failure will reinforce a movement towards the type of compromise envisioned by advocates of negotiation. For example, EPA's enforcement-budget constraint could be eliminated by allowing the agency to pass its costs forward to responsible parties. Such self-financing is generally rejected, since it eliminates a constraint on aggressive enforcement. However, were major generators and environmentalists to believe that strong and rationalized enforcement was key to fair distribution of the toxic debt, support for self-financing could increase by an order of magnitude.[18] The substantial political leverage of opposing interests allows contradictions to be built into Superfund. If united by the prospects of a compromise solution, their leverage would be sufficient to remove or minimize these structural constraints.

NOTES

1 The analysis here draws on Barnett (1994).
2 Superfund Act is a commonly used shorthand for the Comprehensive Environmental Response Compensation and Liability Act of 1980 (CERCLA).
3 The Sewergate scandal was triggered by Administrator Burford's refusal to provide enforcement-sensitive records to Congress. As it ran its course, charges of politically based cleanup decisions, coverup, and perjury dominated media coverage and resulted in resignation of top agency officials.
4 For a fuller discussion of and citation to instrumentalist and structuralist theory, see Barnett (1994, chap. 3).
5 The overall effectiveness of a national program to address problems of hazardous-waste sites is contingent on resolution of other conflicts that do not directly affect Superfund implementation. These include mismatch between Superfund cleanups, on the one hand, and corrective action under the Resource Conservation and Recovery Act and guidelines on cleaning up federal facilities, on the other hand, as well as continuing debate over effective compensation for victims.
6 For fuller discussion of the evolution of EPA's enforcement and of enforcement-first, see Barnett (1994, chap. 9).
7 EPA is attempting to shield municipalities from bearing undue liability and has drafted guidelines to clarify the liability of financial institutions.
8 A RAND Corp. report contains data on the experience of five Fortune 100 firms at hazardous-waste sites where more than $100,000 was spent by these firms between 1984 and 1989. Mixed funding settlements were reached at seven of seventy-three sites (Acton and Dixon 1992, 48).
9 The environmental tax was imposed on corporations subject to the alternative minimum tax on corporate profits as computed under the Tax Reform Act of 1986. Alternative minimum taxable income includes preferences that allow some capital-intensive industries to minimize their profit-tax liability.

10 AIG was effectively denied the opportunity to push this proposal in 1990 when Superfund refinancing was included in that year's budget compromise. Congress wished to avoid repetition of the 1986 funding hiatus and felt that a full debate on the program was premature, given Administrator Reilly's recent introduction of enforcement-first and related program changes.

11 In contrast, the transaction-cost share of general comprehensive insurance outlays is approximately 30 per cent (Acton and Dixon 1992, 16–32). The RAND study estimates that the transaction-cost share of outlays by several very large industrial corporations averages 21 per cent between 1984 and 1989 (Acton and Dixon 1992, 33).

12 Generators that have been held liable for problems created before 1977 would gain at the expense of other policyholders. The former would be more likely to support the proposal than would the latter. Generators who paid premiums in the past may object to paying higher premiums so that insurers could avoid liability for cleanup. In 1989, settlements valued at $1,020 million were associated with insurer and responsible-party transaction costs of roughly $612 million. If insurers' transaction costs are passed forward to policyholders, the average premium would need to rise by an additional 50 per cent to convert all private transaction costs into cleanup funding. (This estimate assumes that transaction costs include the $410 million paid by insurers plus $202 million paid by responsible parties. The latter amount is equal to the $1,020 million in settlements reported by EPA (in its FY87-91 CERCLA Enforcement Data release of 10 September 1991) times the 21 per cent average responsible-party transaction cost reported in the RAND study. Transaction costs of $612 are some 150 per cent as large as the insurers' transaction costs of $410.) The premium increase would be higher for policyholders that can not effectively practise waste reduction and those that do not have self-insurance as an option. These policyholders are unlikely to include petrochemical firms. Other manufacturing interests are thus likely to oppose the tax on equity grounds, while service industries that pay the environmental tax will probably support it under the same banner. The forces of opposition would probably gain from the fact that it is generally easier to increase an existing tax than to impose a new one.

13 Lawyers and consultants are an exception to the statement that no one gains from Superfund failure. The magnitude of their financial rewards depends on the degree of conflict.

14 Clean Sites was established in 1984 in the wake of Sewergate. It conducts a range of activities geared towards improving cleanup of hazardous-waste sites. It also provides direct assistance at sites through mediation among involved parties, allocation of cleanup costs, technical review and management of site studies, and cleanup activities. It is funded by public and private sources.

15 Some of the material in the remainder of this section was originally published in Barnett (1994, chap. 10).

16 For a recent evaluation of negotiation at the regional level, see Church, Nakamura, and Cooper (1991).
17 Debate on this point also serves the interests of members of Congress who, in voicing opposition to greater socialization, can present themselves as promoters of equity.
18 The Senate has passed a bill that allows the FDA to charge drug companies for the cost of reviewing the safety of new drugs and to speed up the review process. The *New York Times* reported: 'The plan is considered feasible because the companies may make millions of dollars at the same time they pay new fees.' EPA is also said to be considering charging companies for the costs of regulation. These user fees set a precedent as a way for federal regulatory agencies to raise money in difficult times. See Hart (1992).

18

Controlling Corporate Misconduct through Regulatory Offences: The Canadian Experience

KERNAGHAN WEBB

Regulatory offences[1] may lack the 'glamour' of crimes,[2] but they are the most effective penal option[3] available to address corporate misbehaviour in Canada.[4] An examination of recent legislative activity[5] and court cases[6] suggests that they will probably remain the preeminent penal tool used to control corporations. While use of criminal sanctions to counter environmental and workplace harm has become the darling of reformers,[7] legislators and enforcement agencies have no such fixation: certain characteristics of crimes render them of little use against corporations, particularly in environmental and workplace contexts.

An apt way of comparing the main features of crimes and regulatory offences is to use the metaphor of the differences between cannons and guns. With crimes – the legal equivalent of cannons – prosecutors have to prove subjective intent in order to obtain a conviction – someone 'knowingly' or deliberately engaged in a harmful act or was criminally wanton or reckless.[8] Satisfying the court that intent exists may be particularly difficult if the accused is a corporation, with a diffuse 'directing mind' and responsibilities divided among many individuals.[9] In regulatory offences (the guns), no proof of intent is required to obtain a conviction. With regulatory offences of strict liability, the corporate accused can escape liability by showing that it exercised due diligence or that there was a reasonable mistake of fact. The onus is thus on the corporation to explain its operations and justify its behaviour. With both crimes and regulatory offences, large financial penalties and imprisonment are available as sentencing options.[10]

No one denies that crimes carry a stigma that is anathema to any law-abiding citizen or corporation. But in most cases, the real question is whether the criminal approach is worthwhile, given the problems of proof associated with it, and in light of an alternative method that is both more appropriate and easier to enforce. Cannons make a lot of noise, but they are cumbersome and miss their target as often as they hit it. Guns are comparatively easy to use, and their lethal precision is well recognized. For good reason, then, outside the Criminal Code,[11] Canadian legislators and enforcement agencies pack guns, not cannons.

A number of debates and developments have occurred in Canada over the past two decades bearing directly on the form, substance, and use of penal offences to control corporate misconduct. These events were shaped by unique features of the Canadian legal landscape, such as the Charter of Rights and Freedoms,[12] but many of the same issues have occurred or are likely to occur elsewhere.[13]

The focus in this chapter is on three controversial issues pertaining to penal offences. The first is the need for new crimes and for increased use of existing crimes to address corporate wrongdoing in such areas as environmental protection and workplace safety. I suggest that such efforts are misguided, given that regulatory offences are more appropriate and are now beginning to be used effectively. The second issue relates to prosecution by enforcement agencies. Analysis reveals that increased use of public compliance and enforcement policies, and of specialized enforcement units, is more effective. The third issue is legal justification for different standards of fault and burdens of proof for regulatory offences, when compared with criminal offences. Courts are developing a distinctive legal approach to regulatory offences, which is being held consistent with *Charter* standards of fundamental justice.

A Word on Terminology

Before proceeding any further, we must define the terms *criminal* and *regulatory* offences. The typology of offences used here is that developed by the Supreme Court of Canada in the landmark 1978 decision *R. v. City of Sault Ste. Marie*. Its three-tiered system divides offences into true crimes, strict liability, and absolute liability and has been essentially upheld in subsequent cases and proven workable. In my opinion, this system is not simply a semantic device resorted to by legally trained individuals to confuse non-lawyers. Rather, it makes important substantive and procedural distinctions that underlie the position taken here – that strict- and absolute-liability offences – the main regulatory offences in use – are both more appropriate and effective in addressing most types of corporate wrongdoing.

In the *Sault Ste. Marie* decision, Mr Justice Dickson (as he then was) described criminal offences as those in which the prosecution must prove both the actus reus of the offence and the subjective intent – the mens rea – of the accused. The vast majority of criminal offences are located in the *Criminal Code*, but there are also mens rea offences in other pieces of federal and provincial legislation, including those pertaining to environmental protection,[14] workplace safety,[15] and consumer protection.[16] Criminal offences, however, are extremely rare outside the Criminal Code and are seldom used.

Most offences contained in non–Criminal Code legislation involve either strict or absolute liability.[17] For this reason, I refer to both types as 'regulatory offences.' With both types, the prosecution need not prove the subjective intent of the accused. With absolute liability, it need prove only the actus reus of the offence, and a conviction will automatically result. With strict liability, after the prosecution has proven the actus reus, the accused is given the opportunity of establishing that due diligence was exercised or that there was a reasonable mistake of fact.

Strict liability offences are often referred to as negligence offences,[18] because of the type of fault element involved. The offence incorporates an *objective* standard of negligence through use of due diligence, so that the mere fact that the accused may have believed that his or her actions were careful or reasonable (a subjective standard) is not sufficient to avoid liability: what matters is whether the courts would consider that a reasonable person in the accused's position would have behaved in a similar manner.

In *Sault Ste. Marie*, the Supreme Court of Canada held that absolute-liability offences, because they impose penal liability without providing an accused an opportunity at least to demonstrate that he or she did everything reasonable, were contrary to the principles of penal justice.[19] More recently, in *Reference Re: S. 94(2) of the B.C. Motor Vehicles Act*, the Supreme Court stated that absolute-liability offences are contrary to the Charter's section 7, where deprivation of liberty such as imprisonment or probation is provided as a penalty. Such offences are comparatively rare in Canadian regulatory legislation.

In *R. v. Wholesale Travel*, a 1992 decision, the Supreme Court of Canada upheld strict-liability offences in regulatory legislation, including offences that may lead to imprisonment. Most regulatory offences in Canada are strict liability in nature.[20] Because such offences with imprisonment have been approved by the Supreme Court, and because of their heavy usage in regulatory legislation, they are the focus of analysis below

CRIMES VERSUS REGULATORY OFFENCES

In Canada, some quarters[21] have called for new crimes, or for more extensive use of existing crimes, to protect the environment or workplace safety. Legislators' reluctance so far to resort to the criminal approach seems to me eminently sensible.

There are three main arguments in favour of the use of crimes. First, the types of harm and suffering caused to humans and the greater environment are serious and deserving of serious denunciation. Second, there are occasions when this harm is inflicted deliberately or with criminal (subjective) negligence. Third, failure to use the criminal law to address this type of wrongdoing, often perpetrated by corporations, reflects an ideological bias in favour of certain powerful classes.

The position against expanded use of the criminal law in these contexts can be summarized as follows. First, there are already numerous criminal offences well suited to deliberate or criminally negligent harm to individuals or property.[22] Second, it is agreed that there may be occasions when harm to workers or the environment is inflicted deliberately or in a criminally negligent manner. However, problems of proof make the criminal approach not as practical or as effective as enforcement through regulatory offences. Third, there are already a wide range of regulatory offences pertaining to environmental or workplace harm, with large penalties attached and the potential for imprisonment.[23] These offences clearly indicate societal disapproval and should be the main penal tool used to control misbehaviour in these contexts.

Fourth, it is considerably easier to enforce these regulatory offences, for both intentional or negligent misconduct, so this should be the preferred route. Fifth, the fact that these regulatory offences exist, and are easier to enforce, reflects societal recognition that regulated actors are in a different position than non-regulated actors – that the former are held to higher standards of conduct and are subject to more demanding legal treatment than the latter. Sixth, development of effective, publicly approved and disseminated compliance and enforcement policies[24] that set out in what circumstances prosecutions will take place should lead to more effective enforcement.

Regulatory offences hold corporations and natural persons to a higher standard than do crimes, for two reasons. First, not only intentional but also negligent behaviour is considered unacceptable.[25] Thus strict-liability offences hold corporations and natural persons to higher standards of care than crimes. Second, the onus is put on the regulated accused to demonstrate the reasonableness of its behaviour. This burden compels regulated persons to put in place preventive measures (e.g., safety or environmental audits[26]) if they wish to be able to establish due diligence to the satisfaction of courts. It is suggested that the largely abysmal enforcement record for criminal offences in addressing harm to workers or the environment,[27] in contrast to evidence of considerable success with regulatory offences,[28] is support for the regulatory-offence approach.

The push for more extensive use of criminality, while well-meaning and eloquently argued, appears to have been motivated more by reasons of doctrinal consistency than any real need. Thus, for example, the Law Reform Commission of Canada seems to have proposed new crimes against the environment and to address workplace harm as part of its suggested revision of the Criminal Code, not because of any pressing demand from the legal community or greater public or because of any deficiencies in the regulatory-offence approach.

Enforcement of Regulatory Offences

Legal and non-legal pressures have led government departments to develop more explicit, open, and effective approaches towards prosecutions of regulatory offences. The due-diligence defence allows accused to raise the issue of the acquiesence of governmental officials to a situation of non-compliance (i.e., 'officially induced non-compliance').[29] This has been one motivation for governments to develop compliance and enforcement policies that set out, for the public, the regulated sector, and inspectors, how and when regulatory offences and other sanctions will be used. The existence of a compliance and enforcement policy, when its terms are followed, decreases the likelihood of officially induced non-compliance and of its being successfully raised as part of a due-diligence defence.

Successful tort actions against government in recent years for negligent law enforcement[30] have led to greater realization in government that a systematic and predetermined approach to enforcement, as through use of compliance and enforcement policies, is desirable. Again, such policies, when strictly adhered to, tend to prevent tortious official-enforcement situations.

The possibility that inconsistent or uneven enforcement could be contrary to Charter principles of justice and equality[31] represents yet another stimulus for development of compliance and enforcement policies, since such policies, if the terms are followed, can lead to more equal enforcement and potentially be a defence to Charter challenges.

Enforcement by citizens or workers can be perceived by the public and government as indicative of governmental ineptitude.[32] Use of compliance and enforcement policies helps to bring citizens into the process earlier and may obviate the need for private enforcement. At a non-legal level, increasing public concern with environmental and health-and-safety matters, coupled with growing scepticism about the motivations and activities of government, has made the public more critical and vigilant. For all these reasons, governments seem to be realizing that the old, ad-hoc approach to prosecution is no longer acceptable.

Compliance and enforcement policies commit government to apply the law in a certain manner. They set out the powers, sanctions, constraints, and approaches of a department and the situations in which various sanctions will be used.[33] To be legitimate and effective, they are developed in consultation with regulatees, the public, other departments, and governments and are made available to the public. Where adhered to, such policies can become the basis for consistent, predictable, and fair implementation of policy. Growing numbers of government departments are developing these policies.[34]

Several environmental departments have set up special enforcement units, separate from the units that engage in day-to-day communications with regulatees.[35] These units have the expertise to bring successful prosecutions where such actions are necessary. They are not impeded by the tactical and practical constraints that might affect officials who regularly communicate with regulatees concerning compliance.

There are indications that limited but consistent use of regulatory-offence prosecutions can be effective against individuals, corporations, and corporate officials. In Ontario, for example, conviction rates for regulatory environmental offences have been high,[36] and empirical studies suggest that corporate officials take the threat of such prosecutions seriously.[37] Officials with the Ministry of Environment note a marked increase in cooperation from regulatees,[38] as well as improved abatement,[39] since the ministry began concerted enforcement of regulatory offences in 1985.[40] Private-sector representatives support this observation.[41]

The trend towards prosecuting corporate directors and officials as well as corporations represents the latest and most aggressive use of regulatory offences.[42] If such offences can survive Charter challenges,[43] a strategy of prosecuting corporate directors and officials will probably be a major additional impetus for corporations to develop effective environmental safeguards.[44]

By imposing a burden on the regulated accused to establish due diligence, the strict-liability offence requires regulated people to put proactive, preventive systems in place that tend to minimize the likelihood of offences arising.[45] Thus, for example, more environmental regulatees are hiring independent 'environmental auditors' to inspect their facilities and alert them to possible violations. If, despite hiring of such an auditor and following his or her advice, a violation does occur and is prosecuted, then the regulated accused can introduce the audits to support a claim of due diligence.[46]

In short, consistent enforcement of regulatory offences, when undertaken pursuant to compliance and enforcement policies, has proven an effective sanctioning tool to control environmental misconduct by corporations and individuals alike. There is no obvious reason why this approach could not be extended to other policy contexts, such as workplace health and safety and consumer protection, with similar positive results. Regular and concerted enforcement of regulatory offences can be an effective backdrop for administrative actions and can lead to regulatees' adopting proactive and preventive strategies.

Regulatory Offences and the Charter

Over the past twenty years, the Supreme Court of Canada has been developing a rationale for imposition of penal liability through regulatory offences,[47] a process greatly accelerated by introduction of the Charter.[48] Because of the status of the Charter, all ordinary legislation must adhere to the rights and principles enunciated in it, or justifications must be put forward to explain why limitations on them would be acceptable.

Courts have developed two main arguments to explain why it is reasonable and fair to impose penal liability (including imprisonment) without requiring proof of subjective intent. The first focuses on practical concerns about enforcement. Because many regulatory offences pertain to potential rather than actual harm, are perpetrated by corporations, and have diffuse victims, evidence of fault or lack of fault is likely to be peculiarly in the hands or mind of the accused.[49] Thus, for example, the adequacy of a preventive program, the fact that environmental or safety audits have been undertaken by a corporation, and the diffuse nature of control over activities evident in corporations are facts in the possession of the regulated accused and may be difficult for prosecutors to find on their own. Thus putting the onus on regulated accused to establish due diligence is a practical necessity, because otherwise it would be virtually impossible to hold regulatees up to the reasonable-person standard of care.[50]

The second argument centres on the distinctive position of regulatees in our society.[51] Regulatees are engaging, often for profit, in potentially dangerous or economically harmful activities. They are thus in an identifiable position of trust and responsiblity vis-à-vis society or a segment thereof. They are officially condoned and controlled risk-takers, and hence it is reasonable and fair to expect that they should bear the burden of demonstrating that they did everything reasonable to avoid contravening the law once the fact of contravention has been proven beyond a reasonable doubt.[52]

The clearest indication that regulatees are in this position occurs where a licence is necessary before persons can engage in a particular activity, such as with a driver's licence. But in many other areas regulatees' heightened social-contractual obligations can be signified through different means. For example, corporate status is mutual recognition between state and corporation that the latter plans to engage in ongoing profit-making activities and must abide by all appropriate laws.[53]

The difficulty with existing decisions on regulatory offences is that there is evidence that justices of the Supreme Court have not univerally adopted as sophisticated an approach to interpretation of Charter principles as is warranted. Thus, for instance, some justices have yet to agree that presumption of innocence has a different content or should apply differently to regulated accused than to criminally accused.[54]

In my opinion, the Charter should continue to be interpreted in a manner that allows for differential treatment of accused and differential safeguards, depending on the situation of the accused. Decisions that have approved of absolute-liability offences in limited circumstances, and have supported the strict-liability offence with due diligence defence, are important and positive developments. The final step may be recognition that the criminal approach should be reserved for situations where there is a possibility for long-term deprivation of the accused's liberty or for deprivation of life.[55] Language in the Charter supports this more nuanced approach to Charter interpretation,[56] and it is hoped that Supreme Court justices will turn to it in order to build on the promising foundation they have already developed.

CONCLUSIONS

Regulatory offences have come into their own in Canada over the past twenty years. They have proliferated in statutes, been strengthened and elaborated on in amendments, and been judicially approved, and they are increasingly being enforced pursuant to coherent and explicit enforcement policies. Prosecution of regulatory offences represents a considerably more practical and effective method to imposing penal sanctions on corporations and other regulated actors than does criminal prosecution. Strict-liability offences, the main type of regulatory offence, impose responsibility for exercising due diligence on regulated actors and are easier to enforce, since the burden is on the accused to establish due diligence. The penalties for regulatory offences can range from million-dollar-a-day fines to imprisonment and probation.

It is both reasonable and fair to impose penal liability through regulatory offences, given the privileged position of regulatees in our society as persons who engage in potentially harmful activity, often for profit, and given the practical difficulties associated with requiring prosecutors to prove lack of diligence.

If courts build on the solid foundations for regulatory offences they have articulated in cases such as *Sault Ste. Marie, Reference Re: S. 94(2) of the B.C. Motor Vehicles Act, Thomson Newspapers, R. v. Wholesale Travel*, and *R. v. Ellis-Don*, the ability of the state to control corporate misconduct will be on considerably more sound footing than if only a criminal approach were available.

NOTES

1 Also referred to by Canadian courts as 'public welfare' offences. Regulatory

offences, as used here and as understood by Canadian courts, are distinct from crimes; They are penal offences adjudicated by the ordinary courts that normally do not require proof of subjective intent to obtain conviction and are usually part of administrative regimes that control rather than prohibit a particular activity (e.g. use of licensing arrangements are common, special powers for inspectors are frequently provided, and reporting requirements are imposed on regulatees). Crimes, in contrast, are penal offences adjudicated by the ordinary courts, which normally require proof of subjective intent to obtain conviction and are often stand-alone offences prohibiting an activity outright, not part of a more elaborate administrative-control regime. This typology is derived primarily from the analysis of Mr Justice Dickson (as he then was) in *R. v. City of Sault Ste. Marie* [1978] 40 CCC (2d) 373–5. More complete discussion of the offences is provided below.

2   The reader may quite justifiably wonder what is 'glamorous' about crimes. The best way to explain this is by referring to a debate over regulatory offences versus crimes in which the author was involved, where I noted: 'I must admit, though, I'm at a psychological disadvantage, in trying to persuade you of the strengths of regulatory offences. The trouble is, when compared with the word "crimes," the phrase "regulatory offences" strikes fear in the hearts of no one. Imagine the blasé reponse of the literary world if Dostoyevsky had entitled his book Regulatory Offences and Compliance, instead of Crime and Punishment.' (Webb 1990, 59).

3   The word 'penal' is used here to denote sanctions with a deterrent and punitive element, including fines, probation, and imprisonment. Both regulatory and criminal offences are penal in nature.

4   I am not suggesting that the penal approach is the only or necessarily the preferable method to control corporate misbehaviour. Other techniques include control orders, licensing arrangements, and warnings. For a discussion of the range of options used to control pollution, see Webb (1988, chaps. 1–3). I believe that adminstrative techniques such as those described above will be more successfully invoked where backed by effective penal sanctions, enforced pursuant to a public compliance and enforcement policy.

5   As evidenced by the offence provisions of the Canadian Environmental Protection Act, 1988, RSC 1985, 4th Supp., c. 16, the Manitoba Environment Act, SM 1987–88, c. 26; 1988 amendments to the Ontario Environmental Protection Act RSO 1980, c. 141, and Ontario Water Resources Act RSO 1980, c. 361.

6   See, especially, *R. v. Wholesale Travel Group Inc.* [1991] 67 CCC (3d) 193, *R. v. Ellis-Don* [1992] 7 OR (3d) 320; *Reference Re: S. 94(2) of the B.C. Motor Vehicles Act* [1985] 48 CR (3d) 289.

7   See Glasbeek (1984); Keyserlingk (1984); Schrecker and Tremblay (1986).

8   Dickson, J., in *Sault Ste. Marie*, 362, states: 'Where the offence is criminal, the Crown must establish a mental element, namely, that the accused who committed the

prohibited act did so intentionally or recklessly, with knowledge of the facts constituting the offence, or with wilful blindness toward them.'

9 See *R. v. Canadian Dredge and Dock Co. Ltd.* (1985) 19 DLR (3d) 161.

10 On penalties available for regulatory offences, see below under the heading 'Crimes
versus Regulatory Offences.'

11 RSC 1985, c. C-46.

12 Part I of the Constitution Act, 1982, being Schedule B of the Canada Act 1982
(U.K.), 1982, c. 11.

13 See U.S. court articulation of non–mens rea regulatory offence in *U.S. Dotterweich*
320 U.S. 277 (1943); discussion of regulatory offences in New Zealand in November
(1990, 236–9).

14 S. 115 of the Canadian Environmental Protection Act.

15 S. 148(5) of the Canada Labour Code, RSC 1985, c. L-2.

16 S. 14 of the Consumer Packaging and Labelling Act, RSC 1985, c. C-38.

17 There are an estimated 97,000 regulatory offences created by federal statutes alone:
see Clifford and Webb (1986, 38).

18 See Dickson, J., in *Sault Ste. Marie* 370.

19 Per Dickson, J., in *Sault Ste. Marie* 363.

20 See comment to this effect re environmental offences in Hughes and Swanson (1990,
159). My own research suggests that legislation on workplace safety and consumer
protection also uses primarily the strict-liability offence. This is in keeping with the
Supreme Court of Canada's guidance in *Sault Ste. Marie* that public-welfare offences
should be presumed to be in the strict-liability category unless there are express legislative indications to the contrary.

21 See Glassbeek (1984); Keyserlingk (1984); Schrecker and Tremblay (1986).

22 See discussion of these in Webb (1988, chap. 4).

23 Under s. 113 of the Canadian Environmental Protection Act, RSC 1985, 4th Supp., c.
16, every person who manufactures or imports a substance in contravention of the act
is guilty of an offence and liable, on summary conviction, to a fine not exceeding
$300,000 and/or up to six months' imprisonment, or, on indictment, up to $1 million
dollars and/or imprisonment for up to three years. In Ontario, corporations that pol-
lute contrary to provisions of the Ontario Environmental Protection Act, RSO 1980,
c. 141, as amended, s. 146a(1), are liable on conviction to fines of up to $100,000 for
repeat-offences, while individual repeat offenders can be imprisoned for up to one
year (s. 146a). Polluters in Manitoba can be fined up to $200,000 per day for repeat
offences and to one year or both, pursuant to section 33 of the Manitoba Environment
Act, SM 1987, c. 26.

24 Compliance and enforcement policies are defined and discussed in greater detail
below.

25 Dickson, J., in *Sault Ste. Marie*, 363, makes the point as follows: 'Where the offence

is criminal, the Crown must establish a mental element, namely, that the accused who committed the prohibited act did so intentionally or recklessly, with knowledge of the facts constituting the offence, or with wilful blindness toward them. Mere negligence is excluded from the concept of the mental element required for conviction. Within the context of a criminal prosecution a person who fails to make such inquiries as a reasonable and prudent person would make, or who fails to know facts he should have known, is innocent in the eyes of the law.'

26 Environmental audits are discussed in greater detail below under the heading 'Enforcement of Regulatory Offences.'

27 As described in Schrecker (1984).

28 As discussed in greater detail below, 'Enforcement of Regulatory Offences.'

29 See *R. v. United Ceramics Ltd.* (1979) 52 CCC (2d) 19.

30 See *Just v. The Queen* [1989] SCR 1228; *City of Vernon v. Manolakos* [1989] SCR 1259; *Tock v. St. John's Metropolitan Area Bd.* [1989] 2 SCR 1181.

31 See discussion of this in Finkle and Cameron (1989, 34).

32 See discussion of the effect of private prosecutions on government enforcement action in Webb (1991, 770).

33 See Environment Canada (1988). This policy is discussed in some depth in Webb (1991, 819–24).

34 At the federal level, the Department of Fisheries and Oceans, in conjunction with the Department of Environment, is developing a compliance-and-enforcement policy for the pollution provisions of the Fisheries Act; the federal Department of Labour has a compliance-and-enforcement policy for the Canada Labour Code; the Department of Consumer and Corporate Affairs is developing such policies for some of its consumer-protection legislation.

35 Ontario, Quebec, and British Columbia have established such units.

36 In 1991, fines against polluters in Ontario totalled a record $2,575,145 on 485 convictions. In conversations of the author (November 1992) with David Kerr, regional supervisor, Investigations and Enforcement Branch, Southeastern Region, Ministry of Environment, he indicated that there is 85–90 per cent success rate for prosecutions (convictions and guilty pleas). There was also a shift in 1991 towards creative sentencing, either as an alternative or in addition to jail terms or fines. Companies have been stripped of profits, required to set up trust funds, and/or establish environmental scholarships. As well, directors and managers are increasingly being directly prosecuted and held liable for environmental offences. During the period 1985–91, the number of prosecutions increased 400 per cent; see Ontario Ministry of Environment (1992a). And see Ontario Ministry of Environment (1991).

37 See Saxe (1990, 91).

38 For example, in a November 1992 telephone conversation with the author, Mr Rob Dunn, district manager, Ottawa District, noted that 'prior to 1985, regulatees used to

say "get off my back" when we came around. Now, they're reporting spills on time, and are much more forthcoming with information. On the other hand, when we do investigations, nowadays they have their their lawyers present.'

39 Because of constantly changing economic, political, and regulatory conditions, officials were not able to supply me with statistical evidence to back up this assertion, but it is the considered opinion of all officials contacted that abatement practices of the private sector have improved since the 1985 enforcement campaign began.

40 Per my discussions with David Kerr. In 1985, the Ontario Ministry of Environment created its Investigations and Enforcement Branch. From fiscal year 1985–6 through to 1991, convictions increased from 100 per year to over 250 per year.

41 Conversations with Tony Pingue, vice president, Regulatory and Environmental Affairs, Philip Environmental Inc., November 1992.

42 Ontario Ministry of Environment (1992b, 2): 'In 1986 provisons were enacted by the Ontario Legislature in the Environmental Protection Act that made all directors or officers of a corporation personally accountable for offences committed against the environment. As a result of these provisons, more and more environmental prosecutions are resulting in the conviction of individuals as well as companies, and senior staff are being held personally responsible for their company's actions. Prosecutors are thinking not only in terms of fines, but also in jail terms – which can't be passed on to someone else.' For a recent example of a successful conviction of corporate directors, see *R. v. Bata Industries Ltd.* [1992] 9 OR (3d) 329.

43 For discussion of defence bar concerns with such prosecutions, and the interpretation of Ontario director offences, see 'The Bata Case – the Inside Story: New Rules for Officers' and Directors' Liability' in Fasken Martineau, *Environmental Law Bulletin* (August 1992), 1.

44 Of course, it may have additional effects, such as reorganization of corporate structures and resignations from boards of directors.

45 Iaccobucci, J., in *R. v. Wholesale Travel*, 235, talks of strict-liability offences as providing an 'effective inducement for those engaged in regulated activity to comply strictly with the regulatory scheme including adopting proper procedures and record-keeping.'

46 For further discussion of environmental audits, their strengths, and their weaknesses, see Edwards (1991, 1).

47 See particularly *Sault Ste. Marie*; *Reference Re: S. 94(2) of the B.C. Motor Vehicles Act*; and *R. v. Wholesale Travel*.

48 For more in-depth discussion of this issue, see Webb (1989, 419).

49 See comments to this effect by Dickson, J. in *Sault Ste. Marie*, and Cory, J., and Iaccobucci, J., in *R. v. Wholesale Travel*.

50 Cory, J., in *R. v. Wholesale Travel*, 225 states: 'Quite simply, the enforcement of regulatory offences would be rendered virtually impossible if the Crown were required

to prove negligence beyond a reasonable doubt. The means of proof of reasonable care will be peculiarly within the knowledge and ability of the regulated accused. Only the accused will be in a position to bring forward evidence relevant to the question of due diligence.'

51 This point is developed by LaForest, J., in the context of a more limited notion of privacy for regulatees than criminal accused in *Thomson Newspapers Ltd. v. Canada Director of Investigation and Research, Restrictive Trade Practices Commission* (1990) 76 CR 129; see also Cory, J., in *R. v. Wholesale Travel*, speaking specifically to acceptability under the Charter of strict-liability offences and the need for a different presumption of innocence for regulated accused.

52 Cory, J., in *R. v. Wholesale Travel*, 213, states: 'Those who choose to participate in regulated activities, have, in doing so, placed themselves in a responsible relationship to the public generally and must accept the consequences of that responsibility. Therefore, it is said, those who engage in regulated activity should, as part of the burden of responsible conduct attending participation in the regulated field, be deemed to have accepted certain terms and conditions applicable to those who act within the regulated sphere. Foremost among these implied terms is an undertaking that the conduct of the regulated actor will comply with and maintain a certain minimum standard of care.'

53 The notion of a heightened social contract for corporations is discussed by Monahan and Petter (1987, 69) and Tollefson (1991, 705).

54 This is evident in *R. v. Wholesale Travel*.

55 This point is elaborated on more fully in Webb (forthcoming).

56 Section 11(f) of the Charter requires that any person tried in an ordinary court and charged with an offence has the right to the benefit of jury trial where the maximum punishment is five years' or more imprisonment. Here is Charter recognition that where longer periods of imprisonment are available, more protection should be available to the accused.

19

Due Process and the Nova Scotia Herbicide Trial

COLIN GOFF

In recent years, scholars (e.g., Jones 1983; Michalowski and Kramer 1987) who study corporate crime have started to look at the conduct of global, or transnational corporations (TNCs), particularly their socially injurious activities towards indigenous peoples. Such actions have been defined by Michalowski and Kramer (1987) as 'any action in pursuit of corporate goals which violates national laws, or international standards such as codes of conduct for TNCs developed within the U.N., which results in social injury analogous in severity and source to that caused by corporate violations of law or international standards.' However, these writers have concerned themselves with First World corporations exploiting Third World (or host) nations.

Yet many TNCs operate – and engage in socially injurious behaviour – within other First World nations. Countries in the First World can be in need of economic investment, and TNCs' offers of monetary infusion may be attractive: 'While the state has grown larger, capital has not been standing still. As well as inexorably centralizing and concentrating, it has, of course, internationalized. The nation state, even it is bigger, has increasingly to go on its knees to international capital, either in the old forms or in the new forms, such as the multinational corporation, to beg for investment' (Mandel 1988, 153–4).

The search for TNC capital is global – it can occur in any nation-state. When a TNC moves into a country, it may relatively easily take advantage of social, political, and economic conditions there. As a result, First World nations must be viewed within a global perspective, as have underdeveloped or economically stagnant regions. And it is these regions that are prime targets for TNCs.

While Canada is viewed as a First World nation, it has considerable regional underdevelopment. One such area is Cape Breton Island, in northern Nova Scotia. It typically has an unemployment rate in excess of 20 per cent and has traditionally relied heavily on federal and provincial monies to improve or maintain the economic base. In order to eliminate this transfer of payments, both levels of government have tried to attract new capital through economic incentives. Much of the resulting economic activity has attracted TNCs to the area. But along with investment, the TNCs have brought socially injurious behaviour.

BACKGROUND: STORA KOPPARBURG AND NOVA SCOTIA

During the early 1960s, a large-capacity pulp mill was built in Cape Breton by the Swedish multinational corporation Stora Kopparburg Berglags AB. Stora's interest in this area began with completion of the Canso Causeway, which linked the mainland with Cape Breton, creating a year-round, ice-free deep-water port 'capable of accommodating the largest supertankers in the world. The Causeway eliminated the threat to shipping by diverting various water currents, and provided a harbour approximately fourteen miles long and one mile wide' (Foote, 1979, 65).

Stora was interested in getting access to the vast forest hinterland, since the ports it relied on to ship its products from Sweden were iced up during winter. Subsequently, it built a $46-million pulp-and-paper mill near Port Hawkesbury, designed to produce 130,000 tons of sulphite pulp annually and employ 350 people. Largely because of the region's need for jobs, Stora was able to negotiate a more-than-favourable deal with the Province, including a free 100-acre (40-hectare) site for the mill, a long-term loan for fresh water from the mainland, exemption from almost all local taxes, as well as a long-term agreement on cheap electricity. The multinational also received a 50-year lease of crown forest lands, which gave it control of 1.3 million acres (0.52 million hectares) of government-held timberland in seven counties of Cape Breton and the northern mainland. In return, Stora agreed to pay the province $1 per cord of softwood cut, with a production limit of 150,000 cords per annum.

In 1969, Stora spent an estimated $86 million on an extension of the sulphite operation as well as adding a newsprint-production facility. It had threatened to leave Nova Scotia unless the provincial and federal governments invested $30 million in a long-term loan from the Cape Breton Development Corp. (DEVCO), a provincial agency. In addition, it negotiated a $5-million outright grant from the Area Development Agency (involving federal money) and provincial assistance in paying the interest on the $30 million received from DEVCO. Twenty thousand acres (8,000 hectares) was added to Stora's forest reserves, which now totalled 1.5 million acres (0.6 million hectares), and it also obtained approval to double production of softwood to 330,000 cords.

In 1976, Stora Forest Industries Ltd, a subsidiary, applied for provincial permits for aerial spraying of an organo-phosphate pesticide to kill spruce budworms that were devouring standing pulp wood in Cape Breton. Opposition to the spraying ran high in Cape Breton, especially after it was made public that a relationship had been discovered between the chemical in question and Reye's syndrome. Ultimately, spray permits were denied, forcing cancellation of the spray program. In 1977, however, the application to spray was once again made after the egg count of spruce budworms skyrocketed. Stora's president flew in from Sweden and claimed that if spraying were not allowed, there would be 'no wood in five years, mills would close and 2,000 people would lose their jobs' (Suzuki, 1989). Once again, however, public opposition ran so high that permits were again denied. The following year, egg counts fell drastically as part of the natural growth cycle.

In 1980, Stora decided that, in order to maximize the yield of softwoods in its forestry reserves, spraying would have to take place. Up to this time, the bulk of the softwood production quota was filled by private contractors working on Stora's crown reserves as well as by owners of private woodlot. In order to increase production, Stora turned to mechanized harvesting – industrial forestry, whereby the forest is viewed as a 'crop' to be harvested as cheaply and inten-sively as possible. This approach involves use of large-capacity machinery and minimization of labour. While one worker with a powersaw can produce two to four cords per day, a mechanical harvester, operated by one person, can cut ten to twelve cords per hour, given the proper physical geography. Because much of the timber in the reserves was hardwood – unsuitable for production of pulp and newsprint – Stora decided that it was essential to spray herbicides on selected areas of timber. This decision ultimately led it into court against fifteen local landowners.

Stora planned to have its wholly owned subsidiary in Nova Scotia (now called Nova Scotia Forest Industries) obtain spray permits from the provincial Department of the Environment. Stora, along with two American-controlled companies, Scott Paper Co. and Bowater Mersey Paper Co. Ltd, requested approval for aerial spraying with *Esteron 3-3E*, produced by Dow Chemical Corp., even though the chemicals in question had not been registered for use in Nova Scotia. This herbicide, in pure form, consists of 50-per cent 2,4-D and 2,4,5-TCDD – phenoxy herbicides that affect only broad-leaved plants, having little or no effect upon conifers. The firm needed the herbicide to kill broad-leaf growth in stands of newly planted softwoods to ensure that hardwood saplings would not smother out the more valuable seedlings. One of the many contami-nants found in 2,4,5-T is the dioxin 2,3,7,8 – tetrachlorodibenzo-p-aradioxin, otherwise known as TCDD, a dioxin. Structurally similar to PCBs, TCDD, along with the other contanimants, is an unavoidable by-products of the manu-facturing process. At the time, TCDD was considered by many authorities to be 'the most lethal chemical ever produced' – 'the equivalent of 5 grains of fine table salt would kill a man. One tablespoon would kill 10,000 chickens.' (Herbicide Fund Society 1983–4, 9).

Dioxins are extremely resistant to degradation and persistent in humans who have been sprayed. Some studies show that TCDD in diluted form is carcinogenic in animals. In addition, it possesses a half-life of at least 10 years, and quantities of the dioxin have been found in Vietnam veterans 12 years after their exposure to Agent Orange, an undiluted 1:1 mixture of 2,4-D and 2,4,5-T.

The area to be sprayed included some 6,000 acres (2,400 hectares) of forest in 12 spray sites – the smallest being approximately 70 acres (28 hectares), and the largest, 3,000 acres (1,200 hectares). The sites were typically several kilometres from habitation in Cape Breton, but the two mainland sites were closer to habitation.

On 21 June 1982, the minister of the environment announced approval of the spray applications, based in large part on the ground inspection conducted by the Ministry's Environmental Assessment Division. Thorough scrutiny of each site had produced detailed reports allegedly indicating that there was no potential harm to inhabitants. Because of demands for copies of these internal reports, the minister reluctantly agreed to release the environmental assessments. It was then found that the reports were one paragraph in length and included significant errors concerning location of homes, streams, and agricultural areas in relation to spray sites.

As a result, individuals located at or close to each site hastily made decisions, in some cases within forty-eight hours, to challenge the permits. Public concern led the minister to announce on 9 July 1982 that all permits for aerial application of the herbicides had been cancelled. However, ground spraying had not been included in the order, and, as a result, Nova Scotia Forest Industries (NSFI) applied for ground spraying permits on 3 August 1982 in order to commence spraying on 11 August. Fifteen local citizens, each located close to one of the sites, quickly decided to mobilize their limited resources, hire a lawyer, and ask the courts for a temporary injunction to ensure that spraying would not take place until they were able to obtain more detailed scientific information about the herbicides in question. After six days of court hearings in August, Mr Justice Burchell granted the plaintiffs a temporary injunction to restrain NSFI from spraying until a complete hearing concerning a permanent injunction could take place, with the trial commencing on 2 May 1983.

THE MEANING OF STANDARD OF PROOF

The trial involved an attempt by fifteen plaintiffs to block permanently, by way of interlocutory injunction, future spraying of Esteron 3-3E on the specified woodland sites close to their residences or farmlands, rather than demanding compensation for past damages. The plaintiffs carried the burden of proof to prove that the spraying in question would cause future 'irreparable harm' and that any damages to be assessed in future would be inadequate compensation. The trial questioned not NSFI's spraying policy but rather the effects of the chemicals to be sprayed. In essence, the herbicides 2,4-D and 2,4,5-T were on trial. And by virtue of having the case accepted in court, the plaintiffs were in fact challenging Dow Chemical Corp. one of the most powerful of all chemical corporations. As the trial judge commented: 'This matter thus reduces itself now to the single question. Have the plaintiffs offered sufficient proof that there is a serious risk of health and that such serious risk of health will occur if the spraying of the substances here is permitted to take place?' In essence, the sine qua non of the case became whether or not the plaintiffs could prove that the chemicals in question are unsafe (Wildsmith 1986, 176).

The interlocutory injunction applied for was '*quia timet*' ('which he fears') – in other words, a plaintiff does not have to wait until actual damage occurs. The legal tests to be met before such an injunction could be granted involved whether or not the claim was frivolous or vexatious, if there was a serious question to be tried, and if there was a real prospect of the plaintiffs' succeeding.

The standard of proof for such a case, as designated by the Supreme Court of Canada, is based on a 'strong case of probability' that the future injury (i.e., health risk) will be both substantial and continued, repeated, or committed at no remote period, and that the damages by themselves will not be an appropriate remedy (*Palmer et al. v. Nova Scotia Forest Industries*, 1983, 347). The plaintiffs contended that the legal test should rest on a sufficient degree of probability that the 'apprehended mischief' would, in fact, arise. In essence, they were arguing for a different test of the burden of proof, which demands that the court support the plaintiff's position if it could be shown simply that future harm would be significantly great in all circumstances (*Palmer et al. v. NSFI*, 1347). The trial judge rejected the plaintiffs' argument, stating that the legal test of 'a strong test of probability' more clearly set forth the proper legal principles. The basis of Mr Justice Nunn's decision was that 'a strong probability' 'does not impose an impossible burden nor does it deprive the court of its ability to consider the balance of convenience or inconvenience or hardship between the parties nor the size or the amount of the injury or distress which might occur. All of these are factors which are woven into the fabric of "a strong probability" and are considered in determining whether the burden of proof has been met.'

Granting of an interlocutory injunction is at the discretion of the judge. 'Any injunction is a discretionary judgment and sufficient grounds must be established to warrant the exercise by the court of its discretion' (*Palmer et al. v. NSFI*, 348). The plaintiffs would therefore have to prove 'sufficient grounds' to persuade the court that the chemicals in question would be harmful in future. And, since none of the plaintiffs could inform the court as to the exact nature of the possible future harm of the chemicals, experts had to be found who would persuade the judge that future harm would, in fact, be a strong probability.

The basis for the outcome of the trial, therefore, was to be over the 'facts' surrounding the nature of the chemicals to be used. And in 'most cases where the facts are disputed, the determination depends on which of the witnesses is believed, there is a tendency to carry this idea of belief over into the drawing of inferences from the facts that are in evidence' (Eggleton, in Harding 1992, 183). And these issues were to be presented through courtroom arguments. This dilemma leads to consideration 'of the utility of distinguishing between normative and pragmatic rules in competitive arenas' (O'Barr 1982, 118). Determining which rules are appropriate for a court decision has far-reaching implications for future cases.

In this trial, the powerful language came from key 'witnesses' for both plaintiffs and the defendant – those individuals who would ultimately decide the outcome of the trial – 'expert' witnesses, specialists in the risks of the dioxin that was the contaminant in the chemicals in question. But the reality was that only one form of powerful language would be accepted by Mr Justice Nunn.

'Expert' Witnesses

Mr Justice Nunn's decision that 'a strong probability' was necessary to prove future harm was a legal criterion for establishing cause and effect. But since this case concerned future spraying, it would involve scientific debates about dioxin. Precedents in the civil courts vis-à-vis expert witnesses had led to the favouring of the evidence of outside experts, usually associated with the project under consideration, leaving citizens directly affected virtually outside the realm of critical evidence-giving (Harding 1992, 184). Indeed, evidence given by scientific experts would ultimately 'tip the scales.' The plaintiffs, according to the court, lacked the expertise to testify about the harmful effects of dioxins. Legal counsel for the defendants stated that since the plaintiffs had the burden of proof, the defendants had, in essence, to do nothing. Dow Chemical, of course, would not dare to ignore the plaintiffs' expert witnesses and their arguments – the Agent Orange hearings were to start soon thereafter in Washington, D.C., and it would not improve its position for the plaintiffs in the upcoming American trial to point to a Canadian court decision where it was established that 'a strong probability' existed that dioxins caused harmful effects on humans. During the trial summation just prior to his judgment, Mr Justice Nunn noted that, aside from the plainitiffs, almost all thirty-four other witnesses were experts: 'This case is unique in part because ... apparently it is the first time that the leading scientists of opposing views regarding dioxin have met in Court where the chemicals involved are at the very centre of the court.'

This case was to be decided not so much on determination of 'a strong probability' but more on the rules of a non-legal entity – scientific research. Such activity is guided by its own logic of cause and effect – the null hypothesis (the proposition that the effect under investigation is not produced by the suspected cause). The null hypothesis for the expert (scientific) witnesses is that dioxin does not produce cancers in exposed subjects or birth defects in their children. By focusing on the null hypothesis, scientific research favours type-II (failing to reject a false null hypothesis) over type-I (rejecting a true null hypothesis) errors (Hays 1973). If an error is going to be made, scientists would prefer to accept a false null hypothesis than a false alternate hypothesis. 'Hence, it is a greater sin in scientific studies of phenoxy herbicides to conclude that dioxin harms health, when it actually does not, than to conclude that dioxin is harmless to humans when it actually is' (Scott 1988).

And as Mr Justice Nunn (*Palmer et al. v. NSFI*, 348) stated, the court is not the arena to determine the truth about the effects of phenoxy herbicides and dioxins: 'A court of law is no forum for the determination of matters of science. Those are for science to determine, as facts, following the traditionally accepted methods of scientific inquiry. A substance neither does nor does not create a risk to health by court decree and it would be foolhardy for a court to enter such an enquiry. If science itself is not certain, a court cannot resolve the conflict and make this thing certain.'

The differences between the expert witnesses concerning the harmful effects of dioxin were outlined in the interlocutory injunction hearing in 1982. The expert witnesses for the plaintiffs made these points. (1) TCDD (dioxin) found in the herbicide 2,4,5-T is the most potent chemical inducer of cancer and birth defects known. (2) TCDD has been demonstrated to produce cancer, mutations, and birth defects in laboratory animals. (3) Studies indicate that humans, if exposed to these herbicides, are subject to cancer and birth defects. (4) It has not been established that there is any threshold below which TCDD will have no carcinogenic effect, and cancer may be induced where even a single cell is affected by one or two molecules of the contaminant. (5) Herbicide-spray drift would reach persons living in the area.

The experts for the defence made these points. (1) The human studies relied on by the plaintiffs have been discredited. (2) Laboratory experiments on animals were not relevant because they involved very high doses, whereas actual use of the chemical would involve only a fraction of the concentrations used in the laboratory experiments; that is, there is a threshold level below which TCDD will not cause cancer. (3) The risk of harmful effects was so small as to be acceptable and in any event outweighed by the benefits of using the herbicides to promote forest growth. (4)There would be no risk of drift.

There was much uncertainty for the court about which of these arguments represented 'true' scientific fact. At the time, scientific studies favouring one side or the other were about equal in number. Most important, however, increasing numbers – in fact, the majority – of studies were concluding their investigations with results that favoured the plaintiffs position. In particular, many of the earliest research efforts did not study the effects of the chemicals in question on humans; instead, they focused on effects on plant life. During the early 1970s, however, studies of the effects of 2,4-D and 2,4,5-T on animals led to the conclusion that 'everyone' involved in the study of dioxins concluded that they were 'exceedingly toxic to laboratory animals' (Scott 1988, 152). This trend in results was recognized by Dow Chemical, and so it sent its best scientific experts to an unlikely setting, Sydney, Nova Scotia, to ensure that the trial judge would side with its arguments.

The Ideology of Scientism

According to Harding (1992, 135), scientism is a common feature in trials using expert witnesses to debate scientific 'facts': 'Ironically, a crude ideology of science (for example, scientism) that gives the experts special authority and contradicts the self-critical activity of science is often used to shore up the proponent's viewpoint. If those controlling the ... procedures believe in a formalistic legal view of impartiality and expertise – which is most often the case – they are prone to accept this ideology and appeal to its authority as a basis of establishing fact and drawing inferences.'

The 'proponents' in this case were the scientists arguing for the defendant's view of the spray, or, to be more specific, for Dow Chemical Corp. Scientism, however, extends beyond scientific 'fact'; it also includes scientists themselves, who are subject to the same crude ideology as are their 'factual statements.' These two components were to play an important role in the final decision reached by Mr Justice Nunn.

Scientific disagreements need to be made over something – that is, they need to be placed in a context to allow the court to decide on the fate of the issue. The debate over the chemicals became a debate over dosage. As the trial judge stated, 'The key to the use of all these is dosage. Where it can be determined that there is a safe dosage, according to acceptable scientific standards, then a substance can be used' (*Palmer et al. v. NSFI*, 353).

The judge evaluated the expert witnesses' testimony on the basis of whether it fulfilled the 'scientific' ideal and was 'objective.' According to his written judgment, the expert witnesses for the defence were more credible 'scientists': 'I did not detect any sense of partisanship. They related their work, their involvement with the substances, the results of their studies and their considerations of other studies in a professional, scientific manner and I therefore found their opinion to be reliable and, indeed, I accepted them as such' (*Palmer et al. v. NSFI*, 354). He singled out one, Dr Michael Newton, a professor of forest ecology at Oregon State University, as giving 'competent' and 'scientific' testimony concerning the dosage level of the chemicals 2,4,D and 2,4,5-T.

The judge considered Newton 'an impressive witness, obviously well qualified and extremely knowledgable in his area of expertise. He was professional in his manner, and competent and scientific in his approach to the evidence that he was giving. I found his evidence to be quite helpful.' Newton's 'objectivity' was not tarnished by the lawyers for the plaintiffs who asked him about his consulting jobs for Dow Chemical. While Newton did admit that he had testified on behalf of Dow on several occasions as an expert witness, his objectivity – in the judge's opinion – was not compromised, since 'he indicated that any fee was turned over to a research foundation and not retained personally by him' (*Palmer et al. v. NSFI*, 316).

What particularly impressed the trial judge was the fact that Newton and several others – including his wife – had conducted a test on themselves to study skin absorption by strapping a one-square-foot cloth, saturated with a normally used concentration of spray, to their thighs and left it for two hours. They concluded that the skin is a very effective barrier for the chemical, with Newton stating 'that even the applicators of the spray are under no risk unless they are spraying over their heads with their mouths open' (*Palmer et al. v. NSFI*, 315).

In contrast, Mr Justice Nunn found the plaintiffs' expert witnesses, particularly Dr Susan Daum, a physician from New Jersey and author of the book *Work Is Dangerous to Your Health*, to be lacking credibility and biased. She 'could give no definite answers despite the quantity used over a relatively long period of time except by extrapolation that dioxin is a very toxic substance and that it does all the things that it does.' In addition, the defence lawyers charged that her book took a 'biased' position vis-à-vis workers. Their charges were based on statements in the book that no safe dosage levels of these chemicals existed. Furthermore, the judge himself was not impressed with her definition of 'probability' – namely, that something could not occur by chance alone: 'Something, given the rules of chance, that would not have occurred by chance alone is significant and it becomes biologically significant if there is a biological explanation for it that is plausible' (*Palmer et al. v. NSFI*, 298).

Mr Justice Nunn held a similar opinion of the other scientific experts for the plaintiffs. He found them enthusiastically espousing a 'cause,' which led to their testimony being inappropriate for the scientific approach:

While I do not doubt the zeal of many of the plaintiffs' scientific witnesses or their ability, some seemed at many times to be protagonists defending a position, thereby losing some of their objectivity. There was a noticeable selection of studies which supported their view and a refusal to accept any criticism of them or contrary studies. Where the study was by anyone remotely connected with industry there was a tendency to leap to the 'fox in the chicken coop' philosophy, thereby ruling out the value of the study as biased. In my view a true scientific approach does not permit such self-serving selectivity, nor does it so readily decry a study on the basis of bias.

The denigration to the status of the plaintiffs' scientific arguments led Mr Justice Nunn to decide against them in his final judgment. He discounted human studies (e.g., of Vietnam veterans) mentioned in the case because of participants' overexposure (i.e., high levels of exposure), while at the same time he declined to make findings of fact in the areas of animal studies, where TCDD was reported to cause cancer and so on, and about the bioaccumulation and persistence of TCDD in both soil and tissue: 'I am satisfied that I have not heard sufficient evidence of a probable risk to health of the furans or pure 2,4-D or pure 2,4,5-T to warrant any fear of risk to health, particularly when considering the quantity of these substances to be used here. The totality of evidence in this regard does not even come close to establishing any probability, let alone a strong probability, of risk to health to warrant the granting of *quia timet* injunctive relief.'

THE JUDGMENT

After finding the plaintiffs to have failed in proving future harm, Mr Justice Nunn's judgment understandably came under enormous criticism. Many individuals in the local and surrounding communities who had given financial and emotional support to the plaintiffs were vocal. A number of legal and environmental criticisms attempted to point to the futility of using the courts to protect the environment. Criticisms were several in number.

Much information was said to have been ignored by Mr Justice Nunn. For example, it was later pointed out that eighteen U.S. federal agencies in a report to the U.S. president had concluded that methods do not exist for determining a 'safe' threshold level of exposure to carcinogens, and established test protocols, which include administration of high test doses to animals, sometimes by a route different than that of expected human exposure, are appropriate and scientifically valid methods for identifying human carcinogens (Castrilli and Vigod 1987, 23).

Cumming (1983) made a number of points. The trial judge had categorized all the plaintiffs' expert witnesses as 'unobjective' scientists. The judgment reeked of a 'scientific-sounding' conclusion rather than just ruling that the plaintiffs had not met the burden of proof to merit an injunction. The judge did not understand the nature of scientific authority, thereby rejecting relevant studies that found the chemicals in question to cause serious harm. The final judgment recognized none of the information given by the plaintiffs' expert witnesses, such as Dr Constable's statement that it is reasonable to use human subjects to determine low-level effects of a very toxic chemical.

However, this trial did benefit Canadian environmental litigation. Wildsmith (1986), who assisted the plaintiffs from the fall of 1982 until the final judgment in 1983, argues that Mr Justice Nunn allowed the fifteen plaintiffs to form a representative (class) action, despite several adverse precedents in the same area – an important precedent for future Canadian environmental litigation.

An Assessment of the Plaintiffs' Arguments

Wildsmith (1986, 167) has argued that on the basis of the evidence in the case 'the plaintiffs probably should have won.' It is then simple to charge that the existing legal system is unresponsive to this type of litigation and that a separate system of assessing the nature of chemicals be instituted whereby the burden of proof is reversed. The producers of chemical would have to prove that the substances in question are safe. Such systems, however, can be criticized in the same way.

The plaintiffs were not able to prove their case largely because of their selection of expert witnesses. In fact, better experts were available, who could have changed the outcome of the trial. The plaintiffs failed to make sufficient counter-arguments about the chemicals; instead, their evidence was in stark contrast to that provided by the expert witnesses for the defence. This approach led Mr Justice Nunn to question the adequacy and reliability of their testimony; indeed, their evidence 'glossed over' many of the issues at hand. As a result, they did not present Mr Justice Nunn with information that would have discredited the testimony of the defendants.

In addition, it was clear that the plaintiffs' expert witnesses did not understand all the circumstances of the studies being discussed by the witnesses for the defence. Instead, they offered the judge little if any basis on which to favour their side. The plaintiffs could have won on the basis of existing information, but they were also the 'victims' of scientific fraud. Studies used by the defence contended that these chemicals would not cause future harm because they were within proper levels of dosage as established by a variety of U.S. federal government agencies – a questionable conclusion.

Implication for the Study of Corporate Crime:
Another Case of Corporate Scientific Fraud

A few years after the trial, the U.S. Environmental Protection Agency (EPA) discovered that many of the scientific studies used to deem dioxins 'safe' within certain thresholds were flawed. Further investigation led the chief of the regulatory branch to send a memo (dated 15 November 1990) outlining the significance and extent of the dioxin fraud. The purpose of his memo was to assess whether or not criminal charges could be laid against Monsanto Corp. for fraud; for criminal charges to be laid, the fraud would need to have affected the regulatory process at the EPA, and the company would need to have knowingly submitted the falsified data and health studies in order to affect the regulatory process. Not surprisingly, the information supplied to the EPA by Monsanto was continually relied on by all offices of the EPA to conclude that 'dioxins have not caused cancer or other health effects (other than chloracne) in humans.' Thus, dioxin has been given a lesser carcinogenic potential ranking, which continues to be the basis of less stringent regulations and lesser degrees of environmental controls. The information has been used as a key component for denying compensation to Vietnam veterans exposed to Agent Orange and their children suffering birth defects from such parental exposures.

The investigation involved Monsanto and allegations 'of a long pattern of fraud' concerning the 2,3,7,8-tetrachlorodibenzodioxin (dioxin) contamination of a wide range of the corporation's products, as well as health studies of its dioxin-exposed workers. All data supplied to the EPA were compiled by the firm's personnel. (The National Institute of Environmental Health Sciences partially funded one of the company's studies, providing a basis for charges of fraudulent use of government funds.)

The investigations conducted by EPA personnel discovered that Monsanto did in fact submit false information to the EPA, which directly resulted in 'weakened regulations,' since these regulations did not take into account dioxin contamination in a number of chemicals, including 2,4-D. In addition, 'Monsanto's failure to report dioxin contamination of the disinfectant in Lysol has prevented any ban or other alleviation of human exposures to dioxins in this product.' The 'charge' against the corporation was that it 'covered-up the dioxin contamination of a wide range of products. Monsanto either failed to report contamination, submitted false information purporting to show no contamination, or submitted samples to the government for analysis which had been specially prepared so that dioxin contamination did not exist.'

The earliest-known efforts by Monsanto to cover up dioxin contamination of its products involved Agent Orange used in Vietnam. Internal documents at the company (dating from the 1960s) reveal knowledge of this contamination and of the fact that the dioxin contaminant was responsible for kidney and liver damage, as well as skin chloracne. Other evidence found in the company's files revealed that samples of 2,4,5-T and other chlorinated herbicides and chlorophenols submitted to the U.S. Department of Agriculture in the 1970s were 'doctored.' Highly contaminated samples were not submitted to the U.S. government, and the Monsanto samples that did arrive did not contain the proper (i.e., contaminanted) dioxin levels. The firm also submitted assertions to the EPA that process chemistry would preclude formation of tetrachlorinated dioxins in any chlorophenolic product other than 2,4,5-T, although memos were found showing that Monsanto did not always use this technology.

These samples and information were subsequently adopted by the EPA for a variety of regulations, and it was recognized in the memo that 'these regulations do not control the chlorophenol/phenoxy acetate products as acutely hazardous due to their contamination of tetrachlorinated dioxins.' Furthermore, the EPA relied on Monsanto's 'process chemistry' studies as a basis for not regulating most chlorophenols and 2,4-D for their tetrachlorinated-dioxin content. The EPA also found that the firm had misled members of the 'Canadian Parliament' to the effect that its products – such as Lysol – contained no dioxin.

Fraudulent scientific studies concerning dioxins were found in a number of epidemiological health studies performed by Monsanto on its dioxin-exposed workers. One study mentioned was performed by Dr Raymond Suskind (of the University of Cincinnati), who was hired by the corporation to study workers at its plant in Nitro, West Virginia. His published reports stated that 'chloracne, a skin condition, was the prime indicator of high human dioxin exposures, and no other health effects would be observed in the absence of this condition.' His unpublished studies indicated the fallacy of this conclusion, as no workers without chloracne were ever examined by him or included in his study. 'In other words, if no workers without chloracne were ever examined for other health effects, there is no basis for asserting that chloracne was the "hallmark of dioxin intoxication."' Suskind's published conclusions have been *repeatedly utilized by the EPA, the Veterans Administration, etc., to deny any causation by dioxin of health effects of exposed citizens, if these persons did not exhibit chloracne.'*

It was also noted that Suskind used statistics on the skin conditions of workers compiled by a Monsanto clerical worker with no independent verification whatsoever. The EPA also discovered another flaw in these studies: the purported 'dioxin unexposed' control group was selected from other workers at the same Monsanto plant who were also exposed not only to dioxins but also to other carcinogens. One of the 'other' carcinogens (para-amino biphenyl) was known by the company to be a human carcinogen, and it was also known that workers were heavily exposed. In addition, the memo discusses another fraudulent study by the corporation that

involved independent medical examinations of surviving employees by Monsanto physicians. Several hundred former Monsanto employees were too ill to travel to participate in this study. Monsanto refused to use the attending physicians' reports of the illness as part of their study, saying that it would introduce inconsistencies. Thus, any critically ill dioxin-exposed workers with cancers such as non-Hodgkins lymphona (associated with dioxin exposures), were conveniently excluded from the Monsanto study.

These same conclusions reached by the EPA were also reached in a study conducted by the National Institute of Occupational Safety and Health (NIOSH). The NIOSH's study found a statistically signficant increase in cancers in Monsanto workers at all sites, when dioxin-exposed workers at the company and other industrial locations were examined as an aggregate group.

CONCLUSION

It is clear that the fifteen plaintiffs in the herbicide trial, while not necessarily arguing a 'good' case, had the chance of winning against one of the major U.S. chemical corporations. Their inability to argue a stronger case was inhibited by scientific fraud on the part of other U.S. chemical corporations. Flawed results were forwarded to various U.S. government agencies, which in turn used these results as the basis of their regulations concerning the same chemicals of concern to the fifteen plaintiffs. Once again, ordinary citizens were victims of a system of 'due process' which allows flawed results to be invoked as a regulatory standard without proper independent verification. If the fifteen plaintiffs were in the same position, ten years later, they probably would have won their case of future harm.

Cases Cited

Andrews v. Law Society of British Columbia, [1989] 1 SCR 143, 56 DLR (4th) 1

Bellis v. United States 1974. 417 US 85

Bichler v. Eli Lilly Co., 436 NE 2d 182 (NYCA 1982)

Brown v. Superior Court, 44 Cal. 3d 1049, 751 P. 2d 470, 245 Cal. Rptr. 412 Cal. SC 1988

Buchan v. Ortho Pharmaceutical (Canada) Limited (1986), 25 DLR (4th) 658, 54 OR (2d) 92 (CA)

Canterbury v. Spence, 464 F. 2d 772 DC Cir. 1972

Ciarlariello v. Schacter, [1993] 2 SCR 119, 100 DLR (4th) 609 (SCC)

City of Vernon v. Manolakos [1989] SCR 1259

Davidson v. Connaught Laboratories (1980), 14 CCLT 251 (Ont. HC)

Distillers Co. (Biochemicals) Ltd. v. Thompson, [1971] AC 458 (JCPC)

Donoghue v. Stevenson, [1932] AC 562 (HL)

Dow Corning Corp. v. Hollis sub nom. Hollis v. Birch. 1990., 50 BCLR 2d. 344 CA

Hale v. Henkle 1906. 201 US 43

Hollis v. Birch (1993), 81 BCLR (2d) 1 (CA), leave to appeal *Hollis v. Dow Corning Corp.* granted 10 March 1994 (SCC)

Hopp v. Lepp, [1980] 2 SCR 192, 112 DLR (3d) 67

Just v. The Queen [1989] SCR 1228

Lapierre v. Attorney General of Quebec (1985), 16 DLR (4th) 544 (SCC)

New York & Central Hudson R.R. v. United States 1909. 212 US 481

Norberg v. Wynrib, [1992] 2 SCR 226

Palmer et al. v. Nova Scotia Forest Industries. Nova Scotia Supreme Court Trial Division. 15 September 1983

R. v. Bata Industries Ltd. [1992] 9 OR 3d. 329

R. v. Canadian Dredge and Dock Co. Ltd. 1985. 19 DLR 3d. 161. RSC 1985, c. C-46

R. v. City of Sault Ste. Marie [1978] 40 CCC 2d. 353 at 373–5

R. v. Ellis-Don [1992] 7 OR 3d. 320; Reference re: s. 942. of the B.C. Motor Vehicles Act [1985] 48 CR 3d. 289

R. v. St. Lawrence Corp. Ltd. 1969. 3 CCC 263; 1 OR 305

R. v. Turpin [1989] 1 SCR 1296, 96 NR 115

R. v. United Ceramics Ltd. 1979. 52 CCC 2d. 19

R. v. Wholesale Travel Group Inc. [1991] 67 CCC 3d. 193

Reibl v. Hughes, [1980] 2 SCR 880, 114 DLR (3d) 1

Reyes v. Wyeth Laboratories 498 F. 2d 1264, 1276 5th Cir. 1974., cert. denied 419 US 1096, 95 S. Ct. 687 1974

Rothwell v. Raes (1989), 54 DLR (4th) 193, 66 OR (2d) 449 (Ont. HC), aff'd (1991), 76 DLR (4th) 280, 2 OR (3d) 332 (Ont. CA), leave to appeal to SCC denied 23 May 1991

Sindell v. Abbott Laboratories, 607 P. 2d 924 (Cal. Sup. Ct. 1980), *cert.* denied, 101 S. Ct. 285

State v. Parsons 1982. 12 Mo. App. 205

Tesco Supermarkets Ltd. v. Nattrass [1971] 2 AU ER 127

Tock v. St. John's Metropolitan Area Bd. [1989] 2 SCR 1181

United States v. Hilton Hotels Corp. 1972. 467 F. 2d 1000 9th Circ., cert. denied, 409 US 1125 1973

Webb, R. v. Wholesale Travel: Case Comment forthcoming

Women's Legal Education and Action Fund. Intervenor's Factum. In *Andrews v. Law Society of British Columbia,* [1989] 1 SCR 143, 56 DLR 4th

References

Abbott, C.C. 1936. *The Rise of the Business Corporation*. Ann Arbor, Mich.: Edwards Brothers

Abegglen, J. 1975. *Management and Worker: The Japanese Solution*. Tokyo: Sophia University Press

Abolafia, M.Y. 1984. 'Structured Anarchy: Formal Organization in the Commodities Futures Markets.' In P. Adler and P. Adler, eds, *The Social Dynamics of Financial Markets*. 129–51. Greenwich, Conn.: JAI Press

Abrahamson, B., and Brostom, A. 1980. *The Rights of Labor*. Beverly Hills, Calif.: Sage

Acton, J.P., and Dixon, L.S. 1992. *Superfund and Transaction Costs: The Experience of Insurers and Very Large Industrial Firms*. Santa Monica, Calif: RAND Corp.

Adams, W., and Brock, J. 1991. *Antitrust Economics on Trial: A Dialogue on the New Laissez-Faire*. Princeton, NJ: Princeton University Press

Addy, G.N. 1991. 'Deceptive Marketing Practices.' *In* R.S. Khema and W.T. Stanbury, eds, *Canadian Competition Law and Policy at the Centenary*. 189–214. Halifax: Institute for Research on Public Policy

AFL-C10. 1992. Department of Occupational Health and Safety. *Death on the Job: The Toll of Neglect*. Washington, DC: Department of Occupational Health and Safety

Aftalion, F. 1991. *A History of the International Chemical Industry*. Philadelphia: Pennsylvania University Press

Aglietta, M. 1979. *A Theory of Capitalist Regulation: The U.S. Experience*. London: New Left Books

Alchian, A.A., and Demsetz, H. 1972. 'Production, Information Costs and Economic Organization.' *American Economic Review*: 777–95

Alderfer, C.P., and Smith, K.K. 1982. 'Studying Intergroup Relations Embedded in Organizations.' *Administrative Sciences Quarterly* 27: 35–65

Alderfer, C.P., and Tucker, R. 1980. 'Diagnosing Race Relations in Organizations.' *Journal of Applied Behavioral Sciences* 20: 35–65

Althusser, L., and Balibar, E. 1970. *Reading Capital*. London: New Left Books

Altschuler, A.W. 1991. 'Ancient Law and the Punishment of Corporations: Of Frank-pledge and Deodand.' *Boston University Law Review*. 71: 307–13

American International Group (AIG). 1989. *National Environmental Trust Fund*. Washington DC: American International Group

American Law Institute. 1956. Model Penal Code. Comment on Section 2.07, Tentative Draft no. 4

Anderson, F. 1985. 'Negotiation and Informal Agency Action: The Case of Superfund.' *Duke Law Journal* 852: 261–380

Annas, G.J. 1989. 'Faith (Healing), Hope and Charity at the FDA: The Politics of AIDS Drug Trials.' *Villanova Law Review* 34, no. 5: 771–97

Apfel, R.J., and Fisher, S.M. 1984. *To Do No Harm: DES and the Dilemmas of Modern Medicine*. New Haven, Conn., and London: Yale University Press

Arendt, H. 1958. *The Human Condition*. Chicago: University of Chicago Press

Arndt, K.A., and Jick, H. 1976. 'Rates of Cutaneous Reactions to Drugs: A Report from the Boston Collaborative Drug Surveillance Program.' *Journal of the American Medical Association* 235: 918–23

Arnold, T.W. 1937. *The Folklore of Capitalism*. New Haven, Conn.: Yale University Press

Asard, E. 1980. 'Employee Participation in Sweden 1971–1979: The Issue of Economic Democracy.' *Economic and Industrial Democracy* 1: 371–93

Australia, Adverse Drug Reactions Advisory Committee. 1992. 'Report for 1980, 1982.' *Medical Journal of Australia* 1: 416–19

Ayres, I., and Braithwaite, J. 1992a. 'Designing Responsive Regulatory Institutions.' *Responsive Community* 2: 41–7

– 1992b. *Responsive Regulation: Transcending the Deregulation Debate*. Cambridge: Cambridge University Press

Backstrom, A. 1988. 'The Role of the Automotive Industry for the Swedish Economy and Labour Market.' In G.M. Olsen, ed., *Industrial Change and Labour Adjustment in Sweden and Canada*. Toronto: Garamond Press

Bacow, L. 1980. *Bargaining for Job Safety and Health*. Cambridge, Mass.: MIT

Bagguley, P. 1991. 'Post-Fordism and Enterprise Culture: Flexibility, Autonomy and Change in Organization.' In R. Keat and N. Abercrombie, eds, *Enterprise Culture*, 151–68, London and New York: Routledge

Bailey, E. 1981. 'Contestability and the Design of Regulatory and Antitrust Policy.' *American Economic Review*, 71, no. 2 (May): 178–83.

Bailey, J. 1992. 'Dueling Studies: How Two Industries Created a Fresh Spin on the Dioxin Debate.' *New York Times* (20 February):

Baker, D. 1981. 'To Make the Penalty Fit the Crime: How to Sentence Antitrust Felons.' In J. Clabault and M. Block, eds, *Sherman Act Indictments* 1955–1980, vol. 2, 529–47. New York: Federal Legal Publications

Barber, B. 1984. *Strong Democracy: Participatory Politics for a New Age.* Berkeley: University of California Press

Barnett, H. 1979. 'Wealth, Crime, and Capital Accumulation.' *Contemporary Crises*, 3: 171–86

– 1982. 'The Production of Corporate Crime in Corporate Capitalism.' In P. Wickman and T. Dailey, eds. *White Collar and Economic Crime*, 157–70. Toronto: Lexington Books

– 1992. 'Hazardous Waste, Distributional Conflict and a Trilogy of Failures.' *Journal of Human Justice* 3, no. 2: 93–110

– 1994. *Toxic Debts and the Superfund Dilemma.* Chapel Hill, NC: University of North Carolina Press

Barney, J., Edwards, F., and Ringleb, A. 1992 'Organizational Responses to Legal Liability: Employee Exposure to Hazardous Materials, Vertical Integration, and Small Firm Production.' *Academy of Management Journal* 35, no. 2: 328–49

Bartlett, D., and Steele, J. 1992. *America: What Went Wrong?* Kansas: Andrews and MacMeel

Baucus, M., and Near, J. 1991. 'Can Illegal Corporate Behavior Be Predicted? An Event History Analysis.' *Academy of Management Journal* 34: 9–36

Baumhart, R.C. 1961. 'How Ethical Are Businessmen?' *Harvard Business Review* 39 (July–Aug.): 5–17

Baumol, W. 1982. 'Contestable Markets: An Uprising in the Theory of Industry Structure.' *American Economic Review* 73, no. 1 (March):1–15

Baysinger, B. 1991. 'Organization Theory and the Criminal Liability of Organizations.' *Boston University Law Review* 73: 341–76

Becker, G. 1968. 'Crime and Punishment: An Economic Approach.' *Journal of Political Economy* 762: 169–217

Beckwith, G.C. 1992. 'The Myth of Injury Prevention Incentives in Workers' Compensation Insurance.' *New Solutions* (winter):

Bell, D. 1976. *The Coming of Post-Industrial Society.* New York: Basic Books

Bender, L. 1988. 'A Lawyer's Primer on Feminist Theory and Tort.' *Journal of Legal Education* 38, nos. 1–2: 3–37

– 1990a. 'Changing the Values in Tort Law.' *Tulsa Law Journal* 25, no. 4: 759–73

– 1990b. 'Feminist (Re)Torts: Thoughts on the Liability Crisis, Mass Torts, Power, and Responsibilities.' *Duke Law Journal.* 40, no. 4: 848–912

Bergman, D. 1991. *Deaths at Work: Accidents or Corporate Crime.* London: Workers' Educational Association

Berman, D.M. 1978. *Death on the Job: Occupational Health and Safety Struggles in the United States.* New York: Monthly Review Press

Bernard, T. 1984. 'The Historical Development of Corporate Criminal Liability.' *Criminology* 22: 3–17

Bernstein, I. 1966. *The Lean Years: A History of the American Worker 1920–1933*. Baltimore, Md: Penguin

Bernstein, R. 1983. *Beyond Objectivism and Relativism: Science, Hermeneutics, and Praxis*. Philadelphia: University of Pennsylvania Press

Beynon, H. 1985. *Working for Ford*. Second edition. Harmondsworth: Penguin Books

Bingham, J. 1992. *Inquiry into the Supervision of the Bank of Credit and Commerce International*. London: HMSO

Bishop, J., Jr. 1968. 'Sitting Ducks and Decoy Ducks: New Trends in Indemnification of Corporate Directors and Officers.' *Yale Law Journal* 77: 1,078–1,103

Bixby, M. 1991. 'Workplace Homicide: Trends, Issues and Policy.' *Oregon Law Review* 70: 333–79

Block, F. 1977. 'The Ruling Class Does Not Rule: Notes on the Marxist Theory of the State.' *Socialist Revolution* 33: 6–28

Block, M., and Sidak, J. 1980. 'The Cost of Antitrust Deterrence: Why Not Hang a Price Fixer Now and Then?' *Georgetown Law Journal* 68: 1,131–9

Block, M., Nold, F., and Sidak, J. 1981. 'The Deterrent Effect of Antitrust Enforcement.' *Journal of Political Economy* 89: 429–45

Bolle, M. 1988. *OSHA Safety Inspection Targeting*. Congressional Research Service

Bonger, W. 1916. *Criminality and Economic Conditions*. Boston: Little, Brown

Bork, R. 1978. *The Antitrust Paradox*. New York: Basic Books

Borkin, J. 1978. *The Crime and Punishment of I.G. Farber*. New York: Free Press

Box, S. 1983. *Power, Crime and Mystification*. London: Tavistock

Boyden, R. 1947. 'The English Business Corporation, 1660–1720.' PhD dissertation, Department of History, Harvard University

Braithwaite, J. 1984. *Corporate Crime in the Pharmaceutical Industry*. London: Routledge and Kegan Paul

– 1985a. *To Punish or Persuade: The Enforcement of Coal Mine Safety*. Albany: State University of New York Press

– 1985b. 'White Collar Crime.' *Annual Review of Sociology* 11: 1–25

– 1989. *Crime, Shame and Reintegration*. Cambridge: Cambridge University Press

– 1992. 'A Sociology of Modeling and the Politics of Empowerment.' *British Journal of Sociology* 45: 445–79

– 1993. 'The Transnational Regulation of Corporate Crime in the Pharmaceutical Industry.' *Annals of the American Academy of Political and Social Science* 525: 12–30

– 1994. 'A Sociology of Modelling and the Politics of Empowerment.' *British Journal of Sociology* 45: 445–79

– In press. 'Inequality and Republican Criminology.' In J. Hagan and R. Peterson, eds, *Crime and Inequality*. Palo Alto, Calif.: Stanford University Press

Braithwaite, J., and Geis, G. 1982. 'On Theory and Action for Corporate Crime Control.' *Crime and Delinquency* 28 (Jan.): 292–314

Braithwaite, J., and Makkai, T. 1991. 'Testing an Expected Utility Model of Corporate Deterrence.' *Law and Society Review* 25: 7–40

Braithwaite, J., and Mugford, S. 1992. 'Conditions of Successful Reintegration Ceremonies: Dealing with Juvenile Offenders.' *British Journal of Criminology* 34: 139–71

Braithwaite, J., and Pettit, P. 1990. *Not Just Desserts: A Republican Theory of Criminal Justice*. Oxford: Oxford University Press

Braithwaite, J., Braithwaite, V., Gibson, D., Landau, M., and Makkai, T. 1991. *The Reliability and Validity of Nursing Home Standards*. Canberra: Department of Community Services and Health

Braithwaite, J., Makkai, T., Braithwaite, V., and Gibson, D. 1992. *Raising the Standard: Resident Centred Nursing Home Regulation in Australia*. Canberra: Australian Government Publishing Service

Bratton, W. 1989. 'The New Economic Theory of the Firm's Critical Perspectives from History.' *Standard Law Review* 41: 1471

Braverman, H. 1974. *Labor and Monopoly Capital: The Degradation of Work in the Twentieth Century*. New York: Monthly Review Press

Brennan, G., and Buchanan, J. 1985. *The Reason of Rules: Constitutional Political Economy*. Cambridge: Cambridge University Press

Brenner, S.N., and Molander, E.A. 1977. 'Is the Ethics of Business Changing?' *Harvard Business Review* 55 (Jan.–Feb.): 59–70

Brickey, S., and Grant, K. 'An Empirical Examination of Work Related Accidents and Illness in Winnipeg.' Paper presented at the Manitoba Federation of Labour Conferences on Workplace Health and Safety, 27 April, 1992

Britain, J.E. 1984. 'Product Honesty Is the Best Policy: A Comparison of Doctors' and Manufacturers' Duty to Disclose Drug Risks and the Importance of Consumer Expectations in Determining Product Defect.' *Northwestern University Law Review* 79, no. 2: 342–422

Brittan, S. 1988. *A Restatement of Economic Liberalism*. Atlantic City, NJ: Humanities Press International

Brown, L.D. 1981. *Managing Conflict at Organizational Interfaces*. Reading, Mass.: Addison-Wesley

Brunsson, N. 1989. *The Organisation of Hypocrisy: Talk, Decisions and Actions in Organisations*. Chichester: John Wiley & Sons

Buchanan, A. 1985. *Ethics, Efficiency, and the Market*. Totowa, NJ: Rowman and Allanheld

Budd, J.L., and Whimster, S., eds. 1992. *Global Finances and Urban Living*. London: Routledge

Burke, Edmund, 1910. *Reflections on the Revolution in France*. London: Dent

Burrell, G. 1988. 'Modernism, Postmodernism and Organisational Analysis. 2: The Contribution of Michel Foucault.' *Organisation Studies* 9, no. 2: 221–35

- 1990. 'Fragmented Labours.' In D. Knights and H. Willmott, eds, *Labour Process Theory*, 274–96. London: Macmillan

Calavita, K. 1983. 'The Demise of the Occupational Safety and Health Administration: A Case Study in Symbolic Action.' *Social Problems* 30: 437–48

- 1984. *U.S. Immigration Law and the Control of Labor, 1820–1924*. London: Academic Press
- 1992. *Inside the State: The BRACERO Program, Immigration, and the INS*. New York: Routledge, Chapman & Hall

Calavita, K., and Pontell, H. 1990. ' "Heads I Win, Tails You Lose'': Deregulation, Crime, and Crisis in the Savings and Loan Industry.' *Crime and Delinquency* 36: 309–41.

- 1991. 'Other People's Money Revisited: Collective Embezzlement in the Savings and Loan and Insurance Industries.' *Social Problems* 38: 94–112

Callinicos, A. 1989. *Against Postmodernism: A Marxist Critique*. Cambridge: Polity Press

Canada. 1984. *Report of the Commission of Inquiry on the Pharmaceutical Industry. Eastman, H.C., Chair*. Ottawa: Minister of Supply and Services Canada

- Office of the Auditor General. 1987. *Report of the Auditor General of Canada to the House of Commons, 1986–1987*. Ottawa: Office
- Director of Investigation and Research, Bureau of Competition Policy. Various years. Annual report for year ending 31 March, published in Ottawa, most recently by Supply and Services Canada
- 1990. 'Restrictive Trade Practices Commission Thomson v. Canada.' 76 CR 129
- Health and Welfare Canada. 1990. *National Health Expenditures in Canada, 1975–1987*. Ottawa: Ministry of Supply and Services
- Health Protection Branch, Health and Welfare Canada. 1991. *Health Protection and Drug Laws*. Ottawa: Health and Welfare Canada
- Review of the Canadian Drug Approval System, D. Gagnon, Chair. 1992. *Working in Partnerships. Drug Review for the Future* (Gagnon Report). Ottawa: Health and Welfare Canada
- House of Commons, 1992. Standing Committee on Health and Welfare, Social Affairs, Seniors and the Status of Women. Sub-Committee on the Status of Women. *Breast Cancer: Unanswered Questions*. Ottawa: Queen's Printer
- Medical Devices Review Committee. 1992. *Direction for Change*. Ottawa: Health and Welfare Canada

Canadian Charter of Rights and Freedoms, Part I of the Constitution Act, 1982, being Schedule B of the Canada Act. 1982 (UK) 1982, c. 11

Canadian Coordinating Office for Health Technology Assessment. 1991. *A Survey of Investigational New Drug and Emergency Drug Release Policies*. Ottawa: Canadian Coordinating Office and Health Technology Assessment

Canfield, G. 1914. 'Corporate Responsibility for Crime.' *Columbia Law Review* 14: 469–81

Caroline, M. 1985. 'Corporate Criminality and the Courts: Where Are They Going?' *Criminal Law Quarterly* 27: 237–54

Carr, C. 1907. *Collective Ownership Otherwise than by Corporations or by Means of Trust.* Cambridge: Cambridge University Press

Carroll, P.N., and Noble, D.W. 1977. *The Free and the Unfree: A New History of the United States.* Harmondsworth: Penguin

Carson, W.G. 1982. 'Legal Control of Safety on British Offshore Oil Installations.' In P. Wickman and T. Dailey, eds, *White Collar and Economic Crime*, 173–96. Toronto: Lexington Books

Carson, W.G. 1970a. 'White Collar Crime and the Enforcement of Factory Legislation.' *British Journal of Criminology* 10: 383–98

– 1970b. 'Some Sociological Aspects of Strict Liability and the Enforcement of Factory Legislation.' *Modern Law Review* 33: 396–412

– 1979. 'The Conventionalization of Early Factory Crime.' *International Journal for the Society of Law* 7: 37–60

– 1982. *The Other Price of Britain's Oil.* Oxford: Martin Robertson

Carter, R. 1980. 'Federal Enforcement of Individual and Corporate Criminal Liability for Water Pollution.' *Memphis State University Law Review* 19: 571–611

Castrilli, J.F., and Vigod, T. 1987. *Pesticides in Canada: An Examination of Federal Law and Policy.* Ottawa: Law Reform Commission of Canada

Chamallas, M. 1992. 'Feminist Constructions of Objectivity: Multiple Perspectives in Sexual and Racial Harassment Litigation.' *Texas Journal of Women and the Law.* 11: 95–142

Chambliss, W.J. 1967. 'Types of Deviance and the Effectiveness of Legal Sanctions.' *Wisconsin Law Review* (summer): 703–19

Chambliss, W., and Seidman, R. 1982. *Law, Order, and Power.* Reading, Mass.: Addison-Wesley Publishing Co.

Chandler, A. 1969. *Strategy and Structure.* Cambridge, Mass: MIT Press

– 1977. *The Visible Hand: The Managerial Revolution in American Business.* Cambridge, Mass.: Belknap Press of Harvard University Press

– 1990. *Scale and Scope: The Dynamics of Industrial Capitalism.* Cambridge, Mass.: Belknap Press of Harvard University Press

Charo, R.A. 1992. 'Who Controls Birth Control?' *Women's Review of Books* 9, no. 9: 18

Chelius, J. 1977. *Workplace Safety and Health.* Washington, DC: American Enterprise Institute

Cherry, R., D'Onofrio, C., Kurddas, C., Michl, T., Moseley, F., and Naples, M. 1987. *The Imperiled Economy, Book 1: Macroeconomics from a Left Perspective.* New York: Union for Radical Political Economics

Christie, N. 1993. *Crime Control as Industry: Towards Gulags, Western Style*. London: Routledge

Church, T., Nakamura, R., and Cooper, P. 1991. *What Works? Alternative Strategies for Superfund Cleanups*. Alexandria, Va.: Clean Sites

Clarke, S. 1988. 'Overaccumulation, Class Struggle and the Regulation Approach.' *Capital and Class*. 36 (winter): 59–92

– 1990. 'The Crisis of Fordism or the Crisis of Social Democracy.' *Telos* 83 (spring): 71–98.

Clean Sites. 1989. *Making Superfund Work: Recommendations to Improve Program Implementation*. Alexandria, Va.: Clean Sites

– 1990. *Improving Remedy Selection: An Explicit and Interactive Process for the Superfund Program*. Alexandria, Va.: Clean Sites

Clegg, S. 1990. *Modern Organizations: Organization Studies in the Postmodern World*. London: Sage Books

Clement, W. 1981. *Hardrock Mining*. Toronto: McClelland and Stewart

– 1988. *The Challenge of Class Analysis*. Ottawa: Carleton University Press

Clifford, J., and Webb, K. 1986. *Policy Implementation, Compliance and Administrative Law*. Law Reform Commission of Canada, Working Paper 51-38. Ottawa

Clinard, M.B. 1983. *Corporate Ethics and Crime: The Role of Middle Management*. Beverly Hills, Calif.: Sage

Clinard, M.B., and Quinney, R. eds. 1973. *Criminal Behavior Systems*. Second edition. New York: Holt, Rinehart and Winston

Clinard, M.B., and Yeager, P. 1980. *Corporate Crime*. New York: Free Press

Clinard, M.B., Yeager, P., Brissette, J., Petrashek, D., and Harries, E. 1979. *Illegal Corporate Behavior*. Washington, DC: National Institute of Justice, U.S. Department of Justice, and U.S. Government Printing Office

Coase, R. 1937. 'The Nature of the Firm.' *Economica* 4: 386

Codrington, C., and Henley, J. 1981. 'The Industrial Relations of Injury and Death: Safety Representatives in the Construction Industry.' *British Journal of Industrial Relations* 19: 297–315

Coffee, J., Jr. 1980. 'Corporate Crime and Punishment: A Non-Chicago View of the Economics of Criminal Sanctions.' *American Crime Law Review* 17: 419–71

– 1981. '"No Soul to Damn: No Body to Kick": An Unscandalized Inquiry into the Problem of Corporate Punishment.' *Michigan Law Review* 79: 386–459

– 1983. 'Corporate Criminal Responsibility.' In Sanford H. Kadish, ed., *Encyclopedia of Crime and Justice*, Vol. 1, 253–64. New York: Free Press

– 1991. 'Liquidity versus Control: The Institutional Investor as Corporate Monitor.' *Yale Law Journal* 91: 1,277

Cohen, M. 1992. 'Corporate Crime and Punishment: An Update on Sentencing Practices in the Federal Courts, 1988–1990.' *Boston University Law Review* 71: 247–80

Cohen, M.A., Ho, C., Jones, E., III, and Schleich, L. 1988. 'Organizations as Defendants in Federal Courts: A Preliminary Analysis of Prosecutions, Convictions, and Sanctions 1984–1987.' *Whittier Law Review* 10: 103–23

Coleman, B. 1975. 'Is Corporate Criminal Liability Really Necessary?' *Southwestern Law Journal* 29: 908–27

Coleman, J. 1985. *The Criminal Elite: The Sociology of White Collar Crime.* New York: St Martin's Press

– 1989. *The Criminal Elite: The Sociology of White Collar Crime.* Second edition. New York: St Martin's Press

Comment. 1979. 'Developments in the Law – Corporate Crime: Regulating Corporate Behavior through Criminal Sanctions.' *Harvard Law Review* 92: 1227–1375

Commoner, B. 1989. 'Why We Have Failed.' *Greenpeace* (Sept./Oct.); reprinted in W. Willers, ed., *Learning to Listen to the Land.* Washington, DC: Island Press

Conklin, J. 1977. *Illegal But Not Criminal: Business Crime in America.* New York: Spectrum Books

Connell, G. 1977. 'A View from the Department of Justice on Jail Sentences in Antitrust Cases.' *Antitrust Register* 22: 259–65

Consensus Workshop to Explore a Framework for Determining Risk of Unexpected Events following Medical Intervention. 1989. *Final Report.* Study sponsored by the College of Family Physicians of Canada and the Drugs Directorate of Health and Welfare Canada. Ottawa

Cook, D. 1980. 'The Patient Package Insert and Its Legal Implications.' *Legal Medical Quarterly* 4 (winter): 258–70

– 1989. *Rich Law, Poor Law.* Milton Keynes: Open University Press

Cook, J. 1989. *An Accident Waiting to Happen.* London: Unwin-Hyman

Cook, R., and Grimes, D. 1992. 'Antiprogestin Drugs: Ethical, Legal and Medical Issues.' *Law, Medicine and Health Care* (special issue) 20, no. 3: 149–270

Cook, R.J. 1991. 'Antiprogestin Drugs: Medical and Legal Issues.' *Mercer Law Review* 42, no. 3: 971–87

Corriveau, C. 1986. 'Devoirs et obligations du fabricant de produits pharmaceutiques.' *Canadian Journal of Women and the Law* 1, no. 2: 470–87

Cotler, V. 1990. 'The FDA, Contraception and RU-486.' *Women's Rights Law Reporter* 12, no. 2: 123–36

Cox, R. 1993a. 'Gramsci, Hegemony and International Relations: A Question of Method.' In S. Gill, ed., *Gramsci, International Relations and Historical Materialism.* Cambridge: Cambridge University Press

– 1993b. 'Structural Issues of Global Governance.' In S. Gill, Ed., *Gramsci, International Relations and Historical Materialism,* Cambridge: Cambridge University Press

Coyte, P., Dewees, D., and Trebilcock, M. 1991. 'Medical Malpractice – the Canadian Experience.' *New England Journal of Medicine* 324, no. 2: 89–93

Crane, M. 1980. 'The Due Process Considerations in the Imposition of Corporate Liability.' *Northern Illinois Law Review* 1: 39–47

Cranston, R. 1982. 'Regulation and Deregulation: General Issues.' *University of New South Wales Law Journal* 5: 1–29

Crawford, R. 1984. 'A Cultural Account of "Health": Control, Release and the Social Body.' In J.B. McKinlay, ed., *Issues in the Political Economy of Health Care*, 60–103. London: Tavistock

Cressey, D. 1988. 'The Poverty of Theory in Corporate Crime Research.' *Advances in Criminological Theory* 1: 31–56

Cumming, P. 1983. *Summary of the Decision in Nova Scotia's Herbicide Case.* Gabarus, NS: Herbicide Fund Society

Curran, D. 1993. *Dead Law for Dead Men.* Pittsburgh, Penn.: University of Pittsburgh Press

Cusamo, M. 1989. *The Japanese Automobile Industry.* Cambridge, Mass.: Harvard University Press

Dahlman, C.J. 1979. 'The Problem of Externality.' *Journal of Law and Economics* 22, no. 1 (April):

Daniels, R. 1991. 'Mergers and Acquisitions and the Public Interest: Don't Shoot the Messenger.' In L. Waverman, ed., *Corporate Globalization through Mergers and Acquisitions.* Calgary:University of Atlanta Press

Daniels, R., and McIntosh, J. 1991. 'Towards a Distinctive Canadian Law Regime.' *Osgoode Hall Law Journal* 29: 863

Danzon, P. 1990. 'The "Crisis" in Medical Malpractice: A Comparison of Trends in the United States, Canada, the United Kingdom and Australia.' *Law, Medicine and Health Care* 18, nos. 1–2: 48–58

D'Arcy, P.F., and Griffin, J.P., eds. 1986. *Iatrogenic Diseases.* Third edition. Oxford: Oxford University Press

Dawson, S., Willman, P., Bamford, M., and Clinton, A. 1988: *Safety at Work: The Limits of Self-Regulation.* Cambridge: Cambridge University Press

De Bardelon, J. 1985. *The Environment and Marxist-Leninism in the Soviet and East German Experience.* Boulder, Colo.: West View Press

Derry, R. 1987. 'Moral Reasoning in Work-Related Conflicts.' In W. Frederick, ed., *Research in Corporate Social Performance and Policy* 9: 25–49

Dicey, A. 1905. *Lectures on the Relation between Law and Public Opinion in England, during the Nineteenth Century.* London: Macmillan

Dill, W.R. 1958. 'Environment as an Influence on Managerial Autonomy.' *Administrative Science Quarterly* (March): 409–43

Donahue, J. 1991. *Workers at Risk: A Survey of OSHA's Enforcement Record against the 50 Largest U.S. Corporations.* Essential Information, Inc.

Donaldson, P., and Farquar, J. 1988. *Understanding the Economy.* Harmondsworth: Penguin

Donnelly, P.G. 1982. 'The Origins of the Occupational Safety and Health Act of 1970.' *Social Problems* 30: 13–25

Doucaliagos, C. 1990. 'Why Capitalist Firms Outnumber Labor Managed Firms.' *Review of Radical Political Economics* 22, no. 4: 44–66

Dowd, D.A. 1977. *The Twisted Dream*. Cambridge, Mass. Winthrop Publishers

Dowie, M. 1979. 'Pinto Madness.' In J. Skolnick and E. Currie, eds, *Crisis in American Institutions*, fourth edition, 4–29. Boston: Little, Brown

Drapkin, L. 1980. 'The Right to Refuse Hazardous Work after Whirlpool.' *Industrial Relations Law Journal* 4: 29–60

Dresser, R. 1992. 'Wanted: Single, White Male for Medical Research.' *Hastings Center Report* (Jan.–Feb.): 24–9

Drucker, P.F. 1992. 'The Coming of the New Organisation.' In G. Salaman et al., eds., Human Resource Strategies, 129–37. London: Sage/Open University

Dryzek, J. 1990. *Discursive Democracy*. Cambridge: Cambridge University Press

Duffin, J. 1989. 'Junk Mail.' *Canadian Medical Association Journal* 140: 112

– 1990. 'Junk Mail.' *Canadian Medical Association Journal* 142: 708

Dukes, M.N., and Swartz, B. 1988. *Responsibility for Drug-Induced Injury: A Reference Book for Lawyers, the Health Professions and Manufacturers*. Amsterdam: Elsevier Science Publishers B.V.

Dunning, J. 1979. 'Explaining Changing Patterns of International Production: In Defence of Eclectic Theory.' *Oxford Bulletin of Economics* 41, no. 4: 269–95

– 1988. *Explaining International Production*. London: Unwin-Hyman

Durkheim, E. 1958. *Professional Ethics and Civic Morality*. New York: Free Press

– 1984. *The Division of Labour in Society*. London: Macmillan

Dutton, D. 1988. *Worse Than the Disease: Pitfalls of Medical Progress*. Cambridge: Cambridge University Press

Eckstein, H. 1975. 'Case Study and Theory in Political Science.' In F. Greenstein and N. Polsby, eds, *Handbook of Political Science*, 7. Reading, Mass.: Addison-Wesley

Economist, 1990. 'Hypocrates Meets Mammon.' 22 (Sept.): 95

Edelman, P. 1987. 'Corporate Criminal Liability for Homicide: The Need to Prosecute Both the Corporate Entity and Its Officers. *Dickinson Law Review* 92: 193–222

Edsall, T. 1984. *The New Politics of Inequality*. New York: Norton

Edwards, J. 1991. 'Confidentiality in Environmental Auditing.' *Canadian Journal of Environmental Law and Practice* 1:

Elkins, J. 1976. 'Corporations and the Criminal Law: An Uneasy Alliance.' *Kentucky Law Journal* 65: 73–129

Elling, R.H. 1986. *The Struggle for Workers' Health: A Study of Six Industrialized Countries*. Farmingdale, NY: Baywood

Elsbach, K., and Sutton, R. 1992. 'Acquiring Organizational Legitimacy through Illegitimate Actions: A Marriage of Institutional and Impression Management Theories.' *Academy of Management Journal* 35, no. 4: 699–738

Elzinga, K., and Breit, W. 1976. *The Antitrust Penalties: A Study in Law and Economics*. New Haven, Conn.: Yale University Press

Environment Canada. 1988. *Canadian Environmental Protection Act Enforcement and Compliance Policy*. Ottawa: Supply and Services

Ermann, D., and Lundman, R. 1980. *Corporate Deviance*. New York: Holt, Rinehart and Winston

– 1982. *Corporate Deviance*. Second edition. New York: Holt, Rinehart and Winston

Ermann, D., and Lundman, R. eds. 1978. *Corporate and Governmental Deviance: Problems of Organizational Behavior in Contemporary Society*. New York: Oxford University Press

Etzioni, A. 1993. 'U.S. Sentencing Commission: A Critical Analysis.' *Annals of the American Academy of Political and Social Science* 275: 147–56

Ewick, P. 1985. 'Redundant Regulation: Sanctioning Broker-Dealers.' *Law and Policy* 7: 421–45

Ewing, S. 1987. 'Formal Justice and the Spirit of Capitalism: Max Weber's Sociology of Law.' *Law and Society Review* 21: 487–512

Faden, R., Beauchamp, T., and King, N. 1986. *A History and Theory of Informed Consent*. New York: Oxford University Press

Fels, A. 'The Political Economy of Regulation.' *University of New South Wales Law Journal* 5: 29–60

Ferguson, J. 1992. 'Is Drug Policy Pushing the Limit?' *Globe and Mail* (25 Feb.): A1, A6

Field, F. 1989. *Losing Out: The Emergence of Britain's Underclass*. Oxford: Blackwell

Finchman, J. 1991. 'An Overview of Adverse Drug Reactions.' *American Pharmacy* n.s. 31, no. 6: 47–52

Fine, B. 1990. *The Coal Question: Political Economy and Industrial Change from the Nineteenth Century to the Present Day*. London: Routledge

Finkle and Cameron 1989. 'Equal Protection in Enforcement: Towards More Structured Discretion.' *Dalhousie Law Journal* 12: 34

Finley, L. 1989. 'A Break in the Silence: Including Women's Issues in a Torts Course.' *Yale Journal of Law and Feminism* 1, no. 1: 41–73

– 1990. 'Laying down the Master's Tools: A Feminist Revision of Torts.' In T. Brettel Dawson, ed., *Women, Law and Social Change: Core Readings and Current Issues*, 53–5. North York, Ont.: Captus Press

Finn, P. 1989. 'Commerce, the Common Law and Morality.' *Melbourne University Law Review* 17: 87–99

Finney, H.C., and Lesieur, H.R. 1982. 'A Contingency Theory of Organizational Crime.' In S.B. Bacharach, ed., *Research in the Sociology of Organizations*, vol. 1, 255–99. Greenwich, Conn.: JAI Press

Fisse, B. 1971. 'Consumer Protection and Corporate Criminal Responsibility: A Critique of Tesco Supermarkets Ltd. v. Natrass.' *Adelaide Law Review* 4: 112–29

– 1980. 'Criminal Law and Consumer Protection.' In A.J. Duggan and L.W. Darvall, eds, *Consumer Protection: Law and Theory*, 182–99. Sydney, Australia: Law Books Co.

Fisse, B., and Braithwaite, J. 1983. *The Impact of Publicity on Corporate Offenders*. Albany: State University of New York Press

– 1988. 'The Allocation of Responsibility for Corporate Crime: Individualism, Collectivism, and Accountability.' *Sydney Law Review* 11: 469–513

– 1994. *Corporations, Crime and Accountability*. Cambridge. Cambridge University Press

Fletcher, A.P., and Griffin, J.P. 1991. 'International Monitoring for Adverse Drug Reactions of Long Latency.' *Adverse Drug Reactions and Toxicological Reviews* 10, no. 4: 209–30

Food and Drugs Act, RSC 1985, c. F-27

Food and Drugs Regulations, CRC, c. 870, ss. C08.007, C08.008

Foote, R. 1979. *The Case of Port Hawkesbury: Rapid Industrialization and Social Unrest in a Nova Scotia Community*. Toronto: PMA Books

Ford, A. 1986. 'Hormones: Getting Out of Hand.' In Kathleen McDonnell, ed., *Adverse Effects: Women and the Pharmaceutical Industry*. Toronto: Women's Educational Press

Foreman-Peck, J. 1989. 'The Privatization of Industry in Historical Perspective. '*Journal of Law and Society* 16, no. 1 (Spring): 00–000

Francis, J. 1924. 'Criminal Responsibility of the Corporation.' *Illinois Law Review* 18: 305–24

Freeman, J. 1989. *Democracy and Markets*. Ithaca, NY: Cornell University Press

Frick, K. 1990. 'Can Management Control Health and Safety at Work?' *Economic and Industrial Democracy* 11: 375–99

Friedland, S. 1993. 'A Medical Study of Older Women.' *New York Times* (4 April): 1

Friedman, M. 1962. *Capitalism and Freedom*. Chicago. University of Chicago Press

Gadamer, H. 1975. *Truth and Method*. New York: Seabury

Garland, D. 1990. *Punishment and Modern Society*. Chicago: University of Chicago Press

Gartner, H. 1992. 'Institutional Investors and the New FinancialOrder.' *Rutgers Law Review* 44:

Geerken, M., and Gove, W. 1977. 'Deterrence, Overload, and Incapacitation: An Empirical Evaluation.' *Social Forces* 56: 424–47

Geis, G. 1967. 'The Heavy Electrical Equipment Antitrust Cases of 1961.' In M.B. Clinard and R. Quinney, eds, *Criminal Behavior Systems*, 139–50. New York: Holt, Rinehart & Winston

– 1972. 'Criminal Penalties for Corporate Criminals.' *Criminal Law Bulletin* 8: 277–92

George, S. 1992. *The Debt Boomerang: How Third World Debt Harms Us All*. London: Pluto Press

Gergen, K.J. 1992. 'Organisation Theory in the Postmodern Era.' In M. Reed and M. Hughes, eds, *Rethinking Organisation: New Directions in Organisation Theory and Analysis* 207–26. London: Sage

Giddens, A. 1972. *Politics and Sociology in the Thought of Max Weber*. London: Macmillan

– 1990. *The Consequences of Modernity*. Stanford, Calif.: Stanford University Press

Gill, C., Morris, R., and Eaton, J. 1978. *Industrial Relations in the Chemical Industry*. Farnborough: Saxon House

Gill, S., and Law D. 1993. 'Global Hegemony and the Structural Power of Capital.' In S. Gill, ed., *Gramsci, International Relations, and Historical Materialism*. Cambridge: Cambridge University Press

Gilligan, C. 1982. *In a Different Voice: Psychological Theory and Women's Development*. Cambridge, Mass.: Harvard University Press

Glasbeek, H. 1979. 'Are Injuring and Killing at Work Crimes?' *Osgoode Hall Law Journal* 17: 506

– 1984. 'Why Corporate Deviance Is Not a Crime: The Need to Make "Profits" a Dirty Word.' *Osgoode Hall Law Journal* 22: 373

– 1988a. 'The Corporate Social Responsibility Movement: The Latest in Maginot Lines to Save Capitalism.' *Dalhousie Law Journal* 11: 363–402

– 1988b. 'A Role of Criminal Sanctions in Occupational Health and Safety.' *In Meredith Memorial Lectures: New Developments in Employment Law*. Cowansville, Que.: Éditions Yvon Blais

– 1991. *Death at Work: Accidents or Corporate Crime?* London: Workers' Educational Association

Glasbeek, H., and Tucker, E. 1992. 'The Westray Story: Death by Consensus.' Centre for Research on Work and Society, Working Paper Series no. 3

Glassman, R. 1973. 'Persistence and Loose Coupling in Living Systems.' *Behavioral Science* 18: 83–98

Goldman, C. 1992. 'The Competition Bureau's New Focus: Increased Risks for Individuals under the Competition Act.' *Canadian Competition Policy Record* 132: 33–43

Goldthorpe, J. 1984. *Order and Conflict in Contemporary Capitalism*. New York: Oxford University Press

Goodin, R. 1980. 'Making Incentives Pay.' *Policy Sciences* 12: 131–45

Goodpaster, K. 1989. 'Note on the Corporation as a Moral Environment.' In K. Andrews, ed., *Ethics in Practice: Managing the Moral Corporation*, 89–99. Boston, Mass.: Harvard Business School Press

Gordon, D., 1988. 'The Global Economy: New Edifice or Crumbling Foundations?' *New Left Review*. 168 (March–April): 24–64

Gordon, A., and Suzuki, D. 1990. *It's a Matter of Survival*. Toronto: Stoddart

Gorman, C. 1992. 'Can Drug Firms be Trusted? *Time* (17 Feb): 26–7

Grabosky, P., and Braithwaite, J. 1986. *Of Manners Gentle: Enforcement Strategies of Australian Business Regulatory Agencies*. Melbourne: Oxford University Press

Granovetter, M. 1973. 'The Strength of Weak Ties.' *American Journal of Sociology* 78: 1,360–80

Gray, W., and Scholz, J. 1991. 'Analyzing Equity and Efficiency of OSHA Enforcement.' *Law and Policy* 13: 185

Great Britain. 1968. *'Report of the Committee on Local Authorities and Allied Personal Social Services*. Command 3703. London: HMSO

Green, F., and Sutcliffe, R. 1987. *The Profit System: The Economics of Capitalism*. Harmondsworth: Penguin Books

Green, M., and Waitzman, N. 1981. *Business War on the Law: An Analysis of the Benefits of Federal Health/Safety Enforcement*. Second edition. Washington, DC: Corporate Accountability Research Group

Griffin, M. 1991. 'AIDS Drugs and the Pharmaceutical Industry: A Need for Reform.' *American Journal of Law and Medicine* 17, no. 4: 363–410

Gross, E. 1978. 'Organizational Crime: A Theoretical Perspective.' In N.H. Denzin, ed., *Studies in Symbolic Interaction*, 55–85. Greenwich, Conn.: JAI Press

Gross, J., and Greenfield, P. 1985. 'Arbitral Value Judgments in Health and Safety Disputes.' *Buffalo Law Review* 34: 645–91

Grunberg, L. 1983. 'The Effects of the Social Relations of Production on Productivity and Workers' Safety: An Ignored Set of Relationships.' *International Journal of Health Services* 13, no. 4: 621–34

– 1986. 'Workplace Relations in the Economic Crisis: A Comparison of a British and a French Automobile Plant.' *Sociology* 20, no. 4: 503–29

Grunberg, L., et al. 1984. 'Worker Productivity and Safety in Worker Cooperatives and Conventional Firms.' *International Journal of Health Services* 14: 413–32

Gunningham, N. 1974. *Pollution: Social Interest and the Law*. Oxford: Oxford Centre for Socio-Legal Studies

Habermas, J. 1984. *The Theory of Communicative Action I: Reason and the Rationalization of Society*. Boston, Mass.: Beacon

Hagan, J., and Nagel, I. 1982. 'White Collar Crime, White Collar Time: The Sentencing of White Collar Criminals in the Southern District of New York.' *American Criminal Law Review* 20, no. 2, 259–301

Hagan, J., and Palloni, A. 1983. '"Club Fed": The Sentencing of White Collar Offenders before and after Watergate.' *Criminology* 24: 603–22

Haines, F. 1992. 'The Show Must Go On. The Response to Fatalities in Multiple Employer Workplaces.'Unpublished paper, Department of Criminology, University of Melbourne

Hall, J. 1982. *Law, Social Science and Criminal Theory*. Littleton, Colo.: Fred B. Rothman

Hall, R. 1982. 'Emile Durkheim on Business and Professional Ethics.' *Business and Professional Ethics Journal* 21: 51–60

Hall, S., and Jacques, M., eds. 1989. *New Times: The Changing Face of Politics in the 1990s*. London: Lawrence and Wishart

Hallis, F. 1930. *Corporate Personality: A Study in Jurisprudence*. London: Oxford University Press

Halpern, J., Trebilcock, M., and Turnbull, R. 1988. 'An Economic Analysis of Limited Liability in Corporation Law.' *University of Toronto Law Journal* 40: 30

Handler, J. 1988. 'Dependent People, the State and the Modern/Postmodern Search for the Dialogic Community.' *UCLA Law Review*. 35: 999–1,113

Harding, J. 1986. 'Mood-Modifiers and Elderly Women in Canada: The Medicalization of Poverty.' In K. McDonnell, ed., *Adverse Effects: Women and the Pharmaceutical Industry*, 51–86. Toronto: Women's Educational Press

– 1992. 'Due Process in Saskatchewan's Uranium Inquiries.' In D. Currie and B. MacLean, eds, *Rethinking the Administration of Justice*, 130–49. Halifax: Fernwood Publishing

Hart, P. 1992. 'Senate Passes Bill to Charge Makers for Drug Approval.' *New York Times* (8 Oct.)

Hawkins, K. 1983. 'Bargain and Bluff: Compliance and Deterrence in the Enforcement of Regulation.' *Law and Policy Quarterly* 5: 35–73

– 1984. *Environment and Enforcement*. Oxford: Clarendon Press

Hays, W. *Statistics for the Social Sciences*. Second edition. New York: Holt, Rinehart, and Winston

Held, D. 1989. 'The Decline of the Nation State.' In S. Hall and M. Jacques, eds, *New Times*. London: Lawrence and Wishart

Hellenier, E. 1994. 'Post-Globalization: Is the Financial Liberalization Trend Likely to Be Reversed?' In D. Drache and R. Boyer, eds., *The Future of Nations and the Limits of Markets*. Montreal: McGill-Queen's University Press

Henderson, J. 1989. *The Globalisation of High Technology Production*. London: Routledge

– 1993. 'Against Economic Orthodoxy: On the Making of the East Asian Miracle. *Economy and Society* 22, no. 2 (May): 200–17

Hepple, B. Hepple & O'Higgins. 1981. *Employment Law*. Fourth edition. London: Sweet & Maxwell

Herbicide Fund Society. 1983–4. *Forest Herbicides on Trial*. Gabarus, NS: Herbicide Fund Society

Hess, H. 1992. 'Jailing of Company President Called Message to Polluters.' *Globe and Mail* (5 Sept): A7

Heyderbrand, W.V. 1989. 'New Organisational Forms.' *Work and Occupations* 16, no. 3: 323–57

Hindess, B., and Hirst, P.Q. 1975. *Pre-Capitalist Modes of Production*. London: Routledge and Kegan Paul

Hirschi, T. 1969. *Causes of Delinquency*. Berkeley: University of California Press

Hirst, P.Q. 1976. *Social Evolution and Sociological Categories*. London: George Allen and Unwin

– 1989. 'After Henry.' In S. Hall and M. Jacques, eds, *New Times: The Changing Face of Politics in the 1990s*. London: Lawrence andWishart

Hirst, P.Q., and Thompson, G. 1992. 'The Problem of "Globalization". International Economic Relations, National Economic Management and the Formation of Trading Blocks.' *Economy and Society* 21, no. 4 (Nov): 357–96

Hirst, P.Q., and Zeitlin, J. 1991. 'Flexible Specialization versus Post-Fordism: Theory, Evidence and Policy Implications.' *Economy and Society* 20, no. 1 (Feb.): 1–56

Hobbes, T. 1949. *De cive*. New York: Appleton-Century-Crofts

Holland, S. 1975. *The Socialist Challenge*. London: Quartet Books

Hounshell, D.A. 1984. *From the American System to Mass Production, 1800–1932*. Baltimore, Md.: Johns Hopkins University Press

Howse, R., and Trebilcock, M. 1993. 'Protecting the Employment Bargain.' *University of Toronto Law Journal* 43: 751

HSE (Health and Safety Executive). 1985. *Deadly Maintenance. Plant and Machinery. A Study of Fatal Accidents at Work*. London: HMSO

– 1987a. *Health and Safety Statistics, 1984–85*, London: HMSO

– 1987b. *Dangerous Maintenance: A Study of Maintenance Accidents in the Chemical Industry and How to Prevent Them*. London: HMSO

Hudson, R., and Williams, A.M. 1989. *Divided Britain*. London: Belhaven Press

Hughes, R. and Swanson, T., 1990. *The Price of Pollution: Environmental Litigation in Canada*. Edmonton: Environmental Law Centre

Hume, David. 1963. 'Of the Independency of Parliament.' *Essays, Moral, Political and Literacy*. Vol. 1. London: Oxford University Press

Hyde, A. 1992. 'In Defense of Worker Ownership.' *Chicago-Kent Law Review* 67: 15

Institute of Medicine. 1994. Anna C. Mastroianni, Ruth Faden and Daniel Federman, eds. *Women and Health Research: Ethical and Legal Issues of Including Women in Clinical Studies*. Vol. 1. Washington, DC: National Academy Press

Itoh, M. 1992. 'Japan in a New World Order.' In R. Miliband and L. Panitch, eds., *The Socialist Register*. London: Merlin Press

Jackall, R. 1988. *Moral Mazes: The World of Corporate Managers*. New York: Oxford University Press

James, W. 1978. *Pragmatism and the Meaning of Truth*. Ed. A.J. Ayer. Cambridge, Mass.: Harvard University Press

Jenkins, C. 1959. *Power at the Top: A Critical Survey of the Nationalized Industries*. London: MacGibbon and Kee

Jensen, P., and Meckling. 1976. 'Theory of the Firm: Managerial Behaviour, Agency Costs and Ownership Structure.' *Journal of Financial Economy* 3:

Jensen, P., and Parker, M. 1992. 'Misleading Advertising and Deceptive Marketing: An Indepth Analysis, October 1988 to December 1991.' Paper prepared for C394, Faculty of Commerce, University of British Columbia, April

Jessop, B. 1990. 'Regulation Theories in Prospect and Retrospect.' *Economy and Society* 19, no. 2 (May): 153–216.

– 1993. 'Towards a Schumpeterian Welfare State? Preliminary Remarkson a Post-Fordist Political-Economy.' *Studies in Political Economy* 40 (spring): 7–39

Johnson, B., ed. 1978. *The Attack on Corporate America*. New York: McGraw-Hill

Jones, K. 1982. *Law and Economy*. London: Academic Press

– 1983. 'Everywhere Abroad and Nowhere at Home: The Global Corporation and the International State.' *International Journal of the Sociology of Law* 12: 85–103

Kanter, R.M. 1989. *When Giants Learn to Dance*. New York: Touchstone Books

– 1991. 'The Future of Bureaucracy and Hierarchy in Organisational Theory: A Report from the Field.' In P. Bourdieu and J.S. Coleman, eds, *Social Theory for a Changing Society*, 63–87. Boulder, Colo.: Westview Press/Russell Sage Foundation

Katz, J. 1979. 'Legality and Equality: Plea Bargaining in the Prosecution of White-Collar and Common Crimes.' *Law and Society Review* 13: 431–59

– 1980. 'The Social Movement against White-Collar Crime.' *Criminology Review Yearbook* 2: 161–84

Katzenstein, P. 1985. *Small State in World Markets*. Ithaca, NY: Cornell University Press

Kazis, R., and Grossman, R. 1982. *Fear at Work: Job Blackmail, Labor and the Environment*. New York: Pilgrim Press

Keane, C. 1991. 'Corporate Crime.' In R. Silverman, J. Teevan, Jr, and V. Sacco, eds, *Crime in Canadian Society*, fourth edition, 223–32. Toronto: Butterworths

– 1993. 'The Impact of Financial Performance on Frequency of Corporate Crime: A Latent Variable Test of Strain Theory.' *Canadian Journal of Criminology* (July): 30–46

Kelman, M. 1987. *A Guide to Critical Legal Studies*. Cambridge, Mass.: Harvard University Press

Kelman, S. 1981. *Regulating America, Regulating Sweden*. Cambridge, Mass.: MIT Press

Kessler, D. 1992. 'The Basis of the FDA's Decision on Breast Implants.' *New England Journal of Medicine* 326, no. 25: 1,713–15

Keyserling, K. 1984. *Crimes against the environment*. Law Reform Commission of Canada, Working Paper 44. Ottawa

King, N., and Henderson, G. 1991. 'Treatments of Last Resort: Informed Consent and the Diffusion of New Technology.' *Mercer Law Review* 42, no. 3: 1,007–50

Knowles, E. 1982. 'From Individuals to Group Members: A Dialectic for the Social Sciences.' In W. Ickes and E.S. Knowles, eds, *Personality, Roles and Social Behavior.* New York: Springer-Verlag

Knox, P., and Agnew, J. 1989. *The Geography of the World Economy.* London: Edward Arnold

Kolata, G. 1992. 'Questions Raised on Ability of FDA to Protect Public.' *New York Times* (26 Jan): 1, 16

Kolko, G. 1976. *Main Currents in Modern American History.* New York: Harper and Row

Kornhauser, L. 1982. 'An Economic Analysis of the Choice between Enterprise and Personal Liability for Accidents.' *California Law Review* 70: 1,345–92

Kram, K., Yeager, P., and Reed, G. 1989. 'Decisions and Dilemmas: The Ethical Dimension in the Corporate Context.' In James E. Post,ed., *Research in Corporate Social Performance and Policy,* 11: 21–54, Greenwich, Conn.: JAI Press

Kramer, R.C. 1982. 'Corporate Crime: An Organizational Perspective.' In P. Wickman and T. Dailey, eds, *White-Collar and Economic Crime: Multidisciplinary and Cross-National Perspectives,* 75–94. Toronto: Lexington Books

– 1983. 'A Prolegomenon to the Study of Corporate Violence.' *Humanity and Society* 7 (May): 149–78

Kreisberg, S.M. 1976. 'Decision Making Models and Control of Corporate Crime.' *Yale Law Journal* 85: 1,091–1,128

Lader, L. 1991. *RU 486: The Pill That Could End the Abortion Wars and Why American Women Don't Have It.* Reading, Mass.: Addison-Wesley

Landes, W. 1983. 'Optimal Sanctions for Antitrust Violations.' *University of Chicago Law Review* 502: 652–78

Laski, H. 1929. *Foundations of Sovereignty.* New York: Harcourt, Brace

Lawrence, P.R. and Lorsch, J.W. 1967. *Organization and Environment: Managing Differentiation and Integration.* Cambridge, Mass.: Harvard University Press

Leadbetter, C. 1989. 'Power to the Person.' In S. Hall and M. Jacques, eds, *New Times.* London: Lawrence and Wishart

Lederman, E. 1985. 'Criminal Law, Perpetrator and Corporation: Rethinking a Complex Triangle.' *Journal of Criminal Law and Criminology* 76: 285–340

Lees, M. 1990. 'I Want a New Drug: RU-486 and the Right to Choose.' *Southern California Law Review* 63, no. 4: 1,113–49

Legge, K. 1989. 'Human Resource Management: A Critical Analysis.' In J. Storey, ed, *New Perspectives on Human Resource Management,* 19–40. London: Routledge

Leigh, D. 1993. *Betrayed.* London: Bloomsbury

Leigh, L. 1969. *The Criminal Liability of Corporations in English Law.* London: Weidenfield and Nicholson.

– 1977. 'Criminal Liability of Corporations and Other Groups.' *Ottawa Law Review* 9: 247–302

Levi, M. 1984. 'Giving Creditors the Business: The Criminal Law in Inaction.' *International Journal of the Sociology of Law* 12: 321–33
– 1987. *Regulating Fraud: White-Collar Crime and the Criminal Process.* London: Routledge
– 1991a. *Customer Confidentiality, Money-Laundering and Police-Bank Relationships.* London: Police Foundation
– 1991b. 'Sentencing White-Collar Crime in the Dark? Reflections on the Guinness Four.' *Howard Journal of Criminal Justice* 304: 257–79
– 1993. *The Investigation, Prosecution, and Trial of Serious Fraud.* Royal Commission on Criminal Justice Research, Study No. 14. London: HMSO
Levine, R. 1988. *Class Struggle and the New Deal: Industrial Labor, Industrial Capital and the State.* Lawrence: University Press of Kansas
Lewycky, P. 1986. 'Increased Severity Rates: Is Unemployment a Factor?' *At the Centre* 9, no. 2: 4–5
Lexchin, J. 1984. *The Real Pushers: A Critical Analysis of the Canadian Drug Industry.* Vancouver: New Star Books
– 1990. 'Drug Makers and Drug Regulators: Too Close for Comfort. A Study of the Canadian Situation.' *Social Science and Medicine* 31, no. 11: 1,257–63
Lindblom, C. 1977. *Politics and Markets: The World's Political-Economic Systems.* New York: Basic Books
Lipietz, A. 1992. *Towards a New Economic Order.* New York: Oxford University Press
Lipset, S.M. 1968. *The First New Nation: The United States in Historical and Comparative Perspective.* New York: Basic Books
– 1990. *Continental Divide: The Values and Institutions of the United States and Canada.* New York: Routledge
Liukkonen, P. 1987. *The Efficiency of Work Environment Activities at a Local Level.* Stockholm: Statistics Sweden
Lofquist, William S. 1992. 'Organizational Probation and the U.S. Sentencing Commission.' *Annals of the American Academy of Political and Social Science* 525: 157–69
Lord, M., Chief Judge. 1986. 'The Dalkon Shield Litigation: Revised Annotated Reprimand by Chief Judge Miles Lord.' *Hamline Law Review* 9: 7–51
Lucey, J. 1992. 'Do You Remember E-Ferol? The Penalty for Selling Untested Drugs in Neonatology: Fines and a Jail Sentence.' *Pediatrics* 89, no. 1: 159
Lynn, J. 1991. 'Implantable Medical Devices: A Survey of Products Liability Case Law.' *Medical Trial Technique Quarterly* 38, no. 1: 44–102
Lynxwiler, J., Shover, N. and Clelland, D. 1983. 'The Organization and Impact of Inspector Discretion in a Regulatory Bureaucracy.' *Social Problems* 30: 425–36
Lyons, N. 1988. 'Two Perspectives: On Self, Relationships, and Morality.' In C. Gilligan, J. Victoria Ward, and J. McLean Taylor, eds, *Mapping the Moral Domain: A Contribution of Women's Thinking to Psychological Theory and Education.* Cambridge, Mass.: Harvard University Press

Macaulay, S. 1963. 'Non-contractual Relations in Business: A Preliminary Study.' *American Sociological Review* 28 (Feb.):

McCormick, A. 1977. 'Rule Enforcement and Moral Indignation: Some Observations of the Effects of Criminal Antitrust Convictions upon Societal Reaction Processes.' *Social Problems* 25: 30–9

McDougall, W. 1920. *The Group Mind: A Sketch of the Principles of Collective Psychology.* New York: G.P. Putnam's

McGarey, B. 1984. 'Pharmaceutical Manufacturers and Consumer-Directed Information – Enhancing the Safety of Prescription Drug Use.' *Catholic University Law Review* 34, no. 1: 117–52

MacIntyre, A. 1984a. *After Virtue: A Study in Moral Theory.* Notre Dame, Ind.: University of Notre Dame Press

– 1984b. 'Does Applied Ethics Rest on a Mistake?' *Monist* 67: 498–513

– 1988. *Whose Justice? Which Rationality?* Notre Dame, Ind.: University of Notre Dame Press

MacKinnon, C.A. 1987a. 'Difference and Dominance: On Sex Discrimination.' In C. Mackinnon, *Feminism Unmodified: Disclosures on Life and Law.* Cambridge, Mass.: Harvard University Press

–, ed. 1987b. *Feminism Unmodified: Discourses on Life and Law.* Cambridge, Mass.: Harvard University Press

– 1989. *Toward a Feminist Theory of the State.* Cambridge, Mass.: Harvard University Press

McMahan, C. 1989. 'Managerial Authority.' *Ethics* 100 (Oct.): 33–53

McMahon, C. 1981. 'Morality and the Invisible Hand.' *Philosophy and Public Affairs* 10, no. 3: 247–77

McMullan, J. 1992. *Beyond the Limits of the Law: Corporate Crime and Law and Order.* Halifax: Fernwood Publishing

Magdoff, H. 1992. 'Globalization – To What End?' In R. Miliband and L. Panitch, eds, *Socialist Register 1992.* London: Merlin Press

Magnuson, J., and Leviton, G. 1987. 'Policy Considerations in Corporate Criminal Prosecutions after People v. Film Recovery Systems, Inc.' *Notre Dame Law Review* 62, no. 5: 913–39

Makkai, T., and Braithwaite, J. 1994. 'The Dialectics of Corporate Deterrence.' *Journal of Research in Crime and Delinquency* 31: 347–73

Malker, B. 1991. 'Occupational Injury Panorama.' *NBOSH Newsletter* 2: 4–7

Mandel, M. 1988. '"Relative Autonomy" and the Criminal Justice Apparatus.' In R. Ratner and J. McMullen, eds, *State Control: Criminal Justice Politics in Canada*, 149–64. Vancouver: University of British Columbia Press

Mann, K. *Defending White-Collar Criminals: A Portrait of Attorneys at Work.* New Haven, Conn.: Yale University Press

Mansfield, P. 1991. 'Classifying Improvements to Drug Marketing and Justifications for Claims of Efficacy.' *International Journal of Risk and Safety in Medicine* 2: 171–84

Marchington, M., and Parker, P. 1990. *Changing Patterns of Employee Relations*. Hemel Hempstead: Harvester Wheatsheaf

Marcotte, P. 1990. 'DES Legacy: Suit Claims Grandchild of Woman Who Took Drug Was Harmed.' *American Bar Association Journal* 76 (June): 14

Martin, E. 1991. 'The Egg and the Sperm: How Science Has Constructed a Romance Based on Stereotypical Male-Female Roles.' *Signs* 16, no. 3: 485–501

Martinson, R. 1974. 'What Works – Questions and Answers about Prison Reform.' *Public Interest* 35: 22–54

Marx, K. 1973. *Capital*. Vol. 1. New York: International Publishers

Mascaro, M. 1991. 'Preconception Tort Liability: Recognizing A Strict Liability Cause of Action for DES Grandchildren.' *American Journal of Law and Medicine* 17, no. 4: 435–55

Matthews, R., and Young. J., eds 1986. *Confronting Crime*. Beverly Hills, Calif.: Sage

Matza, D. 1964. *Delinquency and Drift*. New York: Wiley

May, F.E., Stewart, R.B., Hale, W.E., and Marks, R.G. 1982. 'Prescribed and Nonprescribed Drug Use in an Ambulatory Elderly Population.' *Southern Medical Journal* 75: 522–8

Mayer, M. 1990. *The Greatest Ever Bank Robbery: The Collapse of Savings and Loan Industry*. New York: Charles Scribners' Sons

Medawar, C. 1992. *Power and Dependence: Social Audit on the Safety of Medicines*. London: Social Audit Ltd.

Medline, E. 1992. '$25 Million to Halt Breat Cancer.' *Ottawa Citizen* (16 Dec.):

Medvedev, G., and Sakharov, A. 1991. *The Truth about Chernobyl*. New York:

Meekosha, H., and Jakubowicz, A. 1986. 'Women Suffering RSI: The Hidden Relations of Gender, the Labour Process and Medicine.' *Journal of Occupational Health and Safety – Australia and New Zealand* 2, no. 5: 390–401

Meidner, R. 1978. *Employee Investment Funds: An Approach to Collective Capital Formation*. London:

Mendeloff, J. 1988. *The Dilemma of Toxic Substances Regulation: How Overregulation Causes Underregulation at OSHA*. Cambridge, Mass.: MIT Press

Menell, P. 1991. 'The Limitations of Legal Institutions for Addressing Environmental Risks.' *Journal of Economics Perspectives* 5 (summer): 93–113

Merton, R. 1957. *Social Theory and Social Structure*. New York: Free Press

Merton, V. 1994. 'The Exclusion of Pregnant, Pregnable and Once-Pregnable People (a.k.a. Women) from Biomedical Research.'' *American Journal of Law and Medicine* 19, no. 4: 369–451. Reprinted in the *Texas Journal of Women and the Law* 3: 307–402

Meyer, J., and Rowan, B. 1977. 'Institutionalized Organizations: Formal Structure as Myth and Ceremony.' *American Journal of Sociology* 23, no. 2: 340–63

Michalowski, R. 1985. *Order, Law and Crime: An Introduction to Criminology.* New York: Random House

Michalowski, R., and Kramer, R. 1987. 'The Space between Laws: The Problem of Corporate Crime in a Transnational Context.' *Social Problems* 34, no. 1: 34–53

Miller, D. 1987. 'Strategic Industrial Relations and Human Resource Management – Distinction, Definition and Recognition.' *Journal of Management Studies* 24, no. 4: 347–61

Miller, J. 1988. 'Address Given in Acceptance of the August Vollmer Award.' *Criminologist* 13 (Jan.–Feb.): 7

Minow, M. 1990. *Making All the Difference: Inclusion, Exclusion, and American Law.* Ithaca, NY: Cornell University Press

Mintzberg, H. 1983. *Power in and around Organizations.* Englewood Cliffs, NJ: Prentice-Hall

Mokhiber, R. 1988. *Corporate Crime and Violence: Big Business Power and Abuse of the Public Trust.* San Francisco: Sierra Club Books

Monahan, P., and Petter, A. 1987. 'Developments in Constitutional Law: The 1985–86 Term.' *Supreme Court Law Review* 9: 69

Moore, T. 1989. 'Comment K Immunity to Strict Liability: Should All Prescription Drugs Be Protected?' *Houston Law Review* 26, no. 4: 707–37

Morgan, G. 1986. *Images of Organization.* Newbury Park, Calif.: Sage

Mosco, V. 1989. *The Pay-Per Society: Computers and Communication in the Information Age.* Toronto: Garamond Press

Moser, C. 1992. 'What's New with You?' *Occupational Health and Safety Canada* (July–Aug.): 49–54

Mueller, G. 1957. 'Mens Rea and the Corporation: A Study of the Model Penal Code Position on Corporate Criminal Liability.' *University of Pittsburgh Law Review* 19: 21–50

– 1959. 'Criminal Law and Its Administration.' *New York University Law Review.* 34: 82–116

Murray, R. 1985. 'Benneton Britain: The New Economic Order.' *Marxism Today* (Nov.): 28–32

Murray, T.H. 1988. 'Regulating Asbestos: Ethics, Politics and the Values of Science.' In R. Bayer, ed., *The Health and Safety of Workers: Case Studies in the Politics of Professional Responsibility,* 271–92. Oxford: Oxford University Press

Mytelka, L.K. 1991. 'Technological Change and the Global Relocationof Production on Textiles and Clothing.' *Studies in Political Economy* 36 (autumn): 109–43

Nader, R., Green, M., and Seligman, J. 1976. *Taming the Giant Corporation.* New York: W.W. Norton

Nagel, T. 1979. 'Ruthlessness in Public Life.' In T. Nagel, *Mortal Questions* 75–90. Cambridge: Cambridge University Press

Nagin, D. 1978. 'Crime Rates, Sanction Levels, and Constraints on Prison Population.' *Law and Society Review* 12: 341–66

Nardulli, P. 1979. 'The Caseload Controversy and the Study of Criminal Courts.' *Journal of Criminal Law and Criminology* 70: 89–101

National Safe Workplace Institute (NSWI). 1989. *Unintended Consequences: The Failure of OSHA's Megafine Strategy.* Washington, DC: NSWI

Natural Resources Defense Council (NRDC) 1991. *A Who's Who of Toxic Air Polluters: A Guide to More Than 150 Factories in 46 States Emitting Cancer Causing Chemicals.* Washington, DC: NRDC

Navarro, V. 1983. 'The Determinants of Social Policy: A Case Study: Regulating Health and Safety at the Workplace in Sweden.' *International Journal of Health Services* 13, no. 4: 517–61

Nedelsky, J. 1989. 'Reconceiving Autonomy: Sources, Thoughts and Possibilities.' *Yale Journal of Law and Feminism* 1, no. 1: 7–36

Nelkin, D., and Brown, M.S. 1984. *Workers at Risk.* Chicago: University of Chicago Press

Nichols, T. 1990. 'Industrial Safety in Britain and the 1974 Health and Safety at Work Act: The Case of Manufacturing.' *International Journal of the Society of Law* 18: 317–42

Nichols, T., and Armstrong, P. 1973. *Safety or Profit: Industrial Accidents and Conventional Wisdom.* Bristol: Falling Wall Press

Noble, C. 1985. 'Class, State, and Social Reform in America: The Case of the Occupational Safety and Health Act of 1970.' *Research in Political Economy* 8: 145–62

– 1986. *Liberalism at Work: The Rise and Fall of OSHA.* Philadelphia: Temple University Press

– 1992. 'Keeping OSHA's Feet to the Fire.' *Technology Review* 95 (Feb.–March):

Nonet, P. 1976. 'For Jurisprudential Sociology.' *Law and Society Review* 10: 525–45

Norris, C. 1993. 'Old Themes for New Times: Basildon Revisited.' In R. Miliband and L. Panitch, eds, *The Socialist Register.* London: Merlin Press

November, J. 1990. 'Public Welfare/Regulatory Offences: Judicial Criteria for Definition and Classification.' *New Zealand Law Journal* 236–9

O'Barr, W.M. 1982. *Linguistic Evidence: Language, Power, and Strategy in the Courtroom.* New York: Academic Press

O'Donovan, K. 1985. *Sexual Divisions in Law.* London: Weidenfeld and Nicolson

Ochsner, M. 1977. 'Worker and Community Right to Know: Case Studies in Policy Formation and Implementation.' Unpublished PhD thesis

Oi, W. 1977. 'On Socially Acceptable Risks.' In J. Phillips ed., *Safety at Work.* Oxford: Centre for Socio-Legal Studies

Okin, S. 1989. *Justice, Gender, and the Family.* New York: Basic Books

Oleinich, A., Fodor, W., and Susselman, M. 1988. 'Risk Management for Hazardous

Chemicals: Adverse Health Consequences of Their Use and Limitations of Traditional Control Standards.' *Journal of LegalMedicine* 9, no. 1 (March): 57–8

Ontario. Advisory Council on Occupational Health and Occupational Safety. 1981–8. *Annual Report*

- Legislative Assembly. 1987. 'Standing Committee on Resources Development.' *Report on Accidents and Fatalities in* Ontario Mines. 1st sess. 34th Parl.
- Ministry of Environment. 1991. Offences against the Environment. Environmental Protection Act, RSO 1989, c. 141, as amended, sec. 146a1
- Ministry of Environment. 1992a. 'Environment Minister Ruth Grier Releases Draft Environmental Bill of Rights.' News release, Toronto, 8 July
- Ministry of Environment. 1992b. 'Environmental Offenses – Crimes against the Environment.' In *Environtario Highlights*, 1, 4. Sept.
- Ministry of Environment. 1992c. 'Heaviest Fines Ever for Ontario Polluters.' *Environtario Highlights* 1, no. 4 (Sept): 1–2
- Ministry of Labour. 1991. *Injuries and Illnesses in Ontario's Workplaces: Statistics and Analysis*. Toronto: Policy and Analysis Unit, Health and Safety Policy Branch, Oct.
- Ministry of Labour. Health and Safety Policy Branch. 1990. *Occupational Health and Safety: Facts and Figures*. Toronto, June
- Ministry of Labour. Health and Safety Policy Branch. 1992. *Occupational Health and Safety: Facts and Figures*. Toronto, Dec.
- Pharmaceutical Inquiry of Ontario. 1990. *Report of the Pharmaceutical Inquiry of Ontario: Prescriptions for Health*. Lowy, Frederick H., Chairman. Toronto: Minister of Health. Appendix 7. A. Paul Williams and Rhonda Cockerill. *Report on the 1989 Survey of the Prescribing Experiences and Attitudes toward Prescription Drugs of Ontario Physicians*.
- Workers' Compensation Board. 1987. *Annual Report*

Orchard, D. 1993. *The Fight for Canada: Four Centuries of Resistance to American Expansionism*. Toronto: Stoddart

Orland, L. 1980. 'Reflections on Corporate Crime: Law in Search of Theory and Scholarship.' *American Criminal Law Review* 17: 501–20

Orton, J., Weick, D., and Weick, K. 1990. 'Loosely Coupled Systems: A Reconceptualization.' *Academy of Management Review* 152: 203–23

Ottawa. 1990. *National Health Expenditures in Canada 1975–87*. Cat. H21-99/1990E, 30. Ottawa: Ministry of Supply and Services

Overland, M. 1991. 'No Third-Generation Liability; N.Y. Court Bars Recovery for Granddaughter of Woman Who Took DES.' *American Bar Association Journal* 77 (May): 24

Packer, H. 1968. *The Limits of the Criminal Sanction*. Stanford, Calif.: Stanford University Press

Paehlke, R. 1990a. 'Regulatory and Non-regulatory Approaches to Environmental Protection.' *Canadian Public Administration* 33: 17–36

– 1990b. 'Toward a New Environmental Protection Strategy: A Survey of Options with an Emphasis on Governmental Procurement.' *Business in the Contemporary World* 2: 30–7

– 1991. *Environmentalism and the Future of Progressive Politics.* New Haven. Conn.: Yale University Press

– 1992. 'Environmental Politics and Policy: The Second Wave.' In Max Oelschlaeger, ed., *After Earth Day: Continuing the Conservation Effort.* Denton: University of North Texas Press

Paehlke, R.C. and Torgerson, D.T., eds. 1990. *Managing Leviathan:Environmental Politics and the Administrative State.* Peterborough, Ont.: Broadview Press

Papp, L. 1992. 'Workers Bilking Injury-pay Plan, Companies Say.' *Toronto Star* (9 Jan.): A10

Parris, H., Pestieau, P., and Satnor, P. 1988. *Public Enterprise in Western Europe.* London: Croom Helm and Acton Society Trust

Pearce, F. 1973. 'Crime, Corporations, and the American Social Order.' In Ian Taylor and Laurie Taylor, eds, *Politics and Deviance: Papers from the National Deviancy Conferences.* Baltimore, Md.: Penguin Books

– 1976. *Crimes of the Powerful: Marxism, Crime, and Deviance.* London: Pluto Press

– 1987. 'Corporate Crime.' *Critical Social Policy* 19: 116–25

– 1990. '"Responsible Corporations" and Regulatory Agencies.' *Political Quarterly* 61, no. 4 (Oct.–Dec.): 415–30

– 1992. 'The Contribution of Left Realism to the Study of Commercial Crime.' In J. Lowman and B. Maclean, eds, *Realist Criminology: Crime Control and Policing in the 1990s.* Toronto: University of Toronto Press

– 1993. 'Corporate Rationality as Corporate Crime.' *Studies in Political Economy* 49 (spring): 135–62

Pearce, F., and Tombs, S. 1988. 'Regulating Corporate Crime: The Case of Health and Safety.' Paper presented at the American Society of Criminology Annual Meeting, Chicago

– 1989. 'Bhopal, Union Carbide and the Hubris of a Capitalist Technocracy.' *Social Justice* 36, no. 2, 16 (June): 116–45

– 1990. 'Ideology, Hegemony, and Empiricism: Compliance Theories of Regulation.' *British Journal of Criminology* 30, no. 4: 423–43

– 1991. 'Policing Corporate Skid-Rows: A Reply to Keith Hawkins.' *British Journal of Criminology* 31, no. 4 (autumn): 415–26

– 1992a. 'Corporate Crime and Realism.' In Roger Matthews and Jock Young, eds, *Realist Criminology: Theory and Practice.* Sage

– 1992b. 'Toxic Capital.' *Critical Criminology* 4, no. 2: 1–3

– 1993. 'U.S. Capital versus the Third World: Union Carbide and Bhopal.' In F. Pearce and M. Woodiwiss, eds, *Global Crime Connections: The Dynamics and Control of Organised and Corporate Crime*, 187–211. Toronto: University of Toronto Press

Peltzman, S. 1976. 'Towards a More General Theory of Regulation.' *Journal of Law and Economics* 19, no. 2: 211–40

Pepinsky, H. 1974. 'From White Collar Crime to Exploitation: Redefinition of a Field.' *Journal of Criminal Law and Criminology* 65: 225–33

Permutter, H.V. 1965. 'L'entrepise internationale – trois conceptions.' *Revue économique et sociale* 23, no. 2: 151–65

Perrow, C. 1984. *Normal Accidents*. New York: Basic Books

– 1986. 'Economic Theories of Organizations.' *Theory, Culture and Society* 15, nos. 1–2: 11–45

– 1991. 'A Society of Organizations.' *Theory, Culture and Society* 20, no. 6 (Dec): 725–62

Peters, T.J., and Waterman, R.H. 1982. *In Search of Excellence: Lessons from America's Best-Run Companies*. New York: Warner Books

Petras, J., and Morley 1990. *US Hegemony under Siege: Class, Politics and Development in Latin America*. London: Verso

Pettigrew, A. 1985. *The Awakening Giant: Continuity and Change in Imperial Chemical Industries*. Oxford: Basil Blackwell

Pettit, P., with Braithwaite, J. 1993. 'Not Just Desserts, Even in Sentencing.' *Current Issues in Criminal Justice* 4, no. 3: 225–39

Phillips, K. 1991. *The Politics of Rich and Poor: Wealth and the American Electorate in the Reagan Aftermath*. New York: Harper-Perennial

Phillips, P. 1992. 'Functional Rights: Private, Public, and Collective Property.' *Studies in Political Economy* 38:

Picard, E. 1984. *Legal Liability of Doctors and Hospitals in Canada*. Second edition. Toronto: Carswell

Pijl, K. van der. 1993. 'Soviet Socialism and Passive Revolution.' In S. Gill, ed., *Gramsci, International Relations, and Historical Materialism*. Cambridge: Cambridge University Press

Pizzo, S., Fricker, M., and Muolo, P. 1989. *Inside Job: The Looting of America's Savings and Loans*. New York: McGraw-Hill

Polanyi, K. 1957. *The Greatest Transformation*. Boston: Beacon Press

Polinsky, A., Shavell, M., and Shavell, S. 1984. 'The Optimal Use of Fines and Imprisonment.' *Journal of Public Economics* 241: 89–99

Polinsky, M., and Shavell, S. 1979. 'The Optimal Trade-off between Probability and Magnitude of Fines.' *American Economic Review* 69: 880–

Pontell, H. 1978. 'Deterrence: Theory versus Practice.' *Criminology* 16: 3–22

- 1982. 'System Capacity and Criminal Justice: Theoretical and Substantive Considerations.' In Harold E. Pepinsky, ed., *Rethinking Criminology*, 131–43. Beverly Hills, Calif.: Sage Publications
- 1984. *A Capacity to Punish: The Ecology of Crime and Punishment*. Bloomington: Indiana University Press

Pontussen, J. 1987. 'Radicalisation and Retreat in Swedish Social Democracy. *New Left Review* 165 (Sept.–Oct.): 5–33

Popper, K. 1966. *The Open Society and Its Enemies*. London: Routledge and Kegan Paul

Posner, R. 1976. *Antitrust Law*. Chicago: University of Chicago Press
- 1977. *Economic Analysis of Law*. New York: Little, Brown
- 1980. 'Optimal Sentences for White-Collar Criminals.' *American Criminal Law Review* 17: 409–18
- 1981. *Economics of Justice*. Cambridge, Mass.: Harvard University Press

Powell, W. 1990. 'Neither Market nor Hierarchy: Network Forms of Organization.' In B.M. Staw and L.L. Cummings, eds, *Research in Organizational Behavior*. 12: Greenwich, Conn.: JAI Press

Power, M. 1990. 'Modernism, Postmodernism and Organisation.' In J. Hassard, and D. Pym, eds. *The Theory and Philosophy of Organisations: Critical Issues and New Perspectives*, 109–24. London: Routledge

Przeworski, A. 1990. *The State and the Economy under Capitalism*. London: Harwood Academic Publishers

Public Service Board. 1987. *Review of Drug Evaluation Procedures*. Canberra: Public Service Board

Purcell, J. 1989. 'The Impact of Corporate Strategy on Human Resource Management.' In J. Storey, ed., *New Perspectives on Human Resource Management*, 67–91. London: Routledge

Quinney, R. 1963. 'Occupational Structure and Criminal Behavior: Prescription Violations by Retail Pharmacists.' *Social Problems* 11: 179–85

Raymond, J., Klein R., and Dumble, L. 1991. *RU 486: Misconceptions, Myths and Morals*. Cambridge: Institute on Women and Technology

Reed, M. 1992. *The Sociology of Organizations: Themes, Perspectives and Prospects*. London: Harvester Wheatsheaf

Rees, J. 1988. *Reforming the Workplace*. Philadelphia: University of Pennsylvania Press

Regush, N. 1991. 'Health and Welfare's National Disgrace.' *Saturday Night* 106, no. 3: 9–18, 62–3
- 1992. 'Toxic Breasts.' *Mother Jones* (Jan.–Feb.): 24–31
- 1993. *Safety Last: The Failure of the Consumer Health Protection System in Canada*. Toronto: Key Porter Books

Reich, M., and Frumkin, H. 1988. 'An Overview of Japanese Occupational Health.' *American Journal of Public Health* 78 (7 July): 809–16

Reich, M.R. 1991. *Toxic Politics: Responding to Chemical Disasters*. Ithaca, NY: Cornell University Press

Reich, R. 1983. *The Next American Frontier*. New York: Times Books

Reichman, N. 1992. 'Regulating Risky Business: Securities Regulation and the Mobilization of Bias.' *Law and Policy* (forthcoming)

Reid, J., and Reynolds L. 1990. 'Requiem for RSI: The Explanation and Control of an Occupational Epidemic.' *Medical Anthropology Quarterly* 4, no. 2: 162–90

Reilly, W. 1989. *A Management Review of the Superfund Program*. Washington, DC: Environmental Protection Agency

Ricks, S. 1989. 'The New French Abortion Pill: The Moral Property of Women.' *Yale Journal of Law and Feminism* 1, no. 1: 75–99

Robertson, G. 1991. 'Informed Consent Ten Years Later: The Impact of Reibl v. Hughes.' *Canadian Bar Review* 70, no. 3: 423–47

Robertson, L., and Keeve, P. 1983. 'Worker Injuries: The Effects of Workers' Compensation and OSHA Inspections.' *Journal of Health, Politics, Policy and Law* 8: 581

Robinson, J. 1987. 'Worker Responses to Workplace Hazards.' *Journal of Health, Politics, Policy and Law* 12: 665–82

Robinson, J.C. 1991. *Toil and Toxics*. Berkeley: University of California Press

Rosenthal, E. 1993. 'Drug Companies' Profits Finance More Promotion than Research.' *New York Times* (21 Feb.): 1, 26

Roskill. 1986. *Report, Fraud Trials Committee*. London: HMSO

Ross, E. 1907. 'The Criminaloid.' *Atlantic Monthly* (Jan.): 44–50. Reprinted in G. Geis and R. Meier, eds, *White-Collar Crime: Offenses in Business, Politics, and the Professions*. New York: Free Press

Rosser, S.V. 1986. *Teaching Science and Health from a Feminist Perspective: A Practical Guide*. New York: Pergamon Press

– 1989. 'Re-visioning Clinical Research: Gender and the Ethics of Experimental Design.' *Hypatia* (summer): 125–39

Rothstein, M. 1990. *Occupational Safety and Health Law*. Third edition. St Paul, Minn.: West Publishing

Rubenstein, D., and Woodman, R. 1984. 'Spiderman and the Burma Raiders: Collateral Organization Theory in Action.' *Journal ofApplied Behavioral Science* 10, no. 1: 1–21

Rubin, L. 1990. 'Confronting a New Obstacle to Reproductive Choice: Encouraging the Development of RU-486 through Reform of Products Liability Law.' *New York University Review of Law and Social Change* 18, no. 1: 131–59

Rustin, M. 1989. 'The Trouble with New Times.' In S. Hall and M. Jacques, eds, *New Times*. London: Lawrence and Wishart

Ruttenberg, R. 1989. *The Role of Labor-Management Committees in Safeguarding*

Worker Safety and Health. U.S. Department of Labor, Bureau of Labor-Management Relations and Cooperative Programs, Washington, DC

Sabel, C., Herrigel, G., Deeg, R., and Kazis, R. 1989. 'Regional Prosperities Compared: Massachusetts and Baden-Wurttemberg in the 1980s.' *Economy and Society* 18, no. 4 (Nov.): 374–404

Sabel, C., and Zeitlin, J. 1985. 'Historical Alternatives to Mass Production: Politics, Markets and Technology in Nineteenth-Century Industrialization.' *Past and Present* 108:

Sage, W. 1988. 'Drug Product Liability and Health Care Delivery Systems.' *Stanford Law Review* 40, no. 4: 989-1,026

Salisbury, R. 1979. 'Why There Is No Corporatism in the United States.' In P.C. Schmitter and G. Lehmbruch, eds, *Trends toward Corporatist Intermediation.* Beverly Hills, Calif.: Sage Publications

Saltzburg, S. 1991. 'The Criminal Control of Corporate Conduct in Organizations.' *Boston University Law Review* 71: 421–38

Sandel, M. 1982. *Liberalism and the Limits of Justice.* Cambridge: Cambridge University Press

Sanderson, M. and Stanbury, W.T. 1989. *Competition Policy in Canada: The First Hundred Years.* Ottawa: Department of Consumer and Corporate Affairs

Sargent, N. 1992. 'Mapping the Corporation and Corporate Law.' Paper presented at 'Corporate Crime: Ethics, Law and the State,' Queen's University, 12–14 Nov.

– 1990. 'Law, Ideology and Social Change: An Analysis of the Role of Law in the Construction of Corporate Crime.' *Journal of Human Justice* 1, no. 2: 97–116

Sarno, D. 1991. 'Improving Superfund Remedy Selection.' Bureau of National Affairs. *BNA Environment Reporter – Analysis and Perspective* (3 May): 26–30

Sass, R. 1986. 'Workplace Health and Safety: Report from Canada.' *International Journal of Health Services* 16: 565–82

– 1991. 'Canadian Public Policy in Worker Health and Safety.' *New Solutions* (fall): 39–46

Sass, R., and Crook, G. 1981. 'Accident Proneness: Science or Non-Science?' *International Journal of Health Services* 11, no. 2: 175–90

Saxe, D. 1990. 'The Impact of Prosecution of Corporations and Their Officers and Directors upon Regulatory Compliance by Corporations.' CJELP 1: 91

Scales, A. 1986. 'The Emergence of Feminist Jurisprudence: An Essay.' *Yale Law Journal* 95, no. 7: 1,373–1,403

Schlesinger, S.A. 1992. 'Breast Implants and the Law.' *New York Law Journal* 207, no. 20: 3

Schmitter, P. 1974. 'Still the Century of Corporatism?' *Review of Politics* 36: 85–131

Scholz, J. 1984. 'Voluntary Compliance and Regulatory Enforcement.' *Law and Policy* 6: 385–404

- 1991. 'Cooperative Regulatory Enforcement and the Politics of Administrative Effectiveness.' *American Political Science Review* 85: 115–36
Scholz, J., and Gray, W. 1990. 'OSHA Enforcement and Workplace Injuries: A Behavioral Approach to Risk Assessment.' *Journal of Risk and Uncertainty* 3: 283–305
Schrager, L., and Short, J. 1978. 'Toward a Sociology of Organizational Crime.' *Social Problems* 25: 407–19
- 1986. *The Pitfalls of Standards*. Hamilton, Ont.: Canadian Centre for Occupational Health and Safety
Schrecker, T.F., and Tremblay. 1986. *Workplace Pollution*. Law Reform Commission of Canada. Working Paper 53, Ottawa
Schrecker, T.F. 1984. *Political Economy of Environmental Hazards*. Ottawa: Law Reform Commission
Scott, J.F. 1979. *Corporations, Classes and Capitalism*. London: Hutchinson
Scott, W. 1988. 'Competing Paradigms in the Assessment of Latent Disorders: The Case of Agent Orange.' *Social Problems* 35, no. 2: 145–61
Seebohm Report. 1968. *Report of the Committee on Local Authority and Allied Personal Social Services* No. 3703. London: HMSO
Selwyn, N. 1982. *Law and Health and Safety at Work*. London: Butterworths
Sen, A. 1985. 'The Moral Standing of the Market.' *Social Philosophy and Policy* 2 (spring): 1–19
Shannon, H.S., Walters, V., Lewchuk, W., Richardson, R.J., Verma, D., Haines, T., and Moran, L.A. 1992. *Health and Safety Approaches in the Workplace*. Toronto: Industrial Accident Prevention Association
Shapiro, S. 1980. 'Thinking about White-Collar Crime: Matters of Conceptualization and Research.' *Research on White Collar Crime*. Washington, DC: National Institute of Justice
- 1984. *Wayward Capitalist: Target of the Securities and Exchange Commission*. New Haven, Conn.: Yale University Press
Shavell, S. 1985. 'Criminal Law and the Optimal Use of Nonmonetary Sanctions as a Deterrent.' *Columbia Law Review* 856: 1,232–62
Sherwin, S. 1989. 'Feminist and Medical Ethics: Two Different Approaches to Contextual Ethics.' *Hypatia* 4, no. 2: 57–72
Shover, N. 1980. 'The Criminalization of Corporate Behavior: Federal Surface Coal Mining.' In G. Geis and E. Stotland, eds, *White-Collar Crime: Theory and Research*, 98–125. Beverly Hills, Calif.: Sage
- 1992. 'Cultural Sciences of Corporate Criminal Predisposition and Decision-Making.' Paper presented at conference 'Corporate Crime: Ethics, Law and the State,' Queen's University, 12–14 Nov.
Shover, N., Clelland, D., and Lynxwiler, J. 1986. *Enforcement or Negotiation: Constructing a Regulatory Bureaucracy*. Albany: State University of New York Press

Shrager, L.S., and Short, J.F. 1977. 'Toward a Sociology of Organisational Crime.' *Social Problems* 25: 407–19

Silk, L., and Vogel, D. 1976. *Ethics and Profits: The Crisis of Confidence in American Business*. New York: Simon and Schuster

Silverman, D. 1970. *The Theory of Organisations*. London: Heinemann

Silverstein, K. 1993. 'New young thalidomide Victims Found in Brazil.' *Globe and Mail* (2 June): A10

Simon, D., and Eitzen, D. 1986. *Elite Deviance*. Second edition. Boston: Allyn and Bacon

– 1990. *Elite Deviance*. Third edition. Boston: Allyn and Bacon

Simpson, S. 1986. 'The Decomposition of Antitrust: Testing a Multi-Level Longitudinal Model of Profit Squeeze.' *American Sociological Review* 51: 859–75

– 1987. 'Cycles of Illegality: Antitrust Violations in Corporate America.' *Social Forces* 65: 943–63

Simpson, S., and Koper, C., 1992. 'Deterring Corporate Crime.' *Criminology* 30: 347–75

Slovic, P., Kraus, N., Lappe, H., and Major, M. 1991. 'Risk Perception of Prescription Drugs: Report on a Survey in Canada.' *Canadian Journal of Public Health* 82 (May–June): S15–S20

Smart, C. 1989. *Feminism and the Power of Law*. London: Routledge

Smith, B.E. 1991. 'Black Lung: The Social Production of Disease.' *International Journal of Health Services* 113: 343–59

Smith, D. 1970. 'Sociology and the Sunshine Boys.' In L.T. Reynolds and J.M. Reynolds, eds, *The Sociology of Sociology*. New York: David McKay and Co.

Smith, N. 1984. *Uneven Development*. Oxford: Blackwell

Smith, R. 1976. *The Occupational Safety and Health Act*. Washington, DC: American Enterprise Institute

– 1982. 'Protecting Workers' Health and Safety.' In Robert W. Poole, Jr, ed., *Instead of Regulation*. Lexington, Mass.: Lexington Books

Snider, L. 1978. 'Corporate Crime in Canada: A Preliminary Report.' *Canadian Journal of Criminology* 20: 2–168

– 1987. 'Towards a Political Economy of Reform, Regulation and Corporate Crime.' *Law and Policy* 9, no. 1: 37–68

– 1990. 'Cooperative Models and Corporate Crime: Panacea or Cop-Out?' *Crime and Delinquency* 36: 373–90

– 1991. 'The Regulatory Dance: Understanding Reform Processes in Corporate Crime.' *International Journal of the Sociology of Law* 19: 209–36

– 1993. *Bad Business: Corporate Crime in Canada*. Scarborough, Ont: Nelson Canada

Sobol, R. 1991. *Bending the Law: The Story of the Dalkon Shield Bankruptcy*. Chicago: University of Chicago Press

Somers, E., Kasparek, M., and Pound, J. 1990. 'Drug Regulation – the Canadian Approach.' *Regulatory Toxicology and Pharmacology* 12: 214–23

Sonnefeld, J., and Lawrence, P. 1978. 'Why Do Companies Succumb to Price Fixing?' *Harvard Business Review* (July–Aug.): 145–57

Spelman, E. 1988. *Inessential Woman: Problems of Exclusion in Feminist Thought.* Boston: Beacon Press

Stanbury, W.T. 1976. 'Penalties and Remedies under the Combines Investigation Act, 1889–1976.' *Osgoode Hall Law Journal* 14, no. 3: 571–631

– 1986. 'The New Competition Act and Competition Tribunal Act: "Not with a Bang, But a Whimper".' *Canadian Business Law Journal* 121: 2–42

– 1991. 'Legislation to Control Agreements in Restraints of Trade in Canada: Review of the Historical Record and Proposals for Reform.' In R.S. Khemani and W.T. Stanbury, eds, *Canadian Competition Law and Policy at the Centenary*, 61–148. Halifax: Institute for Research on Public Policy

– 1992. 'White Collar Crime and Competition Policy: Corporations and Conspiracies in Restraint of Trade in Canada' Paper presented at the conference, 'Corporate Crime: Ethics, Law and the State,' Queen's University, 12–14 November

Staple, G. 1993. 'Serious and Complex Fraud: A New Perspective.' *Modern Law Review* March: 127–37

Staw, B., and Szwajkowski, E. 1975. 'The Scarcity-Munificence Component of Organizational Environments and the Commission of Illegal Acts.' *Administrative Science Quarterly* 20: 345–54

Stevens, G. 1992. 'Workplace Injury: A View from HSE's Trailer to the 1990 Labour Force Survey.' *Labour Gazette* (Dec.): 621

Stewart, D. 1992. *Den of Thieves.* New York: Simon and Schuster

Stigler, G. 1952. *The Theory of Price.* Revised edition. New York: Macmillan

– 1955. 'Mergers and Preventive Antitrust Policy.' *University of Pennsylvania Law Review* 104: 176–84

– 1971. 'The Theory of Economic Regulation.' *Bell Journal of Economics and Managerial Science* 2 (spring):

Stinchcombe, A.L. 1990. *Information and Organization.* Berkeley: University of California Press

Stone, C.D. 1975. *Where the Law Ends: The Social Control of Corporate Behavior.* New York: Harper Colophon

Stone, K. 1992. 'Contractual Mechanisms for Protecting Employees with the Nexus-of-Contract Firm.' Paper presented at Ontario Centre for International Business Conference

Storch, R. 1976. 'The Policeman as Domestic Missionary.' *Journal of Social History* 9, no. 4 (summer):

Styles, A. 1991. 'Prescription Drugs and the Duty to Warn: An Argument for Patient Package Inserts.' *Cleveland State Law Review* 39, no. 1: 111–40

Sutherland, E.H. 1949. *White Collar Crime*. New York: Dryden

Suzuki, D. 1989. 'She Helped Keep Cape Breton Free of Pesticide Spraying.' *Globe and Mail* (4 March): D4

Sykes, G., and Matza, D. 1957. 'Techniques of Neutralization: A Theory of Delinquency.' *American Sociological Review* 22: 667–70

Szasz, A. 1984. 'Industrial Resistance to Occupational Safety and Health Legislation: 1971–1981.' *Social Problems* 32: 103–16

– 1986. 'The Reversal of Federal Policy towards Worker Safety and Health.' *Science and Society* 50: 25–51

Taira, K. 1970. *Economic Development and the Labor Market in Japan*. New York: Columbia University Press

Tait, J. 1986. 'Reproductive Technologies and the Rights of Disabled Persons.' *Canadian Journal of Women and the Law* 1, no. 2: 446–55

Tamblyn, R., McLeod, P.J., Abrahamowicz, M., Monette, J., Gayton, D.C., Berkson, L., Dauphinee, W.D., Grad, R.M., Huang, A.R., Isaac, L.M., Schnarch, B.S., and Snell, L.S., 1994. 'Questionable Prescribing for Elderly Patients in Quebec.' *Canadian Medical Association Journal* 150, no. 11: 1,801–9

Teff, H. 1985. 'Drug Approval in England and the United States.' *American Journal of Comparative Law* 33, no. 4: 567–610

Teff, H., and Munro, C.R. 1976. *Thalidomide: The Legal Aftermath*. Westmead: Saxon House

Temin, P. 1980. *Taking Your Medicine: Drug Regulation in the United States*. Cambridge, Mass.: Harvard University Press

Thomas, D. 1990. 'The Impact of Race on Managers' Experiences of Developmental Relationships: An Intra-Organizational Study.' *Journal of Organizational Behavior* 11: 479–92

Thompson, G. 1989. 'Flexible Specialization, Industrial Districts, Regional Economies.' *Economy and Society* 18, no. 4:

Thurow, L. 1984. *Dangerous Current: The State of Economics*. New York: Vintage Books

Tietz, G. 1986. 'Informed Consent in the Prescription Drug Context: The Special Case.' *Washington Law Review* 61, no. 2: 367–417

Toffler, B. 1986. *Tough Choices: Managers Talk Ethics*. New York: Wiley

Tollefson, C. 1991. 'Ideologies Clashing: Corporations, Criminal Law and the Regulatory Offence.' *Osgoode Hall Law Journal* 705

– 1992. 'Corporate Constitutional Rights: Theory and Doctrine in the United States and Canada.' LL.M. thesis, York University, Toronto

Tombs, S. 1990a. 'Industrial Injuries in British Manufacturing.' *Sociological Review* 38, no. 2: 324–43

– 1990b. 'Piper Alpha – a Case Study in Distorted Communication.' In *International Chemistry Symposium, Rugby, IChemE*, 99–111

– 1992. 'Stemming the Flow of Blood? The Illusion of Self-Regulation.' *Journal of Human Justice* 3, no. 2 (spring): 75–92

Trade Practices Commission. 1992. *Promotion and Advertising of Therapeutic Goods*. Canberra: Trade Practices Commission

Tucker, E. 1990. *Administering Danger in the Workplace*. Toronto: University of Toronto Press

– 1992. 'Worker Participation in Health and Safety Regulation: Lessons from Sweden.' *Studies in Political Economy* 37 (spring): 95–127

Tuohy, C., and Simard, M. 1993. *The Impact of Joint Health and Safety Committees in Ontario and Quebec*. Study prepared for the Canadian Association of Administrations of Labour Law, Jan.

Twerski, A. 1989. 'Market Share – a Tale of Two Centuries.' *Brooklyn Law Review* 55, no. 3: 869–82

U.N. Centre of Transnational Corporations. 1984. *The C.T.C. Reporter*. No. 17. New York: United Nations

U.S. Attorney Northern District of Texas. 1990. *Fraud in Financial Institutions*. U.S. Attorney's Report

U.S. Bureau of National Affairs. 1988. *Occupational Safety and Health Reporter* (25 May): 1,877

– 1991a. *Occupational Safety and Health Reporter* (20 March)

– 1991b. *Occupational Safety and Health Reporter* (21 Aug.)

U.S. Congress, House of Representatives. 1977. *To Amend and Extend Authorizations for the Federal Water Pollution Control Act. Hearings before the Subcommittee on Water Resources of the Committee on Public Works and Transportation, March 1, 2, 3, 4, 1977*. Serial No. 95-5. Washington, DC: U.S. Government Printing Office.

– 1987. Committee on Government Operations. Subcommittee on Commerce, Consumer, and Monetary Affairs. *Adequacy of Federal Efforts to Combat Fraud, Abuse, and Misconduct in Federally Insured Financial Institutions. Hearings before the Subcommittee. November 19, 1987*

– 1988. Committee on Government Operations. *Combatting Fraud, Abuse, and Misconduct in the Nation's Financial Institutions: Current Federal Efforts Are Inadequate*. House Report No. 100-1088

– 1989. Committee on Standards of Official Conduct. *Report of the Special Outside Counsel in the Matter of Speaker James C. Wright, Jr. (Richard J. Phelan, Special Outside Counsel)*

– 1990a. Subcommittee on Financial Institutions Supervision, Regulation and Insurance of the Committee on Banking, Finance and Urban Affairs. *When Are the Savings and Loan Crooks Going to Jail? Hearing before the Subcommittee: June 28*

– 1990b. Committee on Banking, Finance and Urban Affairs. *Effectiveness of Law Enforcement against Financial Crime. Field Hearing before the Committee: Dallas, Texas, April 11*

U.S. Congress Senate. 1992. Subcommittee on Consumer and Regulatory Affairs. Committee on Banking, Housing, and Urban Affairs. *Efforts to Combat Criminal Financial Institution Fraud. Hearing before the Subcommittee, February 6*

U.S. Department of Justice. 1990. *Attacking Savings and Loan Institution Fraud. Report to the President*

– 1992a. 'Attacking Financial Institution Fraud.' *First Quarterly Report to Congress. Fiscal Year 1992*

– 1992b. 'Attacking Financial Institution Fraud.' *Second Quarterly Report to Congress. Fiscal Year 1992*

U.S. Department of Labor. 1988. *President's Report to Congress on Occupational Safety and Health.* Washington, DC: General Accounting Office

U.S. General Accounting Office (GAO). 1988. *OSHA'S Monitoring and Evaluation of State Programs*

– 1992a. 'Bank and Thrift Fraud.' Statement of Harold Valentine, Associate Director of Administration of Justice Issues, Subcommittee on Consumer and Regulatory Affairs. Washington, DC: United States Committee on Banking, Housing and Urban Affairs, February 6'

– 1992b. *Problems with the Completeness and Consistency of Site Cleanup Plans.* Washington, DC: U.S. Government Printing Office

– 1993. 'Bank and Thrift Criminal Fraud: The Federal Commitment Could Be Broadened.' Report to the Chairman, Committee on the Judiciary, U.S. Senate. GAO/GGD-93-98. Jan.

U.S. Sentencing Commission. 1991. 'Sentencing Commission Guidelines.' Washington, DC: U.S. Sentencing Commission, Nov.

Vandivier, K. 1972. 'Why Should My Conscience Bother Me?' In Robert L. Heilbroner, ed., *In the Name of Profit.* New York: Doubleday

Vaughan, D. 1982. 'Toward Understanding Unlawful Organizational Behavior.' *Michigan Law Review* 80: 1,377–1,402

– 1983. *Controlling Unlawful Organisational Behaviour,* Chicago: Chicago University Press

Viscusi, W. 1979. *Employment Hazards: An Investigation of Market Performance.* Cambridge, Mass.: Harvard University Press

– 1983. *Risk by Choice: Regulating Health and Safety in theWorkplace.* Cambridge, Mass.: Harvard University Press

– 1986. 'Reforming OSHA Regulation of Workplace Risks.' In L. Weiss and M. Klass, eds, *Regulatory Reform: What Actually Happened*. 234. Boston: Little, Brown

Wade, V.A. Mansfield, P.R., and McDonald, P.J. 1989. 'Drug Company Evidence to Justify Advertising.' *Lancet* (Nov.): 1,261–4

Wainwright, H. 1992. 'The New Left after Communism.' *Studies in Political Economy* 38:

Walters, D. 1987. 'Health and Safety and Trade Union Workplace Organisation – a Study in the Printing Industry.' *Industrial Relations Journal* (spring): 40–9

Walters, V. 1983. 'Occupational Health and Safety Legislation in Ontario: An Analysis of Its Origins and Content.' *Canadian Review of Sociology and Anthropology* 20: 413–34

Walters, V., and Denton, M. 1990. 'Workers' Knowledge of their Legal Rights and Resistance to Hazardous Work.' *Relations industrielles* 45: 531–46

Walters, V., and Haines, T. 1988. 'Workers' Use and Knowledge of the "Internal Responsibility System": Limits to Participation in Occupational Health and Safety.' *Canadian Public Policy* 14: 411–23

War Amputations of Canada. 1989. *Report of the Thalidomide Task Force*. Ottawa

Waring, M. 1988. *If Women Counted: A New Feminist Economics*. New York: Harper Collins

Waters, J., and Bird, F. 1987. 'The Moral Dimension of Organizational Culture.' *Journal of Business Ethics* 6: 15–22

Weaver, P. 1978. 'Regulation, Social Policy and Class Conflict.' In D. Jacobs, ed., *Regulating Business: The Search for an Optimum*. San Francisco: Institute for Contemporary Studies

Webb, K. 1988. *Pollution Control in Canada: The Regulatory Approach in the 1980s*. Ottawa: Law Reform Commission of Canada

– 1989. 'Regulatory Offences, the Mental Element and the Charter: Rough Road Ahead.' *Ottawa Law Review* 419:

– 1990. 'On the Periphery: The Limited Role for Criminal Offences in Environmental Protection.' In D. Tingley, ed., *Into the Future: Environmental Law and Policy for the 1990's*, 58–69. Edmonton: Environmental Law Centre

– 1991. 'Taking Matters into Their Own Hands: The Role of Citizens in Canadian Pollution Control Enforcement.' *McGill Law Journal*: 36: 770

Webb, Forthcoming.

Weber, M. 1946. *From Max Weber: Essays in Sociology*. Ed. H. Gerth and C. Wright Mills. New York: Oxford University Press.

– 1961. *General Economic History*. New York: Collier-Macmillan

– 1964. *The Theory of Social and Economic Organisation*. New York: Free Press

– 1978. *Economy and Society*. Berkeley: University of California Press

Weber, M. 1980. 'National State and Economic Policy.' *Economy and Society* 9, no. 4 (Nov.): 428–49

Wegner, D., Giuliano, T., and Hertel, P. 1985. 'Cognitive Interdependence in Close Relationships.' In W. Ickes, ed., *Compatible and Incompatible Relationships* 253–71. New York: Springer-Verlag

Weick, K. 1976. 'Education Organizations As Loosely Coupled Systems.' *Administrative Science Quarterly* 21 (March): 1–19

Weil, D. 1991. 'Enforcing OSHA: The Role of Labor Unions.' *Industrial Relations* 30: 20–36

Weisman, R. 1993. 'Reforms in Medical Device Regulation: An Examination of the Silicone Gel Breast Implant Debacle.' *Golden Gate University Law Review* 23: 973–100

Wells, C. 1993. *Corporations and Criminal Responsibility*. Oxford: Clarendon Press

Werden, G.J. and Simon, M.J. 1987. 'Why Price Fixers Should Go to Prison. *Antitrust Bulletin* 234 (winter): 917–37

Wetston, H.I. 1990. 'Canadian Competition Law: Current Issues in Conspiracy Law and Enforcement.' In *Meredith Memorial Lectures*, 30 Nov. Montreal: McGill University

– 1991. 'Notes for an Address to the Canadian Corporate Counsel Association.' Department of Consumer and Corporate Affairs, Ottawa, 19 Aug. Mimeo

– 1992. 'Decisions and Developments: Competition Law and Policy. Remarks to the Canadian Institute, Toronto, June 8. mimeo

Wheeler, S., and Rothman, M. 1982. 'The Organization as Weapon in White-Collar Crime.' *Michigan Law Review* 807: 1,403–26

Wheeler, S., Weisburd, D. and Bode, N. 1982. 'Sentencing the White Collar Offender: Rhetoric and Reality.' *American Sociological Review* 47: 641–59

White, H. 1981. 'Where Do Markets Come From?' *American Journal of Sociology* 87, no. 3: 517–47

Whitfield, D. 1983. *Making it Public: Evidence and Action against Privatisation*. London: Pluto Press

– 1992. *The Welfare State*. London: Pluto Press

Wildsmith, B. 1986. 'Of Herbicides and Humankind: Palmer's Common Law Lessons.' *Osgoode Hall Law Journal* 24, no. 1 (spring): 161–86

Willer, D., and Willer, J. 1973. *Systematic Empiricism: A Critique of Pseudo-Science*. Englewood Cliffs, NJ: Prentice-Hall

Williams, A.P., and Cockerill, R. 1989. See Ontario, Pharmaceutical Inquiry of Ontario (1990).

Williams, G. 1956. In American Law Institute, *Proceedings, 33rd Annual Meeting*, 19: 104–9

Williams, K., Williams, J., and Haslam, C. 1990. *Economy and Society.*, 19, no. 4 (Nov): 456–90

Williams, P. 1991. *The Alchemy of Race and Rights*. Cambridge, Mass.: Harvard University Press

Williams, T. 1990. 'Re-Forming Women's' Truth: A Critique of the Royal Commission on the Status of Women in Canada.' *Ottawa Law Review*. 22, no. 3: 725–59

Williamson, O. 1983. 'Organizational Innovation: The Transaction Cost Approach.' In J. Ronen, ed., *Entrepreneurship*. Lexington, Mass.: D.C. Heath

– 1984. 'Corporate Governance' *Yale Law Journal* 93: 1,197

– 1975. *Markets and Hierarchies: Analysis and Anti-Trust Implications*. New York: Free Press

Wilson, G.K. 1985. *The Politics of Safety and Health: Occupational Safety and Health in the United States and Britain*. Oxford: Clarendon Press

Wilson, J. 1980. *The Politics of Regulation*. New York: Basic Books

Wilson, L. 1979. 'The Doctrine of Willful Blindness.' *University of New Brunswick Law Review* 28:

Wilson, W.J. 1992. 'Another Look at the Truly Disadvantaged.' *Political Science Quarterly* 106: 639–56

Wokutch, R. 1992. *Worker Protection, Japanese Style: Occupational Health and Safety in the Auto Industry*. Ithaca, NY: ILR Press

Wolff, M. 1938. 'On the Nature of Legal Persons.' *Law Quarterly Review* 54: 494

Women's Legal Education and Action Fund. 1989. Intervenor's Factum. *Andrews v. Law Society of British Columbia*. 1 SCR 143, 56 DLR 4th

Woodiwiss, A. 1991. *Rights v. Conspiracy: A Sociological Essay on the History of Labour Law in the United States*. New York: Berg

– 1992. *Law, Labour and Society in Japan*. London: Routledge

– 1993a. *Postmodernity USA*. London: Sage

– 1993b. *Human Rights, Labour Law and Transational Sociality around the Pacific Rim*. City University of Essex

World Bank 1989. *Sub-Saharan Africa: From Crisis to Sustainable Growth*. Washington, DC

Wrong, D. 1961. 'The Oversocialized Conception of Man in Modern Sociology.' *American Sociological Review* 26: 183–93

Yeager, P. 1986. 'Managing Obstacles to Studying Corporate Offences: An Optimistic Assessment.' Paper presented at the Annual Meetings of the American Society of Criminology, Atlanta, Ga.

– 1987. 'Structural Bias in Regulatory Law Enforcement: The Case of the U.S. Environmental Protection Agency.' *Social Problems* 34: 330–44

– 1988. 'The Limits of Law: State Regulation of Private Enterprise.' Paper presented at the Annual Meetings of the American Society of Criminology, Chicago.

– 1991. *The Limits of Law: The Public Regulation of Private Pollution*. Cambridge: Cambridge University Press

408   References

- 1993. 'Industrial Water Pollution.' In Michael Tonry and Albert J. Reiss, Jr, eds, *Beyond the Law: Crime in Complex Organizations*, vol. 18 of *Crime and Justice: A Review of Research*, 97–148. Chicago: University of Chicago Press

Yeager, P., and Kram, K. 1990. 'Fielding Hot Topics in Cool Settings: The Study of Corporate Ethics.' *Qualitative Sociology*. 13 no. 2: 127–48

Young, J.E. 1992. 'Mining the Earth.' In L. Brown, ed., *State of the World 1992*. New York: Norton

Zeitlin, M. 1989. *The Large Corporation and Contemporary Classes*. New Brunswick, NJ: Rutgers University Press

Zey-Ferrell, M., and Ferrell, O.C. 1982. 'Role-set Configuration and Opportunity as Predictors of Unethical Behavior in Organizations.' *Human Relations* 35: 587–604

Zey-Ferrell, M., Weaver, K., and Ferrell, O.C. 1979. 'Predicting Unethical Behavior among Marketing Practitioners.' *Human Relations* 32: 557–69

Author Index

Subject Index

product liability, 91–2; and the adequacy of information, 96–7; Canadian disclosure standard, 94; and compensation, 103–4; and the duty to warn, 92–5, 105; and feminism, 94, 105–7; goals of, 91; and the learned intermediary rule, 92, 95–6, 107; legislation, 91–4, 107; principles of, 92–4, 105–8; and risk, 92, 94; and the standard of reasonableness, 94, 105; and women, 107–8
public enterprise, 27
Public Service Board (Australia), 66

Reagan, Ronald, 203, 207, 323, 329
recognized professional bodies, 190
regulation: and capitalism, 23–6, 30–2, 38–9, 41, 268; and corporate crime, 4, 9–11, 181–4, 186, 190–4, 208–12, 339–46; and the corporation, 10, 23, 117, 159–63, 268; effects of, 23–4, 339–46; functions of, 190–5, 208–13; and the pharmaceutical industry, 99–101, 105, 107–8; political economy of, 181–3, 194–5; and republicanism, 4–5, 51–2, 54–5
regulationist model, 31–2; criticisms of, 32; and the perpetuation of capitalism, 31–2
regulatory law, 159–61; as distinct from criminal law, 329–33; assumptions of, 159, 339–46; corporate perceptions of, 159–61; criticisms of, 159–61; moral nature of, 159–63; and professional standards, 161–2; proposed changes in, 162–3; and public policy, 162–3
Report of the Fraud Trials Committee (U.K.), 182
republicanism, 4–5, 48–54, 65, 68–70; and accountability model, 65; and Australia, 48–50; and community, 52; conception of citizenship, 54–5, 69–70; conception of liberty, 50, 68; and corporate crime, 4, 51–5, 68; and the definition of crime, 50–1; and individual empowerment, 53–5, 69; philosophical foundation, 52–3; and regulatory compliance, 51–2, 54–5; and tripartite enforcement, 65
Resolution Trust Corp., 200, 205, 210–11
Resource Conservation and Recovery Act, 336
Richardson-Merrell, 104
Royal Commission on Criminal Justice, 185

Savings and Loan scandal, 10, 30,
Schumpeterian workfare state, 38
Securities and Exchange Commission, 206–7
Securities and Futures Association (U.K.), 192
Securities and Futures Authority (U.K.), 191
Securities and Investments Board (U.K.), 184, 186, 190–1
Seebohm Commission (U.K.), 85
self-regulatory organizations, 190
Senate Banking Committee, 206–7
Serious Fraud Office (U.K.), 182–3, 187–9, 190–1, 193–5, 198
shareholding, inequalities in, 20
Sherman Antitrust Act (U.S.), 73–4, 214, 216
Silverado Savings and Loan, 205
social bond theory, 176
social constructionism: and definitions of risk, 284; and organizational morality, 147–8
Solomans Carpets: and administrative